"Don't look here for a scripted, mapped-out program of how to be⌐ ⌐sionary. It's packed with practicalities, helping you discover your distinctive part in God's mission. The stories of how others have been finding their way in God's mission mean that you are no longer alone in figuring out your own journey. Essential equipment for anyone coaching others to live effectively for God's purposes."

Steve Hawthorne, coeditor, *Perspectives on the World Christian Movement*

"There is no other resource equal to the *Global Mission Handbook*. The combination of topics, authors and approaches stands alone as a comprehensive compendium related to crosscultural action. *Global Mission Handbook* guides the reader through stages of preparation and involvement—all toward the goal of helping each reader investigate and discover the unique ways that we belong in serving the world in Jesus' name. I recommend it to every person who wants something larger out of life—a sense of understanding where we fit in God's global purposes."

Paul Borthwick, senior consultant, Development Associates International

"God is still calling people to serve as missionaries, but this process can be confusing and even intimidating. *Global Mission Handbook* demystifies the call to missions while capably exploring and unpacking its spiritual essence. With sound practical advice and profound insight from a wealth of global voices, I can think of no better preparatory resource for those considering service in the fields that still remain white unto harvest."

Jason Mandryk, editor, *Operation World*

"It's with great delight that I commend to any pastor, organizational leader or trainer, missionary candidate, or missions executive the book *Global Mission Handbook*. The authors—Steve Hoke and Bill Taylor—are among the most experienced, respected and beloved missions practitioners of our generation, and they truly provide a serious, comprehensive guide for crosscultural service. The handbook divides the missionary preparation process into ten phases to guide the missionary-hopeful through the rigors of the many steps to the field. Nothing like this handbook exists to date, and it fills a huge hole in the missionary training process for churches, schools and agencies alike. It is my prayer that thousands of copies are used in the coming years to guide the next generation preparing for missionary service to honor God with their lives."

Dr. Monroe Brewer, president, The National Association of Missions Pastors, and director of Church Connections, CrossGlobal Link, Wheaton, Illinois

Steve Hoke & Bill Taylor

Global Mission Handbook

A GUIDE FOR CROSSCULTURAL SERVICE

IVP Books

An imprint of InterVarsity Press
Downers Grove, Illinois

InterVarsity Press
P.O. Box 1400, Downers Grove, IL 60515-1426
World Wide Web: www.ivpress.com
E-mail: email@ivpress.com

InterVarsity Press® is the book-publishing division of InterVarsity Christian Fellowship/USA®, a movement of students and faculty active on campus at hundreds of universities, colleges and schools of nursing in the United States of America, and a member movement of the International Fellowship of Evangelical Students. For information about local and regional activities, write Public Relations Dept., InterVarsity Christian Fellowship/USA, 6400 Schroeder Rd., P.O. Box 7895, Madison, WI 53707-7895, or visit the IVCF website at <www.intervarsity.org>.

All Scripture quotations, unless otherwise indicated, are taken from the Holy Bible, New International Version®. NIV®. Copyright ©1973, 1978, 1984 by International Bible Society. Used by permission of Zondervan Publishing House. All rights reserved.

You Can So Get There from Here was originally published by MARC in 1969 and was reprinted through 1991. In 1991 it was revised by Steve Hoke and Bill Taylor as Send Me! Your Journey to the Nations, by permission of MARC/World Vision International, 800 W. Chestnut, Monrovia, CA 91016-3198.

Permission to adapt Send Me! Your Journey to the Nations by InterVarsity Press has been granted by World Evangelical Alliance Mission Commission and William Carey Library.

Permission to reprint material was granted by the following: All the writers of "My Journey"; all the writers of "Global Perspectives"; all the writers of additional articles and sidebars; Wherever magazine, published by TEAM, P.O. Box 969, Wheaton, IL 60189-0969; Perspective, Focus, and Mentoring workbooks by Terry Walling. Carol Stream, Ill.: CRM Publishers/ChurchSmart Resources, 1996 (phone: 1-800-253-4276); Public Relations, Columbia International University, P.O. Box 3122, Columbia, SC 29230-3122; Missions Today, The Short-Term Mission Handbook and The Great Commission Handbook, Berry Publishing, 701 Main St., Evanston, IL 60202.

Table 4 on p. 275 is reprinted from Paul Stanley and J. Robert Clinton, Connecting (Colorado Springs: NavPress, 1992), p. 42. Used with permission.

Photography is thanks to and with the personal permission of Taylor Martyn; Peter Shrock, CRM; Andy Silk, CRM; and Bill Taylor.

Design: Cindy Kiple

Images: grid: iStockphoto
mature woman hiking: Image Source/Getty Images
man with suitcase: ZenShui/Frederic Cirou/Getty Images

ISBN 978-0-8308-3717-5

Printed in the United States of America ∞

Library of Congress Cataloging-in-Publication Data

Global mission handbook: a guide for crosscultural service /
[compiled by] Steve Hoke and Bill Taylor.—Rev. ed.
    p. cm.
  Includes bibliographical references.
  ISBN 978-0-8308-3717-5 (pbk.: alk. paper)
  1. Missions. 2. Intercultural communication—Religious
aspects—Christianity. 3. Christianity and culture. 4. Cultural
pluralism. I. Hoke, Stephen. II. Taylor, Bill, 1940-
BV2063.G563 2009
266'.023023—dc22

                                                                2009021521

P	21	20	19	18	17	16	15	14	13	12	11	10	9	8	7	6	5	4	3	2	1
Y	27	26	25	24	23	22	21	20	19	18	17	16	15	14	13	12	11	10	09		

Dedication

Steve Hoke

To Don and Martha Hoke, my missionary parents, whose selfless commitment to a person-drawn cause over a lifetime modeled for me the purpose-driven life, and whose appropriate nurture and unfailing encouragement have guided my journey to the nations for the past fifty years. I still cannot come close to their levels of people-centered ministry and flat-out love for people.

To Stephenie and Christopher, my only children, whose pursuit of their God-given calling in very different spheres of influence continue to challenge me with their responsibility, availability to people and radical commitment to incarnationally live out the gospel in this generation. I still do not even begin to have their eagerness to share life in covenant community with the poorest of the poor.

Bill Taylor

To Bill and Stella Taylor, my missionary parents, with deepest respect for their example as lifelong servant-leaders and long-term crosscultural veterans, having "permanently changed their addresses," enjoying their eternal reward. To Yvonne, my life-partner since 1967, my mentor and muse, source of wisdom, full partner in life and ministry. To my children and their spouses, Christine and Cliff, David and Phaedra, Stephanie and Scranton, for loving me, keeping me honest and being such a vital part of my life and work.

In memory of those who have finished their race well, among them Phyllis, Jerrell Dean, Mac.

In honor of that cohort of faithful missional, crosscultural servants, all friends, too many of whom have already paid an incredibly high price. Among them Dave and Janet, Stanley, Ray and Gwen, Jan and Roy, Dottie and Carlton, Dave and Barbara, Caren and David, Rose and Dick, Kirk and Sarah, Matt and Michelle, Rod and Jennifer, Sergio and Linda, Doug and Lisa, Bertil and Alzira, David and Dora Amalia, Mike and Stephanie, Kees and Els, Younoussa and Alphonsine, David and Wendi, Keith and Suzanne, K and Pramila, David and Hunbok, Richard and Irene, Ramiro and Sonia, Marcos and Rosangela, Willie and Lydia, Dwight and Sandi, Pam, Jamie, Rudy, Reg, Alex, Piers, Steve, Jim and so many others.

With gratitude to the parents—later grandparents—who released their children into world mission.

With anticipation to the generations to come and those en route as we write, among them Brendan, Sarah, Taylor and Allison, Anne, Wendy and Aaron, Travis and Leslie.

Steve and Bill

To those who have completed the "Perspectives on the World Christian Movement" course, have attended at least one Urbana, Passion or other missions conferences and celebrations . . . and who want to know what to do next. You are the future servants, gifted, empowered, equipped, released, tested, willing to serve and to suffer in countless kinds of teams and ministries. You will serve short term, mid-term and long term within and beyond your geography and your culture.

Contents

About the Authors

Steve Hoke, *People Development, Church Resource Ministries*

Growing up as a missionary kid in Tokyo, I committed very early to lifelong involvement in world evangelization. I wanted to be a part of what God was doing around the world; it just took me a while to discover how God had wired and gifted me and to find the niche God had carved out for me.

Through college, serving in several churches, and graduate study, I realized my gifting was not as an evangelist or church planter but as an encourager-equipper and teacher. Through serving as a missions professor and director of campus ministries at Seattle Pacific University, director of field training for World Vision International, president of LIFE Ministries (Japan) and presently as vice president of people development for Church Resource Ministries, my gift mix has been confirmed—I'm a Barnabas, not a groundbreaking church planter like Paul.

In my present role, I help mobilize, prepare and encourage international teams for ministry around the world. My passion is to equip and encourage frontline crosscultural workers to minister with spiritual authority in the difficult places of our world. That involves face-to-face and distance coaching and mentoring, spiritual direction, training design, live teaching and training, and writing and coordinating various distance-learning modules. In raising up the next generation of mission leaders from across North America and the world, I want to do all I can to ensure that they are effective as intercultural servant-leaders.

I've been married to Eloise since 1972, and we now minister out of Fort Collins, Colorado. Our daughter, Stephenie, is a veterinarian, and our son, Chris, is chaplain to gangbangers with Tierra Nueva in Burlington, Washington.

Bill Taylor, Global Ambassador and Senior Mentor, World Evangelical Alliance

Born and raised in Latin America of missionary parents, I committed my life to missions at an early age. As a third-culture kid, I definitely found it challenging to move to the United States in my senior year of high school. But I survived and finished my university and seminary studies while working as an InterVarsity staff member in Texas. A Ph.D. in Latin American studies from the University of Texas, Austin, came some years later. After marrying my young artist wife, Yvonne, in June 1967, we moved to Guatemala, where I taught leadership development for seventeen years at CAM International's Seminario Teológico Centroamericano.

During those years we joined a church-planting team that led to a dynamic, mission-minded congregation geared toward the emerging professional class in the capital city. In addition to discipling new believers and having a ministry of intercession, Yvonne used her gifts as a classical pianist in pre-evangelism outreach.

Based in the United States since 1985, I teach missions courses at various seminaries. From 1986 to 2006 I served as executive director of the Mission Commission of the World Evangelical Alliance (WEA), a worldwide network of global leaders from the older and younger missions sending nations. Since 2006 I have continued with the Mission Commission as senior mentor while also serving the WEA international director as global ambassador.

Yvonne is my full partner and muse, serving as a critical thinker and sounding board, editing my writings and ministering with me locally and internationally. A long-time student of Christian spirituality, her calling from God has been to minister in spiritual formation, spiritual direction and mentoring.

Our life has been committed to crosscultural missions. Our three kids—all now married—were born in Guatemala; we also have six grandchildren.

My passion: to serve as mentor and sage, and to finish well with integrity.

Preface

Many have asked why we have produced a revised edition of what used to be called *Send Me! Your Journey to the Nations*. Well, the reasons are clear and relatively simple.

First, the world has changed in radical ways. When we first wrote, Christians weren't talking much about globalization. Global terror was not a daily news item; 9/11 had not yet happened. The idea that a clash of civilizations might be happening was relatively new; to name it as such was to clarify a reality for many of us. The devastating impact of endemic diseases and global pandemics was just coming full force onto our screens. Internet technology was young. Ours is now a *glocal* world—the global and the local have converged on us, with all kinds of implications.

Technology has exploded and changed the world. My new back-up hard drive for my computer has a brief thirty-one-page manual in sixteen languages! Technology through the Internet has also given us a *new* language: Wikipedia, iPod, iMac, iPhone, iTunes, YouTube, Facebook, MySpace, Twitter, The Cloud, Friendster, blogs and biospheres; and it has given us new categories, like social networking sites, or new verbs, like I just *Googled* "Christian martyrdom." However, by the time you read this, this new language may be passé. More seriously, though, is the question, will the Internet make us smarter, wiser or more civil? Probably not.

Ours is a more dangerous world. Anybody thinking seriously about a short-term to midterm to long-term mission must have a practicing theology of suffering, persecution and martyrdom. (We will address these issues as we move along.)

In short, we wrote *Send Me!* before the end of the twentieth century and the start of the third millennium. That's enough to require some changes.

Second, the category of generations has changed. In North America countries, we speak now of at least four generations, with approximate dates for each:

- Builders: born 1945 or earlier, experienced World War II, the Cold War, the beginning of the civil rights movement

- Boomers: born 1946–1964, experienced the Vietnam War, Watergate, the civil and women's rights movements

- Generation X: born 1965–1976, experienced the Reagan presidency, the collapse of the Soviet Union and the Berlin Wall, the advent of HIV/AIDS, globalization

- Millennials: born 1977–1994, experienced the tsunami, the presidencies of Clinton, Bush and Obama, 9/11, terrorism, the Iraq War, hurricanes Katrina and Ike

Our desire is that this new edition will be applicable to all generations.

Third, the world of the global church and missions has also changed radically. Most of the world's Christians are in the Global South. Mission does not belong to the West (Global North) alone. It's from all nations to all nations. We must learn from each other and not be naïve (believing such things as "everything from the Global South is good news") nor judgmental ("there is no longer any need for missionaries from the Global North"). Old dichotomies ("home" versus "foreign" missions; near and far; within culture and crosscultural; evangelism and social concern) are passé.

Many peoples of the world are now found far from "home" due to refugee realities and global immigration. These people have come to stay, bringing with them language and culture, faith systems (Islam, Buddhism, Hinduism, animism—and vibrant Christianity, hope for the weak churches of Europe and North America) and unique cuisine. We are plunged into new worlds all around us.

Contrary to popular thinking, the sending of long-term North America missionaries through established mission agency structures is not in decline. It is now growing, slowly. Sending peaked in the late eighties, then took a dip in the early nineties due to the retirement of a host of post-World War II missionaries. That coincided with the collapse of the Marxist-Russian-Central European system.

But in the mid-nineties we saw a noticeable increase in sending, which continues. This comes with major new trends worldwide: the technology explosion and the rise of the younger and more globalized Christian generations with a heart for the world and its multiple needs. But ultimately, it comes as the Spirit of God is at work.

Missions language, definitions and categories have changed. The new vocabulary in missions today includes *missional* in company with the use of a broader term *mission*. Regretfully, both words are used to describe almost everything Christians do in the world, so they risk losing their core meaning. In both the secular and the Christian worlds, the term *glocal* is increasingly used to refer to involvement and commitment both to the local and the global arenas. A Google search of *glocal* in late 2008 brought up 493,000 references. Glocal mission is in!

While short-term mission is a hot item (in 2005, 1.6 million Americans had some kind of short-term mission experience), long-term vision is changing. Missions from the Global North are increasingly more expensive, and funding patterns and structures must adapt. More and more local churches are determining the nature and focus of global mission, and clearly they set the budgets. Too many in North America have "missional ADD," that is, a very short missions attention span. Some churches are radically and unwisely changing their focus—sometimes it's the "missions flavor of the decade," sometimes it conforms to the passions of the current missions team leader.

Fourth, so much of what we said ten years ago needs to be said in a better and clearer way, and we have tried to do this. We have included many new voices in this global pilgrimage: those telling the story of their journey to the nations, those expressing the needed but changing role of missionaries from the Global North and those commenting briefly on vital issues.

And finally we, Bill and Steve, have changed. We are clearly older, more scarred, hopefully wiser. Our age gives us the advantage of having seen a lot of life, a lot of the world, a lot of missions and our fair share of mistakes. We have battled personally to stay in close contact with the living God. We have both faced unanswered prayers. But some things have not changed in either of us—the passion for God and the commitment to the centrality of Jesus the Christ, unique among all saviors, and the Christian faith, unique among all world religions. We are deeply committed to the life-transforming gospel of Jesus, and we long for every person in every generation to have at least one thoughtful opportunity to hear and understand the full claims of Jesus Christ. We long for the arrival of the full kingdom of God in Christ.

So for those reasons we present to you this second edition. We are delighted that InterVarsity Press has taken it on, with all of their creativity and commitment to the global cause of Jesus. We hope it will serve you more effectively in your own passion for the living, triune, missional God. We deeply want you to discern and engage your role in his eternal purposes for the human race.

Read on! Mull over the material, and let it mull you over.

Beginning Your Journey to the Nations

A PERSONAL FITNESS ASSESSMENT

INTRODUCTION
What Does It Take to Be Prepared?

STEVE HOKE AND BILL TAYLOR

This book covers the three major phases of missionary preparation and training that you need to consider before starting on your journey. Each of these has a number of steps.

Phase 1: Getting Ready

Before you get started, it's essential that you take a few moments to assess who you are and where you are now. The introductory "personal fitness assessment" (see the section "Grounding the Journey: Four Personal Fitness Assessments," pp. 38-39) helps you measure your present readiness to start on the journey on three levels—self-awareness, sensitivity and practical skills—a yardstick by which to measure and evaluate your present position and readiness.

This first section of the book will further define what a crosscultural missionary is and will give you a clear profile of several distinct crosscultural missionary roles still needed today.

First, personal spiritual formation. Who you are—your character and spiritual formation as a disciple of Jesus Christ—is essential to the role you will play and your effectiveness in missions, for ministry flows out of being. Clarifying your basic commitment, your "call" and your spiritual gifts, and making sure your spiritual foundation is solid, are foundational first steps to ensure an effective journey. Finding a personal mentor early in this journey is critical to starting well.

Second, discovering your ministry identity in the body of Christ. Understanding your church's or community of faith's unique missions vision and finding your place and gifted role in it are critical to your effectiveness in extending the church into other cultures. Experiencing God's power in making disciples in your home culture will hone your ministry skills and help sharpen your spiritual effectiveness *before* you serve in a crosscultural setting. You'll learn where you are spiritually powerful and where you need others in the body. Beginning to invest financially in missions now will accelerate your education and establish a lifelong habit.

Third, exposure to other cultures. Growing up in only one culture limits our ability to understand others, appreciate diversity and learn languages. Frankly, being monocultural is really boring for today's global citizen in a pluralistic society. So gain some early crosscultural exposure. Go beyond your comfort level by relating to people from widely different cultures. Forge intercultural friendships where you are. It will stretch your mental, physical and spiritual muscles and will help you understand and accept people of other cultures. It will introduce you to the intercultural differences that can be a block or a bridge in relationships across the cultural gap. It's also an invaluable crucible for testing your gifts, your passions, your dreams and your capacity for a long-term commitment.

Fourth, critical issues in schooling and support raising. Foundational academic preparation for a short- or long-term ministry needs to be considered and customized to your experience, skills and gifts, and to the demands of where you will serve. Not every effective crosscultural servant is a college grad. What kind of formal schooling and education do you need for missions today, whether vocational or professional? When would formal education genuinely contribute to your effectiveness? We'll sort through the steps you can take at this point that will broaden your worldview and enrich your basic educational background. We'll explore specific training for crosscultural ministry later.

Phase 2: Getting There

Fifth, church and agency connecting and courting. Your best work is not a solo effort. What sending group or "team" (church or agency) is the best fit for you? Making the connection with the right agency is similar to the courting process: both sides are getting to know each other. Who are you looking for and what are they looking for? What essential support systems do you need to put in place? What kind of team do you need to help make you most effective and to help you grow the most? What kind of team leader do you need to help you stay focused and effective? What are the options, and how do you think through them?

Sixth, ministry role and assignment search. Related to the question of the sending group are the questions of location, people group and the specific role God is asking you to fulfill in reaching others with the gospel. What is your ministry burden or passion? Who are those you'll reach? Where are they? How can your gifts be used in building up the national church? What is your initial assignment in God's overall game plan?

Seventh, hands-on missionary training. Language and culture learning are part of a missionary's "basic training." What are the various ways to gain the most practical ministry training outside the classroom? We'll explore a range of emerging models for just-in-time training that promises holistic skill training to prepare for your initial assignment.

Phase 3: Getting Established

Eighth, apprenticeships and internships. Effective missionaries don't just emerge fully formed from their church or educational experience. On-the-job ministry either at home or on the field tests what you've learned, provides models in ministry and helps you develop your own approaches to "telling the story" and establishing vital communities of faith. Being mentored in initial ministry ensures a healthy start, and come-alongside mentoring is more and more common.

Ninth, lifelong learning. When missionaries stop learning, they often wither or get stuck. Assuming a posture and establishing a pattern of lifelong learning early in your career is essential to finishing well over the long haul. How intentional and discerning can you be in designing your own annual learning projects that keep you on the leading edge?

Tenth, finishing strong and well. Crosscultural ministry is a crucible for character development. Understanding what it means to finish well is crucial, particularly in an activist Christian subculture that values task accomplishment and activity. Why do so many leaders *not* finish well, and how can we anticipate pitfalls? We want to help you become intentional in your spiritual development so that you can grow stronger *from* and *in* service, rather than weaker, so that during your entire Christian pilgrimage you will walk the long path of obedience in the same direction—whether you are in missions or not.

Navigating your journey is not about planning a vacation; it is about becoming intentional in joining God's foreign-policy team. It's taking time to pray and plan how you are going to get actively involved. It's about taking specific steps forward in sync with the Spirit rather than being shoved around sideways by peer, family and career pressure. It's about moving from the grandstand to the playing field, whether as a grower or as a goer.

Your own journey will be unique. Charting it will be a life-changing process. These ten steps, energized by the Holy Spirit, will help you transform your ideas and commitments into a powerful plan for spiritual change.

A Note About the "My Journey" and "Global Perspectives" Pieces

As we dreamed, prayed and planned this revision, we wanted to listen to the voices of some of our friends and colleagues from other cultures. We have done this in the fifteen "My Journey" narratives and in the fifteen "Global Perspectives" (on four key questions).

 Out of many **"My Journey"** narratives in our files from women and men of both Global North and South, we have selected these representative few. Each summarizes how God led her or him into crosscultural mission. You will listen to younger as well as older, women as well as men. They speak of special influences, challenges, struggles, arenas of services and, especially for the veterans, reflections during the latter season of life.

North Americans have their own brand of nearsightedness. We tend to see the world from our perspective, and know little else. To remedy that myopia, we asked some of our friends and colleagues who play important roles in the global church to share their perspectives on four critical questions. Sprinkled throughout the book, the "Global Perspectives" pieces may further stretch your understanding of what God is doing around the world.

 For the **"Global Perspectives,"** we asked leaders to respond to these four key questions:

1. What is the *role of the missionary from the Global North,* that is, the West (North American, Europe, New Zealand and Australia)?

2. What kinds of global ministries are *attracting the attention of the next generations* (younger, middle and older) going into mission today?

3. What kind of *prefield training* would you recommend to this next group of Western partners to have?

4. What are the prime *character and spirituality qualities* you would want them to demonstrate or be committed to?

Some responded to all four questions; others focused on two or three. Again, allow these global colleagues to speak from their experience into your own life and future.

We trust these will encourage you as you read and as you identify with your sisters and brothers who are walking or have walked their own pathway into the world.

My Journey

TAYLOR MARTYN
SIM (Serving in Mission), United States, Sudan

I had always pictured myself making lots of money and being able to actively be a "sender." My father was a successful businessman, and I never saw myself doing anything different. During my freshman year of college, I participated in the missions course "Perspectives on the World Christian Movement." My class was administered by a retired SIM missionary who is now a professor at John Brown University. I believe God had me attending this class to soften my heart to a message I would hear toward the end of that semester at school.

Late in the semester I had the opportunity to hear from a group representing Mercy Ships at an evening event. As I listened to what they had done while on mission, my attention focused on one of the guys who had participated as a videographer. My degree was in media, and I knew I wanted to do video production. In the midst of their sharing, I realized God turning on a light bulb in my head. I came to a realization that not all missionaries are church planters. Teachers, engineers, bankers and nurses are just examples of the myriad of skills needed on the mission field. In this moment, I realized God wanted me on the mission field, capturing the stories of missionaries to tell back to the American church. I had no idea when, where or how I would come to be a missionary, but that night I started my journey toward a life of missions.

My major was digital media, minor in graphic design. Allison, my wife, was majoring in intercultural studies with an emphasis in community development. We both took the Perspectives class. Allison's degree is built around the idea that it will be used overseas in a missions environment, so many of those classes were taught from that vantage point. I took a few classes with her and got a heavy missions emphasis/application on everything I was learning.

This Handbook Is for You!

STEVE HOKE AND BILL TAYLOR

This hands-on workbook has been designed for two kinds of people: those who have a deep desire to serve God crossculturally (whether within their geography or further away) and those who want to invest in them. We aren't trying to persuade people to become missionaries. Rather, we assume an initial interest—an early indication or drive somewhere inside that God may have invited you into an intentional missional future. It might be a long-term desire or a recent stirring in your heart. We assume that you sense a holy discontent in staying where you are in life and lifestyle, but neither are you running away from life and personal problems. We also assume your initial and serious commitment to explore the options before you.

We are aiming at a variety of readers, but with two primary ones: younger adults (students and young career women and men) facing an open future and older adults facing the challenge of an early retirement or career change.

Some of you have had the sense for a long time (perhaps since childhood or early youth) that God has invited you into world mission, to serve him in another culture, country, language, religion or worldview. And now you desire to engage this future with follow-through commitments. This handbook is for you.

What we advocate here will also help churches, mission "events," campus groups, schools, missionary training centers and agencies to think and pray through short-term and long-term plans with those responding to the voice of the missional God. While we are profoundly committed to the right kind of short-term missions, at the same time we also challenge our gifted and mobile younger adults to make long-term commitments. This will require some of you to stand against some of the driving values of your generation. The final ingathering of the fulfillment of Matthew 28 and Revelation 5:9-10 will not be accomplished without women and men willing to invest their gifts in substantial, longer-term service.

Who else might be our readers? *Global Mission Handbook* is written to help those who have attended an Urbana student missions convention and have made watershed decisions for missions and for those who have been met by God at a Passion conference or another radical gathering of younger or older Christians dedicated to God's global purposes. We also have designed this new edition for those who have taken the Perspectives course with its dense DNA of the heart of God, the history of mission and some of the strategic issues we face in missions today.

This handbook is also written for the "finishers," that generation of older servants who have completed one or more careers and now long to be used of God in another culture for the sake of the gospel. It's crafted to apply to those going into restricted-access nations as teachers, engineers or person with the skills and experience to begin a viable business venture that will create jobs and contribute to national development.

Finally, we have structured this book to best serve mission mobilizing teams, missional churches, sending structures (mission agencies) and schools and training centers that help prepare missionaries for long-term, effective crosscultural service.

So if you know of someone who has made a serious and significant commitment to crosscultural mission, this book just might help him or her to move forward toward the goal of serving in a crosscultural setting.

A Few Key Items

First, short-term or longer-term? The terms for lengths of mission service are debatable. While many mission agencies do not call a two-week (or less) mission trip "short-term," this is probably the most popular use of the term in church missions programs. Missions researcher Michael Jaffarian wrote to Bill personally that

> long-term missionaries are those whose length of service is expected to be more than four years. Short-term means a term of service expected to be at least two weeks up to one year. In fact, almost all who are counted as "short-term" serve for at least a month. Most mission agencies, in their reporting for the *Mission Handbook,* don't count 1-2 week mission trip participants in the short-term category here. Middle-term means a term of service longer than one year but shorter than 4 years.

Where do we stand on these definitions? We tend to think of short-term as something less than two years; mid-term, two to four years; longer-term, four years or more.

We have been asked whether we are writing for the short-term missionary or the longer-term one. The answer, in a sense, is both. But we are profoundly convinced of the need for long-term crosscultural servants of all varieties who will invest a decade or more of their lives to give every person a viable opportunity to respond to the person of Christ. Our dream is to become coworshipers with all peoples, languages, tribes and nations. This will happen in part through the work of short-term workers, their service and later intercession and mobilizing.

But, historically, the advance of the kingdom of Christ in the earth and the establishing of his church among the peoples and cultures of the world is due in large part to those willing to leave their homes and cross language, cultural and geographic barriers to share Christ and see his church come to maturity. So we have to be upfront with you. Yes, as writers, we are both committed to short-termers. But our heart's desire is to see vast new cohorts of young and older adults in longer-term crosscultural servant ministries.

Second, traditional or nontraditional? Others have asked us whether we are writing for the more "traditional" church-planting missionary or for somebody going into other kinds of crosscultural work, such as "business as mission" or relief and development. Well, we really hope this tool is valuable for the whole range of options and possibilities.

What crosscultural roles might be for you, and how would this workbook help you? If you are anticipating any of these crosscultural contexts, we think you will find *Global Mission Handbook* both practical and encouraging. You may be, or hope to be, someone going into . . .

- mid-term service somewhere in your mother tongue but in another culture
- long-term service as part of a church-planting team, having to learn a new language and culture
- business as mission assignment, creating jobs and contributing to national development
- missionary mobilization and training in another culture

- medical missions and training
- literacy and/or Bible translations
- arts and mission, ethnomusicology or some other creative expression
- relief, development or transformational work
- partnering and grass-roots service to the national church
- developing high-tech facilities for national ministries
- leadership development or training ministries
- bivocational tentmaking, as a teaching or engineering
- mentoring and nonformal leadership formation
- any other of dozens of categories

Third, what or who really is a missionary? The term *missionary* generates diverse definitions, so let's take time to grapple with the issues. For some, "everybody is a missionary." But then, if everybody is a missionary, nobody is a missionary. If everybody is a teacher, nobody is a teacher. A few argue that only a select and highly spiritual group of people should be honored with this title; still others discard the title totally and substitute "apostolic messenger" or "crosscultural partner" instead.

What can we then suggest? In part we are guided by a biblical theology of vocations, natural abilities and spiritual gifts, all coming from Father, Son and Spirit.

As you read through our material, you will see a consistent use of the broader term *mission,* which speaks of the most encompassing and holistic task that God has given his church to fulfill in the world. This term is the key descriptor used by those of us who are committed to the global missionary task.

In the New Testament, the Greek term *apostello* emerges in two major categories: first, as a broadly used verb, meaning to send in one form or another and by different senders (132 times);

and second, as a more specifically used noun connoting the apostolic person (80 times). The core New Testament concept clusters around ideas related to sending or crossing lines, to those being sent, the sent ones—whether the original apostles or others who serve with some kind of apostolic authority or function. The New Testament affirms that the apostolic messenger (the missionary) becomes the person authoritatively sent out by God and the church on a special mission with a special message, with particular focus on the Gentiles, the "nations." Authors such as Alan Hirsch accurately capture this biblical dynamic when they speak of "the apostolic genius" of the early church. The apostolic motivation was part of the "missional DNA" of the early church.

In Jewish records, this term describes authorized messengers sent into the Hebrew Diaspora for special assignments. The New Testament adopts some of these ideas, as well as a broader concept from Greek culture: divine authorization. It then injects new meaning into the work of the missionary apostles: diverse, long-term service and Spirit-empowered ministry, with particular focus on the missionary task, that is, the extension of the kingdom of God in Christ. The New Testament uses the term for the original twelve disciples, but opens it up to other authorized messengers, which include the apostle Paul and some others.

In the post-apostolic era, *apostello* was used when speaking of itinerant ministers. In A.D. 596, Gregory the Great sent the Benedictine monk Augustine to lead a "missionary delegation" to the British Isles. Roman Catholics use the term "sent ones" in reference to their monastic orders.

As the Latin language became the common church translation in the Western, the Latin synonym *mitto* became the dominant word. This term is the root of the English "missionary." Thus an "accident" of linguistic history replaced the original Greek concept, with all of its richness and depth.

The Protestant Reformation, partially in reaction to Roman Catholicism, minimized the "missionary" term and concept. In their zeal to eliminate other excesses, the Reformers tossed the structure and language most essential to maintaining an outward focus—that of the missionary orders of the Roman church. This missional impulse reemerged in the Protestant churches starting with the Moravians in the early eighteenth century, who used the term *missionary* for their broad-spectrum enterprise. It was then adopted by the Protestant missionary pioneers William Carey, Adoniram Judson, Robert Morrison, David Livingstone and their successors in the late 1790s and into the 1800s.

We are convinced that *missionary* is not simply a generic term for all Christians doing everything the church does in service to the kingdom of God. We do a disservice to the term by universalizing its use, oversimplifying a rich vocabulary and theology of gifting and vocation. While all believers are witnesses and kingdom servants, not all are missionaries. While all believers must be committed to and involved in mission, not all are missionaries. We do not glamorize nor exalt the missionary, nor do we ascribe higher honor in life or in heaven, nor do we create an artificial office. In an attempt to get away from the old, worn-out images of "missionary," some of our good friends are introducing new terms, such as "partner" and "crosscultural servants." No problem! Just be sure you define this key term and concept.

How do we draw this discussion to a close? Both of us are committed to a robust biblical *theology of vocations* (God has given us diverse vocations and all are holy, but not all vocations are the same); a *theology of gifts* (not all are apostles, nor do all do miracles [1 Cor 12:29], therefore, not all Christians are missionaries); and a *theology of callings* (the sovereign triune God calls some to this position and task). These women and men are crosscultural workers who serve within or outside their national boundaries, crossing some kind of linguistic, geographic or cultural barrier in obedience to God.

Charting Your Pilgrimage

Becoming an effective crosscultural servant is not easy. Regardless of where you live, what culture you claim, what language you speak, whether you want to travel far or not, whether woman or man, whether younger or older, the road toward effective crosscultural service is full of roadblocks, detours and false starts. It's easy to get discouraged. That's why we have offered a "journey" template to help you chart your course "from here to the nations."

A lifetime cannot be planned in one sitting or more, with a workbook or just a program, alone or with a group, or with the latest broadband wireless technology (backed by iChat, Twitter, Facebook or any other global social-networking option). With some grasp of the available information, you can gain an overview of what lies ahead. You will need to stay tight with the living God and be led by his empowering Spirit as you embrace the future God has for you. This workbook attempts such an overview. It also provides several checklists and worksheets so you can put dates on the benchmarks you pass along the way. It will also periodically ask you to reflect critically on the journey and to journal—intentionally—to write out what God is saying to you, what you are learning and becoming and how you are growing and preparing.

This handbook describes three phases of missionary development with foundational components that should be worked through as you move through each phase. Although these components are ordered sequentially, this is not a lock-step, mechanical ordering. You will be able to adapt the sequence to your personal circumstances. There are also side paths we suggest for you to take as you integrate personal information and creative opportunities.

The format is simple: after we discuss the background of each component, you are invited to engage them through a number of questions. These will guide your reflection on what you have been thinking and will help you keep a journal of where you are on this thoughtful pilgrimage. Each element along the way has external resources from which you can draw.

All the way through, you will find articles by some of our global colleagues, telling their own story. Other sections will challenge and encourage you to engage current questions—for example, is there still a role for the Western missionary?

Let's be honest. Heading into any variety of crosscultural mission is challenging, especially if it calls for long-term commitments. You may see it as a long road, a winding path, a pilgrimage into the unknown. But that's what life is, and trying to walk in step with the Spirit in a radically changing world is what the Christian life is all about.

For a thoughtful, comprehensive summary of key terms, see Christopher J. H. Wright, *The Mission of God; Unlocking the Bible's Grand Narrative* (Downers Grove, Ill.: IVP Academic, 2006), pp. 22-25.

🌐 Global Perspectives

REUBEN EZEMADU
International Director,
Christian Missionary Foundation, Ibadan, Nigeria

Role of the Missionary

Though the Global South is rapidly transforming from a "mission field" to a "significant mission force" in the twenty-first century, this does not mean that missionaries and missions from the West (Global North) no longer have a role to play in today's global mission needs. Western missions and missionaries still have a stake in global mission for some obvious reasons.

What might be some of the advantages of veteran crosscultural workers from the Global North?

- They bring years of experience in crosscultural ministry.

- They may have easier access into many countries.

- They bring strong support mechanisms and resource bases from churches with centuries of a sending culture.

- They provide availability and affordability of strategic resources, tools and facilities.

But the roles will change in many areas, from

- pioneers to supporters of national initiatives

- solo players to team players

- experts to coaches and fellow learners

- going only themselves to sending and supporting nationals partners

- masters to servants

- parents to grandparents

What would be some complementary roles of these older workers?

- They should be marked by encouraging, strengthening and resourcing existing mission and church structures as well as local initiatives in areas where the church is strong and already engaged in missions. What is God already doing in this "mission field" that can be affirmed?

- They should also become pioneers in those areas where the church is still weak but which are still easily accessible by Westerners with appropriate expertise, resources and diplomatic privileges to penetrate such areas.

- They must focus mainly on places where the gospel has not penetrated or where there are no local efforts toward such.

- They can model Christian unity by promoting efforts in working and relating better with other Western missions in the same country or area of assignment.

Attracting the Next Generations

Some of the global ministries attracting the attention of the next generations going into missions today include the following:

- ministries that are related to their professions

- ministries that involve the application of highly technical skills and facilities

- ministries that need their intellectual ability

- ministries that afford them opportunities for rapid social mobility

- ministries that are not too boring and do not tie them down for a long period

- ministries that are adaptable and reproducible

The Global Canvas
How Your Story Fits into the Big Picture
BILL TAYLOR AND STEVE HOKE

Living in a context of constant change can be exhilarating and disturbing, challenging and exhausting. It's exhilarating to live life to the fullest and to do it in the context of eternal truths in a rapidly changing world. It's deep joy to know that we serve Jesus Christ the Lord, the unique Son of the living God. But we are bombarded by too much information, too many experiences and too many decisions. The swirl of life and history at times seem too random; life is chaotic! It's exhausting because the stimulus dazzle is so much more than we can absorb, much less sort into meaning and significance.

Just consider some of the realities we face as citizens of our world today. Danny Hillis, a computer designer and inventor, says Google changes the way we think: "Knowing things is very twentieth century. You just need to be able to *find* things."

But is this really the full story? No. But exploding technology and the Internet substantially affect the way we think, read, find information, learn, decide and act. The jury is out on the power of the Internet: is it making us wiser or dumbing us down? Do Google and Wikipedia give us knowledge and wisdom, or are they just information sources?

We are deeply committed to both the younger and the older generations. We affirm the broadening concerns of our younger friends, which includes a commitment for the preservation and protection of life as well as the environment; the clarity of the gospel of Jesus as well as understanding that people today approach God differently; the protection of religious liberty, racial harmony and the reform of immigration policies in the United States; the defense of marriage and family as well as the desire to alleviate global hunger and poverty.

We rejoice in the living God who shares these multiple concerns. But we ask with the jailer in Philippi, "What must I do to be saved?" Let us not fall into oversimplifications of the gospel, into fuzziness about what the transforming Grand Story of God in Christ is to all generations and all cultures. Let us not fear telling truth and Truth, even as we narrate our stories and the Epic.

In the global mission enterprise, we experience yet more levels of change. So let's grapple as thoughtful Christians with some of these global and local (glocal) issues and trends. Mull over the following list of issues and trends and grade them in light of how they might impact you as a Christ-follower committed to world mission. A high score is 5 and low is 1.

First brush strokes: What are some of the *macro issues* facing us in our global community, the human race on planet Earth?

Triad 1

The reality of globalization (a global whole, the intensification of worldwide interrelations), with its winners and losers. Friends in North America lose their jobs to India and friends in India get new jobs. But what about Nigeria and Nicaragua? Globalization as the grand disrupter is a Hydra with many faces—economic, cultural, technological, media, terror and faith systems, to mention only a few. Globalization is good-bad, helpful-hindering, invigorating-deflating all at the same time. And anti-globalization reactions are for real.

The clash of civilizations, with 9/11 a symptom of a much larger reality. We will see tensions and wars following the civilizational "fault lines" of our planet—tribal, religious, economic, political. Where will tribalism end up? Danger will increasingly threaten the global Christian mission movement, so we need a theology and practice of suffering, persecution and martyrdom.

War and injustice are daily bread for too many, with certain regions and nations most threatened. Slave trafficking is on the rise. You can purchase a young Haitian girl today for a mere fifty dollars. Yet, in some nations where peace has emerged, Christians have the unique opportunity to contribute to national reconciliation and healing, restoration and development.

Triad 2

The technological explosion continues unabated and shapes us personally and globally, hopefully for good. It redefines information flow and economics, communication and travel, medicine and human relationships, education and entertainment, personal and family life, employment and a sense of the future.

A massive worldview shift has taken place, affecting the entire globe—from modernity to post-modernity and now to post-postmodernity. Progress and science are questioned, and spirituality is in, but there are too many dabblers in transcendence. Postmodernity has major implications at the level of lifestyle, the arts and literature, science and technology, spirituality and religion. Life is fluid, commitments are tenuous; all belief systems are equally valid, or not; metanarratives are out, but there is space and a hearing for authentic truth telling of the epic Christian story. People will come to faith in Jesus as they transition over a series of "thresholds."

Apparently random natural physical disasters unleash uncontrollable chaos, whether tsunamis, earthquakes or advancing deserts.

Triad 3

The reality of endemic disease confronts us, whether it be malaria, HIV/AIDS, Ebola or the threat of some other random and ravaging virus. Malaria, which can be eradicated, kills more people than HIV/AIDS. The younger generations, in particular, seriously want to make a change here.

Populations explode and cluster most clearly in the cities—whether small or world-class in size, particularly in nations with limited natural and economic resources to feed, nurture, educate, employ and keep their people healthy.

Christians around the globe constantly grapple with *systemic injustice, disproportionate wealth distribution and poverty.* They wonder, "What can I do?" Again, these are hot issues for the younger generation.

Triad 4

An historic migration of peoples is taking place due to shifting economics and political violence. In China alone, 150 million migrant workers have surged into the cities. Consider global migration: the nations are everywhere. Even in small Western towns you can find clusters of peoples from around the world, many of them holding on to customs, culture, faith systems and language.

The Muslim populations in Europe, and to a lesser degree in North America, will continue to change the historic landscape of these countries, where the Christian church struggles for vitality and renewal.

New and sophisticated systems of globalized terror threaten in every nation. No one is safe anywhere.

Triad 5

Economic crises in one region inevitably ripple around the world, impacting the global family, all linked to the borderless economy—another face of globalization.

Resurgent world religions (some clearly missionary, such as Islam, and other newly so, such as Hinduism and Buddhism) are on the move, with attractive adaptations to "win the West" by immigration, birth rate and conversion.

Islam in particular becomes a global faith, in head-on competition with Christian mission and presence.

And again, engage. Mull the following list of issues and grade them in light of how they impact and concern you personally as a Christ-follower committed to world mission. A high score is 5 and low is 1.

Let's switch the global lens and focus on some of the *macro issues* facing our global Christian community. Here we have to examine ourselves and our Christian faith, evaluating the status of the Christian faith, its various communities and its missionary movement. Each region or country has its own particularities, so we will focus primarily on North America.

Triad 1

The church of Jesus is globalized today as never before, and with it comes a parallel missional heart from all the nations of the world. This face of globalization demonstrates the valued interconnected nature of the global family of Christ, with resources and passions, with struggles and victories. There is a growing sense that God is at work in history and that we may be either on the cusp of a global meltdown or on a journey into the last major phase of history.

The anemic, fractured church in the Global North is now recognizing as a mixed bag—with huge strengths and resources, but with structural flaws. Something is wrong. We have not experienced authentic transformation of worldviews. We need a radical openness to the Spirit of God, as well as a heart that listens to and learns from the church in the Global South. But we also know that not all is well and healthy in the Global South churches, which face their own particular challenges today.

We grapple with *philosophical and religious*

pluralism. Christians in North America, especially younger ones, hold to their singular truth but also seem to affirm a gentle and persuasive universalism. All crosscultural workers must be prepared to suffer, to face persecution and even martyrdom because of the Name above all names.

Triad 2

Harassment and persecution is a daily reality for some 200 million Christians around the world, especially in Islamic, Hindu, Buddhist, animist and militant secular contexts. Militant Islam, Hinduism and Buddhism have carefully targeted Christians, and the number of martyrs is not complete.

Many thoughtful younger and older mission partners and leaders are concerned about a dangerous *evangelical tendency to minimize theology,* opening the doors to a "gracious universalism." Is Jesus just singular—like the choice between Coke, Pepsi or Sprite—or is he unique—there is no one like Jesus the Christ?

The younger generations are passionately *pro-justice* and concerned about poverty, modern slavery and global trafficking, consumerism and the environment—and rightly so.

We live today as players in a prolonged season of radical transitions. What might some of them be?

Triad 3

The transfer of creativity, responsibility and authority from the older to the younger Christian generations, including the unprecedented transfer of wealth from their elders.

The emergence of a new wave of young leaders who passionately desire to live as practicing supernaturalists in a secular world, willing to play a high-risk game in following Jesus. They are also creatively starting new Christian ventures in the name of Jesus. They are hardwired, but also need a strong dose of long-term commitment to finish well what they have started.

The tectonic shift of Christianity from the Global North to the Global South teaches us that the Spirit is moving South without abandoning the North. And the new glocal mission call is "from all nations to all nations." Our global missional partners truly reflect "from every tribe, nation, tongue and people."

Triad 4

The nations of the world have come to the West, a great opportunity to tell them the great Story of Christ. It is also an invitation for Western churches to be infected with the family and celebratory values of these younger Christian communities now implanted in the West.

The surprising faces of "mission from the margins," from the nobodies, from the "underside of history," from the Christians migrating around the world—legally or otherwise. They are on the move, following freedom, jobs and a better place for their families, and they take the gospel with them. The revitalization of the Christian church of Europe will come in part from the vital faith and conversion of migrant peoples, especially from Africa and Latin America. Some of you, in the name of Jesus, may be called to serve with these unusual servants, on the margins of history and society, on behalf of the poor and oppressed. Just don't be naive about it or go it alone.

The shift of ownership of the missions movement from parachurch groups to churches, with all kinds of partnerships emerging. This means greater church involvement in selection and screening, testing and equipping, supporting and interceding, strategizing and shepherding of the mission force. It also calls for strategic alliances between churches and training schools and field-based agencies. The wisest churches are those who realize that they cannot do missions on the fly, a "McMissioned" variety of the Great Commission of Jesus. The smartest churches engage in strategic cooperation in thoughtful prefield mis-

sionary training, sending structures and on-field systems of shepherding and strategizing.

Triad 5

The explosion of short-term missions as significant appetizers of crosscultural reality and ministry for thousands of young and older adults, some of whom will be forever changed and others who will return to invest longer seasons of their life in mission. In 2005, 1.6 million American Christians had a short-term mission experience. But this raises many questions. Have these crosscultural trips significantly changed values, behavior and commitment to long-term mission services? Have short-termers influenced the mission vision of their churches? Have these trips touched budgets and lifestyle? And have the funds used for 1.6 million short-termers affected budgets for long-term workers and projects?

A reworking of missions language and definitions, such as "terms of service" from the traditional to meanings that allow greater geographical mobility; a greater flexibility of vocational change during a lifetime; more focus on teams; and sequential terms of service with longer periods at "home" for ministry, equipping and restoration.

Business as mission and other varieties of bivocational workers require creative skill sets and gift mixes for ministry in open as well as restricted-access nations. We need originality to develop new "creative access platforms" for long-term ministry. Before you launch into a business-as-mission venture, be sure you can do it in your home culture. We need skills here, as well as a robust theology of vocation and work.

A Final Quad

We must avoid oversimplification (reductionism) of complex missions realities: the Great Commission is more than just evangelization; the unreached/less-reached/hard-to-reach world is vast; people-group thinking is only one paradigm of the need; short-terms are great, but not a substitute for the long-term crosscultural servant.

Future crosscultural, long-distance, long-term servants must prove themselves in their own geographies, which are increasingly multicultural. In the United States, the younger generations (shaped by postmodernity) as well as the newer immigrants are open to spirituality, to relationship, to authenticity. And younger Americans will come to Christ over a series of "thresholds" of conversion, from distrust to trust, from complacency to curiosity, from being closed to change to being open to it, from meandering to seeking. Only then will they cross the threshold of the kingdom of God in Christ. If you cannot wisely tell the story of the gospel in your own culture, what says you will anywhere else in the world?

Our next generation of Western missionaries must go out as servants, able to serve alongside and under the leadership of other cultures and mother languages. We must allow others to set the agenda and then serve with them.

We will grapple with realities, needs and desires as we try to fund mission into the future. The older model of personal support raising, will continue, but we need new ones—creative, realistic, functional. Perhaps it will mean more kingdom companies (designed to make a profit, of which a significant percentage goes for global mission) or more bivocational and business-as-mission servants, or more strategic alliances between churches and agencies. But we must find a new way. Who are the thoughtful incubators here?

So there you have it. This is our reading of history and our role in God's story. Thank God that his story is going somewhere, and so is your life. But we must take the time to make the connections between events and trends that some observers might describe as random.

Drawing to a Close

Ultimately, no one else but you and the eternal God can connect the dots and sketch out the landscape of your life and future. You've got the ball in your court, but you are not alone. You must be empowered by the Spirit, counseled by God's people and grounded in your values and commitments. The wisdom of others' experience, as well as knowing the story of how the church has gotten to this point, will assist you in your journey.

For that reason you'll want to work with others in this project. It's in community that God truly wants to reveal himself. We need one another. Invite into your story the community of friends, of family, of a spouse, of your spiritual leaders, of veteran missionaries and crosscultural workers.

Come, walk this lifelong, global pilgrimage of long obedience in the same direction. We are convinced that you will witness the greatest spiritual harvest of history. But it will not come easy, so prepare to serve and suffer in ways you could not imagine. Prepare to encounter the evil one in his diabolical attacks. Be ready to get sick and perhaps never get well. Prepare to die but die well. Countless thousands like you are already engaged in this crosscultural pilgrimage of the epic Story. They are not all North Americans or Europeans. Today's missions movement is a truly globalized mosaic, with servants from Africa, Asia, Latin America, the Caribbean, the Middle East and the South Pacific.

These broad strokes on a global canvas make us think of the book of Revelation—written by a persecuted pastor-apostle-poet-prisoner to persecuted Christians. In the midst of the most horrific experience for true followers of Jesus, God was in control; worship would happen; believers would suffer; evil would be judged; there would be a triumphant end to this chaotic history.

So let's encounter this same living and triune God of the book of Revelation and enter into our own missional story for planet Earth.

The next generation of history belongs to you!

Ancient Principles for Our New World of Partnership

DAVID RUIZ

Partnership for us in the Global South means something different for those in the Global North. We define it differently; we view human and financial resources differently (money is not that important in the South); and we measure success differently. The main challenge for those who want to see healthy and spiritually driven cooperation is to return to Scripture to define what authentic partnership really is. That will allow us to evaluate how it functions and what we call success. Here are two key concepts to consider.

First, there is no substitute for character as the prime characteristic of those who want to see effectiveness in partnership. This means that above all we want to see

- humility that recognizes that we all are part of the same church but that there are new patterns of doing things and new players in the global scenario

- simplicity to discern respectful arenas of cooperation in unexpected places

- wisdom to share lessons that help others people, groups and churches to become more effective and faithful in mission

- a gracious learning attitude to discern how Global South Christians understand the mission of God, as well as missions and cooperation

Second, we are convinced that spiritual business needs spiritual principles in order to function and succeed. We all need to commit ourselves to be faithful to the biblical principles of cooperation as seen in 2 Corinthians 8:

- The believers first "gave themselves to the Lord and to us" (v. 5 NASB, and paraphrased).

- "Not as one who orders but who serves" (v. 8). We cooperate in order to join God's plan, not because we have more and richer resources or a better plan to solve all the problems.

- "Not as one who has, but who gives everything" (v. 9). We are not to exhibit wealth but to experience the joy of giving.

- Based on concrete actions that provide benefit to those with whom we partner (v. 11). Alliances do not begin when we sign an agreement but when we are in true relationship, where we know each one and love each other. Only then are we ready to work together.

- The result of truly good partnership provides mutual benefit (v. 14). As a result of cooperation, we understand and practice equity and worthiness, where each person has something unique to provide and to complement the other.

Cooperation/partnership is an act of love that introduces us to a two-way path where we must encounter the quality of love of 1 Corinthians 13. John 13 profiles Jesus as the model of love, and John 17 establishes its measure of success. As we move into a century of cooperative, multicultural mission partnerships, Jesus' model is our clearest, finest and only proven pattern. God's ancient principles once again set the stage for a new world of partnerships.

David D. Ruiz is a Guatemalan pastor who served for ten years as president of COMIBAM (the Ibero American Mission Movement). He is currently an associate director of the Mission Commission of the World Evangelical Alliance.

Missions in a World That Is Flat and Tilted

PAUL McKAUGHAN

New York Times International Affairs correspondent Thomas L. Friedman wrote a seminal book emphatically announcing to everyone living on it that their world is flat.[1] The two salient characteristics of Friedman's flat world were the ubiquitous and quasi-universal access to unimaginable knowledge, and the ability to collaborate in real time with anyone anywhere, at anytime.

Honestly, we all know that the world is not truly flat. Flat is merely a metaphor that enables us to see a global reality. There are the frustrated billions of poor, disenfranchised people who live in vast pockets of need all around the world. They have neither access to global knowledge nor the ability to enter into distant collaborative ventures. However, the flat-world metaphor is helpful to describe a dominant reality you and I live each day.

The world into which I came as a young missionary sure didn't seem flat. It still featured long voyages by sea to reach one's field of service. A month between my written question and the home-office response was considered normal. My world of missions back in the Brazilian jungle seemed like the missionary stories I heard from the 1800s. However, the forces that would flatten our missional world were already in play.

In those earlier days, that flattening world was definitely tilted in our direction. We in the West had the masses of church members, money, education and status, and quite naturally we imposed our missional priorities and models on the rest of the world. In spite of our feelings of entitlement, God blessed and, over the years, he raised up millions of new Christ-followers on every quadrant of our still flattening world.

Throughout the world this flattening process has been going on for many decades. Only recently have we realized the extent to which the process has impacted the church and its mission. Leverage and the tilt of the flattening world shifted toward the church in the Global South.

The number of Christ-followers in the Global South is growing exponentially while the churches in the old sending countries are in decline, both in size and vibrancy. The revival of his church is the West's only hope to reverse our negative trends.

Churches in countries that were once recipients of our missional focus send missionaries in numbers already surpassing ours. In the West we find it disconcerting to be considered the focus of missionary passion from churches in Asia, Latin America and Africa.

The once-assumed moral ascendancy of the West is vividly and constantly debunked through our narratives and lifestyles viewed by billions on global TV, movies and the Internet. Sadly, the United States is seen by the world's masses as a corrupt, oppressive war machine enforcing economic dominance.

Not many years ago our technological edge helped tilt the world in our direction. However, nations that were technologically deficient catapulted right over the intermediate stages of technology into the digital age. Their countries are now manufacturers and purveyors of our technological solutions. In some instances, missions from the West are forced to play technological catch-up.

Even financial resources that once ensured that our missional agenda found receptivity have been diminished by the weak dollar, increased costs and the economic ascendancy of emerging market countries. Today many strong national churches, and their missions, have the financial resources to do what they want to do. Our money, though we still have more of it than anyone else, doesn't have the impact that it once had. The flat world is now tilting in their direction, not ours.

Since we live in this metaphorically flat new world that is tilted away from us, what is our place; how should we function? To withdraw as though our job were done is not an option. To assume others can now accomplish the task and that somehow we have been absolved of responsibility would be criminal. To turn inward and concentrate on meeting our own needs would be self-serving, disobedient and sinful. The masses of people who need to experience Christ and his grace are the most numerous in human history.

Flatness was new to Friedman, but it is a very old biblical concept. The Bible says that in Christ there is no male or female ascendancy. There is no advantage to slave or free. There is no Jew or Greek superiority. We are all one in Christ and are part of the same body. The church is one global-local reality. We knew this, yet we assumed that somehow our education, history, money and technology conferred on us the right for the flat world and Christ's church to be tilted in our direction.

The first necessary step toward operating in the new flat world is to repent of our superior attitudes. Repentance means we have to act differently. Rather than always pushing our agenda, we need to take time to listen more and truly hear the burdens and agendas of the Majority World church. Where do we fit in the agenda God has given them?

The apostle Paul says the body, Christ's church, works through its differentiation and functional collaboration. That is a very flat-world concept. He asks the Corinthian church, can we all be eyes or hands or feet? No! Collectively we are a body and can function well only when all the parts work as designed by the Creator. God has gifted individuals and, I believe, also cultures and peoples so that together we can be a more complete and dynamic collaborative representation of Jesus Christ, God's Son. We must know the things we do well and stop doing things others are gifted to do better. This demands great honesty and humility. We collaborate best when our limitations and differences are recognized and accepted as complimentary to the strength of others.

There is another biblical fact relevant to doing missions in a flat world. All we are and have is God's. There is nothing we possess that God did not give us for his glory and for the advance of his reign. Accountability is ultimately to him for the use of his resources. We must be good stewards; however, stewardship and control are not the same thing, no matter what the IRS may say. In this flat world, all our structures must enhance collaboration, not merely efficient self-service. Even internal administrative processes must improve collaborative kingdom output. We must give up our control mentality, no matter how subtly it manifests itself. To do otherwise is to choose the path to missional redundancy.

We must look to him and, in faith, aggressively seek our unique and productive place as servants in his flat world. They are rightly assuming more responsibility for leadership. We may no longer control the agenda. So what! The proper stance for a Christ-follower is, and always has been, that of a humble servant. We must look to him and to our brothers and sisters, and in faith aggressively seek our unique and productive place as servants in his flat world. That is an awesome privilege!

We are on a mission with our God in the most exciting and exhilarating time his church has ever known. The world is flat. Almost universal access and the ability to collaborate with few limitations are global characteristics on this flat world. This divinely ordered context holds the potential for unimaginable kingdom synergy. Let us thank our Lord for the privilege of serving him and his church in such a day as this, and let us take full advantage of the flat and tilted world.

Paul McKaughan served as a missionary to Brazil for twelve years before returning to the States to help direct Mission to The World for a decade. After serving for fifteen years as president of EFMA, Paul assumed new responsibilities as The Mission Ex-change (formerly EFMA) ambassador at large. Paul and his wife, Joanne, now travel coast to coast and continue to serve the mission community through speaking, teaching, coaching and mentoring mission leaders.

[1]Thomas L. Friedman, *The World Is Flat* (New York: Farrar, Straus and Giroux, 2007).

Participate in the Story of His Glory

BILL TAYLOR

It's an experience forever etched in my memory. Yvonne and I were standing that evening under a large tent pitched on the Youth With A Mission base just outside Auckland, New Zealand, during one of the evening sessions of the South Pacific Prayer Assembly. We had been honored to join believers from eight South Pacific nations for a week-long event. The worship had been rich, the prayer powerful, the diversity of peoples, languages, cultures and streams of Christian faith simply glorious.

That night, Michael Maelieu, a spell-binding storyteller from the Solomon Islands, narrated God's historic and epic work in the islands, thanking the Westerners present for bringing the gospel to their isolated region and paying with the high cost of their very lives. He shared the story of the dramatic advance of the gospel among his own people—people who one hundred years before had been an unreached, cannibal group.

But then Michael's focus changed. "Now we island believers have heard God calling us to share with you, our Australian and New Zealand brothers and sisters, the flaming missionary torch of the gospel you so lovingly brought to us." He called all the Papua New Guinea and South Pacific islanders to the front, and then the Aussie and Kiwi leaders, inviting his island peo-ples to encircle and minister to their Western colleagues.

The heavenly sounding cacophony of prayer, singing, weeping, glossolalia and worship was incredible. Islanders prayed fervently for Australians and New Zealanders. The former mission fields had been converted into new prayer and sending bases for world evangelization in the form of what was called "the deep sea canoe mission movement." We sensed deep in our spirits that this would be a transformational transaction that would radically shape history in that region.

Flash Forward to Heaven

In my mind I was transported to that majestic series of more than seventeen worship scenarios that play out in the drama of the book of Revelation. In chapters 4–7, John the apostle, prisoner, pastor, poet and prophet offers us magnificent scenes that center attention on our glorious, sovereign God and his Son. These scenes range from the four mysterious creatures to the twenty-four elders, from angels to all creation and from heavenly choirs to an unprecedented worship procession, which John describes in Revelation 7:9-10:

> After this I looked and there before me was a great multitude that no one could

count, from every nation, tribe, people and language, standing before the throne and in front of the Lamb. They were wearing white robes and were holding palm branches in their hands. And they cried out in a loud voice: "Salvation belongs to our God, who sits on the throne, and to the Lamb."

But, how did all these peoples get there? The story of God's glory begins before creation in the mystery of the Holy Trinity. It dramatically unfolds in the opening chapters of Genesis. Our first parents are the prototype of all humanity, created in God's image, loved by the Father, to be redeemed by the Son in the power of the Spirit. The entire biblical record reveals both gradually and in narrative spurts God's passionate heart for all his creation, for all people made in his image, loved in spite of their rebellion.

Israel, God's select community, is chosen and set apart to be a light to the nations, a testimony to the world of the one true God. They were to do this within their ethnicity, their geography, their language, their holy city and temple. By their example and testimony they were to extend an invitation to other peoples to "come and see," to encounter the living God. Sadly, they did not obey, came under judgment and were scattered among the nations. Yet God was not finished with his plan.

Through the incarnation and arrival into the earthly realm of the holy Son of God, Jesus Christ, both Israel and the nations around her would encounter the Messiah, the suffering Savior. Following his death, resurrection and ascension, the Spirit would come upon the apostolic band of faithful disciples with power and authority. The rest of the New Testament records the emergence of the new missional people of God (Jew and Gentile). But this time the movement is to and from all ethnicities, languages, geographies, cities and nations. Very

soon the early church became both polycentered and multidirectional—a preface to what we see today around the entire world.

Embedded in the heart of our loving God is an invitation to participate with him in his grand redemptive plan. Children, youth and adults have sensed with conviction (through some kind of "calling" or invitation) that God is asking them to leave their culture and family to cross barriers. They do this in order to present the claims of the risen Christ and to establish worshiping communities among all the peoples of the world.

In obedience to his call, they have been willing to pay the costly price of leaving home and family to serve in difficult, even dangerous, contexts—whether in cities or rural areas. Jesus made it clear that to follow him we must be willing to take up his cross. And the two-thousand-year history of the advance of Christ's kingdom and the establishment of his church is filled with stories of heroic courage, losses, suffering and glorious victories. Satan does not relinquish his captives nor his power and control easily! Missionary biographies reveal plenty of tough times, bitter and sweet tears, gut-wrenching pain and loss, darkness and despair, as well as joy and victory. But these servants, motivated by love, persevere so that the Lamb, who is worthy to receive all praise and worship, "might receive the reward of His suffering"—in the words of the Moravians.

Central to the seer-pastor's vision is the reality of persecution and martyrdom for some because of Christ. Remember that the New Testament was written by persecuted Christians to persecuted Christians.

When he opened the fifth seal, I saw under the altar the souls of those who had been slain because of the word of God and the testimony they had maintained. They called out in a loud voice, "How long, Sovereign Lord, holy and true, until you judge the inhabitants of the earth and avenge our blood?" Then each of them was given a white robe, and they were told to wait a little longer, until the number of their fellow servants and brother who were to be killed as they had been was completed. (Rev 6:9-11)

Well did the ancient Celtic Christians speak of a tricolored martyrdom: white for leaving hearth and home, clan and land, going into exile for Christ's sake; green for self-denial and penitential acts that led to personal holiness; red for persecution, bloodshed or martyrdom.

The Importance of Worship

The prime and ultimate business of heaven is worship. John Piper's words resonate in our hearts: "Missions is not the ultimate goal of the church. Worship is." So why do we still have missions? "Missions exists," Piper reminds us, "because worship doesn't." The task of claiming worshipers for God and his Lamb is unfinished business. We come to understand that worship and mission merge as overarching passions, motivating and sustaining us as we labor to pack heaven with worshipers.

As we make our way into the unknown future of the third millennium, the stunning truth is that we are privileged to see what the prophets of old longed to see: God's plans and purposes coming to fruition and fullness. Against tremendous odds, the church of Jesus Christ has advanced and become truly globalized. The mission of God is now flowing *from* all nations *to* all nations. We stand at an incredibly significant crossroads. This is a *kairos* moment, and we're privileged to be a part of it. Thousands of faithful disciples have preceded us and participated in the harvest. The Holy Spirit calls us to minister in word, deed and power, and he fills us with himself to enable us to do so.

But in order to see heaven filled with the final ingathering of worshipers from all the people groups and nations, we will need a new wave of vibrant, courageous, long-term, crosscultural workers. We must identify, equip and deploy a new generation of radically committed servants and partners who will live anywhere, who will identify with the oppressed, the widows and orphans, the trafficked women and children, and will cry out for justice in the name of Christus Victor—Christ our Champion. Working in multinational teams, they will be willing to stay long enough to learn the language well, to understand the culture and to love the people. God will show them how to narrate the full saving Story, how to incarnate the gospel so that the church can be established and strengthened. They will stay long enough to see not only converts, but mature disciples whose worldviews have been transformed by the empowering Spirit of God. They will have the inexpressible joy of seeing those whom they served join the vast multitudes already surrounding the throne of God, who worship the Lamb.

We will all have the privilege of presenting the once-unreached peoples to our Lord as our offering of praise. That's where history is going, and that's our part in the story of his glory.

A Final Story

Some years ago, Yvonne and I stood on the cold, windswept, sandy shores of the wee island of Iona, a center of Celtic Christianity and missions, where St. Columba of Ireland had arrived in A.D. 563 with his mission team of 140 colleagues. Iona first, then England's Holy Island and countless other centers throughout the British Isles became seed beds of gospel and community, education and art, creation-keeping and mission teams. The Celts developed the singular concept of *peregrinatio,* combining spirituality and pilgrimage in order to explore the unknown and to carry the gospel to those who had not heard. Their symbol for the Spirit was the wild goose, and in his power they evangelized the wild Picts (in Scotland), much of England, France, Italy, Switzerland and as far away as the Ukraine and Byzantium.

As we spent time on the island of Iona, we were struck by the power of this ancient expression of Christianity that flowed out into the world in obedience to Christ's commission. It was yet another historic example and inspiration to us in our own pilgrimage of faith and mission. We were strengthened in our resolve to live lives of holy abandon to the Spirit, journeying wherever he leads, willing to walk the costly path of discipleship so that Christ may be known and honored near and far.

As you move forward in your commitment to serve in crosscultural missions, be prepared to live to the fullest, to be tempted to the worst, to be challenged in your health and in your spirituality, even to doubt your faith (just be sure to doubt your doubts!). You will at times wonder about the relevancy of the very work you do, wonder if it's worth it. Just hang in, learn and grow, honor your marriage vows and love your children, laugh and worship, befriend and cultivate deep friendships, serve people and the church, stay long enough to see the fruit of some of your investment.

Back to Iona. One dark, cold, windy night in March, as we lingered in prayer after a quiet service in the abbey, we experienced an almost mystical presence of those Celtic saints of old, those who in their time followed the call of the wild goose to make Christ known in far-off places. We felt in those moments a deep connection to them across the barriers of "clock" time. For we, too, like they, had said yes to Christ's call to the nations. As devoted followers of heaven's High King, we are all part of an ancient and unbroken line of splendor—from Pentecost to today—whereby the kingdom has spread and penetrated the human realms of this world.

It is a beautiful mystery that God would invite frail and broken humans to participate with him in this glorious Story begun in Genesis and culminating in Revelation. As our individual stories are caught up into his story, we become part of a grand adventure with a certain ending. For all these reasons and more, we will press on until our role is done on this earth. And then we will join all those who have gone before, where the story of his glory continues from everlasting to everlasting. Amen.

Mission in Contexts of Suffering
BILL TAYLOR

It's an increasingly dangerous world, especially for those who thoughtfully claim the uniqueness of Jesus Christ and the uniqueness of his epic Story. We estimate that today some 200 million Christians live in pockets of intense persecution. In no country is anyone exempt from suffering for the cause of our Lord, whether from militant Islam, Hinduism, Buddhism, animism or secularism. The recent tally of modern martyrs finds them in Turkey and Jordan, in Mexico and Indonesia, in Afghanistan and Nigeria, in India and Sri Lanka, in Somalia and Pakistan, and in the United States. Do we need to recall and study the words of Jesus in John 15:20:

"Remember the words I spoke to you: 'No servant is greater than his master.' If they persecuted me, they will persecute you also."

Marv Newell gave a helpful survey of these themes in November 2008 in Thailand at the global consultation convened by the Mission Commission of World Evangelical Alliance. Using Matthew 10, he made a number of observations about the universal, uneven and unabating persecution of Christians. In this chapter, Jesus commissions his disciples for their ministry starting in Israel but ultimately extending to the entire world. It is rigorous prefield training for all who would experience transformational discipleship.

Note the degrees of opposition:

- rejection (v. 14)
- detention (vv. 17, 19)
- violence (v. 17)
- persecution (v. 23)
- martyrdom (vv. 21, 28)

Note the sources of persecution:

- family (vv. 21, 35-36)
- society and secular powers (v. 18)
- religious powers (v. 17)
- demonic powers (v. 28)

So here are a few questions to ponder:

- What are your thoughts about physical suffering because of the name of Christ?
- What is your theology of suffering, persecution and martyrdom?
- What Bible passages help you the most as you think about these themes?
- Who can best teach us about these topics?

You will find a worldwide gold mine of helpful information on this challenging topic in a recent issue of *Connections: The Journal of the WEA Mission Commission* with forty writers from twenty-seven nations. Articles range from a theology of persecution and martyrdom to codes of best practices to stories of persecution and martyrdom in countries like Turkey, as well as resources and information on the Web at <http://www.weaconnections.com/index.php/articles_archive/list/category/missions_in_contexts_of_suffering_violence_persecution_and_martyrdom/>. There you will find Newell's article and a review of his book *A Martyr's Grace* (Moody Press, 2006).

Grounding the Journey
Four Personal Fitness Assessments

STEVE HOKE

Like mountain climbing or even backpacking for a day hike, long-term mission takes careful planning and preparation. If you "train" right and "pack" well, you'll be better able to handle the unexpected and weather the difficulties. Before you get started, here's a personal fitness assessment with three levels: self-awareness, sensitivity and practical skills. Greater self-awareness will lead to greater sensitivity, which in turn will help you to develop greater insight into yourself and to hone practical ministry skills.

Self-Awareness Level

You carry your culture with you—whether you're conscious of it or not. Until you see yourself as you really are, you'll see both yourself and others from a distorted point of view. The first part of your personal preparation program helps you gain a balanced perspective with the use of some important and simple tools.

1. Taking a cross-sectional view: Profile of a critical role needed today. The first self-assessment tool ("Assessment One: The Missionary Needed Today," pp. 39-40) allows you to see how *who* you are today matches with the profile of one critical role needed in missions, that of a crosscultural church planter, regardless of your public identity or job assignment or specific function in mission.

This role is only one of a variety of important ones needed in missions today, including Bible translator, provider of technical services, mentor-coach, business entrepreneur, relief and development worker, video producer or bivocational servant, to name but a few. Some of the new roles include serving as facilitators, trainers, leader developers and side-by-side encouragers. But we've chosen the core role of church planter as a

baseline profile because it takes into account some of the most important personal spiritual formation and character traits, ministry skills and knowledge areas you will need to have.

Each person will have the privilege and challenge of customizing this to his or her specific field role. So don't be alarmed if you are not heading into church planting and don't stack up against those who do. This profile is to give you an idea of the range of attitudes, skills and knowledge you want to pray through as you prepare for ministry in another culture.

2. Evaluating your readiness. The second self-assessment tool ("Assessment Two: Evaluating Your Readiness with Real-Life Case Studies," pp. 46-51) asks a series of questions as you read through the case studies of others preparing for their journey. Their stories and the issues raised may give you a framework from which to see the importance of evaluating your own readiness at this time.

3. Taking a spiritual gifts inventory. In "Assessment 3: Discovering Your Blueprint for Living" (pp. 84-97), we introduce a third assessment: a spiritual gifts inventory. Spiritual gifts are the areas where God is powerful through you. A spiritual gifts assessment is available online to help you assess where God has made you strong (and weak) and to help you see from the outset what other people and giftings you need. It is not about what you are good at, but rather about what the Spirit of God empowers you to do. It is not your natural abilities or skills that make the difference, but rather the dynamic power of God at work in you and out from you, so that he gets the glory and not you.

Spiritual gifts emerge as you are serving. This starts in your home culture and home church.

There you minister and are affirmed by others as they see where you are effective. These abilities are relational gifts that only come into play as you relate with others in communities of faith. Depending where you are in your faith journey and how much exposure and experience you have in ministering in the body of Christ, this simple gifts inventory will help you identify three to four of your areas of most effective ministry.

4. Using journal worksheets. The fourth self-assessment tool is a journal worksheet at the end of each section of this book, asking guiding questions for you to think and pray about in all three related areas: self-awareness, sensitivity and practical skills. Dialoguing with God, listening to his voice and jotting down your honest assessment of where you see yourself now will serve as a helpful benchmark as you continue to grow spiritually, mentally and relationally. The more brutally honest in a self-evaluation at this initial phase, the better you will be prepared to respond honestly and thoughtfully to the questions of others as you take your first steps toward missions involvement.

Once you've taken these steps, you might even think that you are almost packed and ready to go. You'll have a sense of, "Hey, I've already thought and prayed about that. I'm ready to take the next step."

Just stay humble!

ASSESSMENT ONE

The Missionary Needed Today

STEVE HOKE

Before you get started on your journey, it may be helpful to take a look at the kind of missionary needed today. In the past, many missionaries were sent out by agencies after receiving formal education at colleges or seminaries. Knowledge—the accumulation of useful information and methods a student might need in missionary ministry—was emphasized. Everything thought important was front-loaded. It was assumed that once on the field, a graduate would be able to draw on this reserve of information. It was also assumed that future education would be difficult and inconvenient, so why not get it before going? It was a compelling argument . . . fifty years ago. But our world has changed since the 1950s.

The trouble with this approach is that much more is required of a missionary than knowing the right stuff. Crosscultural service is a crucible that tests one's character, probes one's spirituality and stretches one's ministry skills, while also demanding a wide range of background knowledge. The best way to develop a sound missionary training curriculum is to begin with the end in mind—what a missionary needs to *be*, to *know* and to *do*—and then build backward to design the learning experiences needed to reach those goals.

Notice the balance between knowing, being and doing. This description of qualities and competencies creates a verbal picture—a profile—that defines goals in a holistic manner, specifically focusing on the character qualities (including spiritual formation), ministry skills and knowledge needed for effectiveness in ministry. It's an approach that treats the learner as a whole person and sees the relational task of missions as having those three dimensions as well. It is an important shift from concern only with what individuals need to *know*, to who they *are* and what they can *do* as a result of training.

One word of warning: effective missionary service has little to do with "competency" in the way the world uses the term. It is more than what you know, what and where you have studied, and what skills you've developed. Ministry (doing) flows out of being. Crosscultural servanthood arises out of your very identity in Christ, not your academic training or professional skills. The critical factor will always be a vibrant spirituality empowered by the presence and power of the Holy Spirit. No matter how well a missionary may be trained, if the presence of the Holy Spirit is not in that person's life, she or he will just be going through the motions.

In the past several years, a consensus has emerged among stakeholders in the missionary training arena: effective missionaries are those best able to identify the qualifications necessary for missionary service. So quality and "competency profiles" have been designed based on the input from these experienced missionaries. A forum of missionaries, trainers, mission agency leaders, sending pastors and leaders of receiving churches has prayerfully described what a missionary profile should look like. This consensus approach is critical in creating commitment to change in training programs. The single profile generalizes (for the sake of space) the most critical elements for parallel roles, including the crosscultural

mentor-coach and tentmaker.

We present an abbreviated profile of one distinctive role North Americans can fill in the global missionary enterprise: church planter.[1] This is only one of a variety of important missionary roles needed today, including the tentmaker, the mentor-coach, the Bible translator and the provider of technical services. Yes, the North American crosscultural servant-leaders of the future will carry out differing roles. Some of the new emerging force will be facilitators and trainers; others will be leadership developers; yet others will be specialists. Most will work side by side with colleagues from other nations. Some will work under non-Western leadership.

Many of you will serve on teams, and this is good news. It means you don't have to have all the qualities desired in the church-planting profile. But you must major on the character and spirituality issues, as well as on those critical skills and knowledge components that you don't want to serve without. So as you evaluate these profiles, do it in light of the particular role you are considering in each one.

---

[1]See Robert W. Ferris, ed., *Establishing Ministry Training* (Pasadena, Calif.: William Carey Library, 1995); updated in Integral Ministry Training: Design and Evaluation, ed. Robert Brynjolfson and Jonathan Lewis (Pasadena, Calif.: William Carey Library/WEA Missions Commission, 2006).

How Can This Training Profile Serve You?

BILL TAYLOR

Welcome to a profile of a long-term, crosscultural servant, one that combines the most critical cluster of characteristics sought in missions, focusing on three areas: character qualities, ministry skills and knowledge goals.

Let me make three initial observations on this profile.

First, don't be overwhelmed by the apparent detail you will discover. Relax! This profile is the product of a series of training projects around the world. It's not an American deal. It suggests a set of tested markers that have been put into practice in India, the Philippines, Korea, Nigeria, Argentina and North America.

Second, one profile obviously cannot identify all the necessary competencies for every possible missionary role, especially those specific skills needed in areas such as literacy and Bible translation, community development, theological education, business as mission, pandemic relief, medicine, technology, the arts and other specialized ministries. But it does identify the core competencies needed by most missionaries as we read history and look to the future.

Third, some of you say, "But I'm not going to be a church planter, so this really doesn't apply to me." Let's look at it from another angle. One of my good friends, Kent Parks, is the leader of a very creative agency-team that focuses on the less-reached people groups of the world. They have staff dedicated to ministry to the "discarded ones" of India, the handicapped. They are seeking some of the crucial "redemptive analogies" that may lead to spiritual breakthroughs in resistant people groups.

But my friend expresses a broader vision when he speaks to his team and to future servants who would say, "This is who I want to work with." Kent asks, "What's your passion? We want to share it. Your heart beats for the oppressed in Thailand, the children captured in the slave trade? The Dalits of India? So you want to invest your life in national development or business as mission or teaching English as a second language? Great! Here's the comprehensive vision: we ultimately want to see worshiping communities of Jesus' disciples in these contexts. We want innovators in ministry who know that the heart of Christ is to see people experience freedom from their bondages—material, spiritual, physical, emotional. Jesus is passionate about his church also—these wor-shiping communities—and we challenge you to think how best to see new fellowships established among the people you love and serve. This is the broader perspective; this is the ultimate picture we want to see: Jesus followers and worshipers here, who will join those worshiping throngs ultimately in heaven. So go to the hardest areas, the least loved, the toughest to reach, the least-less-unreached peoples of the world. Serve them fully and play your strategic role to establish these creative faith communities of transformed Jesus disciples."

This week, Yvonne and I spent a memorable evening in the home of some friends, dedicated to bless and pray for a gifted and committed single woman in her forties. Lois was headed off to Rwanda to serve as a teacher-mentor in a series of community schools whose students had come out of the genocide. Lois, who had left a very successful teaching career in a high-quality, private, Christian school in Texas, had now signed up for a first two-year term, but her future was radically open. This is the kind of risk-taking I love to witness, some twenty-four years after her first Urbana student missions convention, where the Spirit of God first touched her.

With this in mind, we see at least six different groups of people who will profit from this profile.

1. Those who plan to enter long-term crosscultural work, that is, the missionary candidates. Raquel and David, a young couple thinking about long-term mission, saw an initial draft of the profile. As David began reading the material, he said, "This is what I need right now! It will help me to evaluate who and what I should be in terms of character, skills and knowledge, and our pastor will be encouraged to see the important role our church has in shaping us for crosscultural ministry." Ultimately the sovereign God led them into the pastorate, and it fit their particular gifts. But their heart pulses with God's heart for the peoples, near and far. They are truly glocal, rooted in the life of a vibrant local church in a very secular city.

You as a future crosscultural servant have the primary responsibility for your own development and ministry effectiveness, but you will want to do this in a spiritual community of mutual accountability. If you are being sent by your home church or through an agency, this profile becomes a very helpful tool for evaluating your process of preparation for crosscultural ministry. Potential tentmakers or those going into business as mission will also find the profile helpful in identifying the general competencies needed, though not specifically applied to those unique roles. You will want to be careful to build on the character qualities basic to all serious missionaries.

2. Local sending churches. A radically new attitude is transforming churches as they recognize and reaffirm their essential role in the selection, screening, equipping, sending and field supporting of their own missionary candidates. At the same time, many churches realize there are some tasks they should not tackle alone, so they engage in a variety of strategic alliances with other churches, schools, agencies, groups and key individuals. Other tasks can be delegated in the wisest manner, such as specialized training (linguistics, TESOL, business as mission, anthropology, technology courses) and more substantial biblical, theological and missiological study (such as in crosscultural communications and contextualization, comparative religions or the study of a specific religion, and church planting in difficult areas). Instead of sending missionaries under-prepared, the wise church utilizes all available resources.

3. Mission agencies or sending organizations. Regardless of the kind of sending group, it's important that the organization think critically to determine as carefully as possible what kind of missionary it wants to send. It is imperative that agencies work in gracious dialogue and interdependence with their missionaries' sending churches. Careful use of the profile, with its specific adaptations, will help. Each group will need to modify the profile to fit its specific parameters and requirements.

4. Missions mobilizers. The key men and women gifted with ability to encourage, envision, stimulate and motivate now have an additional tool. It will help them balance their passion with a serious evaluation of the kinds of missionaries the world will need as we move in obedience to Christ into the future.

5. Missionary training schools and programs—whether based in the sending or the receiving culture. The profile challenges leaders and faculty with a more holistic set of learning experiences: formal (classroom-focused, exams, degrees), nonformal (field-based, out-of-school learning) or informal (incidental learning through life experience) that will enable the school to provide the right kinds of learning experiences that lead to the crosscultural workers needed. The profile can also help professors identify the teaching and learning objectives they should focus on in their knowledge-oriented courses. At the same time, schools and training programs must realize they are partners with candidates and their churches and sending agencies.

6. Field-based receiving and partnering churches or ministries. Where there is a receiving church or others already committed in the same area, its leaders play a key role in the entire process of equipping the missionary. Obviously, this won't apply to countries or people groups where there is no existing church.

Overall, the greatest benefit in the profile comes when all six players involved enter into mutual dialogue and interdependence in understanding their roles.

Personalize the Profile

The profile is designed to assess your readiness

and suitability to serve as a crosscultural worker. It is divided into three sections: character qualities, ministry skills and knowledge goals. Each row lists subcompetencies or qualities for each category, listed in the left column. Entry-level qualities begin in column one on the left, progressing toward more advanced ones in the numbered columns to the right. Spend time reading through the basic profile. It is designed as a self-assessment tool.

Once you've completed the profile, take a few minutes to look back over each category to see what it tells you about your level of spiritual experience, maturity and ministry skill. Consider the following questions:

1. What are the several areas in which I am strong? Is there a pattern that links my church experience with my area of ministry skill? What areas of strength can I continue to build on?

2. What are the areas in which I am weak and need further development? Which ones do I want to work on first? How can I begin to make progress on them now?

To evaluate your progress in each of the categories, you can reassess yourself periodically during your preparation. Each time you reassess your progress, check off or highlight the areas in which you have grown, and then note your total score and the stage in your preparation.

Training Profile of a Crosscultural Servant

STEVE HOKE

While this profile examines the characteristics that lead to effective establishers of worshiping communities of Jesus followers (that is, churches), don't think of this as a straight-jacket that will limit who you are and how the Spirit wants to use you. Most of these qualities apply across the board to everyone deeply committed to long-term crosscultural servanthood.

Instructions. Remember that this profile is designed to help you assess your readiness and suitability to serve as a crosscultural church planter. It is divided into three sections:

1. spiritual formation/character qualities

2. ministry skills

3. knowledge goals

Each row lists subcompetencies or qualities for each category listed in the left column. Entry-level qualities begin in column one on the left, progressing toward more advanced ones in the numbered columns to the right.

1. Score one "point" for each box that describes an area in which you are experiencing growth or now feel competent. Leave it blank if it is still an area for substantial growth.

2. Tally your scores for each row in the "Total" column on the far right.

3. Sum your row totals in the box at the bottom right. This is a somewhat arbitrary number to help you establish a benchmark, which indicates areas of present strength as well as areas for personal growth.

TRAINING AREA	1	2	3	4	5	6	Total
SPIRITUAL FORMATION / CHARACTER QUALITIES The missionary . . .							
Spiritual Formation	Knows and loves God and exhibits fruit of Spirit	Spontaneously worships God, growing in personal and corporate worship and power	Is responsive to God's guidance; exhibits endurance and personal transformation	Recognizes God's lordship and leadership; evidences obedience and submission	Is committed to world evangelization; has a clear vocational calling	Grows in exercise of spiritual gifts and disciplines, including prayer, fasting, love and time in the Word	
Spiritual Power in Ministry	Consistent experience of God as source of quality and fragrance in relationships	Experiences God's forgiveness, evident in grace-giving and acceptance	Evidences the fruit of the Spirit consistently and gives off the aroma of Christ in relationships	Evidences an attitude of brokenness and forgiveness to others	Hears God's voice clearly and consistently to discern ministry direction and share wisdom	Evidences a growing spiritual authority and power in prayer and ministry	
Family Wholeness (for couples)	Both spouses practice mutual submission and loving service	Freely expresses feelings and empathizes with others	Nurtures and trains children lovingly	Protects planned time for holidays and recreation for family; plans "margin"	Encourages each family member in spiritual and ministry growth	Relates well to the larger mission family and community	
Single Wholeness (for singles)	Accepts single status, yet is open to change	Expresses feelings and empathizes with others; no unresolved conflict with friends	Able to give and receive in nurturing relationships	Protects planned time and recreation; plans "margin"	Is aware of the particular challenges of being single in a crosscultural context	Healthy relationships with singles and married, whether expatriates or nationals	
Servant's Heart	Accepts God's love and forgiveness, growing in grace	Submits to Christ's lordship in trust and obedience	Puts others above self; actively serves to meet needs of others	Serves others with diligence, joy and faithfulness; can easily forgive	Gravitates to the needy	Models the example of Christ	
Adaptability	Recognizes God's sovereignty	Gladly accepts difficult circumstances	Adapts flexibly to new situations and is resilient	Appreciates various personalities and styles of leadership	Evidences contentment in various settings	Distinguishes between what's "wrong" and what's "different"	
Cultural Sensitivity	Appreciates and values the host culture	Is sensitive to host culture's expectations and mores	Is sensitive to host culture's models of learning and leading	Recognizes the importance of language learning as ministry	Takes responsibility for lifelong language learning	Recognizes social structures and areas of cultural captivity and strongholds	
Commitment to the Church	Models active participation in a local church at home and in host culture	Reflects Christ's love for the church—the communities of Jesus' followers	Partners with and serves the national church	Stewards relationships and activities for maximum long-term impact on planting reproducing creative expressions of communities of faith (churches)		Values the heritage of a people and church, and learns from past	

TRAINING AREA	1	2	3	4	5	6	Total
MINISTRY SKILLS The missionary . . .							
Language Learning	Recognizes the importance of language learning	Listens actively and discerns language sounds and patterns	Disciplines self to practice regularly; grows "bonding" relationships	Takes personal responsibility for lifelong language learning	Accepts failures and learns to laugh at mistakes	Uses language effectively in living, learning and ministry	
Cultural Adaptation and Contextualization	Appreciates and values aspects of the host culture	Copes with cultural differences; lives incarnationally	Understands the natures of the cities, cultures and communities	Conversant with needs and concerns of prayed-for ministry groups	Collects relevant data; analyzes and interprets findings accurately	Adapts behavior and "contextualizes" appropriately	
Evangelism and Discipleship	Shares Christ in culturally appropriate ways	Leads people to Christ and enfolds them in local cells or churches	Disciples new believers in Word, prayer, witness and fellowship	Equips believers to reproduce and have a heart for people in local communities	Motivates others to use their spiritual gifts; engages in spiritual warfare	Empowers and releases disciples to personal ministry	
Church Planting and Maturation	Prays strategically	Analyzes the social environment	Builds relationships; can grow cell groups of new believers	Develops an effective evangelistic strategies	Trains small-group leaders to train others and multiplies cells	Establishes a reproducing cell and/or faith communities	
Leadership Development	Identifies, selects, nurtures and equips potential leaders	Helps believers interpret and apply the Word in their context	Equips believers in appropriate Bible study methods	Empowers and entrusts others for responsibility; builds intentional partnerships	Plans and equips for transitions in partnership with national leaders	Contextualizes biblical leadership styles	
Leadership Follower-ship Skills	Envisions new ministries; enlists others in vision	Uses historical insights to teach churches	Motivates, recognizes and celebrates others' contributions	Matches appropriate biblical leadership style with the situation	Functions as team player and servant-leader	Ministers in Word, deed and power of the triune God	
Interpersonal Relationships	Affirms others; not monopolizing or domineering	Willing to listen, especially when corrected	Builds accountable relationships; respectful of spiritual authority	Properly relates to nationals and coworkers of opposite gender within cultural guidelines	Experienced in community living; manages conflict without explosion	Relates well to people of different personalities and cultural backgrounds	
Professional Bivocational Competencies and Skills, i.e., Tentmakers	Demonstrates a strong biblical, theology of vocation, work and ethics	Has appropriate professional qualifications to match openings in host country	Integrates occupation with ministry; has mindset of application to host culture	Manages self effectively; organizes work efficiently	Maintains personal and organizational accountability	Appropriately engages in multiple simultaneous tasks	

TRAINING AREA	1	2	3	4	5	6	Total
KNOWLEDGE GOALS The missionary should comprehend . . .							
Foundational Bible Truths	The flow of the biblical story and the missional nature of Scripture	Biblical holism; life and ministry of Jesus; "apostolic genius" of the church	Bible study and interpretation principles and methods	God, Christ and Holy Spirit; spiritual gifts; human nature and destiny	Salvation (including sanctification, victory in Christ, ethics, and so on)	Principles of Christian living; the church; apologetics, and so on	
Ministry and Missions	Church / mission partnership theory and strategies	Evangelistic methods and strategies	Developmental principles of spiritual growth and formation	Understands church planting, growth theory and strategies	Religious history of target people; missions history	Christian spiritual classics; religious dynamics; pluralism	
Leadership and Servanthood	Biblical bases, values and leadership development	Principles of spiritual growth and spiritual empowerment	Mentoring processes; motivational strategies	Team-building and coordination strategies	Stewardship of relationships; unique time and event orientation	Servanthood and followership	
					Your personal total for today:		

ASSESSMENT TWO

Evaluating Your Readiness with Real-Life Case Studies

BILL TAYLOR

I've known David and Christine, Karl and Susan, Mark and Mary, Jean, Michelle and Stanford, Jay and Anne for many years. They represent different generations: the first with over forty years of service; the second with nineteen; the third with a few years; and the others about to depart for their long-awaited field of ministry. These are prime crosscultural servants working in challenging to extremely difficult contexts. They minister on three continents: Asia, Latin America and Africa.

Let's ask some questions: How did they get there? How do their stories compare or differ? What kinds of prefield equipping did they have? Are they still doing what they thought they would at the beginning? How can their story encourage you as you walk into your own future with the missional God?

Ultimately, it is the sovereign seeking and sending God who thrusts us into high-risk (personal or contextual) long-term ministries. But this God also uses childhood and youth experiences like Sunday school, camps and short-term mission trips; he uses the Perspectives class to open hearts and minds to the world; he uses venues like the Urbana Student Mission Convention and the Passion conference. God utilizes university campus ministries to challenge and disciple us and to equip us in foundational evangelism and spiritual maturity; he uses formal and nonformal college studies, graduate school and seminary; he uses the local church.

In the process, each of the above-mentioned individuals came to a profound conviction—some call this "the call"—that the Lord of the universe wanted them in long-term crosscultural ministry. David invested his training and gifts in leadership development, and Christine in the arts. Karl served as an anthropologist and Susan as a med tech. Mark became an engineer and grew a viable business; Mary ministered as a teacher. Both David and Mark spent a few years in student ministry to gain maturity and experience. Mary discipled younger women. Jean is a magnificent servant; Stanford an M.D.; Michelle a mother and intercessor. Jay is a film and media guru, and Anne studied community development in college. All used a variety of means to prepare for crosscultural service. All had significant experience in local church ministry, and all were sent out by their churches, with most serving under established mission agencies. All have a passion for the living God and desire to walk with integrity and to finish well.

After college and seminary David and Christine invested a year in language study before embarking on their field ministry. Their children were born in Latin America and are now third-culture adults. Jean finished her Bible studies and began engaging with the seculars of her "passport culture." Stanford and Michelle, just out of university and single, each taught English in Hungary for two years, and then they married. While Stanford finished med school, they both worked hard to prepare for their future through a series of strategic short-term mission experiences, reading, study and local church involvement. Jay and Anne have a challenging road ahead of cultural adaptation and language learning in a volatile area of the world.

Mark and Mary spent two intensive years of nonstop language study in Asia before moving with a team to the extremely resistant people group God had placed on their hearts. They then began the long process of building relationships of trust while gradually becoming immersed in the local culture. Their three children were born in their country of service. Just daily living, however, was extremely stressful due to various factors. That and the intense spiritual darkness and warfare of that area converged to make it impossible for them to stay. In spite of everything, they wanted to stay, but their children's health was so threatened that they had to return home. They were brokenhearted. The aftermath of all this was long and difficult as they healed from the trauma they had experienced. The good news is that the "seeds" they planted have flourished in that hostile environment; what they went to do has not only survived but is growing and blossoming. These two faithful servants continue their commitment to global, crosscultural ministry from their base now in the United States.

All of my friends have invested a lot of time and financial resources in their prefield and early-field preparation. Our multination studies of mission attrition and retention have shown us that the prime reasons for early return from mission service are these:

- inadequate spirituality and lack of tested commitment to mission
- inadequate ministry competencies, including problems with "relationality," that is, the ability to get along with others
- inadequate prefield equipping and training, especially that which combines formal, nonformal and informal education

In other words, take prefield preparation seriously. You will never regret it.

In what way is your story similar to or different from the account of these friends mentioned above?

What do you pick up from them about their long-term commitment to crosscultural ministry?

What insights for *your* training and preparation emerge from their journeys?

Equipping for the Long Haul

Seek equipping and training specifically applicable to your ministry goals. Choose your ministry: evangelist, church planter, relief and development worker, leader developer, youth worker, tentmaker, teacher, coach-mentor, writer, nurse, doctor, medical technician, graphic artist, computer wizard, radio/television producer, general servant—whatever. No matter what you desire to do, you'll need equipping and training in order to serve with long-term effectiveness and fruitfulness.

David and Christine's target population and ministry goals called for them to seek training beyond the university. For this reason, they sought a graduate school and seminary with a strong missions curriculum. Susan worked long hours in the hospital to put bread on the table and pay Karl's school bills. Karl painted houses and hung wallpaper for a year so his wife could fulfill her dream of a year of intensive biblical study. Because they would be serving in the Muslim world, they wanted substantive working knowledge of Scripture, theology and missions before embarking on their career overseas. I won't forget Karl's statement to me: "It will take me ten years to get proficient in Arabic, and I want to know the Qur'an thoroughly to effectively communicate the story of Christ."

Regardless of your future ministry, prepare adequately. If you want to be a church planter, be sure you have the experience of evangelism and discipleship (even church planting) in your home congregation. Also, seek a team with a strong combination of gifts and training. All team members should have strong church experience, including a supervised internship in their home culture. Some team members would benefit from one to four years of solid biblical, theological and missiological study, whether at home or in their adopted culture. If you want to be involved in business as mission, be sure you have the experience and preparation to do this in a different country.

None of our friends regret the years spent in preparation, particularly when they see that preparation applied in a variety of ways on the field.

Into what kind of ministry do you feel God may be leading you? Why?

How did you come to these conclusions? What confirmations have you seen already? Who else affirms this leading and passion?

Many people think that life in a local church, university or Bible college or seminary will do the complete job of preparing them for missions service. It won't. Most churches have an informal equipping process, if anything at all. Most formal schools tend to focus on knowledge first and on skills for ministry second. Very few have distinguished themselves for their commitment to character development, spirituality and relationality.

You do need a strong component of knowledge for effective ministry. But you also need mentoring directed toward holy living, character formation, spirituality and ministry skills. Ask your pastor or spiritual mentor how best to prepare wisely for the stress and demands of crosscultural living. In addition to the profiles on the previous pages, here are some "competency categories" to keep in mind:

- character: personal walk with God, spiritual discipline, self-discipline, personal and spiritual maturity, moral purity, personal and family wholeness, servant's attitude, teachability, adaptability, compassion, spiritual gifting

- ministry competency: relational abilities, evangelism and discipleship gifts, church-planting and development skills, language and culture training, communication aptitudes, leadership and followership ability, practical talents, professional or vocational expertise

- knowledge: biblical and theological truth, culture basics, communication and language-learning principles, ministry and missions foundations, leadership and followership development, an understanding of global partnership, a basic grasp of human personality and health issues, professional or occupational training and bivocational issues

In which of the *character* traits above would you say you are relatively strong today?

In which do you need strengthening?

In which *ministry skills* are you strong today?

Which skills need strengthening?

In which *knowledge* areas do you feel you are strong?

What knowledge areas need strengthening?

Mark and Mary's target population required them to enter the country as professionals working with a corporation. Along with their well-developed theology of vocation, their academic preparation as an engineer and a teacher opened doors, facilitated visas and legitimized their "work" as all part of God's call on their lives. Their years of practical ministry had honed their spiritual skills and endurance. And their years of preparation equipped them for the discipline of two years of study in their adopted nation.

Seek equipping and training in nonformal, formal and informal contexts. All three of these aspects of learning are very important, though we tend to think that training must come in formal school contexts.

- *Nonformal education* refers to out-of-the-classroom learning, yet it is designed and purposeful. It includes supervised field trips, internships and mentoring relationships. Some nonformal equipping is taught; some is simply "caught."

- *Informal education* refers to the dynamics of living, observing and learning within community. Much of this is "caught."

- *Formal education* is what we know best. It's what we call "school"—planned, supervised, academic, primarily theoretical, classroom-oriented, graded by examinations and ending with graduations and degrees. Certain components of knowledge are best and most efficiently communicated in formal settings.

Where can you get the necessary educational balance? Use the worksheet below to think through your own best learning and experiences and to identify in which category (nonformal, informal, formal) they fall. Notice that some learning experiences overlap into two or even three categories.

Think in terms of seven different learning contexts that mold a future missionary:

- The home shapes us.

- The job teaches and hones skills.

- The church stimulates development of character and long-term spiritual formation, ministry skills and important knowledge.

- Formal schools focus on knowledge and some skills.

- Mission agencies take a careful look at character, competencies, skills and knowledge. They may offer or require their own specific equipping.

- The national church you may serve with will shape you in all areas of your life. There is a good chance today that you can do more biblical, ministry and missionary training in your adopted context as well.

- Our interpersonal relationships mold us too.

Now go back to the character, ministry skill and knowledge dimensions. Where are these best learned in relation to the seven learning contexts above? The following exercise can help you determine the best route(s) to follow in your own equipping and training process as you contemplate missions.

1. In which *informal* contexts have you learned important lessons?

List two to three key lessons you've learned.

2. Which *nonformal* contexts have provided significant learning for you?

In what areas?

3. List the *formal* schools you've studied in (starting with kindergarten), and total the years. That's the part of your life that you've spent "institutionalized."

In what ways has this been good and not so good for you?

4. What other kinds of *formal* learning contexts could be valuable to you as you prepare for cross-cultural service?

A Final Word

Does this seem too complicated for you, requiring too much time and too many resources, when the world is coming unglued, unjust, violent and going to hell in a handbasket? Don't worry about it. Relax. Chill. Consider how many years Jesus lived and worked before launching into his public ministry. Evaluate the same with the apostle Paul.

Consider your prefield preparation a lifelong investment. You won't regret it. But if you cut it short, you may. Don't minimize this crucial phase of your lifelong development.

Our Journey

MALCOLM AND LIZ McGREGOR
SIM (Serving in Mission), Scotland, Nigeria, Ethiopia, United States

This has been a pilgrimage of discovery for Liz and me. Our route into missions did not include the usual mileposts of seminary or Bible school or a "Macedonian call." We have a business background and came into missions through this route.

We first traveled to Nigeria in 1975. We did not see ourselves as missionaries and had no thoughts in that direction. We were young, both twenty-four years old and ready for adventure; we wanted to stretch ourselves by living in another culture. We were Christians and had been actively involved in our church, especially in youth work, but had a lot of growing and learning to do.

I am an architect by training, and Liz is a musician. I went to work for a Nigerian firm of consultants when the country was undergoing a massive growth surge following the huge hike in oil prices by OPEC in 1973. When we arrived there, Liz got involved with Nigerian Television and teaching music. We spent seven years in

Nigeria, working in these capacities, and during that time were mentored and discipled into missions by a series of godly SIM and Navigators missionaries who accepted us, believed in us and invested in us.

Our missions training was "on the job." It was a wonderful apprenticeship as we listened to others, observed their lives and got involved alongside men and women of God who took us as we were, saw some potential in us and intentionally sought to develop us.

God was also in the business of refining us in Nigeria. We went through some very tough situations: two ectopic pregnancies for Liz, our house robbed four times, great ethical struggles with the corrupt business world of Nigeria and how we should handle the practical realities of this every day. But right through these circumstances, God placed people beside us to helped us grow in our understanding of him, and a desire to serve him in new ways began to grow.

Our seven-year "on the job" missions apprenticeship in Nigeria led us into commitment to work with SIM. We moved to Marxist Ethiopia during the 1984–1985 famine and stayed there for eleven years. With SIM we committed ourselves to establish a discipling movement among university students. This was a very difficult time in Ethiopia's history. Again we used our training in architecture and music to do this. For part of the time I taught at Addis Ababa University and Liz taught music.

Looking back I believe one of the most significant things we engaged in was helping young men and women who had come to faith in Jesus establish their own businesses founded on godly principles. These businesses are still functioning today and are the financial backbone of the discipleship ministry that continues under Ethiopian leadership.

We continue to be learners as we carry leadership responsibilities in SIM. We love to listen to others, observe what God is doing around the world, seek to understand the times we live in and read widely, but our burning passion is to disciple others and see them reach their full potential for God.

The future of
Southern Sudan

"We will get there."

Phase One

GETTING READY

ONE

Personal Spiritual Formation
STEVE HOKE AND BILL TAYLOR

You're a growing Christian. You know Jesus Christ as your Savior and are getting to know him as Lord of your life and as hope of the world. You're his disciple, and you want to grow as a global Christian—a believer with a heart for the world and a passion to take the gospel to all peoples.

You've made a commitment. You love God and want to serve him. You believe he may be leading you to take on one of the most rewarding roles in the world—to become a crosscultural servant-messenger-missionary.

But dedication is not enough. Raw zeal is not enough. Commitment is not enough. Not even high-octane spiritual gifts are enough! We need to constantly grow in intimacy with Christ and experience the unmistakable, transforming power of the Spirit in our lives.

We are concerned with changed lives, with transformation in Christ. "Transformation" points us toward God's own concerns in his relationships with mankind. But we also want to understand how we might facilitate that formation in ourselves and others. While *transformation* refers to the process of Godward change flowing from relationship with him, *spiritual formation* refers to the human side of the relationship, those means by which we seek to "work out" the transformation that the Spirit "works in."[1]

Paul told the Philippians they needed to look forward, not back. He pushed them to forget the past and to press toward the goal of knowing Christ more intimately (see 3:12-14). Growth in Christ takes place as you nurture your faith relationship through prayer, the study of God's living Word, spiritual disciplines, Christian witness and fellowship with other Christians in the church community.

Relationship is everything. This is true from the Trinity on through to Christ and his disciples, to the church today. Who you are is more important than what you do. For that reason alone, it's critical to get your relational priorities straight from the outset. As you prepare yourself in right relationship with the Lord of the universe, you'll find that your ministry will flow out of your being—your internal spiritual character and your intimacy with Abba.

Spiritual formation is often used as a synonym for discipleship, spiritual growth and sanctification. Biblically, "'spiritual formation' focuses our attention on the dynamics of how the Holy Spirit works in us, among us, and through us." It is *dynamic* in its emphasis on the divine power and *deep* in its focus on the interior growth of the human heart. It is primarily the "shaping work of the Holy Spirit, carried out according to the will of God the Father, for the purpose of confirming us to the image of Christ. The trinitarian pattern is clear in Romans 8:27-29."[2]

We cannot actually "do" spiritual formation on our own, but the Holy Spirit can. He does it by working deeply and powerfully in our spirit, thereby transforming every dimension of our life—heart, soul, mind and behavior. This Spirit-powered transformation includes even our personality and behavior. Paul paints this word picture: "The fruit of the Spirit is love, joy, peace, patience, kindness, goodness, faithfulness, gentleness and self-control. . . . Since we live by the Spirit, let us keep in step with the Spirit" (Gal

5:22-23, 25). It is clear "that the various aspects of the fruit of the Spirit are primarily relational, not privatistic."[3]

Are you learning to enjoy God—to abide in him? That means that even though the Spirit places us within environments of grace to grow, we must not miss the absolute necessity of solitude and private devotion with the Lord for our spiritual growth. Just as Jesus moved away from the disciples in the early hours of the morning to spend private communion with Abba, we too must find solitude. Without it, we cannot develop the intimate relationship with him that is so essential for crosscultural ministry.

The "Perspectives on the World Christian Movement" course being taught in many churches in the world helps students see that the Bible is "The Story of His Glory." From Genesis through Revelation, the Bible is the unfolding story of God drawing a people to himself—into a relationship of love, acceptance and forgiveness. Eugene Peterson has expressed the worship dimension in even more obvious terms: "God is personal reality to be enjoyed. We are . . . so redeemed that we are capable of enjoying him."[4] His grace evokes our gratitude.

Richard Averbeck highlights the primacy of worship in these words: "Worship is one of the most transforming activities for us to engage in as Christians." Gradually—or sometimes dramatically

> when we become duly impressed with God our lives change because the things that matter to us change. . . . True worship happens when we get a glimpse of God—who he is and what he is about—and just stand there in awe of him, being impressed and transformed down to the very depths of our being by the magnificent vision of the glory of our heavenly Father.[5]

Missions, then, is "his-story"—God's process of calling disciples from every nation to follow him and give him glory as true worshipers. So as we go and make disciples, our essential task is to call the peoples and nations of the world to worship him too. And when Christ finally returns, all of us who follow him will get to take part in the massive international worship service that's previewed in Revelation 5:7 and that's going on right now!

Are You Learning to Pray?

The Bible tells us that the way to *be* anything, to *get* anywhere and to *do* anything is to pray. Pray-ers become white-hot worshipers. Pray-ers become lovers. Pray-ers become doers. The same disciples whom Jesus commanded to pray for workers for the harvest (see Mt 9:37-38) were the ones he sent to reap the harvest (10:1-23).

Every surge of missionary activity in history has grown out of revitalized personal prayer and personal renewal. If you're serious about being sent, your concern for those who need to be reached will drive you to pray for them and for the missionaries who are trying to reach them. Pray alone. Pray with others. Get involved in some of the prayer events in the worldwide prayer movement for world evangelization, such as concerts of prayer, prayerwalking or Prayer Summits.

Prayer is fed by passion and reality. Fuel your prayer with well-focused information. Constantly try to discover and define the needs of this world God loves. Use material like *Operation World* or a daily prayer journal to pray for peoples and nations.

One of the best ways to give meaning to facts is to relate them to individuals you know. So take part in supporting expatriate or national missionaries. Get to know them by reading their prayer letters and corresponding with them.

Talk to them by e-mail or when they're on home leave. Pray for their work.

But prayer is not just intercession for the overwhelming needs of our world. Prayer is—at the core—your heart-to-heart communication with your loving Abba. If you have not found Abba to be your hiding place in personal conversation, if you have not found joy in extended times of meditation in solitude, if you cannot find strength in contemplative prayer in wordless silence, then you are still growing in understanding all that prayer can be in your personal spiritual formation.

Are You Learning to Give?

One of the quickest ways to heat up a lukewarm heart is to begin investing in the kingdom of God. Somehow linking your wallet to what's on the heart of God is the first step toward "[storing] up for yourselves treasure in heaven" (Mt 6:20). Have you considered living more simply now so that you can give more to advancing God's kingdom? Have you started supporting someone in missions? Are you investing financially in the ministry of a friend? Are you supporting someone behind the scenes as well as on the frontlines? You don't have to wait until you are on a missionary income to live within a missionary budget. A "faith" missionary becomes a steward of the gifts of others. You give up the luxury of generating a predictable income in exchange for vocational involvement in God's worldwide purpose. As an expression of wise stewardship, the missionary embraces a "wartime" living allowance according to need.

Are You Sitting in, Soaking up and Studying God's Word?

Have your discovered the joy of being in God's presence in his Word? David the poet wrote, "You have made known to me the path of life; you will fill me with joy in your presence" (Ps 16:11). Do you have a consistent approach to exposing yourself not only to what the Bible says but also to what it calls you to do? Are you able to feed yourself from the Word for extended times without depending on the input or preaching of others? Are you adjusting your life to what it demands of you? Are you in a study group with others who are attempting to understand God's will for them through studying his Word? Are you holding each other responsible for obedience? Are you memorizing portions of God's love letter to you? Are you growing in your foundational understanding?

What Is Your Sense of God's Call on Your Life?

Call is a commonly used and often misunderstood term. The Spirit uses various routes to thrust us into missions. Do you have a clear sense of ministry burden or passion? Whether our heart's desires lie in bivocational tentmaking or in long-term vocational missions, we relate to a God who loves us and knows us intimately, and who wants to work with us according to our uniqueness. The reflection exercise below will walk you through a listening and discernment process as you wait on the Lord to identify just what burden or passion he is putting on your heart.

You will find a letter later on giving an actual response to a young couple seeking clarity on what their call might be and how to deal with it.

Are You Involved with Other Christians?

First Corinthians 12 tells us that when we become Christians, we not only join God's family as adopted sons or daughters, but we also become part of a marvelous organism called the body of Christ. Each of us has been gifted to build up the others. Christians simply cannot live without other Christians.

How are you experiencing Christian fellowship? Are you seriously plugged into a local congregation where you're growing in your commitment to the body of Christ? Are you involved in a cell group? Are you serving with your gifts? But more on this later; this will be the core of our section on finding your place in the body of Christ.

Are You Telling the Story of the Reality of Christ in Your Life?

The most effective way the gospel can be communicated is through telling others what Christ has done for you. It's essentially storytelling. To want to speak for Christ "out there" without sharing him with others "here" would be inconsistent, to say the least.

Skills in storytelling and communicating are developed in practice. Your actions reinforce your values and make them meaningful. You become what you do. Becoming a crosscultural witness means being a witness right here, right now. The more crosscultural you can make your witness now, the better equipped you'll be to interact with people of other cultures in the future.

Is There Unmistakable Evidence of God's Presence in Your Life?

The history of Christian mission is strewn with the well-meaning but misdirected lives of people who thought of mission primarily as a task— crusading, preaching or ministering—and not essentially as *relationship.* They got started on the track of *doing* before their life had a quality

of *being* that made them attractive. Paul reminded his readers in 2 Corinthians 3:2 that they are living "letters"—people whose lives will be read by those around them. He also wrote that through us Christ spreads the fragrance of his knowledge and love to others (see 1 Cor 2:16).

Is your life becoming increasingly more fragrant and attractive? Who are the people you have recently attracted to wanting to know more about Jesus? Does the way you live convey a kind of message the world finds attractive and see? Is God's touch on your life becoming more evident with each year of your Christian experience?

Winsome, fragrant living is the basis of incarnational ministry. It's what Hugh Halter and Matt Smay call "the tangible kingdom"[6]—creating incarnational community wherever you're planted—on campus, in the marketplace, in international relationships or in your neighborhood. "To *be* the faithful church in small pockets throughout our city."[7]

---

[1]Evan Howard, "Reflections on the Study of the Christian Spiritual Life," *Journal of Spiritual Formation and Soul Care* 1, no. 1 (spring 2008). 11-13.

[2]Richard Averbeck, "A Biblical Theology for Spiritual Formation," *Journal of Spiritual Formation and Soul Care* 1, no. 1 (spring 2008): 28.

[3]Ibid., p. 35.

[4]Eugene Peterson, *A Long Obedience in the Same Direction,* 20th Anniv. ed. (Downers Grove, Ill.: InterVarsity Press, 2000), p. 198.

[5]Ibid., p. 38.

[6]See Hugh Halter and Matt Smay, *The Tangible Kingdom* (San Francisco: Jossey-Bass, 2008).

[7]Ibid., p. xxi.

**Prayer is ministry:
Asian spirituality in action**

Longing for God at the Heart of Mission
BILL O'BYRNE AND TOM ASHBROOK

Discerning a Deeper Calling

The yearning to do great things for God too easily becomes a substitute for knowing God himself. Arriving in post-communist Russia in the early nineties, we saw a myriad of mission agencies hit a wall. Many of us became discouraged as the huge response and the great opportunities were simply not translating into the significant church planting or growth we had expected.

After holding a missionary Prayer Summit in 1995, our team led citywide and monthly prayer gatherings to seek God's heart for this field and the ministry. We soon realized that God was more interested in drawing *us* deeper into himself than showing us what to *do*. He made us attend to our hearts, our sin and our love for him, and in doing so he poured out his overflowing love on us.

Like many missionaries, we had begun to find our meaning and significance in what we would *do* and accomplish, rather than in who we are and were made to *be*. Indeed, achievement and activist-oriented Christianity can get empty very quickly, especially if your reception is not nearly as warm as you hoped or your agency, supporters and host country do not seem to appreciate your efforts and sacrifices.

How do we learn to keep the love of God ahead of our service for him? We need to be defined by our relatedness and relationship to him, finding our peace and our strength in his love (see Deut 30:6; Rom 5:5). The pursuit of a deeper life with God, in Christ, through the Spirit in community is what will help missionaries survive the difficulties and endure the discouragements and isolation of ministry.

First-Order Calling Accessed Through Longing

This "first-order" call to intimate relationship with God is the true source of our "second-order" calling to service. Since God is the knower and revealer of hearts (see 1 Sam 16:7), he will constantly be revealing our hearts to us, as his servants "entrusted with the gospel" (1 Thess 2:4), and our hearts for him, as his children (see Gal 4:6). The longing that he places in us for himself keeps ministry in its proper place. From this longing flows an authentic, powerful service that mirrors his love to a frenetic, lonely world.

Our longing is the desire to love God more, which continues to deepen along with our intimacy with the Trinity in ongoing spiritual formation. It is this longing that God uses to woo and call us forward in our relationship with him. Longing can inspire a holy dissatisfaction with status-quo Christianity, but it always stimulates greater degrees of hunger and thirst for him. Augustine begins his *Confessions* with a statement that the rest of his story explains: "Thou hast made us for thyself, and restless is our heart until it comes to rest in thee." Through gaining a clearer understanding of this longing, we can better interpret God's actions and purposes in our daily lives and cooperate with him more fully as we follow our "second-order" callings to "go and make disciples."

Longing for God Draws Us into Deeper Intimacy

God draws us into deepening relationship by placing a deep longing within us, a longing to experience the fullness of his love. Expressions of this longing for God are found throughout

Scripture and are indications of the spiritual vitality of his servants in mission. It was not enough for Moses to convince God to keep his presence with Israel; he said "Now show me your glory" (Ex 33:18). David acknowledged that his heart's deepest desires themselves came from, were found and were satisfied in God alone (see Ps 37:4). Many of the psalms are filled with the images and language of longing (see Ps 23:1; 42:1; 61:4; 131:2). Isaiah recognized the deeper source of his desire for justice: "At night my soul longs for You, indeed, my spirit within me seeks You diligently" (Is 26:9 NASB). Jesus' own desire for intimacy with us only the divine Community can provide (see Jn 17:24).

It is God's desire to make that longing an increasing reality in our relationship with him. Paul takes the concept of longing a step further in his longing-instilling prayer: that his disciples may know "the love of Christ which surpasses knowledge, that you may be filled up to all the fullness of God" (Eph 3:17-19 NASB). Paul's spiritually forming and missional longing for others comes from a heart that lives in that longing itself. A deeper love and longing for God always leads to greater spiritual maturity and to a more authentic, humble, enduring and effective service of him.

Longing Is Foundational for Missions

It is vital to attend to this first-order calling at the beginnings of pursing a call into ministry and to return to it again and again, for this is how God allows our heart for him to grow, mature and expand. In our zeal to follow God's call into ministry of any sort, but especially "to the ends of the earth," it is all too easy to presume or ignore God's continuous call to deeper fellowship with him. The longing for God deep in our spirits is frequently the impetus that God uses and responds to in order to inspire personal renewal and spark revival in others. But God must be loved for his own sake, not as a means to another end, not even kingdom expansion.

When we consciously attend to the longing that the Spirit places in our heart for God, we find that what we have to give others is primarily what he is doing in us. God's desire is that everyone be saved *and* come to a mature, intimate knowledge of him. That means listening to the Spirit's longing, sensing his presence and desire in and for others. God teaches us all of these, as we learn to pay attention and respond to our longing.

Living into the Whole Calling of God

We can use a simple exercise to identify the longing that God has placed in our hearts for himself. Imago Christi suggests going on a "longing retreat" to formulate a "longing statement" (see "Longing Retreat" on p. 60). Though our longing for God continues to develop as we mature, this exercise helps us express our present longing as best as we presently understand it. Imago Christi's Discovery process provides an opportunity to identify your longing and goes on to integrate it into the overall spiritual formation journey.

Those of us who are in the process of discerning, following or even reevaluating our second-order callings to serve Christ and "go to the ends of the earth" must learn to be attentive to our hearts in order to proceed on the first-order journey of deepening intimacy with the triune God. Exploring, expressing and engaging the longing that God has placed in our hearts for himself needs to be recognized as a vital aspect of the discernment process for crosscultural ministry, an integral part of the spiritual journey of vocational missions and a crucial factor that shapes our vision and activity in mission.

(Adapted from a module of Imago Christi's Spiritual Formation Discovery for Leaders, a three-day intensive spiritual formation event designed to engage participants at the intersection of their own journey and a historical paradigm of spiritual formation, so that they may more intentionally cooperate with the desire of God for the heart of his servants. (Visit Imago Christ's website at <www.imagochristi.org>.)

Longing Retreat

Prepare. Understanding our longing requires time for reflection and processing, as well as the faith to embrace it. The longing of our hearts for God cannot be recognized by a busy mind, cluttered with schedules and worries.

- Find an appropriate, quiet place and set aside an extended time, even a full day, to explore your longing for God. Enlist the prayer and intercessory support of the spiritual friends and mentors closest to you.

Listen. Understanding your longing is an exercise in listening. It calls for listening to your heart and to God's still, small voice to discern the nature of your passion for God and his passion for you.

- Reflect on how God has been drawing you nearer to him in the past, and journal your insights.

- Then prayerfully offer God the meditations you have just written. Do not try to think them up, just remain open to his voice, his stirring in your heart. Ask him to "enlighten the eyes of your heart" to reveal your desire to know him (Eph 1:17-18).

Record. When you feel ready, start writing.

- Start with an image that came to mind, perhaps from Scripture, a picture of what intimacy with God looks or feels like to you. "The relationship I long to have with God is like . . . " or "I long to be . . . "

- Use that image to create a helpful metaphor

to describe the quality of relationship you desire. Sometimes nothing comes until you decide to put pen to paper.

It is often helpful to repeatedly return to a prayerfully listening posture before God during this process, especially whenever you feel stuck or done. Allow God to show you the nature of your personal longing for him that is presently in your heart. This type of listening is not easy. Putting words to our most intimate thoughts and feelings is not natural for all of us, but it helps us engage the heart relationship that is central to our identity.

Here are two examples of longing statements that demonstrate the variety of images that can express our desire for intimacy with God:

- I long to be like a flower in the garden of the Lord: responsive to the rising glory and magnificent beauty of the Lord each morning, lifting up my face and opening my heart to him, following his movement through the course of daily hours, having my way, my movement correspond in all things to his will, at night to rest, rooted and sustained in the provision of his love.

- I long to live in you, Lord, to dwell in your Temple of Light, to behold your beauty, to taste your love and to wait upon your every desire. I long to enjoy you both in solitude and in the community of my brothers and sisters of Light where you, oh Holy Fire, make me a "porch light" for those who seek your face.

In a listening posture, journal the image of longing the Spirit gives you.

Pray. Turn the longing statement itself into a prayer, asking God to illuminate whatever glimpses of longing you have gained and to make this longing a reality.

Share. Take the opportunity to share your

longing statement and retreat with a trusted spiritual friend or mentor. Share your experience of the exercise itself, and then share its fruit.

Revisit. Because our understanding of intimacy with God is dynamic, we suggest that you plan to repeat this exercise regularly, perhaps a few times in the next year, to bring its ideas into focus and make its fruit more evident.

Keep a copy in your Bible or prayer journal and make it a part of your prayer life to express your profound longing to know your loving God.

Then in a year or two revisit the retreat and see how God has refined and matured your longing for him.

God uses the longing of our heart to draw us into ever-deepening intimacy with himself, the source of our spiritual formation. Those of us who are in the process of discerning, following

or even reevaluating our second-order callings to follow Christ "unto the ends of the earth" cannot afford to ignore discerning and engaging the first-order longing God has placed in our hearts for himself.

Bill O'Byrne is a Church Resource Ministries (CRM) missionary in Russia, one of the three cofounders of Imago Christi, the covenant community of spiritual formation ministry in CRM that provides spiritual formation and direction resources for Christian church and mission leaders.

Tom Ashbrook is the director of spiritual formation for Church Resource Ministries, and he leads CRM's spiritual formation team Imago Christi. He give spiritual direction and coaching for pastors and missionaries in various parts of the world and leads spiritual formation discovery retreats for Christian leaders in many places in the United States and abroad. He lives with his wife, Charlotte, in Centennial, Colorado.

What's Your God Language?

MYRA PERRINE
Church Resource Ministries

As the ability to personalize everything grows—from iPod playlists to RSS feeds to Bibles—wouldn't it be nice if believers were empowered to worship God out of their unique personalities instead of being squished into a one-size-fits-all spirituality?

Enter Myra Perrine, a spiritual director who specializes in helping believers figure out their unique spiritual temperament and then suggesting specific spiritual practices ideally suited for that temperament. Perrine's insight is available in her book *What's Your God Language?* (Tyndale House, 2007).

"Serving as a pastoral counselor and spiritual director," Perrine explains, "I've observed that there is a real need for permission among those who are serious about Jesus to meet him in ways that don't exactly correspond with how others are meeting him in their homes or communities of faith." She adds, "In fact, this theme continually emerges in my conversations: *I want to connect with God more deeply, but I don't know how.*

Both profound and practical, *What's Your God Language?* contains tools that will enable believers to find renewed passion and pleasure in their relationship with God, including

- a spiritual temperament inventory (fifty-four questions)
- a spiritual practices inventory (fifty-four questions)
- detailed descriptions of nine spiritual temperaments (or preferences), with biblical examples of each

  1. The Activist—loving God through confrontation with evil
  2. The Ascetic—loving God through solitude and simplicity
  3. The Caregiver—loving God through serving others
  4. The Contemplative—loving God through adoration
  5. The Enthusiast—loving God through mystery and celebration
  6. The Intellectual—loving God through the mind
  7. The Naturalist—loving God through experiencing him outdoors
  8. The Sensate—loving God through the senses
  9. The Traditionalist—loving God through ritual and symbol

- Four weeks worth of specifically tailored spiritual exercises for each temperament, allowing readers to grow spiritually through both their strong and weaker spiritual preferences
- Discussion and reflection questions ideal for individuals or groups. In addition, readers can go to <http://files.tyndale.com/thpdata/BookGuides/guides/13221_guide.pdf> for a PDF of eight weeks of additional exercises at the intermediate and advanced levels, corresponding with the strength of their distinct spiritual temperaments.

Dr. Myra Perrine has a passion for intimacy with God and has been speaking and teaching on this subject for more than thirty-five years. Currently on staff with Church Resource Ministries, Myra offers pastoral counseling and spiritual direction to some of CRM's 350 missionaries in twenty-five nations. With a doctorate in theology and spiritual formation, Myra is also an adjunct professor at Azusa Pacific University, where she teaches a variety of classes, including spiritual growth and leadership.

I Pledge Allegiance to the Kingdom of God

CHRIS HOKE

When Jesus sent out his disciples the first time, to their own people, they were told to give only a one-sentence sermon: "The kingdom of heaven is near" (Mt 10:7). It was not a message of reviving the kingdom of Israel. They were not calling God's people back to their forefathers' faith, reforming the government for God. They were announcing the approach of another, alien, invading nation: the direct governance and boundary-less kingdom of *heaven*.

I think this is important. If there were ever a nation blessed by God, it was Israel. And yet Jesus gave them no room to promote their interests as a nation. The annunciation of the kingdom of heaven's arrival is almost a threat: Israel's day is done. No more patriotism for Israel. Nor for the Roman Empire. If you're with Jesus, it's only for the kingdom of heaven.

Many American Christians go into all the world proclaiming two kingdoms: making disciples of Jesus and teaching his ways . . . and the ways of the United States, teaching the American Way. When Jesus sent his disciples out of Israel, the second and *Great* Commission, he again gave no room for the promotion of Israel as a nation or as a culture. He actually limited what they were to teach: only "to observe all that *I* commanded you" (Mt 28:20 NASB, emphasis added)—not temple sacrifice, economics or any of their cultural customs otherwise assumed to be best. That goes for American culture today as well: worship, ways of doing church, economics, politics, foreign policy, technology, how to run a meeting or what language to use.

The point of the Great Commission is to wash—baptize—*all* people of their temporal allegiances, from all nation(alism)s (see v. 19). That begins with us!

Chris Hoke ministers among migrant workers and gang members in Burlington, Washington, and commutes between Central American jails and the Skagit County Jail to forge bridges for youth on the margins. He recites a different pledge of allegiance now than he once did in school.

✎Creating Your Personal Calling Statement

STEVE HOKE, GARY MAYES AND TERRY WALLING

Run water through a pipe six feet in diameter and you have great volume with great potential. Force that same water through the nozzle of a fire hose and you have great impact. You were created for a life that makes that kind of impact. You are being shaped and positioned by God himself to make a unique contribution for the kingdom. The apostle Paul said it this way: "For we are God's workmanship, created in Christ Jesus to do good works, which God prepared in advance for us to do" (Eph 2:10).

How do you discover what those "good works" are supposed to be? With all the options for significant ministry, how do you discover nozzle-like focus for your life and ministry?

This series of exercises, which leads to a personal mission statement, will help you discover and articulate your unique contribution. At the core, a personal mission statement is all about destiny, and destiny is about living out God's purposes for your life.

About Your Personal Calling Statement

What exactly is a personal calling statement? It is a dynamic statement that captures your best understanding to date of the unique contribution for which God has created you. Effective statements weave together your biblical purpose, life-ministry values and personal vision.

How will a personal calling statement help you? It provides encouragement and fulfillment, helping you stay on track during times of stress or testing in ministry. It also provides a decision-making grid that helps you assess various ministry opportunities. It points out areas where intentional growth and mentoring are needed to achieve full impact. And it serves as a personal call to arms, helping you stay mission-minded amid the plethora of daily distractions.

Creating your personal calling statement will involve tackling the following three focus questions and then weaving the three strands together:

1. Why do I exist? (biblical purpose)

2. How has God shaped me? (unique shaping and life-ministry values)

3. What is God calling me to accomplish? (vision)

1. Why Do You Exist? (Your Biblical Purpose)

Biblical purpose articulates your best understanding of why you exist. It takes into account the mandates of Scripture and then captures in your own words what you believe about the life God created.

What has God taught you? What verses has God used to shape your sense of purpose in life, verses that now serve like a compass, keeping you on the right track?

Personal reflection. Write a response to the following questions to help you begin personalizing your thoughts about biblical purpose.

• Why did God create me? Why do I exist as a person?

• What does God say should provide my greatest joy?

• What is my response to God's work of grace and salvation on my behalf?

• What is my personal response to the lordship of Christ?

Your biblical purpose. Based on your understanding of Scripture and your reflections above, write out what you perceive to be your biblical purpose. A healthy biblical purpose statement should be concise and reflect the biblical mandate that we have as believers. While your understanding of biblical purpose may apply to all believers, the way you express it should be personally significant to you.

Scripture search. Push your reflections a bit further by reviewing the verses listed below. Read each passage and write out your response to the question, what insights does this passage provide regarding the purpose of my life from God's perspective?

Scripture	*Insight*
Matthew 16:24-26	
Matthew 22:37-40	
Matthew 28:18-20	
John 13:34-35	
Romans 15:6-7	
Ephesians 2:8-10	
Philippians 3:7-14	
2 Timothy 1:9	
1 Peter 2:1-5	
2 Peter 1:5-9	

My biblical purpose:

2. How Has God Shaped You? (Your Unique Shaping and Life-Ministry Values)

The next step in developing your personal calling statement is to reflect on your unique shaping as a leader. Life-ministry values are the key to understanding this unique shaping.

Life-ministry values are the beliefs, assumptions and preferences that guide your behavior and actions. Values often show up first as lessons or beliefs, but they are forged into core convictions through experience, often the painful kind. While there are many things we may identify as generally true or important, our core values shape actual and ongoing behavior. Life-ministry values should encompass:

- your personal journey with Christ
- family, relationships and accountability
- biblical convictions and principles
- insights concerning ministry and mission
- insights related to leadership
- character formation and effectiveness
- unique calling and contribution

As you think about the priorities and convictions that guide your life and ministry, you will want to identify six to ten values in regard to the topics above. Capture each in one or two words and then describe them concisely.

Examples of life-ministry value statements:

- Kingdom: I value the kingdom, not just local church growth.
- The church: I value the primacy of the church as God's vehicle of mission in the world.
- Change: I value change, helping the church and God's people move forward.
- Teamwork: I value people, team ministry and relational empowerment.

Write out your values. Using the space below, write out your values. Work hard to keep your value statements concise and direct (ideally ten words or less).

3. What Is God Calling You to Accomplish? (Vision for Your Personal Life and Ministry)

Vision—the ability to see God's preferable future—is the heartbeat of the personal mission statement. *Vision* is a word picture that describes what you believe God desires to accomplish. It flows from the heart of God as he invites us to participate in the redemptive work of his kingdom. Our task is to invent neither the future nor our calling; our task is to discover what God is doing and join him in it. Vision describes that work.

Vision involves passion! It motivates and captivates the leader. It is what the heart yearns to see accomplished. Healthy vision is specific, not general. Personal vision answers this question: if you knew that you would not fail, what would you do, in your lifetime, for the glory of God?

Discovering your personal vision. The following questions provide multiple lenses into the things God has stirred inside you. Finish the statements below and allow them to stimulate fresh thinking about your own vision.

Some of the people and circumstances that have most shaped my life include . . .

When I think about ministry in the future, the area of ministry I would love to concentrate on is . . .

The qualities of character I most admire and desire for God to shape into my life include . . .

People who know me believe I am most used by God when I am involved in . . .

Why? What is it that motivates me?

My ministry activities that contribute most to God's kingdom include . . .

Why?

When people talk about passion for ministry, I often begin to think about giving my life to accomplishing . . .

Why?

Based on the way God has shaped you in your past, your reflections above, and your passion for ministry, write out your answer to the question, if you knew you would not fail, what would you do, in your lifetime, for the glory of God?

Vision is often the hardest of the three components of personal mission to articulate. Typically, we know the most about biblical purpose, some about life-ministry values and the least about personal vision. Ask these questions as a means of sharpening your work on vision.

- Can you see it? (True vision is a word picture that describes what God will accomplish. The vaguer it is, the less motivating.)
- Is it bigger than you? (Godly vision demands faith, and faith implies risk.)
- Is it anchored to God's work in your past?
- Does it engage your passion?
- Would you do it if you didn't get paid, or would you pay for the chance to do it?

Weaving It All Together: Your Personal Calling Statement

You are ready to put the pieces together. A personal mission statement is the interweaving of your *biblical purpose,* your *life-ministry values* and your *personal vision*. Using the work you have done, try to blend together these three elements into one comprehensive statement. It should be no longer than two or three paragraphs. We have found that crafting the elements into one paragraph is not vital to the impact of this exercise. The key is to have thoughtfully and carefully reflected on each component—purpose, values, vision and passion—and attempted to articulate those at this stage of your journey.

A Suggested Method

1. Begin on another piece of paper. At the top of the paper write down your biblical purpose.

2. Skip a line or two and write down your personal vision.

3. Attempt to weave your values into these other two components as modifiers and clarifiers, personalizing what your contribution looks like. Don't worry about crafting it into a final version at this initial stage. But an attempt at integration will give the document passion and make it uniquely personal. Make a copy and keep it with you for daily reference.

My Biblical Life Purpose:

My Core Values:

My Vision for Life and Ministry:

Peter Scazzero. *Emotionally Healthy Spirituality.* Nashville: Thomas Nelson, 2006.

Terry Walling. *Vision: Your Personal Calling Statement.* St. Charles, Ill.: ChurchSmart, 1998.

Dr. Gary Mayes serves as a vice president of Church Resource Ministries (CRM), overseeing more than one hundred staff and the twelve teams on which they serve throughout the United States. Gary has been speaking to and training church leaders since 1983. He has written three books and given leadership to the development of numerous resources and training processes used by CRM staff worldwide.

Dr. Terry Walling is a former pastor and missionary to Australia with CRM, who designed a systemic training and coaching approach to pastoral leadership development known as ReFocusing Leaders. Terry currently coaches leaders through life transitions with Leader Breakthru. (See <www.leaderbreakthru.com> for more information.)

✎ Discovering Your Ministry Passion

STEVE HOKE

This exercise is designed to help you prayerfully reflect on your past experiences and conversations with Jesus to distill the essence of the passion that God has given or is giving you for your life and ministry.

Definition

Passion—the vision or heart concern that captivates your whole life and motivates you to extraordinary levels of sacrifice. What is your vision or heart to develop a ministry or serve to meet the needs of either Christians or non-Christians?

Etymology

Middle English, from Anglo-French, from Late Latin *passion-, passio* suffering, being acted upon, from Latin *pati* to suffer—4a (1): COMPELLING EMOTION (his ruling *passion* is greed) (2) *plural:* the emotions as distinguished from reason, b: intense, driving, or overmastering feeling or conviction, c: an outbreak of anger; 5a: ardent affection: LOVE, b: a strong liking or desire for or devotion to some activity, object, or concept, c: an object of desire or deep interest. Synonyms PASSION, FERVOR, ARDOR, ENTHUSIASM, ZEAL mean intense emotion compelling action.[1]

Isaiah: "Here am I, send me."

Count Zinzendorf: "I have but one passion—it is He, it is He alone. The world is the field and the field is the world; and henceforth that country shall be my home where I can be most used in winning souls for Christ."

John Knox: "Give me Scotland, or I die!"

Jim Elliot: "He is no fool who gives what he cannot keep to gain what he cannot lose."

Amy Carmichael: "O for a passionate passion for souls, O for a pity that yearns! O for the love that loves unto death, O for the fire that burns!" (She spent fifty-five years in India, dedicated to rescuing children from temple worship.)

Observations

Passion is related to the core of our emotions, hence it is deep, possibly obscure and initially inexpressible. Passion is sharpened over years on the anvil of life experience and spiritual intimacy with Abba; it is not merely cognitive, and it is not often discerned immediately.

The Holy Spirit seems to reveal passion gradually as you are ready and as it is needed to proceed (just in time). It can emerge or come into the light only gradually and into a receptive heart. Recognizing your passion is a dawning experience that often takes weeks and months.

Passion is recognized most readily in a posture of listening, reflection, ruminating, meditating and receiving, not merely in isolated creative writing.

Questions for Personal Reflection and Listening

Where have you sensed a tug of the Holy Spirit toward a person, a group of people or an area of need (for example, Mother Teresa—the dying in Calcutta; Billy Graham—mass evangelism; Sue Lloyd—young prostitutes in Cambodia; John Knox—all of Scotland; Joni Eareckson Tada—the disabled)?

Where has the Holy Spirit touched your heart with areas of need in the world, in the church or with a particular person or group of people (for example, Patrick McDonald—children at risk; Craig and Mary Hendrickson—helping churches become multicultural; Iliya and Becky Majam—helping leaders in West Africa)?

What people or opportunity for ministry has the Holy Spirit put before you, if any, in years past (for example, Bob Ekblad—Honduran farmers and migrant workers; Jim and Kimberley Creasman—unreached peoples groups in Asia; Nate and Jenny Bacon—immigrant gang members in San Francisco's juvenile hall)?

What areas of your ministry to others has the Spirit blessed with fruit or affirmed with effectiveness over the last few months or years of your life (for example, Diane Moss—hospice care offered for HIV/AIDS victims by Cambodian Christians and churches; Paul and Mariah Nix—homeless street kids in San Francisco; Chris Hoke—gang members in Burlington, Washington)?

So, how does your sense of passion become clearer as you connect the dots of your experience in the past, your spiritual gifts, your ministry experience to date, recent revelation from the Lord and confirmations from the Holy Spirit or others?

In the space below, craft a first draft of your passion statement in one sentence or a short paragraph.

If a sense of ministry burden or passion is not clear at this time, don't be frustrated or concerned. Abba is not in a hurry to reveal it yet. Commit to praying regularly for God to reveal his passion for you and to listening regularly to hear with clarity just what he will tell you.

---

[1]*Webster's Universal College Dictionary* (New York: Random House, 1997), p. 579.

 Global Perspectives

STEVE MOORE
CEO/President, The MissionExchange

Role of the Missionary

What missionaries do on the field must be connected with where the people group is on a basic continuum. It ranges from no access to the gospel (least reached) to lots of access (reached). Here's one way to look at it:

No access   Lots of access

← —————————————————————————————————————— →

Evangelism and church planting   Discipleship   Leadership training   Mobilization

Of course this is never truly linear; all these activities happen to some extent simultaneously, but we must establish the right priorities in relation to the continuum.

The biggest changes for workers from the Global North are connected to the reality that there will often be people from the Global South serving in similar roles wherever we go. How we relate to those peers is critical. I believe there is still need for workers from the Global North across this continuum, where we engage in everything from pioneer evangelism to mobilizing new mission movements. But increasingly we do that in the spirit of interdependence with servants from the Global South.

Attracting the Next Generations

My experience with next-generation workers is that they are naturally holistic, with an integrated view of mission that weaves together issues of justice, poverty, disease and evangelism in a seamless garment of compassion in the name of Christ. They are often much more environmentally conscious than their parents or grandparents and may look disparagingly on an organization that has not given any consideration to reducing its carbon footprint.

Recommended Prefield Training

Cultivate increasing levels of self-awareness in terms of your personality, strengths, skills, spiritual gifts, passions and dreams. Know your temperament well enough to help others understand what they need to know about you to work together effectively. Identify your natural strengths and skills so you can actively leverage them for kingdom good. Engage your spiritual gifts with focus and energy, and be proactive about developing them. Reflect on what triggers your passion and compels you to act. Formal and nonformal training modes will combine to give you the right preparation.

Character and Spiritual Qualities

The most gifted leader in the world is of little use for the kingdom without humility, a teachable spirit, a grace-awakened interpersonal life, spiritual and emotional resilience, self-discipline and perseverance. These basic qualities are not readily championed in our success-at-any-cost world. But they are absolutely essential for the Christian worker, especially in crosscultural and multicultural settings.

Reflections on the Missionary "Call"
A Letter to James and Maria

BILL TAYLOR

Dear James and Maria,

Your great letter just arrived, and it's good to hear from you again. How we praise God for the deep conviction the two of you have to serve Christ in long-term crosscultural work in Central Europe. You have asked a tough question: "How do we know we are called?" To be honest, I'm not sure I can fully answer it. You're touching on deep and heavy stuff! It involves critical issues that relate to who we are, how God has made us, our understanding of who God is and how he directs us today.

Unfortunately, there's a lot of confusing and sometimes contradictory talk about the "missionary call." Beware of the extremes. Some good people expect you to have had your own mystical "call," or voice, from God. I don't deny this happens to some, but don't let others over-spiritualize the process then force it on you as normative. Other Christians approach it from an overly rational, dry, mathematical model that requires gathering the facts, praying and then making a logical decision.

I've concluded that the Spirit uses various routes to thrust us into crosscultural mission. Whether our heart's desire is to be inner-city youth ministers, bivocational workers establishing a viable business in a restricted-access country, Bible translators or long-term church planters, we all relate to a God who loves us and knows us intimately and who wants to work with us according to our uniqueness.

In a sense we're all "called" believers in Jesus the Christ. We are called to Christ, called to worship and serve him, called to walk worthy of our calling in him, called to obey the biblical creation mandates, called to share Christ with oth-ers. *Call* is a rich biblical term with a multifaceted use.

So, why make a big deal of the "missionary call"? Well, it's partly to clarify matters. I personally try to eliminate unbiblical teachings that falsely dichotomize vocations and life into "secular" and "sacred." Everything we touch and do, we do for the glory of God. But I am also seeking to find a balance as we consider the biblical theology of creation and vocation alongside the overarching challenges of using our vocations in crosscultural service. This applies to "tentmakers" and "home missionaries" as well as "regular" missionaries or "national" missionaries.

What are some of the ways God leads people into mission, especially long term?

The Four Paths

Path one. A few have had some kind of personalized call, vision, powerful encounter or voice from the Lord. They feel a deep sense of having received a mandate from God. It's incontrovertible. They step out in straight-forward obedience to the Spirit. Some of these folks may quote Paul's Macedonian call to validate their experience.

But we need to check this out. The fact is, Paul was already functioning as a field missionary when this call came to him. The Macedonian call served to reroute Paul in a different geographic direction than he had been headed. Frankly, I don't use this passage much in terms of the missionary call.

Missionaries who had a strong call like this report that it helps sustain them when the going gets rough. But remember that a personal call is not a guarantee that one will be a successful missionary.

Path two. Other friends tell me that their story was not so much one of a personalized call to mission. Rather, it was a matter of obedience to God. In some cases a woman discerned that the Lord was leading her to marry a man, knowing that he was (and therefore, they were) going into mission. My wife, Yvonne, had a clear call to full-time ministry, but the specific of crosscultural mission was clarified when we fell in love and later married.

God's will thus becomes clear through a combination of circumstances and relationships. Some have called this the Ruth/Naomi model. (You may want to reread that story in the book of Ruth.) This route isn't easy. One woman said that had she felt her own call to missions, separate from her husband's, it would have made her less susceptible to doubt and questioning during the difficult times on the field. But the call to follow God sustained her, and God blessed her commitment.

Path three. Still others find that they end up in missions after a serious evaluation of their commitment and obedience to Christ, plus a personal assessment of interests, gifts, experience and dreams, combined with a heart of compassion for the poor, the abused, the lost or the seekers. They want an opportunity to make a difference in the world. These all converge to create a path into mission. This is more a case of the best job fit, with conclusions made after wise counsel, prayer and self-evaluation.

Path four. Some report that the prime factors leading them into missions were rather simple: a radical obedience to Christ that meant a willingness to do anything, go anywhere, pay any price—plus an identification of their gifts and the needs of the world. Discovering those needs provided the final indicator of where and what would constitute a strategic investment of their life and gifts.

Common Factors in the Four Paths

In all four paths, certain common components are crucial. In all there is a passion to serve Christ in a risky venture larger than one's own life; all call for radical obedience to God; all involve a process of wise evaluation and of confirmation and guidance from trusted colleagues and spiritual leaders. And in all there is a final, profound, unshaking conviction from the Spirit of God that "this is what God truly has for me." It may be short-term or long-term, far away or just on the other side of town, but there's a conviction: "This is what I've got to do with my life."

These are some of my musings after forty-four years in crosscultural mission. I've seen and evaluated good missionaries and poor missionaries from all four calling categories. As you have further questions come up, let's keep in touch as able.

With anticipation,
Bill

The Call to Missions

PAUL BORTHWICK

"No aspect of the Christian mission is more puzzling than the problem of a call."

That's how J. Herbert Kane starts his book *Life and Work on the Mission Field* (Baker, 1980). He knows that nothing needs to be said about ministering in a crosscultural situation until the issue of "the call" is settled in people's minds.

Yet we still flounder around. What is the "call"? How do I know if I'm called? Where do my desires fit in? If I'm called, how do I know where I am called to?

Some message-bearer leaders have tried to deal with the problem of the call by discounting it. Back in the early 1980s, Keith Green's pamphlet "Why You Should Go to the Mission Field" reaffirmed his belief that "we don't need a call; *we need a kick in the pants!*"

Others seem to imply that common sense is enough: "if the needs are greater overseas, then every one of us should be planning to go until God directly intervenes and calls us to stay home." Still others take the "the Bible says it; that settles it" approach: "just read your Bible and God will show you." But this still leaves most of us confused when it comes to where we should go, what we should do and what team we should join.

My experience has shown that people's sense of call often falls into three categories. People sense a call to (1) a location or a people group (as in Paul's desire to go to Spain or Hudson Taylor's zeal for China); (2) a task (for example, pioneer evangelism or healthcare or Bible translation or church planting); or (3) a team (as illustrated by the couple who said, "We love Frontiers, and we just want to go with them." (These three directions for the call, however, should be the subject of a separate article.)

The problem with negating the concept of the call is that it overlooks the Scriptures, for many disciples and message bearers were indeed "called." On the other hand, the Scriptures can be abused when we all want to be called in the same dramatic, miraculous way that Isaiah was (see Is 6:1-8) or Jonah was (see Jon 1–3).

So where do we find the answers? Do we just imitate our understanding of message-bearers of the past and try to feel called as they were? Where do the Scriptures fit in? And how does our expanded base of knowledge about the world fit?

For guidance, let's look to the book of Acts, the primary message-bearer text of the Scriptures. In the accounts in the book of Acts, we have at least three types of calls, and by evaluating these calls, we can learn the various ways God may lead us out into crosscultural ministry.

Call 1: The Mysterious Call

This call comes directly (and even audibly) from God himself. Peter received a direct dream (three times!) from God, which commanded him to go to the Gentiles with the gospel (see Acts 10). Paul heard the Lord's voice and became a Christian (see Acts 9), and later he went to the Macedonians in response to a dream from God (see 16:9). These (like the call of Isaiah or Jonah referred to earlier) were mysterious, miraculous interventions by God.

The problem with mysterious calls is that everyone wants one. When someone says, "God hasn't called me into missions," they often mean, "I have received no dream or revelation to go." But the error here is that these mysterious calls are *exceptional,* not normal. There are other, more common ways that God calls us into missions.

Call 2: The Commissioned Call

This type of call occurs in Acts 13, when the church in Jerusalem specifically identifies (through prayer and fasting) two individuals to go out as missionaries to Antioch. In this case, there is not so much mystery; instead, it is the Holy Spirit speaking through the church leaders. (Read Michael Griffith's book *Who Really Sends the Missionary?* [Moody Press, 1974] based on this text.)

How does this apply to today? Those interested in ministry get involved. Church leaders and elders can affirm and identify spiritual gifts and leadership abilities. And then, in the spirit of prayer and reliance on the Holy Spirit, the leaders affirm and commission the person or people for crosscultural outreach. So, if an elder or church leader tells you that you have crosscultural gifts that could benefit the church of Jesus Christ, don't take these words lightly. It may be God's words to you, designed to be part of God's call on your life.

If we are to be serious about this commissioning type of call, we must be open to the advice of others. Perhaps we should go to the elders to ask them to pray for us as we seek God's direction. Perhaps we need to request the prayers of our pastors or even the missions committee regarding where God wants us. If we do this, we can be assured that more people are listening to God with us and for us, and when we get sent out, we'll know that the church is behind us.

Call 3: The "Common-Sense" Call

In this case, the example of Acts shows us how God works through our minds, our knowledge and our common sense. When Philip was put into the presence of the Ethiopian eunuch (Acts 8:26-40), the Holy Spirit told him to go up to the guy's chariot. Philip did not pray, "Now Lord, what should I do?" No, he did the obvious; he opened his mouth and beginning from this Scripture he preached Jesus to him.

When Paul and Barnabas were selected out, the church made some other decisions regarding sending Judas and Silas. Although there was a strong sense of the Holy Spirit's leading when they sent the first two, they sent the second two because it seemed good to the apostles and the elders (see Acts 15:22).

Imagine doing something because "it seemed good." Perhaps, as we build our own relationships with Christ and are assured of the Spirit's guidance, we too can make decisions because "it seemed good to us." Perhaps some of us will see needs and respond to them because our common sense tells us that we can meet these needs. If God keeps putting Kurds in your path, use your common sense: God could be calling you to work with Kurds. If your e-mails and reading are always exposing you to the spiritual hunger of the Muslim world, use your mind: this could be the way God will direct you into crosscultural service.

So how does God call us? Maybe it will be a miraculous voice out of heaven. Maybe it will be a result of the counsel of others. Or it might just be God speaking through our common sense telling us, "This seems to be the right thing to do." It might actually come as a combination of all three. Not everyone hears the call in the same way, and we fall short when we overlook the various ways that God may call us into missions around the world.

(Adapted from "The Call to Missions," *SVM2 Times* 3 [October 2006].)

Paul Borthwick, D.Min., along with his wife, Christie, serves on the staff of Development Associates International (www.daintl.org), focusing on leadership development in the Majority World. In addition, Paul teaches missions at Gordon College

(Wenham, Massachusetts), serves as an Urbana/ missions associate with InterVarsity Christian Fellowship and mobilizes others for crosscultural missions. Rick Warren, author of The Purpose Driven Life, *cites Paul's books* A Mind for Missions *and* How to Be a World-Class Christian *as "books that should be read by every Christian."*

 My Journey

TONICA VAN DER MEER
Principal, Center for Evangelical Missions, Brazil

I grew up in a Christian family, but I experienced the beautiful, personal love of God at a student camp and became active in ABU, the Brazilian Student Movement. ABU organized the first mission conference in Latin America in 1976, and then I believed that the Lord was calling me to serve him in student work.

My conviction that God was leading me into crosscultural service kept growing. The confirmation came in 1979, but then I wanted training to do good missionary work and not make as many mistakes. God led me to All Nations Christian College, and in the United Kingdom, and there I understood that I was being led to serve in Africa.

In late 1983 I was invited by IFES (International Fellowship of Evangelical Students) to serve in Angola, where a new Christian student group needed help. I was convinced this was the Lord's guidance, but felt afraid because the country was at war, with a Marxist government.

But I served there for ten years, loving the people and my work with students, as a teacher at Bible schools, with churches, with the Angolan Evangelical Alliance and visiting victims of the war in hospitals.

During those years, Brazilian missionary friends were facing difficulties because of a lack of training and member care. I determined that when the Lord led me back to Brazil, my future ministry would be in training and member care.

When I was advised to return to Brazil because I had prepared national leaders, in 1996 I began my work as a missionary trainer at the Evangelical Missions Center (EMC) in Viçosa, Brazil. The EMC is a school with a thorough program, and it also allowed me to become involved in member care. I finished my doctorate in missiology in the Philippines and wrote my dissertation, "Understanding and Supporting Missionaries Serving in Contexts of Suffering."

Answers to Questions About Women in Missions

LISA HORN

1. What are some of the natural ways in which women are spiritually sensitive or attuned to the voice of the Spirit, and what are the ways to tap into that wiring to go deeper with God?

Thirty years ago, evangelical Christians seemed to emphasize two concepts. The first was that listening to one's emotions and intuition was not as significant in knowing God as comprehending God through reason. Intellectualism and rationalism reigned supreme in the faith. However, the Holy Spirit touches us spiritually, emotionally and physically, not just mentally or rationally. Women seem to connect more naturally with God in all areas of their lives, not just with their minds. A clear caution is that women (and men) need to fill their lives with the Word of God through study and memorization so that, as God speaks, we can hear him and filter out what is from our own minds, the world system or the evil one.

For many, salvation in Christ is focused on the personal, even private, decision to accept the truth about Christ and less on joining a faith community to live and learn about God. We heard about having a relationship with God but that mostly involved our minds. Again, for many women this was unnatural because they tend to experience life on many levels of awareness. Women also gravitate to relational and communal living. God in his essence as Trinity is communal and relational. In the past ten years or so, evangelicals seem to be reacquainting themselves with these less rationalistic ideas about God. The result has been a reawakening of a desire to hear from God and more intimately know him.

2. What are your top five suggestions for young women, single or married, heading into cross-cultural missions that you wish someone had shared with you twenty years ago?

1. Do not complain around your family or those you live with. A negative outlook is sadly contagious, especially to children.

2. Cultivate a sense of humor about yourself and the frustrations of living. Laughter is truly good medicine (see Prov 15:30).

3. Avoid too much contact with people from your home country. You will need fellowship with your team, but it might become easy to "hang out" with other expatriates who are not in the country for the same reasons as you. In other words, don't join the American club!

4. Ask God to give you a close friend who is native to the country. If you are in a country with an established church, ask God for a prayer partner. Praying weekly with someone from your host country who loves the Lord will surely bind your heart with the people.

5. Expect discouragement, homesickness and spiritual warfare. Do not be surprised. Acknowledge the reality of your situation and believe God for help and change. Remember that he who is in you is greater than he that is in the world (see 1 Jn 4:4).

Dr. Lisa Horn is a graduate of Dallas Seminary with a master's in biblical studies (1983). She and her husband, Tom, were missionaries in Singapore from 1988 to 1995. While raising three children, she has been involved in prayer ministry, mentoring, coaching and teaching women. She has been a spiritual formation group leader at Denver Seminary since 2001. Presently, she is working for the Navigators International Missionary Group and is coaching and mentoring missionary appointees as they prepare to leave for the field. She has a D.Min. in spiritual formation from Denver Seminary.

🌐 Global Perspectives

RICHARD TIPLADY
British Director, European Christian Mission

The rapid growth of evangelical missionary movements from Latin America, Africa and Asia has led some to claim that the missionary from the Global North is being eclipsed. I think that there is sometime more rhetoric than wisdom in this kind of assertion. While northern missionaries are sometimes seen as having an ongoing contribution to global mission in areas like theological teaching and administration, that feels to me like the same kind of ethnocentrism that would confine Africans and Latinos to evangelism "because they have more enthusiasm for the gospel than Westerners do." The gifts of the Holy Spirit are not allocated by nationality; they are given to the whole church and to those from every people and nation.

As the CEO of a church-planting mission agency working in Europe, I am seeing a new generation of young missionaries from the United Kingdom, committing themselves to working in church-planting teams across Europe and doing so for the long haul. They recognize their need for biblical and theological training, for crosscultural sensitivity and self-understanding, and for lifelong learning and training. They need to be flexible and creative, diplomatic and visionary, able to receive (sometimes unjust) criticism, willing to work under local leaders and possessing a strong sense of personal security based on who they are in Christ. These criteria apply to all from the Global North, just as they apply in equal measure to those from the Global South.

✏️ Journal Worksheet One

STEVE HOKE

Where Are You Now?

How would you describe your conversations with God?

What do you most enjoy doing in your time with God?

How do you keep track of specific requests? Answers? Promises?

How specifically and knowledgeably are you praying about your involvement in missions?

Describe how you spend time in the Word, including your Bible reading and study routine.

What significant financial investment are you making in God's global purposes? If you aren't, how could you begin?

Describe what other spiritual disciplines or practices help you experience God more personally.

Where are you now in sensing a specific call from God—a clear sense of burden or passion for a people or ministry?

How are you growing in your ability to witness to others about your experience with Christ?

How would you describe your "fragrance" and the evidence of God's presence in your life?

What Do You Need to Do Next?

I will explore getting to know God better by . . .

I will explore listening to God in my times of prayer by . . .

I will practice the presence of God in my life by . . .

I will deepen my understanding and application of God's Word by . . .

I will increase my financial investment in God's purposes by . . .

I will seek to be a more natural and fragrant witness to Jesus' great love by . . .

What Will the Future Look Like?

What kind of person will you become if you obediently carry out your desire to be more focused in intentional time alone with God, in conversation with God, in Bible reading and study, in sharing life with others, in lifestyle witness and in living out God's presence in your life?

What marks of true spirituality would you like to see developed in your life over the long term?

TWO

Discovering Your Ministry Identity in the Body of Christ

STEVE HOKE AND BILL TAYLOR

Just as you need to grow in your commitment to Christ, you need to grow in your commitment to the body of Christ. Individual Christians become a part of a larger Christian family when they accept Jesus Christ as Lord. The Bible never describes Christians as being whole unless they're linked in authentic fellowship with one another. Romans 12 and 1 Corinthians 12 tell us that we are part of one another, parts of the body of Christ. We need each other. We're linked together.

You want to be seriously involved in a church or a community of faith—worshiping, fellowshiping, learning and serving with a local community of faith wherever you are. If you're a college student, this my mean relating to two church bases: the one at home and the one at school.

The Church: God's Design for Discovering Gifts

Lest this sound like a harsh command, it may be helpful to take a fresh look at how God designed his bride—the body of Christ—into communities of faith (whether a home group or a megachurch) that are the environment in which believers discover their God-designed gifts and thus their "fit" in the body of Christ.

Below, in "Discovering Your Blueprint for Living," Paul Ford describes the simple elegance of how the Spirit wired interdependence into his new family. Committing to life together is a necessary second step if you want to grow in intimacy with Abba and experience the dynamic power of the Holy Spirit that is unleashed only through his body.

Those preparing for missionary service need to be involved in many ways: they need to be with other Christians on the campus, in the marketplace, on the job, in the training school and on the field. They need to be in contact with a mission sending body. They need to be engaged and serving in a local community of faith.

This is not because their serving is indispensable, but because their faith needs a relational context in which to grow.

You need the body. You cannot expect to launch into crosscultural outreach without a rock-solid foundation in a local body of Christ. You may lead a Bible study. You may host a weekly gathering of young Christians for prayer and fellowship. You could be part of an evangelism team. You could (should) serve in a home or cell group. You could be a summer intern in a church. You may serve weekly alongside other believers in meeting needs of the poor in your community.

Ministry is relational. As you minister in one area and then another, you will begin to receive affirmation from others about your effectiveness. You detect your gifts through this feedback from other discerning believers, not through isolated prayer in a closet. "You were really effective in teaching that class," a friend may tell you. Or when another person says, "When you host our small group in your home, you make everyone feel safe and welcome," it may be an indication of a gift of hospitality.

Ministry is organic. If you are a new believer, volunteer for several different kinds of ministry. If you have been a believer for some time but don't yet know your gifts, start with any ministry that presents itself. Ask others for feedback as to your suitability and effectiveness. Within a relatively short time, you will be directed to or will find a ministry that seems to fit your spiritual interests.

As you serve in that role, whether it be helping people move, teaching a class, leading a small group, participating in or initiating outreach, offering hospitality or gathering people together, you will begin to receive feedback as to whether you are spiritually powerful in that area of service. Mature believers will be able to advise you whether it is an area of ministry to keep working on or you should try another. That's body life.

Ministry is mutual. You must build into the church and make a contribution with your life before you can expect to receive from that community or church. From local communities of faith come not only the people, but also the intercession, counsel, encouragement and finances that make the worldwide missions enterprise possible.

Share Your New Commitment

Tell your family and local community of faith. Start with your parents, family and the pastoral team. Share with your shepherds any decisions or commitments you've made about missions. Ask them to give you the spiritual guidance and help every Christian needs.

Too many young mission zealots neglect their parents and family in the critical early steps of mission enthusiasm. But what do you do if your parents or other family members disagree with your decision and think you're crazy to consider leaving your home and job to transition crossculturally? That question along with a myriad of others are answered for you on the AskAMissionary website (www.AskAMissionary

.com). Visit it frequently to get the flavor of the seasoned responses to the practical and sometimes gut-wrenching questions you'll be asked.

Ask your faith community for specific prayer support. Since they are your most natural supporters, don't neglect nurturing the relationship and communication until you come asking for money. Involve them as active participants early in the process. Ask, "If you were me, how would you prepare for crosscultural service?" Let the pastor know that you're genuinely seeking input and that you are available and teachable, desiring to be prepared within the church for effective ministry.

Find a fruitful senior saint who can serve as a practical spiritual guide or mentor. Ask leaders in your church and your community if there is a special person or couple who can mentor you and pray with you. This doesn't have to be a golden-ager, but an experienced and mature Christian who may be several steps ahead of you on this journey.

This will involve much more than just counseling. Seek a mature person whose kingdom values are evident in his or her lifestyle and who would be willing to spend regular time with you as a kind of spiritual director. Some churches have a procedure for taking pastoral or missionary candidates "under care" while they are in training for ministry.

Be Involved in Missions in Your Church

Offer to join (or start) a missions or global outreach committee for your church. Many issues will be clarified in your own mind as you join others in your church as they seek to obey God's foreign policy for the church. Discussion and study of church missions policy and giving will enlarge your own understanding and enlighten your personal giving.

Don't be afraid to ask questions about things

that are new to you or that might appear out of sync with what God is teaching you about missions. You may be able to play a helpful role in increasing the energy and effectiveness of your church's involvement in missions.

Increasingly, local churches are assuming greater responsibility in training their missionary candidates. This usually involves an intentional internship or apprenticeship in which specific character qualities and ministry skills are nurtured. The church recognizes such people as having been called to the Christian ministry and seeks to support them through their training period and into their future career. It is also during such a trial period that a church decides whether or not to confirm and stand behind your future ministry.

If your church does not have a strong missions training program, share a copy of this workbook with the leaders. Share what you've learned about yourself through it. Even if your local church is in the dark about the whole process of how to help a person move into crosscultural ministry, you still need their prayers and counsel. Take the initiative to inform them of your growing interest and motivation. Don't expect them to detect it from afar.

Develop Accountable Relationships

Two dynamics are critical to your spiritual maturation: relationship and accountability. Our culture's extreme stress on individualism has left Western Christianity weak in relationships. Mentoring relationships for growth should include a relational network that embraces mentors, peers and younger Christians to ensure development and a healthy perspective on life and ministry. (We discuss this further in "Developing Your 'Thrival' Strategy" [pp. 94-99], as well as in "Exercise: Finding Personal Mentors" [pp. 281-84].)

Second, you need mentoring relationships for *accountability*. You should also seek "later-al," or peer mentoring relationships with friends and colleagues with whom you can enter mutually supportive relationships for encouragement and protection—relaxed, open and relevant relationships with peers that enable you to stimulate, interact with and hold one another accountable at a personal level. A circle of accountability is the safeguard for finishing well.

Demonstrate Your Commitment in Financial Stewardship

Missions will become more real to you as you invest yourself practically in prayer, financial support and encouragement for someone in whose shoes you may someday walk. When you are on support yourself, your experience in supporting others will enhance your own ministry to your donors. And the challenge of investing wisely will stimulate you to learn more than you might otherwise.

"Travel" Crossculturally

Western Christians travel internationally at an increasing rate. Link up with some of these travelers and ask them to share their experiences with you. It will help both you and them to deepen your understanding of crosscultural issues and ministry. Talk with missionaries. Invite international students into your home; study with them; hang out with them. Take the initiative to develop international friendships right in your community and city (see Dan Brannen's "International Students: Crosscultural Witness at Home," pp. 102). Don't wait until you take a short-term trip to another continent.

Get on-the-Job Training

Don't overlook the value of the training you will receive from your on-the-job experience in the body of Christ. Important lessons can be learned and values developed from any job, no matter how menial.

Missionaries must be people who can become self-sufficient. The next generation of missionaries may have to use their skills to generate income to stay on the field. They must be imaginative and find ways to do routine tasks effectively.

Look at every job as a learning opportunity. Approach it with an open mind and the simple belief that God has placed you in it for a purpose and expects you to do your very best. Learn about taking directions from others. Learn about working on a team. Experiment to see if your drive and passion for starting new communities of faith in the difficult places of the world is genuine. Take initiative. Innovate. Start new ministries.

Western young people are not considered "adult" until they have actually gone out and supported themselves. Too often our society, including our schools, treats young adults as if they were not yet ready to accept major responsibility. Don't fall into this trap.

You develop responsibility by proving yourself over time in the various roles you fill. Appreciate what other people say about responsibility and missions. But use every opportunity to sharpen your professional skills while gaining work experience in the marketplace.

As you pray and plan, listen for God's voice and feel God's touch. Try to discover his path for you. As your congregation helps you, they too will catch a vision. They'll be stretched to seek for more.

ASSESSMENT THREE

Discovering Your Blueprint for Living

PAUL FORD

It has taken me over fifteen years, but I finally have found a way to help Christians and Christian leaders to discover the whole of who they are, from baseline personality to powerful spiritual gifts, from underlying motivational needs to gift liabilities. It is with great joy that I and hundreds of other Your Leadership Grip/Birkman Blueprint coaches assist others to discover their blueprint for living, God's natural and supernatural design for each person to play her or his Spirit-empowered part in the body of Christ.

One foundational piece must be firmly set in place before I share with you my own pilgrimage to discovering the Grip/Birkman Blueprint process. Because of the overt individualism that drives certain cultures, including American culture, I realized early that I had to develop a lens through which each individual believer would see himself or herself with an authentic, biblical worldview. I call that view the Body Life Design Team. In others words, as each of us seeks to understand how God has prepared us for ministry, we must first understand how we fit into the bigger picture of God's purposes with others.

You and I are a special part of God's Body Life Design Team. What does this mean? These words give clear definition as to who I am, where I fit and how I best serve.

First, *Body Life* reveals the core of what living in Christ means for who I am. *Body Life* means that, before anything else, I am absolutely significant because of the cross of Christ. There is nothing I can do or say, nothing I can write or preach, no award or position, no honor or any human relationship that will make me any more significant than I already am in Christ. Because of the cross, I become truly special in the eyes of God, received as his child—Abba's child. That which I cannot do on my own—prove my worth and value—Jesus does for me, and he releases to me a life full of significance and meaning that no one can steal or destroy.

Second, *Design* means that I have a unique, God-designed part to play because of supernatural spiritual gifting. Not only am I absolutely significant as a Christian but, completely separate from that, I have a part to play in the body of Christ that no one else can play. My role is so important that all three persons of the Trinity are involved with the design and enactment of my body life function: the Father determines gifts (see 1 Cor 12:18), the Son gives the gifts (see Eph 4:7) and the Spirit empowers them (see 1 Cor 12:11). That is how strategic we are in kingdom purposes!

Thus it is imperative that I seek to understand and live out my ministry identity, since no one else can fulfill the blueprint that is mine and mine alone. Once I understand my design and my powerful strengths, I also am able to see my areas where I need others to play their powerful parts. I understand not only who I am but also who I need in the body.

Team adds a third and often-forgotten piece to the puzzle of understanding how I best serve as one who is both absolutely significant because of the cross and has a unique role to play. *Team* means that I choose to work for unity in the body. In an individualistic culture, each of us is tempted to want "my own thing," apart from others whom God has brought into the body. Only in *Team* can I find the unity that Jesus prayed for in John 17:20-26. He not only prayed for unity among his present disciples, but also for us who would believe in the future. Jesus knew from his experience on the mount of temptation that the devil would encourage each of us at times to see the "I" of self as more important or above the "we" of the body.

Unity is not an accident or something across which you stumble. It is an active choice. It is my conscious, intentional decision to move from a self-focused, entitled "I" to becoming a member of *Team*—"we." We make sense and are most powerful together. I choose to serve others in the body so together we can serve outside the body. That is what moves us into missional living and ministry. This is the home base for "apostolic genius"—it is housed in the body of Christ. It is not an independent, individualistic, entrepreneurial impulse we attempt to exercise on our own where we discern there to be a need. That is the blatant individualism that has characterized too much of North American missions around the world. God reveals his purposes most powerfully as together we become a place where he lives by his Spirit (see Eph 2:22).

So then, with the all-important issues of significance in the cross and the will to unity now meaningfully wrapped around my design through the Body Life Design Team moniker, let us go back to my search to help believers more deeply and intently understand their blueprint design.

In the eighties I started developing tools for lay Christians to discover and fulfill their God-designed roles in or beyond the local church. The title of one of the workbooks telling the story: "Getting Your Gifts in Gear." Organic body life began for many Christians and churches, with many believers discovering and playing their God-prepared parts for the first time.

But by the mid-nineties it became shockingly clear to me that thousands of Christian leaders were the ones blocking the door to effective lay mobilization. So I started facilitating team-building seminars with ministry teams to help leaders build strong teams by first understanding the ministry identities of their players.

As they first became good stewards of their own gifts, leaders also became more intentional in equipping and releasing others to play their gifted parts. They became good stewards of "who we are" as a group of individuals who each possess God-given spiritual gifts. To date, I seldom if ever have seen a leadership training model that meaningfully trains a leader to steward the gifts and passions of his or her teammates.

Through this process, many a leader quit worrying about how to be that "visionary leader" and got back to the biblical business of equipping and releasing the saints for the work of ministry. We utilized a workbook process called "Discovering Your Ministry Identity" for helping leaders to assess themselves and their team members in six different areas—from spiritual gifts to ministry burdens or passions—and therein discover how "who I am affects who we are." Body life functioning realized its dependence on every person playing his or her part.

The blueprint for the "I" and the "we" was starting to take shape. But I continued to be incredibly frustrated with leaders as I assisted them in effective lay mobilization and intentional team building. Then, in 1999, I got to the heart of why many leaders were not equipping and releasing others: the majority of Christian leaders—and this includes pastors and missionaries (as high as 70 percent)—do not clearly understand who they are in Christ! Many were never trained to be good stewards of their gifts.

The Assessment

It was out of this frustration that I developed "Your Leadership Grip," a workbook that gives the Christian leader a chance to identify her or his spiritual gifts from three different angles through five different assessments. In addition, the leader is able to identify weaknesses and who he or she needs alongside to be a better teammate. My goal? *Leader, rather than trying to be a visionary leader, a manager by objectives or a leader who looks just like your mentor, how about first making a sober estimate of who you already are—powerful strengths—and also your weaknesses, which simply reveal who you need.* Thousands of leaders, pastors and missionaries are doing just that.

The Whole Blueprint

Over the years of this developmental process, it slowly dawned on me that a Christian has two distinctive patterns going on in her of his life at the same time. Every believer has a baseline personality—your natural abilities crafted by God—but also functions powerfully with a mix of two or three dominant spiritual gifts—spiritual empowerments from the Holy Spirit—where you are truly dynamic in the Spirit. I began to observe the pattern of how the gifts flow out from baseline personality. I used to think that the two areas of our lives—gifting and personality—just blended together into one form. But then I observed scores of leaders whose personality and gifting appeared to be different in part or in total. And for some, the attempt to understand gifting was confused by certain personality qualities. Which is it: talent or gifting?

How could I help leaders come to grip with the reality of both worlds colliding within? It was then I realized that the Lord had already given me the two major puzzle pieces. "Your Leadership Grip/Birkman Blueprint" is an assessment set that helps individuals and teams gain a clearer understanding of their personality and natural abilities using the Birkman Method, a sophisticated personality and behavior profile, while also gaining insight into their supernatural spiritual makeup of spiritual gifts. It's a path to help people identify, more deeply and profoundly than ever before, the differences between their natural personality and powerful gifting, their talents and their supernatural empowering. It's an approach for each person to discover his or her "blueprint for living" as God has designed naturally from birth, then empowered supernaturally from conversion.

So then, our overarching purpose with the Your Leadership Grip/Birkman Blueprint is to help Christians become more intentional stewards of who they are. It also helps those who train or encourage others in their ministry role to become intentional stewards of their teams—who "we" are. Let's start with what God has already prepared in each of us before we add vision or competencies that may steal from God's already-prepared design specs.

Simply including a basic spiritual gifts inventory in this book with no other explanation seemed short-sighted. We have designed a way for readers to complete an online set of assessments to gain an accurate understanding of their God-given wiring. Your Leadership Grip provides a computer-generated report on your spiritual gifting by the Spirit, and the Your Leadership Grip/Birkman Blueprint provides a more comprehensive correlation of your gifts with your personality and behavior patterns.

An online version of Paul Ford's "Your Leadership Grip" combining the Spiritual Gifts, Team Style Primary Functions assessments is available to readers of this book at a reduced rate of just six dollars. The more complete Your Leadership Grip/Birkman Blueprint inventory is available directly from ChurchSmart Resources as well for thirty-nine dollars. Go to <www.churchsmart.com> and click on the "Hot Deals" link at the bottom of the home page to order these assessments, or call ChurchSmart Resources at 800-253-4276 for assistance.

Paul Ford is a leadership and team-building specialist with Church Resource Ministries. He and his wife reside in Albuquerque, and they have one college-age son, Stephen.

E-mail paul.ford@crmleaders.org for more information.

For Best Results

STEVE HOKE

If you want to best prepare yourself for future crosscultural ministry, follow this suggested prefield conditioning program. You can't do every exercise every day; you'd kill yourself. So prayerfully consider which exercises and activities will best limber you up and build spiritual and relational muscle for long-term servanthood. A few critical books are listed to assist your further investigation.

Be accepting of others' opinions. Acceptance, openness and trust are three of the most important values you can carry into intercultural relationships. When you talk to people who hold viewpoints different from yours, ask questions like, "Can you help me understand why?" instead of trying to convince them that your opinion is better.

Refine the art of conversation. Commit yourself to making new acquaintances. Take the initiative. Ask good questions. Be a responsive listener. Observe what topics are most effective in getting people to open up and talk about themselves and their interests. Hone your skill at asking open-ended questions that spark conversation.

Practice adapting and stretching. Develop

flexibility. Consider alternatives. Look for more than one way to accomplish tasks, and practice praising others for their creativity. For example, an ever-present crosscultural irritant to learn to accommodate is the differences in time: long, free-flowing meetings or meetings with rigid agendas; long worship services or tightly planned sixty-minute events; unannounced drop-in visits or specific appointments at Starbucks.

Be informed about world events. Read international news and of materials on intercultural relations. Sharpen your perception of patterns and principles relating Scripture to cultures and peoples' behavior. Step out of the box of the typical and traditional interpretations of global change, chaos and world religions. Learn to hone your reasoned opinions on moral dilemmas and global issues. This will undoubtedly mean you'll need to become a more avid reader of international news magazines and at least one daily newspaper with a significant international section, such as the *New York Times, Los Angeles Times* or *Chicago Tribune.*

Study other cultures. Ted Ward's practical handbook *Living Overseas* (Free Press, 1984) is an excellent primer containing tips for learning about other cultures. More recent books include study books on cultural anthropology; also look for magazine articles describing peoples from other cultures. Build a file on the region of the world to which you sense compassion or the initial whispers of a call. It's never too soon to start studying other cultures.

- Duane Elmer. *Cross-Cultural Conflict: Building Relationships for Effective Ministry.* Downers Grove, Ill.: InterVarsity Press, 1993.

- Myron Loss. *Culture Shock: Dealing with stress in cross-cultural living.* Winona Lake, Ind.: Light and Life Press, 1993 (3rd printing).

- Craig Storti. *The Art of Crossing Cultures.* Yarmouth, Maine: Intercultural Press, 1990.

Get accustomed to another language. Tune your car radio or television to a foreign-language station. Learn basic phrases in another language. Practicing any new language sharpens your mental capacities and makes you more responsive to the particular language you will learn overseas. Check out the missions language-acquisition classic by Betty Sue and Tom Brewster, *Language Acquisition Made Practical* (Lingua House, 1976).

Build a friendship with a person from another country. Establish a long-range relationship with an international student or internationals living in your community. Learn some of your new friends' language and try to understand their perspective. Visit their home or apartment, sharing meals in their comfort zone, not your own. Be attentive to the ideas or topics that open their hearts to you.

- Patty Lane. *A Beginner's Guide to Crossing Cultures: Making Friends in a Multicultural World.* Downers Grove, Ill.: InterVarsity Press, 2002.

- Tim Stafford. *Friendship Across Cultures.* Grand Rapids: Zondervan, 1986.

Strengthen spiritual unity by yielding your rights. Paul said that all things are permissible, but not all things are beneficial (see 1 Cor 10:23). Although some behavior isn't inherently wrong or evil, it doesn't build unity. Paul was willing not to insist on his rights in every situation (see Phil 4:11-12). He accepted certain limitations or conditions (see 1 Cor 9:12, 15, 19). Look for ministry opportunities in which you can yield rather than demand your rights in areas as mundane as music or dress, or as vital as worship patterns and witness.

Commit to a team ministry in your community or church. Learn to become an effective and appreciated team player. Learn how to most effectively share ideas, raise questions and explore goals on a team of diverse people.

Teamwork emerges from costly and timely practice. Take leadership responsibility. You must learn to deal graciously with interruptions and ambiguity, give and receive feedback and have your ideas rejected. Read Paul R. Ford's *Knocking Over the Leadership Ladder* (Church-Smart, 2006).

Keep a journal. This is a practical way to reflect on your ideas, inner thoughts and feelings in a consistent, organized manner. Record what you saw and felt, why you responded the way you did and what you learned about yourself. Keeping a journal will sharpen your critical thinking and is one way of becoming more intentional and responsive on your spiritual journey. Look into Richard Peace's *Spiritual Journaling: Recording Your Journey Toward God* (NavPress, 1998).

Develop physical stamina. Physical endurance affects every area of life, especially the spiritual. The physical and emotional demands of entering and adjusting to a new culture can be countered through a consistent conditioning program. We're not talking about Olympic competition here, or world-class body building; rather, stretch muscles and strengthen your cardiovascular system in preparation for the rigors of living outside your comfort zone.

Invest financially in advancing God's kingdom—both on the frontlines and behind the scenes. Develop the hilarious and holy habit now of investing in kingdom ministry through people and projects that touch your heart. Research where this giving can be most effective, then accompany it with prayer.

(Adapted with permission from *Wherever,* a publication of TEAM, 1995.)

Why Wait Till You Get There?

MALA MALMSTEAD

Mission service today offers incredible opportunities to experience the world while sharing Christ. Sometimes our desire for adventure can blind us to the fact that being a missionary for any length of time is hard work. It demands many skills and an uncompromising clarity of purpose.

Just living crossculturally is often tougher and far more stressful than living at home. Communication barriers, the complications of obtaining basic necessities like food and clean water, and the difficulties of getting along with coworkers and adapting to a new culture may be daily challenges.

On top of all this, your purpose isn't just to survive—it's to point others to Christ. So the more ministry experience you have at home, the more effective you'll be in a foreign context.

Minister at Home

Preparing for your missions experience is the key to adapting well and being a useful instrument, available for what God wants to do through you. If you aren't sure you want to go through the preparation process, maybe you need to reconsider your missions plans. Consider traveling instead—experiencing the world without the express purpose of sharing the gospel.

You can test your missions motivation by examining the activities you're involved in now. The most important way to prepare for the rigors of missions is to live a life of service at home first. Whether you have a year before your proposed missions trip or just a couple of weeks, you can get involved in ministry. Any opportunity that takes you out of your comfort zone is good preparation for the foreign field.

Here are a few ways you can begin to get actively involved in ministry right now, so you'll be better prepared for your future as a missionary.

Find Crosscultural Environments

While in college, I was involved in various inner-city outreaches. As I worked at shelters for the homeless, I learned to listen to people from backgrounds and situations vastly different from my own. By volunteering with a kids' mentoring program, I met children from another ethnic group. They spoke an English lingo that I didn't know. Even their jokes and concepts of morality were foreign to me. Learn to laugh at your mistakes, and don't underestimate the power of gestures and pantomime. The most important thing is not how you communicate—it's that you do communicate.

As a result of these experiences, I was better prepared later to do child evangelism in Spain and to work in orphanages in India and Uzbekistan. Opportunities for ministry abound! Finding one that suits your personality and interests should not be too difficult. Literacy programs, Sunday schools, church youth groups, crisis pregnancy centers, drama, music and prison ministries are just a few of the hundreds of options that will help prepare you for overseas ministry.

Practice Telling the Story

Witnessing to friends and strangers in your own country is difficult for most Christians. Knowing your culture and caring what others think can be hard barriers to overcome. But the more you learn to share your faith at home, the more effectively you'll share your faith overseas. It's important to know some basic evangelistic tools and methods, to know how to verbalize your testimony and to be familiar with some Scripture that may speak to non-Christians.

Suzy Schultz is one example of how this works. Before Schultz went to Poland, she spent time witnessing in a local park. She talked with total strangers and shared with them how they could receive Christ. Later, when two artists she was witnessing to in Poland wanted to receive Christ, Schultz was prepared to explain salvation to them.

Make International Friends

Spending time with international students or with foreigners at your workplace is excellent training for developing friendships abroad. Scott DeVries spent two years in Czechoslovakia. He says some of his closest friends were international students whom he met while in college and seminary. "They helped me see the world from their eyes," he explains.

Broadening your perspective on the world is crucial to understanding a foreign culture. If you talk to a person from your country of interest, you can learn a great deal about that person's culture long before you enter it. Knowing as much as you can about the culture you are planning to enter will not only minimize your culture shock, it will also help you avoid some painful blunders. The country you enter may be nothing like your own. You cannot expect it to be.

You can follow these guidelines to prepare for missions right now. You can also take specific steps toward making your transition to the mission field smoother. Below are some suggestions I have found helpful.

Study the Language

I recently returned from a year in Tashkent, Uzbekistan, where two languages are spoken: Russian and Uzbek. I struggled through that year, at times feeling isolated and helpless due to my lack of language training. Making friends was tough too. I felt inhibited by the difficulty of communicating. I cannot emphasize strongly enough the importance of spending time learning your target language.

While you're still at home, listen to language tapes regularly. Teach yourself from a book or the Internet. Or hire a tutor to help you with the language. Find a national of that country to practice with you and give you pronunciation tips. At the very least, learn a few important phrases. Not only will you be able to communicate (even if it's only a little bit), but the people you meet will be touched by your efforts with their language.

Study the Country

A very useful book that can give you an overview of the continent and of the specific country you're heading for is *Operation World* by Patrick Johnstone and Jason Mandryk (Zondervan, 2001). Filled with information about the various religions in each region, the state of the church and the country's key prayer needs, it is an excellent way to learn about "your" country and to begin praying faithfully. Find a world map or atlas so you can visualize the country and familiarize yourself with its geography, cities and so forth.

While you're at it, get on the Internet. Take a trip to the local library and research the history, traditions, philosophers, famous writers and scientists of the country. People are extremely proud of their cultural heritage. They may expect you to know their countrymen's accomplishments. Ignorance about their country can strongly offend them.

Involve Your Family and Church

If you're seriously considering a mission trip, you may have approached your family and church already for counsel, service, prayer and finances. For others to be involved in and con-

tributing to your trip, you have to do a lot of networking and sharing your vision. Missions service is not the place for showing off your independence or proving your own capabilities.

As David Hicks of Operation Mobilization puts it, "Your mission trip should not only impact you, but should impact lots of people who can't go."

Be a Servant

No matter how much you prepare for crosscultural work, there will still be things that surprise, challenge, disgust and disturb you. And though you may try to be the most culturally sensitive person in the world, you probably will end up offending people more than once. These experiences are normal. Maybe the best thing to remember is that the key to effective ministry is servanthood. Veteran crosscultural specialist Duane Elmer gives practical guidance for serving with sensitivity and humility in *Cross-Cultural Servanthood* (InterVarsity Press, 2006).

One mission leader says that when he looks for recruits, he looks for people who are teachable, flexible and humble in spirit. "Character is more desirable than competence," he says. "If your attitude is [one of] seeking after God, then your life will reflect that in service."

Heading overseas with a warm, caring attitude and finding practical ways to serve the people you want to reach will go a long way toward making your mission experience successful. Cultivate these skills and attitudes now, and you'll be better prepared for crosscultural service—whenever and wherever God leads you.

Mala Malmstead is a freelance writer who was raised on the mission field. She and her husband, Greg, recently spent a year teaching English in Uzbekistan.

Four Building Blocks for Lifetime Service

ROBERTSON McQUILKIN

God sent his only Son as a missionary to people who were without hope. It was a sacrificial plan, a costly one—but such is his love. The apostle Paul spoke of himself as a colaborer with God. In God's primary work of redemption, the career missionary is a special apostolic emissary—a credentialed ambassador of the King of all kings!

There are four important building blocks for a life of missionary service. To discover and shape them, you need a team. God has provided this team in his church.

1. Heart Preparation

If your attitudes and behavior don't give people a valid picture of the character of Jesus Christ, what kind of salvation will you have to offer? The key is continual personal sacrifice, ever moving toward a greater likeness to the Savior. The path for this constant personal growth is a solid prayer life—a discipline that should grow for a lifetime.

2. Active Involvement in Ministry

Gifts of the Spirit are needed for any effective service for God, and certainly for full-time missionary service. For example, the gift of evangelism is needed for church-planting work. There's only one way to know if you have the gifts you need: minister. Try it, find out what your abilities are, and develop them.

But be patient. Give the process time. Don't decide too soon that you don't have a particular gift you think you need. I made this mistake. I assumed that if I had the gift of evangelism I must become a little Billy Graham. I pleaded with God to give me the gift of evangelism and expected people to respond to the gospel in droves when I spoke to a crowd. If I didn't have this kind of gift, how else could I be a pioneer missionary?

Finally, I realized I had restricted my definition of evangelism. I discovered that God was preparing me for evangelism in Japan, where mass meetings were not the best way to communicate the gospel. I could settle among unevangelized people and love them to Jesus Christ.

3. Formal Preparation and Basic Education

One of the normal contemporary routes to an effective ministry includes formal study of God, Scripture and missions. Even those going into support roles in missions, like medicine and technology, can benefit from a year of Bible study. These support people must be able to function as part of the team and participate in winning others to faith and building up the church.

A degree program at a Bible college or seminary is valuable for those pursuing a career in evangelism or Bible teaching. Find a school that has a strong reputation for preparing full-time missionaries—just as you would choose the best possible medical school if you were preparing to become a doctor. Consult with missions leaders to determine the relative quality of the schools that interest you.

4. Language and Cultural Studies

Don't skimp on these. Of the hundreds of missionaries I've known, there is only one exception I've found to the rule of careful language and cultural study. Don McAlpine arrived in Japan with the conviction that the Communists would take over momentarily or the Lord would return. He never paused long enough to learn the language—or the culture either.

Using an interpreter for more than thirty years, he became a premier church-starting evangelist. He compensated for his lack of language and his occasional lapses in cultural sensitivity by maintaining a strong prayer life and a deep love for people.

A Church Home

To fit these four building blocks of a missionary career together properly, build a relationship with at least one church that will give you partnership in vision and prayer. For confirmation of your call, for supervised experience in ministry, for prayer and financial support, for accountability and reinforcement while on the field, there is no substitute for a strong sending church.

When you are ready to choose a mission body and a place of service, one will follow the other. Some feel called to a particular location and look for the mission best suited to reach that particular people. Others choose the agency first, to be sure of the "team" before deciding on the "playing field." If your church sends all its missionaries through a single board, your choice of a board is predetermined. If not, your church can help you find the best mission agency for you—one that matches your doctrinal and philosophical views of missions, your gifts and your calling.

If God calls you, he will prepare and empower you. What a glorious calling—to spend your life in partnership with the missionary God, reaching those he loves and has chosen!

Robertson McQuilkin is president emeritus of Columbia International University in Columbia, South Carolina, and served as a church-planting missionary in Japan. Both Steve and Bill consider him a singular veteran sage.

Downtown Muslim prayer

My Journey

PIERS VANDER
Cedar Springs Presbyterian Church,
United States, Zimbabwe, France, South Africa

How is it possible for someone growing up in a non-Christian home in a small African town in Zimbabwe, having spent most of his life in the business world, to then become the director of Global Mission at a large Presbyterian church in the American South? Only God could develop a script like this. And that is what he did.

God called me to his Son as a nineteen-year-old student by convicting me of my sin over a period of about six months. Oddly enough, it started in France, far away from any church or Christians. It eventually culminated through hearing a sermon on Romans 1:18-32 by a stand-in preacher.

God ensured that I obtained a strong mix of business skills plus a wide range of church and mission experience. It took about ten years for God to strip me of my love for success and acclaim, but in the process, my desire for deeper involvement in ministry got stronger and stronger.

Then God made it crystal clear to me that this is what he wanted. How? First, I got to know Mac Sells, my mentor and predecessor (now with the Lord) at Cedar Springs Presbyterian Church in Knoxville, Tennessee. I recognized that the role of director of Global Mission was something I felt I could do and enjoy.

Second, the call came from the church; fellow believers with whom I lived in community were telling me I should transition into full-time ministry.

Third, the people who knew me best—family members—felt that God was leading me in this way. My brother-in-law revealed to me that he had predicted that God would call me to missions, long before I had begun to realize the same thing.

Fourth, God miraculously cleared roadblocks—some seemingly very large. The most significant was my immigrant status in the United States.

The combination of these factors made the call irrefutable. Failure to respond would have been disobedience.

Developing Your "Thrival" Strategy

STEVE HOKE AND MYRA PERRINE

Have you ever wondered what Jesus meant when he said, "I have come that they may have life, and have it to the full" (Jn 10:10)? I'm pretty sure he wasn't talking about what we refer to as the "prosperity gospel"—naming and claiming new cars, homes and all things monetary. Jesus means for our life (zoe, spirit life) to be abundant, he uses a word that is not often found in the New Testament, perissos, which means "all the more, with every advantage, beyond all that's expected, in excess." It is the word Paul used when he wrote, "Now to Him who is able to do far more abundantly beyond all that we ask or think, according to the power that works within us, to Him be the glory in the church and in Jesus Christ to all generations forever and ever" (Eph 3:20-21 NASB, emphasis added).

The word *abundantly* leaves us with the same picture Jesus gave when he said that all who believe in him would have *rivers* of living water flowing within, a river of abundant life, water, grace, peace, love, compassion and all that God's Spirit brings flowing into and through us to a dry and thirsty world (see Jn 7:38). That is God's intention for his children, no matter where we live or what our circumstances. Jesus intends for us to *thrive,* not merely survive. Abundance and thriving flow naturally out of the depths of the character of God.

When you think about your own "thrival," not just survival, but living with abundant *zoe* life, what comes to mind? When we've asked our own incoming staff (missionaries) that question, we've gathered a varied list of the elements they perceive as vital. The following is a sampling of their suggestions:

- close connections with friends and family
- supportive home churches
- strong peer relationships on the field
- a caring and effective team leader
- clear communication channels with the home office
- regular physical exercise
- a strong and steady base of financial supporters
- people who pray for us consistently
- resources to help with children's schooling
- time and space to get away and be with God on a regular basis
- people and resources to help us keep learning and growing

What additional elements might you add?

Working together as a Staff Development and Care Team to equip and nurture our staff around the world to transition to international living, we've found that it takes a "thrival strategy"—a personal strategy for thriving in another culture or wherever God sends them to serve Jesus—for our staff to be the people God calls them to be and to do the work he calls them to do.

We have identified four critical support systems that build on one foundation, each being essential to long-term thrival. These support systems do not come together on their own. They must be carefully, prayerfully and intentionally constructed, person by person, until they become the bedrock of everything we intend to accomplish in a crosscultural setting. This is as vital as the pillars to a bridge, the foundation to a skyscraper, the bedrock of a railway.

Intimacy with God

The thrival foundation of the four support systems is, of course, a deep, vital relationship with Jesus Christ. This relationship is growing, progressive and developmental. Jesus' last words to his disciples clearly informs us regarding what eternal life (*zoe*) is all about: "And this is life eternal, that they may know thee, the only true God, and Jesus Christ, whom thou hast sent" (Jn 17:3 KJV). Knowing God is the meaning of our life; it is the beginning and the end, as well as the middle. When we forget that all of life is about a dynamic, personal, one-on-one love relationship with a living Person, we dry up quickly.

The same happens when we put anything before that abiding connection, including ministry. I (Myra) like to paraphrase John 15 this way:

Jesus is the Vine, we are simply his branches. We can't expect ourselves to produce the life we need without him—a life that is powerful wise, and lovingly courageous. We just weren't created to generate any aspect of that life apart from him. He is our Life-giver and we are his Life-receivers. He has attached us to himself forever, but we must live in conscious awareness of that permanent relational connection, allowing his life to flow through us mightily and without pause. The fruit of his Spirit will be abundantly produced in us, even in excess. But we won't make it even one day without him, we really won't. Only his life in us brings the overflowing peace and grace we need.

Yes, it's true: only his "river of living water" within can bring thrival to our souls! Apart from him, we can do nothing!

Upon the indispensable foundation of an ongoing life-connection with God himself we build four supportive components.

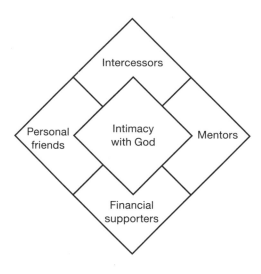

1. An Intercession Team

This is team of five to fifteen individuals (and possibly prayer groups) that have agreed to pray for you on a consistent basis, whether that be daily, weekly or on a certain time of day each week. We don't assume that everyone who gives to you financially necessarily tracks with your specific requests. This is the primary team to form as you prepare to raise personal support and to transition overseas.

Patty M. learned the importance of having a personal team backing her in prayer in the early nineties. She writes:

> I had been thinking about starting a personal intercession team since Sam and I were in leadership and felt it would be important. However, I felt a bit sheepish about asking others to pray regularly for me, thinking, "Who am I to ask for this? I'm nobody special." However in 1990, as I was dealing with a serious illness, my spiritual director told me that she felt this prolonged illness could be broken by two weeks of prayer and fasting, and she encouraged me to form a personal intercession team. I called together a small group of close friends, explained the situation and asked them to consider being part of this team.
>
> They each felt called by God to do this, and they became my core intercessors. Most of these women are still on the team today (2008), and the number of people on the team has increased to about twenty. Apart from the triune God and my own family, this team is God's greatest gift to me. I don't know what I would do without their partnership in life and ministry.

2. A Financial Support Team

A team is anywhere from 50 to 150 individuals and churches who pledge to send financial support into your account in a mission agency on a monthly or annual basis. Almost every mission agency trains its new missionaries how to develop their financial support team. The primary approach is to meet with individuals and couples face-to-face in their home and invite them to prayerfully consider becoming a part of your personal prayer and financial support team. [Note: Some few denominational agencies provide full financial support when you enlist as a member of their denominational sending organization, like the Southern Baptists and Christian and Missionary Alliance, among others.] (For more information, see "Keys to Raising Your Personal Support" on pp. 143-46.)

3. A Personal Support Team

In addition to prayer and financial support, the next vital system to have in place is a group of carefully selected, close friends whom you ask to be available to you for personal interaction and support, whether it is face-to-face, over the phone, by e-mail or through Skype. These are people with whom you can be "off," have fun and hang out, without thought of ministry or giving out. Many women already have this group in place, those close friends they call to talk through a pressing issue, pray with about the children or share a heart concern. For guys, it's often the men they go fishing with or buddies they call to do something fun. These are people who know and love you—even when you are down or look nothing like the spiritual giant others expect you to be. We have found it challenging yet mandatory to construct this group by personal invitation, explaining to them why their friendship will be vital when you are living in another culture.

I (Myra) have found that when our care team goes to the field to visit a missionary who is not "thriving," it is often this support system that is missing, especially for women. We tend to neglect our souls, those places in us that need human connection and downtime to be listened to, laughed with and just take time to play. The Benedictines insist that there is enough time in each day for prayer, work, study and play. Without time away from ministry to have fun, we truly cannot thrive.

4. A Personal Mentoring Cluster

Mentors are godly men and women who can pour into your life even while you are living at a distance from them. Paul Stanley and J. Robert Clinton identify nine distinctive types of mentors in their excellent book *Connecting* (NavPress, 1992). Do you need a spiritual director, a counselor, a discipler or a coach, to name four? Don't assume that every church or agency will provide all the mentoring and input you need while living overseas. We coach staff to find and invite key people to serve in their "mentoring cluster"—a group of two to four people who agree to serve as resource people to them in areas of selected need or personal growth. (See "Finding Personal Mentors," pp. 281-84.)

I (Steve) discovered the life-changing impact of selecting personal mentors almost forty years ago. Since 1971 I've always had one or more godly men whom I have asked to serve as advisers or mentors in specific areas of my life. During grad school I spent monthly time with a local pastor I respected. Early in my teaching career I had regular conversations with my doctoral mentor. For years I've had at least one peer mentor—a close friend who models a vital spiritual maturity—to meet with me weekly or monthly to keep me focused on my life and ministry goals. They continue to breathe energy, vision and encouragement into my often parched inner life.

It's that simple—constructing four interrelated relational support systems that will nurture your spiritual, emotional, physical and psychological health while serving in another culture. But it takes prayer, planning and some intentional conversations with people you know.

Can you imagine the impact of having those support systems in place in your life right now? When we ask participants to draw what it would look like and feel like to be fully supported for the duration of their time on the field, their group drawings are extremely informative. Visualize each of the following images that have been drawn by previous teams:

- a safety net
- a fully loaded airplane with adequate fuel, filled tires and happy passengers
- a carefully constructed extension bridge
- a chair with four legs
- a human body that has a digestive, circulatory, reproductive and excretory systems

What image comes to your mind that best depicts a comprehensive thrival strategy?

Constructing Your Four Support Systems

Use the space on the following worksheet to list specific names of people you want to contact to be on your support systems. Use additional paper to write or create your lists on your computer. Come back to it several times over several days to capture the names the Spirit will bring to your mind.

In the days and weeks ahead, begin to call and speak to people directly about becoming a part of one of your support teams.

Yes, you might survive without having each of these systems in place. But your thrival will depend on the strength and solidity of these four interlocking systems to provide long-term support. Don't be content to merely survive; trust the Lord to come back stronger as a result of growing in accountability and dependence.

Developing Your Four Support Systems

Intercessor team. List the people who are now praying or whom you will ask to pray for you regularly.

1.

2.

3.

4.

5.

6.

7.

Personal support system. List the people who are or will be part of your personal support team, that is, those who nurture you.

1.

2.

3.

4.

5.

6.

7.

Mentors. List the people inside and outside of your sphere of work or ministry you would like to mentor you. (Consider working through the questions in "Finding Personal Mentors," pp. 281-84, to help you make this list.)

1.

2.

3.

4.

5.

6.

7.

Jesus' Words About Family

CHRIS HOKE

I work with gangs. Latino gangs. There's a word they have for each other, a term of endearment: *carnal* (car-NAHL). Like, "of the flesh." Or "of my blood. You're family to me. Closer than a brother." One of the gang's highest leaders began calling me—a white kid with glasses from the suburbs—this in his letters to me from prison two years ago. I have since accepted: we are indeed brothers.

Most of the criminal youths I pastor were abandoned by their biological fathers. Their mothers might be too busy at work, hooked on drugs or trying their best to please the new boyfriend. Their older brothers beat them up, mock them. The home is not a safe place for these kids, and the streets adopted them. Fellow gang members take them in, stick up for them, give them a new name.

They've found that there is something thicker than blood, even in their family-focused Hispanic culture. Despite lip service to the importance of their families, the *homies* in their gang come before their homes. It is the dynamic of adoption. That's why they're growing—without books, conferences and multimedia outreach.

A similar dynamic is at work when we are called into the ministry of Jesus. The New Testament can be read as the story of God explicitly cracking open the chaff of the Hebrew race, the descendents (*sperma,* in Greek, e.g., Jn 8:33) of Abraham, to cast the "seed" of his promise—not loins—into all peoples, races and nations. It is a scandal at all levels: Jesus calling individual disciples away from their homes (see Mt 10:34-39) on up to Paul trying to convince Roman Jews that God is grafting the rest of the world of Gentiles and odd-looking pagans into the same family as "children *[tekna]* of God" (Jn 8:39; Rom 8:21; 1 Jn 3:1). I imagine this is hard to do from God's perspective. Both then and now.

It is a scandal because it is not of this world. It is heavenly. This world is forged by ancient, biological, Darwinian principles of species propagation. Nurture the nest. Defend the cave and cubs. Maintain a vigilant distance from other-looking creatures. It's built into our flesh, our instincts. It's normal.

But to respond to Jesus' call into this mission is to be on the frontlines of *changing* what's normal. We are crossing cultural, social, racial, national and familial lines. To be missional is antithetical to the status quo.

This is where I've seen many Christians' potentially thrilling apostolic callings practically die in the womb. They follow the natural instinct to put a buffer between their home—their spouse and children—and the foreign people God sent them to live with and die for. I believe almost all the Bible studies, sermons and social services added up do not have the transformative power of the gospel on a human life that the radical spirit and experience of adoption does. Biological instinct causes parents to lay down their life for their progeny. But Jesus says, "Greater love has no one than this, that he lay down his life for his friends [that is, nonfamily loved ones]" (Jn 15:13).

One of my heroes is Father Greg Boyle of East Los Angeles. Hundreds, maybe thousands, of LA's gangsters of every stripe and color know him as the father they never had. It's not his homilies or evangelistic events. He's a white guy with a funny white beard who's put himself repeatedly between the gunfire of tattooed, feared brown youths, shouting that he loves them. He's been up all hours with them, their tears, problems, drugs, guns and dreams. For years. Made space on his floor, his couch, his schedule, his heart, his whole life.

His fruit is so big in his mission because he has ignored the instinct that stops most young missionaries so early: he doesn't have to think about his family first and so protect his floor, his schedule, his kids or his own life from the gangsters God adores. He's a Jesuit, and those believers learned centuries ago that sending priests out into the world with missions was most powerful if they were celibate. Their love for the people would not be relegated to a "work" schedule outside the home; it would be their entire lives. In Father Greg, I see that the idea of being a "man of the cloth" is not about purity, abstinence, self-denial or being down on the ol' hanky panky. It's about having missional power to the greatest degree—to be able to live out most freely the Father's heart of wildly open adoption among the world's peoples.

Whether we have spouses and kids or not, I believe Jesus' call to the apostolic life is to be able to give yourself without precaution.

When Jesus is giving his life in the most complete and risky way—taking the foreign, Roman death penalty on the cross—he forges a new family: "Woman," he says to his mother, "here is your son," and he points to his friend and disciple John (Jn 19:26). He tells the same to John. Biologically, this is the worst: to lose your oldest son. But Jesus demonstrates the kingdom of heaven's dynamic: as he gives his life freely in love, Mary's family grows!

We too with Jesus and Mary, are able to live out our fatherly and motherly instincts more fully with dozens more spiritual children than our loins and trust funds could ever support. As you step out into your calling, today tell God he has permission to pop the bubble of your nuclear home. Then taste the variety, the adventure and the bigness of the good news in your own growing home. I believe that as we take down such barriers and allow God to grow our families in this way, we will see the growth of the kingdom on earth as we never imagined.

Chris Hoke moved away from his biological family to start his new family among migrant workers and gang members in Burlington, Washington, and commutes between Central American jails and the Skagit County Jail to forge bridges for youth on the margins. His biological parents still love him deeply, but adopted him out to join a much broader family of the world's peoples.

My Journey

MIN-YOUNG JUNG
Wycliffe International,
Korea, Indonesia, United States, Singapore

I was born into a Christian family. My maternal grandfather was one of the first Korean pastors trained by Western missionaries a century ago and sent to work in Jeju Island, where my mother spent a few of her teen years. Jeju Island was regarded as a mission field at that time, so I guess I inherited a missional gene from my own mother and grandparents.

But my actual journey to the nations is inevitably connected to the corporate pilgrimage of the Korean church. When you talk about ethnocentrism, it's hard to beat Koreans, known as "the hermit nation" for centuries. The Korean church had not been particularly missional until the 1970s, when God, almost a century after the gospel was first introduced, began to open their eyes to notice something bigger than the Korean peninsula.

As God began to stir up our sense of indebtedness to the nations, the church I attended, later our sending church, became one of the first to catch the vision and obey the mandate. The senior pastor has been an ardent champion of missions, and I have been tremendously in-fluenced by the missional zeal of this church.

God then led me to several important people who guided my next steps. Among them was an American Bible translator visiting Korea in time for my decision for the future. My love of the Bible made it impossible for me to refuse God's call to bring the gospel into languages of unreached people groups, who are still without God's Word in their mother tongue.

So we joined Wycliffe Bible Translators and were sent to Indonesia to translate the Bible into one of her seven-hundred-plus tribal languages. Despite ups and downs, it was worth it to witness this people group finally getting God's Word in its heart language.

Since there still are more than two thousand languages to go, I have been involved in mobilizing the church worldwide for the cause, and especially Asians. Following in the footsteps of numerous spiritual predecessors, I will continue my journey to the nations until all of them are given a fair chance to know the Lord, to read the gospel in their own languages.

International Students
Crosscultural Witness at Home

DANIEL BRANNEN

Ever consider how to be directly involved in the Great Commission without leaving home? God has given us a wonderful way to reach the nations of the world in our own living rooms while broadening our vision at the same time. He has brought the world's peoples to us. Over 725,000 international students and scholars from more than 175 different countries are studying on the university and college campuses in our communities. These students often represent the brightest and most gifted of their country.

International students come to the United States not only to achieve their educational goals but also to experience life in Western culture and to develop crosscultural friendships with Americans. However, making friends with Americans is usually a greater challenge than most expected. Language, cultural differences and the face-paced American lifestyles are major obstacles for our international visitors to overcome.

This provides a great opportunity for individual Christians and churches to welcome these students into their hearts and homes. Christian hospitality is one of the best ways for students to experience firsthand the love of Jesus. Sharing our faith in the context of authentic friendship is the most effective way to invite international students into Christ's kingdom.

As international students are transformed by the gospel and are captured by a vision of how God wants to use them, they return to their countries and help the spread of the gospel to their nations.

American volunteers have played significant roles as conversation partners, friendship families, culture guides, Bible study leaders and by just including students in their family holiday celebrations, vacations and everyday activities. Many students remember these friendships as the highlight of their experience during their sojourn in the United States. Maybe this is your chance to make a friend and influence a nation.

For information on how to get involved and find support in getting started with international students in your community, contact International Students, Inc., <www.ISIonline.org>, 1-800-ISI-Team.

Daniel Brannen spent his teen years as a missionary kid in Japan. Since the late seventies, he and his wife, Carolyn, have been serving with International Students, Inc., in Seattle.

Global Perspectives

JIM TEBBE
Director, InterVarsity Missions and Urbana

Role of the Missionary

We know for sure that all Christians are called to be part of God's global mission. That is scriptural. So there is no question that there is a place. In my opinion there are at least five major ways of being involved.

The first is to visibly be part of international teams working together toward a common purpose. One of the best messages that can be communicated through modeling even more than through words is the universality of the gospel. Multinational church-planting teams, multicultural development teams, multicultural seminaries and multicultural support services for missionaries like schools all bear witness to this truth. It isn't easy, but it is important, and it can help temper the bad effects of cultural dominance that can happen when a "team" comes from only one country.

Second, the North has a contribution to make in missiology—the theory and practice of missions. We have learned much over the years, and this now is reflected in our formal teaching and is ever more available internationally. It is not at all perfect, but something can be learned.

Third, we can offer professional expertise. Education in the North is of a high quality. The professionalism that can come with that can be of significant help in the mission effort.

Fourth, the whole area of business as mission is something the North can offer (as can many other countries). The free-trade practices of the North have produced many capable business people. The establishment of Christian, ethical businesses can do much to strengthen the fledgling church.

And, finally, all of us in the North can pray. We should encourage one another in prayer and learn to pray for other peoples.

Attracting the Next Generations

Groups that send out teams are very attractive to the younger generation. I believe there is a movement among young people today that calls them to sacrificial, incarnational living to reach the urban poor. (See Scott Bessenecker's *The New Friars,* InterVarsity Press, 2006.) Compassion ministries are very popular and compelling to young people today. Issues of justice and social concern are huge. The growth of the International Justice Mission is but one example of this. The stewardship of creation will be a next big wave of interest in missions. However, what seems to be missing is the conviction of the lostness of humanity without Christ and the urgent need for the gospel message.

✎Journal Worksheet Two

STEVE HOKE

Where Are You Now?

Describe your current involvement in a local community of faith. How is the church benefiting from your involvement in it?

After completing the Your Leadership Grip Spiritual Gifts Inventory online (and receiving your test results; see "Assessment 3: Discovering Your Blueprint for Living," pp. 84-87), list your top three or four spiritual gifts and briefly describe where you are currently using these gifts in your church or community.

1. _____:

2. _____:

3. _____:

4. _____:

In what ways do you need to grow as a believer? In what ways do you need to grow in your ministry skills?

What are the most natural opportunities for ministry in your church where you could both exercise and use your gifts as well as stretch your range of ministry skills by volunteering to minister outside your comfort zone?

Who is the person in your church you would like to have as a mentor in the process of becoming a crosscultural servant? With which of your church's missionaries could you discuss your aspirations?

With which friends could you enter into accountable relationships?

How are you investing your own finances in local church ministry and in missions? Are you currently supporting a missionary working crossculturally? If not, who would be the most appropriate person(s) for you to begin supporting now?

What is your church's understanding of the task of missions, and what does your church do to pray for, promote and finance missions and missionaries? What is your church's expectation for people who want to be missionaries?

What kind of work experience do you have, and what kind of professional skills do you want to develop? What does this suggest for the type of training you will need to develop these skills?

Who could you ask to offer to serve on (or start) your church's mission committee or help launch a local or global outreach effort?

What Do You Need to Do Next?

If you're living away from home, where will you be actively involved in a local fellowship? How could you serve in a local church?

What short-term mission trips is your or an area church offering in the next year in which you could participate?

How can you best share your decision with your parents and family?

When and how will you share your new commitment with your local church?

How do you plan to grow in your knowledge of and involvement in world evangelization?

How can you help educate others in your church about world evangelization?

When can you form an accountability group? Whom might you include in it?

With your family, spouse, other Christians you respect and your advisers at school (as applicable), discuss work opportunities that will complement your plans to become a missionary. Consider your training needs and financial situation.

What Will the Future Look Like?

Where do you envision yourself five to ten years from now? What do you picture yourself doing?

What are some of the critical steps necessary to get there?

How would you like your church to participate in this venture with you?

What habits or activities do you need to change now in order to be more effective for God in the future?

THREE

Exposure to Other Cultures
STEVE HOKE AND BILL TAYLOR

It's been observed that people don't really understand themselves or their culture until they have a chance to step outside their own culture and look back. That distance gives them a fresh perspective. Simply put, that is the great benefit of exposure to other cultures during the early phases of your missionary preparation: gaining perspective and stretching your vision.

Cultures are neither right nor wrong; they're just different. Behaviors, language, social systems, cultural values and worldviews all vary depending on your location and the people around you. People who go to live in a culture very different from their own almost universally experience something called "culture shock." That's the stress experienced as a result of losing all the familiar cues from our home culture. Not until we have actually experienced another culture by attempting to live as part of it do we understand the tremendous differences that exist.

Some are better equipped than others to be bridges between their own culture and the culture in which they are attempting to communicate Christ. God has apparently gifted these individuals with a unique ability to cross cultures. Nevertheless, almost everybody can learn to be more prepared for culture adjustment by deliberately broadening their exposure to other cultures.

Crosscultural experience cannot be obtained through books, although these will help in your preparation. You need to gain actual experience. It's important that as soon as possible you have an opportunity to live and work in another culture. Even better is a program that permits you to have a series of experiences like this. One experience may not be a true test.

There are many ways this can be done. A number of colleges have a year- or semester-abroad program in which one studies for a year, usually living in the home of nationals. Other colleges offer an interterm or summer study trip to selected mission fields. These forays into other cultures pay rich dividends both academically and relationally.

There also are myriad short-term missionary experiences available. They vary in length from two weeks to two years. The two-week trips are primarily for exposure and getting your feet wet. Summer mission projects lasting eight to ten weeks allow you to do ministry, usually using English or a language you may already know. The longer one- and two-year experiences actually place you in roles where you engage in long-term ministry alongside experienced career missionaries or supervisors.

Some groups are specifically designed to place young men and women in short-term ministry experiences crossculturally. Others are part of a larger mission organization. Some short-termers do specific work. Others go primarily as learners.

Caution: do no harm! As some of the following firsthand stories suggest, you go as a humble learner, to discover what God is already at work doing in that place. You do not go to teach or to solve anything. Short-term missions at this phase are purely exploratory and, as Robert Reese suggests, are primarily a spiritual exercise through which the Spirit will further shape your character.

Don't overlook crosscultural experience in your home country. You may be surprised how many people of different ethnicities and cultures live around you. God has brought the unreached peoples to our back door. Visit ethnic neighborhoods in major cities. Look for opportunities to work and to serve in multicultural settings. This will sharpen your sense of the delightful differences between cultures and heighten your awareness of the need to build bridges. (See "Why Wait Till You Get There?" on pp. 89-91.)

Look through the resources available. Choose specific cultural exposure programs that fit your overall career plan. If possible, choose an agency or project among a people with whom you think you may eventually like to work.

Consider inner-city summer internships with groups like World Impact (www.worldimpact

.org), InnerCHANGE (www.crmleaders.org/ministries/innerchange) and CityTeam (www.city team.org).

Youth With a Mission (www.YWAM.org), OMF International (www.OM.org) and International Teams (www.iteams.org) are notable examples of groups that specialize in short-term missions for young people.

Tim Dearborn. *Short-Term Missions Workbook: From Mission Tourists to Global Citizens*. Downers Grove, Ill.: InterVarsity Press, 2003.

Laurie Fortunak, ed. *Engaging the Church: Analyzing the Canvas of Short-Term Missions*. Wheaton, Ill.: Evangelism and Missions Information Service, 2008.

J. Mack and Leeann Stiles. *Mack & Leeann's Guide to Short-Term Missions*. Downers Grove, Ill.: InterVarsity Press, 2000.

Take the Short Step

GENE SMILLIE

It's a great time for short-term missions! There are more opportunities than ever. If you pay attention during your short-term mission trip, you can learn a lot. And these lessons will apply to the rest of your life, paying dividends over and over.

Full disclosure: I'm addicted to short-term missions. On my first short-term mission, when I was twenty, I spent a year in Colombia. Young, single and adventuresome, I immersed myself in the culture and picked up the language quickly, simply by living with Colombians. I came back to the States eager for more crosscultural experiences and helped start a Chinese church while in graduate school. In seminary, I continued my pattern of short-term commitments.

The Attractions

What are the attractions of short-term missionary service? First, the obvious: it's short. You aren't making a lifetime commitment. This is attractive if you aren't sure what you want to do with your life. It's a way to explore God's will—to "get your feet wet" on the mission field and decide whether long-term service is for you.

Another attraction is the romanticism of it. Going off to New Guinea or Japan or Eastern Europe for a summer is pretty exciting. Let's admit it: while it may not be a very spiritual motivation, short-term missionary work presents a colorful alternative to those other summer jobs you were considering. Sometimes it's a matter of getting out of a rut and seeing things from a different perspective. The plethora of choices of breakfast cereal on the shelves at your neighborhood supermarket will never look the same after you've lived overseas a few months. This can be a wonderful catalyst for creative thinking—for shaking up your life and getting on with it.

Short-term mission trips are also attractive if you know you want to work in a crosscultural setting, but you don't know exactly where or how. A short-term assignment allows you to search out the form and location of your personal missionary calling.

A few generations ago, the "missionary call" usually indicated a lifelong assignment to one place or one ethnic people group. This concept has largely given way to the idea that God offers us several options and that we may respond to those options as we go along. Mission boards have adapted to the changing circumstances and attitudes with a variety of missionary service opportunities.

Effectiveness

Mission agencies also understand the cost-effectiveness of short-term missions. Studies show that a disturbing percentage of first-term missionaries don't return for a second term. There's a great loss in invested time and money when someone decides, "I was wrong. God didn't call me to do this." On the other hand, when a person "tries it out first" on a short-term basis, and that person decides to return to the field for a more serious long-term commitment, a mission board knows it has a solid missionary who will likely stick with the project.

What's the actual effectiveness of a short-term missionary? It depends largely on you. Almost everything about your success depends on your attitude. If you expect to serve, you'll have a great ministry. If you expect to be served, the experience will be hard on everyone. This is true in most areas of life, but it's especially true for short-termers.

The work you do on a short-term trip usually contributes in some way to the work being done by career missionaries or national Christians. These people have been in a location for a long time before you get there, and they will be there a long time after you leave. Your time with them is an opportunity for you to learn as well as to serve. Or it can be a time of chafing and impatience. The difference is all in your attitude.

Language and cultural barriers can't be bridged in a few weeks. If you don't speak the language, the limits of what you can do as a short-term missionary are clear. Cultural barriers—especially subtle ones—are just as real. But if you see yourself as a support person, ready to contribute to an ongoing ministry in *any way you can,* you will make a valuable contribution to the crosscultural ministry of whoever is your host.

Take Heart

Don't be surprised to find yourself facing depression after you arrive on the mission field, particularly if there are significant differences in what you thought you were going to be doing and what you are actually doing. This happens to everybody. So does culture shock. As you begin to discover how different the new culture really is from the one you're used to—how superficial the similarities are that you thought you recognized at first—you may begin to feel discouraged, feeling "I don't belong here." You're right; you don't. Get over it.

But take heart. Your very newness will attract some people to you, and they will excuse you for most of your cultural faux pas. Very likely they will laugh with you and forgive cultural "bloopers" that would be unforgivable in others.

The depression you may experience will give way to acceptance of yourself and your limitations in your new surroundings. You will make good friends, gain a deeper understanding of what God is doing in the world, lighten the load of fellow workers and see yourself in a new light. Be forewarned: a short-term mission can change your life. But that's partly why you want to go, isn't it?

Gene Smillie spent a one-year short term in Colombia, helped start a Chinese church while in gradu-

ate school and helped churches in Alaskan Indian villages one summer. He spent a year as an inner-city pastor, worked with international youth on an army base and put in one day a week as a prison chaplain. He later served ten years in Côte d'Ivoire, West Africa, and then pastored a Chinese church in the Chicago area while working on his Ph.D. Most recently he worked in Spain with African, Latin American and Chinese immigrant churches.

Let's Grow!

LINDA OLSON

As Prema limped into the room where I was waiting to counsel teenage girls, her brown eyes, full of tears, caught mine. Earlier in the day, I had spoken to her South Indian school group about God's unconditional love. Now our interpreter beckoned Prema to join us and began asking questions. Finally, the interpreter turned to me with the story.

Prema had become a Christian—much to the horror of her devout Hindu family. After beating her severely when they heard of her new faith, they forbade her to attend afterschool Bible club meetings. Still, the thirteen-year-old studied the Scripture whenever possible.

"Should I obey my parents and continue to wear the vermilion dot on my forehead, symbolizing my allegiance to the god Shiva?" she asked me now. "Or should I be bold for Christ, refuse to wear it and risk another beating?"

Then she raised her sari and exposed a small leg, badly swollen from the beating. Stunned, my heart was filled with sympathy, anger and confusion. What could I tell her? It seemed nothing in my training had prepared me for this. None of the answers fit. I wanted the right thing for her. I wanted "living for Jesus" to mean goodness and wholeness and

love and laughter. Oh, what some parents back home would give to have a daughter so committed to Christ. I fumbled through an answer emphasizing the Lord's love for her and knowledge of her heart. Then I went back to my Indian host family and cried.

A New Shade of Lenses

Until this point, I had been on a short-term mission in India, hoping to share the Lord. Now I had to wrestle with the realities of what it meant to be a Christian and an Indian. I still wanted to share Jesus, but I now knew I would have to take off my own culture-tinted glasses and put on an entirely different shade of lenses.

When God takes us on a journey like mine in India, there is tremendous opportunity for personal growth. Like me, many Christians have a naive view of servanthood. We want to serve where we know we are using our gifts, we know what is required and we are sure we'll make a difference.

A short-term venture—where the norms of culture and the ways of people are not our own—often shakes our minds and hearts loose from our assumptions about being a servant for Christ. It can redefine and enrich our view of discipleship and of the Lord we serve. We find ourselves more attuned to God's agenda for the world, less concerned about ourselves and more open to the leading of the Holy Spirit.

Whether we feel we have nothing to offer or feel we can change the world, a short-term experience puts our personal usefulness to God into a balanced perspective. Few short-termers return claiming to have changed the world in the two weeks or two years they've been gone. But most return with a humble sense that God has used them in his great kingdom gathering. When that humility is in place, the Holy Spirit can do great things through us.

The benefits of a short-term mission go beyond those experienced by the short-termer. When careful planning and training are part of the venture, the receiving community profits greatly. Many ministries around the world badly need the resources we sometimes hoard and even take for granted. They need buildings for shelter and worship. Wells to unite a village. Life-saving technology too long withheld for lack of profit. Evangelism with a creative new twist. Discipleship training from in-depth biblical resources. This and much more can be offered in loving servanthood by those who come, do a job and return home to pray.

Christians outside our culture have a wealth of gifts for us as well—vision, wisdom, simplicity, commitment—often born of struggle. As we honor the church God is building outside our sociopolitical boundaries, short-term mission can provide a strong network of prayer and care across cultural lines.

A Ripple Effect

Home churches enjoy a tremendous ripple effect from short-termers. The sending process often involves people who might never have given missions a thought. As friends invest personally in the lives of those going and returning in a short time, their own vision for missions is challenged and renewed. In turn, those returning bring a more realistic understanding of the needs of nationals and career missionaries. They come home to lead others in prayer and support.

There is a powerful contagion spread by the Holy Spirit from those who return to the community of believers who sent them. Through the stories and lives of returning short-termers, God calls more and more to join his team of followers—people committed to seeing the good news extend throughout the world.

After watching several peers make sacrifices for short-term ministry, a young man in my church accepted the Lord's call. He gave up a fine job and entered seminary to prepare for long-term crosscultural service. A student group that sent several members on a summer mission project began praying regularly and passionately for the community they had visited. Some retirees—after spending a month away investing their professional gifts—returned to recruit others for a program benefiting the homeless right in our own city.

God is using short-term mission to awaken the church worldwide. He is using the Premas of the world to change the hearts of his people and to give them a humble passion for making his name known.

Dr. Linda Olson worked with InterVarsity for over twenty years, developing intercultural communication curriculum and training students and staff to become biblical citizens of the world. She is now faculty director of an academic minor in leadership studies at the University of Denver, where she educates and trains undergraduate leaders with a focus on social responsibility and community engagement.

Discover the Best Short-Term Mission for You
STEVEN C. HAWTHORNE

You have an "option overload" problem in missions. Hundreds of mission agencies have opportunities. Many of them want you—or someone like you. And yet each of them is different. Which one is right for you? Which one will best fulfill God's call on your life? I've learned to take note of six decision areas that need to come together for the best missions "fit." Everyone works through them in a different order and in a unique way.

The sequence in which you consider each area, however, makes a great difference. For example, someone who assumes he or she will go overseas for the summer (term) to play basketball (talent) with a sports ministry (team) may or may not then be able to choose between going to Mexico City or to Muslims in Indonesia (target).

Switch those priorities to spending a summer (term) among Muslims in Indonesia (target), and you may find yourself doing an entirely different ministry with a very different team.

What are *your* priorities? How flexible are they? As you read through the following six decision areas, try to identify your priorities. Then complete the Decision Points Checklist on the following page.

1. Target

Consider your target. What need will you touch? To which country will you go? What people? Which city? For some individuals, targeting is the main event. Perhaps they feel that God has called them to a particular country. Others figure that it is important to go where they are most needed. Of course, the word *target* doesn't simply imply that you are on some kind of military campaign or that you are shooting at someone. It's more about toward what geographic or ethnic arena you are directing your attention.

Others have learned to put their finger on places and people groups that are strategic in light of the big picture of world evangelism. For example, some persons get their heart set on going to Kenya, and all their other choices follow from that. Others may find themselves interested in the Muslim world. Others "eat and sleep" China.

2. Task

Consider your task. What kinds of activities will you be doing from day to day? What goals will you accomplish? Some people are open to serve in just about any way. But others start out fixed on a particular job description. You may have your heart set on digging wells or church planting or nursing or doing literacy work or helping in churches or playing with orphans or doing street evangelism or even building runways in the jungle. Get acquainted with the range of fascinating possibilities. Dream boldly, but beware of spinning scenarios in your mind that are out of reach. Don't get excited about novelty. Widen your willingness to serve by accepting a challenge.

3. Team

Consider your team. With whom will you go? What sending group, mission agency or church? What relationship will you have with national churches? To step into a short term usually means that a team is taking you on. Suddenly, you will be involved in something larger than yourself or your own career. It's really a matter of trust.

Mission agencies or your church will probably accept you, believing that you will contribute to the task God has given them. You need to trust the leaders of that sending body to help guide your service. If you choose your team first, they will usually be heavily involved in determining your target, task and term.

Carefully consider several sending groups. Don't get stuck on one mission just because you knew someone who served with them or because you have supported them in the past. Develop some criteria and go shopping.

A large part of your total team is your family and the church that is sending you. Don't leave them out of your decision at any point. Many of them have developed a strategic vision and program of short-term mission trips that are part of their long-term strategy. Let them be a part of your Body Life Design Team.

4. Talents

Step back and take a good look at yourself. Consider your talents, gifts and strengths. What spiritual gifts or natural abilities are called for? What do you like to do most? What weaknesses do you have? Many people start here on the search. There may be something they're good at, like playing guitar or basketball. Some are pleasantly surprised that their special ability can be put to use in missions. Others, however, get trapped by their own gifts and put undue expectations on mission leaders to assign them duties only in areas in which they excel or have interests. They can easily find themselves disappointed and resentful when they are given tasks that do not give them that magic feeling of "self-fulfillment."

Do not get involved in missions, even short-term, if you merely seek to feel satisfied and good about yourself. Missions work is *work*. It is fundamentally service, not self-fulfillment. The "vacation with a purpose" can be astoundingly devoid of God's purpose. The currents of our self-seeking culture can drift overseas quite easily. It's a subtle tendency.

Short-term missions become expensive summer camp, a career-shopping expedition or an alternate context for personal soul-searching and career searching. Be careful of viewing your short-term mission for what it will do for *you,* the short-termer. On the other hand, try to find something that fits you best. You may not feel that you have much to offer. You do. You may believe that you don't have many well-developed expectations of your time. Silent expectations are the most dangerous. Get in touch with them.

5. Training

Consider your training. What are you equipped or prepared to do? You may begin the short-term selection process by examining your education, experience and qualifications. These are worthy considerations, but sometimes a poor place to start. Although you might find something that fits you, you will probably miss several key opportunities because you're limiting your options to your own current abilities.

Be sure to inventory all your qualifications. You may be more prepared than you think! Check to see if different church and mission structures offer training as part of the short-term experience.

6. Term

Consider your term of service. How long a commitment will you be making? Are you thinking of spending a couple of weeks, a summer, a semester or a year? Do you want an option to extend your term? Are you seriously exploring how to spend most of your life overseas, should this short term work out well?

Consider how much more you may gain and give if you were to commit yourself for a year or two instead of just a summer. Be wise about severing ties and quitting jobs. You probably shouldn't burn all your bridges. But do keep in mind that short-term missions *is* missions. *Expect* that you'll need to give up something to give something. Beware of trying to work missions into your schedule only when it seems convenient. It is rarely convenient to change the world.

Decision Points Checklist

Use these statements to find out how you've already begun to decide which opportunity might be right for you. How certain you are in some areas will influence your decisions in other areas. First, simply read through the entire list and check each statement that reflects most closely your hopes and desires.

	Certain	Some Idea	Unsure
Target (the people, city or country I'll touch):			
I want to work with a particular people or kind of people.			
I already have a particular country or city in mind.			
I want to avoid certain places or kinds of people.			
Task (the kind of work I'll do):			
I hope to do evangelistic activities.			
I want to focus my time on the needs of churches.			
I want to be involved in people's physical and social needs.			
Team (the organization I'll go with):			
I want to link up with my church or denomination.			
I'm leaning toward one mission agency already.			
I know what kind of organization I want to go with.			
Talents (the skills and gifts I'll use):			
It's important to use my special skills and experience.			
The job has to mesh with my known spiritual gifts.			
I want to do things I haven't done before.			
Training (the schooling I have or need):			
I want further training as part of my short term.			
I have professional training that could be used.			
I want to do something that won't freeze my career.			
Term (the length of time I'll be gone):			
I just have the summer.			
I want something with long-term options.			
I have to set a limit on the length of time.			

Now return to those statements you checked and decide how certain you are about each. In which of the six areas (target, task, team, talents, training, term) do you have the most certainty? The least? Rate how strongly you want each of them to influence your decision-making regarding your short term. In which areas could you use a little more flexibility?

In what areas should you probably be more decisive?

(This article is adapted from *Stepping Out: A Guide to Short-Term Missions,* YWAM Publishing, 1992. Used by permission. For information, search <www.ywampublishing.com>.)

Steven C. Hawthorne helped design the "Perspectives on the World Christian Movement" textbook and course. He launched a research and mobilization effort called Joshua Project, leading exploration teams in Asia and the Middle East. As part of his vision to mobilize united prayer for Christ's glory in a prayed-for, soon-to-be evangelized world, he coauthored the book Prayerwalking: Praying On-Site with Insight. *He lives with passion for the greater glory of Christ and says of his life work: "I like to commit arson of the heart."*

▣ My Journey

PABLO CORTES[1]
Philippines, Philippine Missionary Association

I started getting burdened for the unreached peoples while attending a missions conference in 1993. By divine design, I met an American missionary who got me involved in reaching the Punjabi Sikhs in the Philippines. I then began mobilizing other churches as well as the one I pastored to reach the Punjabis.

Later I took a six-month missionary training course. I went on to host a missions radio program right after graduation. Within the same year, I was invited to join the organization that has trained me as its sending director and later, as COO. Over the next five years, we established nine training centers in the Philippines that equipped close to four hundred individuals and facilitated deployment of two hundred of them to twelve countries in Asia and Africa. Filipino missions bases were set up in several of these countries. My country being the only predominantly Christian country in Asia and the only country that was converted from Islam, I strongly feel that the Filipino church must be fully engaged in world evangelization.

Then in 1997 the Lord showed me the strategic value of mobilizing the Filipino Christian diaspora working in restricted-access countries. This is most evident in the Arabian Peninsula, where there are 1.5 million Filipino contract workers. I believe that the movement of Filipinos to the nations has been orchestrated and facilitated by God. Now, under the Philippine Missions Mobilization Movement, we have been training Filipino contract workers and raising bivocational teams to reach their host peoples and other migrant worker communities. We have developed training materials to fit our context and have connected our networks with Filipino churches locally and globally to produce greater synergy in missions.

---

[1]The author's name has been changed to protect identity.

Short-Term Missions as Spiritual Exercise
ROBERT REESE

North American short-termers tend to come across as secular, even if they are trying not to be. The sheer amount of technology and "stuff" North Americans travel with and their compassionate natures cause them to be seen as agents of Western civilization instead of ambassadors for Christ.

How does compassion come to be seen as secular? This happens when compassion drives North Americans to try to solve people's perceived problems with American solutions instead of biblical ones. People in developing countries sometimes give Americans star status, as representatives of the sole global superpower, but that can be a hindrance to a spiritual short-term experience. How can the cross be inserted into short terms? How can short terms become more of a spiritual exercise?

Making the cross central to short terms comes from intentional preparation. Preparation before going on a short term can make all the difference, because it determines whether you go as an ambassador of Christ or as a secular agent. Spiritual preparation, in particular, allows you to open up to what God hopes to achieve through your short term. The cross was the most unselfish act of personal sacrifice, laying down life for the sake of others, counting them as worthy of eternal life on the basis of their faith. Although Jesus paid for the sins of his disciples on the cross, he did not produce heaven on earth for them; rather he expected them to take up crosses too.

Many, if not most, short terms involve North Americans among people who believe in spiritualism. Ironically, spiritualists are more open to the work of spirits, including God, than are most North Americans. Table 1 lists some areas of potential misunderstanding between North Americans and people who hold a spiritualist way of thinking.

Issue	North American Thinking	Spiritualist Thinking
Time	Time is for tasks.	Time is for relationships.
Sickness	Healing is by medicine.	Healing is by magic "medicine."
Problems	Use natural reasoning.	Problems have a spiritual cause.
Criterion	Judge by technology.	Judge by strength of social ties.
Decisions	Individual decides.	Group decides.
Power	Power is in things.	Power is in spirits.

North American thinking is heavily influenced by secularism, which is not biblical thinking. By intentionally bringing the cross into the situation, the short term can become a spiritual exercise instead of a secular one. This comes by replacing secular thinking with biblical (see table 2).

Issue	North American Thinking	Biblical Thinking
Time	Time is for tasks.	Time is for relationships.
Sickness	Healing is by medicine.	Healing is both physical and spiritual.
Problems	Use natural reasoning.	Problems may have a spiritual cause.
Criterion	Judge by technology.	Judge by strength of social ties.
Decisions	Individual decides.	Group decides.
Power	Power is in things.	Power is in God and Christ.

Biblical thinking is much closer to spiritualist thinking than to secular thinking. The power of the cross does not depend on our resources but on God's. It does not depend on our actions but on our dependence on God. How much then do we take time to pray before acting in our missions? This may show us whether we think secularly or spiritually.

If the first reaction of a short-termers to situations he or she encounters is to pray and depend on God for answers, then true success of the project is much more likely, because this shows that the short-termer values God's agenda more than her or his own. This means something to people of less secular cultures, who struggle daily with problems they have no solution for. If they can see that even North Americans must depend on God for answers, then the short term has been successful.

For secular-thinking North Americans, spirituality is not automatic. Deliberate spiritual preparation can make a great difference in the short-term experience. Of course, "short-term" and "cross-bearing" do not really go together, so our prayer is that learning to do short terms in the way of the cross will create a new style of discipleship that will pervade all aspects of life. Increased Christian spirituality will always give the glory to God for whatever it does, because it operates with the real source of all power. Our task is not merely a short-term project, but to "preach the gospel—not with words of human wisdom, lest the cross be emptied of its power" (1 Cor 1:17). To God be the glory!

For a fuller description of the spiritual preparation Robert speaks of, see his longer article in *Evangelical Missions Quarterly,* April 2008. Also see the complete book of *Evangelical Missions Quarterly* articles on short-term missions: Laurie Fortunak, ed., *Engaging the Church: Analyzing the Canvas of Short-term Missions: An EMQ Short-term Mission Compilation* (Wheaton, Ill.: Evangelism and Missions Information Service, 2008).

Robert Reese was born and raised in Zimbabwe, the son of missionaries. He was a missionary there from 1981 to 2002 and now takes short-term teams to Zimbabwe every year. He teaches missions at Roanoke Bible College in Elizabeth City, North Carolina.

Eyes Wide Open
Developing Cultural Intelligence

DAVID LIVERMORE

Long before Starbucks was selling lattes in Bangkok and centuries before you could fly virtually anywhere in the world in twenty-four hours or less, Christian missionaries were engaged in transcontinental work. Missionaries have been leaving their homelands to serve Jesus for nearly two thousand years. The challenge of encountering a new culture with all its values, norms and rituals has been one of the most daunting tasks facing any missionary. As a result, missionaries have traditionally been trained as lifelong professionals who spend years studying local languages and customs.

However, the crosscultural challenges facing today's missionary are growing increasingly complex. Missionaries from Iowa and Florida are serving alongside missionaries from Nigeria, Korea and Brazil. These servants must adjust to the cultures of their colleagues as well as to the people living in the places where they serve. In addition, by consuming up-to-the minute information available in a the flattened world of technology, locals gain impressions of what Americans or Aussies are like long before they ever meet them. Missionaries of all stripes must open their eyes to the ubiquitous influence of culture on how they serve. More than ever before, missionaries need cultural intelligence to effectively embody Jesus in the twenty-first-century world.

Researchers have been studying the crosscultural engagement of missionaries for many decades. Most of the research has concentrated on examining the work of more-traditional missionary efforts, such as American church planters in Kenya or Bible translation among tribal people. Increasingly, a growing number of us have also been examining the crosscultural engagement of less-traditional missions efforts, including short-term missions, church-to-church partnerships and business as missions efforts.

Many of the findings from studying the crosscultural behavior of these relatively new expressions of North American missions parallel the findings from studies that have examined more-traditional missionary efforts. Consider a few of the comments made by local pastors in twenty-two countries when asked to describe what it's like to be on the receiving end of North American missions efforts, including those done by long-term and mid-term missionaries and by short-term missions teams. The following quotes represent the kinds of attitudes that surfaced with unusual frequency among the pastors surveyed:

- You act as if the American church is the true trendsetter for how we should all do church.

- You're so concerned over the evil spirits ruling our land when so much evil breeds in your own backyard.

- You live so far above our average standard of living, and you behave as if you're still in North America.

- You conclude that you're communicating effectively because we're paying attention,

when we're actually just intrigued by your foreign behavior.

- You're obsessed with picture taking and making videos during our evangelistic programs. It's really quite embarrasing for us.

- You underestimate the effectiveness of our local church leaders.

- You talk about us to your churches back home in such demeaning ways.

- You too quickly get into the action without thinking through the implications on our churches long after you go home.

- You call us backward for having little regard for your music, no palate for your green salads, no IQs for your advanced technology—and the list goes on. We are not naive and backward. Instead we are your brothers and sisters in Christ.[1]

Many of the pastors surveyed also had plenty of generous things to say about the North American Christians they've encountered. Some pastors credited North American missionary efforts for the unprecedented vibrancy of the Christian church in the southern hemisphere today. But even if the above statements are only part of the story, surely we want to pay attention to how we might more effectively go about serving and representing Jesus in the world.

Furthermore, most of the missionaries studied didn't initially come off as "ugly Americans." In fact, most of them passionately expressed a desire to be culturally sensitive and to posture themselves as learners. Yet they often defaulted to behavior that didn't align with the message of Jesus they were hoping to embody and express. Their good intentions often got lost in translation. Most crosscultural servants love the people they're seeking to serve. But the desire to love and the ability to express that love are two different things.

One of the most promising tools for dealing with the increasingly complex challenges of crosscultural work is cultural intelligence. Cultural intelligence is the ability to effectively reach across the chasm of cultural difference in ways that are loving and respectful. It's both a measurement (cultural intelligence quotient—CQ) and an overall framework for dealing with the array of issues involved in crossing various cultures—often many cultures at the same time.[2]

Cultural intelligence is just a way of describing our interaction with the Other, a term popularized to mean "those not like us, including ethnically, geographically, economically or ideologically different people." The emerging domain of cultural intelligence was developed using some of the same ideas used to develop IQ, EQ and the theory of multiple intelligences. However, though there's little we can do to change our IQ, an enhanced CQ can be learned and developed over time.

Most approaches to crosscultural sensitivity focus primarily on learning different cultural values. For example, there are many books and training programs that outline these various values (such as individualism vs. collectivism, and event time vs. clock time) and describe how they affect personal life, work and ministry. Certainly cultural values are an important point of understanding, but more is needed.

Other approaches to crosscultural effectiveness place more emphasis on an individual's need to be a humble learner when moving across cultures. This kind of training focuses on the importance of humility and being a learner. But even if I'm a learner, will I know how to translate my learning into loving expressions of friendship and service? Not necessarily.

Still other approaches place primary emphasis on the practices and taboos of various cultures, such as appropriate gestures, gift-giving protocols and how to exchange business cards. All of these contributions are important for thinking about how we lovingly interact crossculturally. But the value of these varied emphases is enhanced when wed together with a coherent framework for understanding the relationship of cultural values with an individual's personality, with one's motivation for service and with how to translate all that understanding into behavior that expresses Jesus in loving and respectful ways.

Cultural intelligence combines these varied approaches and emphasizes the importance of looking within ourselves in order to more lovingly behave crossculturally. A call to inward transformation is the primary distinction of cultural intelligence from other approaches to crosscultural work. The pathway toward loving the Other stems most from our inward transformation rather than from mere information or, worse yet, from artificial political correctness. Simply learning more about cultural differences or even gaining the ability to navigate cultural differences is not enough. *We have to actually become more multicultural people so that we might better express the love of Jesus to the Other.* This kind of transformational approach is essential for the challenging nature of missionary work in the twenty-first century. We can't become experts about every culture we encounter, but we can internally grow in our ability to adapt to the varied cultural contexts we encounter day in and day out.

There are four key dimensions to cultural intelligence: knowledge CQ, interpretive CQ, perseverance CQ and behavioral CQ. All four of these are interrelated, and one without the other not only hinders effectiveness but might even be counterproductive to overall cultural intelligence.

Knowledge CQ: Understanding Crosscultural Differences

Knowledge CQ refers to our understanding about crosscultural issues and differences. It's understanding what culture is and how it shapes behavior. And it's where the specific cultural values emphasized in many other approaches to crosscultural work need to be included. The objective is to develop a growing repertoire of understanding how culture influences the behavior of others and us. Knowledge CQ needs to include both a general understanding of how cultures shape behavior and specific information about the cultures with which we consistently interact. This dimension is the one most often emphasized In missionary training.

Interpretive CQ: Interpreting Cues

Interpretive CQ is simply the degree to which we're mindful and aware when we interact crossculturally. It's turning off the "cruise control" we typically use as we interact with people in our own culture, and stepping back to question intentionally our assumptions about what we observe in a new cultural context. It's becoming more aware of our personal emotions as we interact crossculturally. Knowing what kinds of questions to ask ourselves and others, reflecting on what we observe and testing our interpretations are all included in interpretive CQ. This is the dimension that was most lacking among the North American missionaries studied. Learning to reflect in the midst of action is essential for becoming more culturally intelligent.

Perseverance CQ: Persevering Through Crosscultural Conflict

Perseverance CQ refers to our level of interest, drive and motivation to adapt crossculturally. It's a missionary's robustness, courage, hardiness and capability to persevere through cultural differences. A person high in perseverance CQ draws great satisfaction from being in new places and interacting with people from different cultures. A person low in perseverance CQ avoids engagement with the culture as a whole

and tends to avoid or deny the pain in working through conflict and misunderstanding. For example, short-term missionaries with low perseverance CQ hope to stay in comfortable hotels, interact primarily with their fellow teammates and eat familiar foods. In contrast, short-term missionaries with high perseverance CQ want to adapt to the new culture not only to do short-term missions well but also because they're genuinely interested in learning about life in a different place. Of course missionaries faced with the prospect of making a new culture their home for an extended period have their perseverance CQ tested at much higher levels than short-term missionaries do.

Behavioral CQ: Acting Appropriately

Finally, behavioral CQ is the extent to which we can flex our behavior to adjust to a crosscultural situation. This is when we actually translate our understanding, interpretation and motivation into words and actions. Everything from how fast we talk to what we talk about is part of behavioral CQ. Cultural taboos such as talking with our hands in our pockets or pointing are some of the endless actions included in observing behavioral CQ. Behavioral CQ is being sensitive and appropriate with our actions and behavior as we engage in a new culture.

The point isn't to act as chameleons wherever we go. In fact, behavioral CQ is as much knowing when *not* to adapt as it is when to do so. In an attempt to empathetically relate to our fellow human beings, we want to learn how to interact and behave in loving and respectful ways.

The biggest problems for most missionaries are not technical or administrative. They lie in communication, misunderstanding, personality conflicts, poor leadership and bad teamwork. These are issues that can be addressed, in part, through cultural intelligence. At the end of the day, mastering CQ isn't really the point. Rather, it's a tool to help us communicate the love of Jesus to people in ways they understand.

When we do the hard work of inward transformation required by cultural intelligence, we more closely align ourselves with God's redemptive work in us and thus in the world. Cultural intelligence provides us with a framework for addressing the complexities associated with our increasingly diverse relationships and work.

Most importantly, it helps us do what we were created to do—to join God in his mission to the world—and to live it out in ways that come across as loving and respectful to the Other. Mission—short-term, long-term, overseas, next-door—is about giving people a living picture of who God is, what he cares about and how he acts. Cultural intelligence is a promising skill for widening our perspective in order to more effectively engage in God's mission in the flattened world.

(Adapted from Livermore's *Cultural Intelli-*

gence: Looking In Before Reaching Out [Baker, 2009].)

David Livermore, Ph.D., is the executive director of the Global Learning Center at Grand Rapids Theological Seminary, where he also teaches intercultural studies. David is widely published on youth ministry, missions and issues of contextualizing the gospel. His book Serving with Eyes Wide Open: Doing Short-Term Missions with Cultural Intelligence *(Baker, 2006), was awarded the 2006 Mission Book of the Year by* Outreach *magazine.*

---

[1]Findings generated from responses of 250 local pastors in twenty-one different countries.

[2]Cultural intelligence is a research construct originated by Soon Ang and P. Christopher Earley as described in their book *Cultural Intelligence: Individual Interactions Across Cultures* (Stanford, Calif.: Stanford University Press, 2003), and applied and tested in missional work by David Livermore as described in *Serving with Eyes Wide Open: Doing Short-Term Missions with Cultural Intelligence* (Grand Rapids: Baker, 2006), and *Cultural Intelligence: Looking In Before Reaching Out* (Grand Rapids: Baker, 2009).

Global Perspectives

KIRK FRANKLIN
International President, Wycliffe Bible Translators

Role of the Missionary

The retirement of people who are now in their late sixties and early seventies is a significant threat to Western-founded missions having enough people resources to fill critical staffing. Recruitment of new workers does not seem to keep pace with retirements. Compounded with this fact are messages being heard in the West, like "send more money, not people" or "Christian nationals can do it better, faster and cheaper."

However, serving in missions takes place in an increasingly "borderless" world, so being from the West or of retirement age are second-

ary issues to one's attitude and willingness toward living and working in multicultural and multifaith circumstances. Such situations are often under non-Western leadership but certainly in partnership with local Christians. This requires "bold humility." Humility precedes boldness, because the only boldness we can claim is our humility before Jesus Christ, who holds all authority.

Attracting the Next Generations

Integral mission that incorporates poverty alleviation, aid and development including literacy, medical ministry including HIV/AIDS and microenterprises are of increasing interest because these grapple with many of the urgent crises facing the poorest of the poor. True transformation of individuals and communities requires the gospel to be integrated into all forms of mission. Therefore, roles that holistically integrate discipleship training, mentoring and capacity building of church leadership of the Global South are essential.

The prime character and spirituality qualities you would want them to demonstrate or be committed include

- a personal relationship with Jesus Christ and the assurance that he is the only means of reconciliation with God
- a dependence on the Holy Spirit as the Spirit of mission who empowers God's

children for life and ministry

- a confidence in the Bible as the Word of God, made available to all people and appropriate in all matters pertaining to salvation, transformation, fruitful living, relationships and the problems facing humankind
- a willingness to serve others (for example, local communities, national and local churches, mission organizations, nongovernmental organizations) by being willing to listen
- a willingness to serve under national leadership
- a heart of humility that seeks to develop others and see them succeed
- · a willingness to work with Christians of all persuasions in light of the rich diversity of God's global church

Prisons, Pilgrims and Transformation
Understanding Your Cultural Captivity
SHERWOOD LINGENFELTER

Members of each society hold a collective worldview and participate in structured social environments. Learning from parents and peers to accept and live in accord with certain values, beliefs and procedures for action, they create a collective this-worldliness, which becomes a prison of disobedience. So entangled, they live a life of conformity to social images that are in conflict with God's purpose for humanity. Paul suggested that human beings are in a prison, a cell of disobedience: "God has imprisoned all human beings in their own disobedience only to show mercy to them all" (Rom 11:32 NJB). In Galatians 3:22, paraphrasing Psalm 14:1-3, he observed that "the whole world is a prisoner of sin." God has penned up all people in their self-created cells of culture, including Jew and Gentile, pagan and missionary.

I reject the notion (held by some Christian anthropologists and sociologists) that culture or worldview is neutral. We can say culture is more like a slot machine found in Las Vegas's gambling casinos than a wrench or a screwdriver. Culture, like a slot machine, is programmed to ensure that those who hold power win and the common players lose; when or if the organized agenda is violated, people frequently resort to violence to reestablish the programmed advantage. Every cultural system brokers power to its members, although the power advantage may be held by either individuals or groups. The structures and organizations of cultures are not neutral; people define and structure their relationships with others to protect their personal or group interests and to sustain or gain advantage over others with whom they compete.

Culture is created and contaminated by human beings; culture is the pen of disobedience from which freedom is possible only through the gospel.

The gospel, in contrast, liberates men and women from the cell of disobedience. Peter wrote, "You were redeemed from the empty way of life handed down to you from your forefathers . . . with the precious blood of Christ" (1 Pet 1:18-19). The gospel brings a contradictory message to the peoples of the world, challenging their social order and beliefs. Peter again clarified, "But you are a chosen people, a royal priesthood, a holy nations, a people belong to God, that you may declare the praises of him who called you out of darkness into his wonderful light. Once you were not a people, but now you are the people of God" (2:9-10).

The Scriptures show clearly that Jesus challenged the accepted society and worldview. Although he was living as a Jew in the Jewish world, he shattered that world with his preaching and teaching. His good news brought conflict and change. People in Judea and Samaria hated him and plotted to kill him because he challenged their system. They did everything they could to destroy Jesus and his followers.

Mission anthropologist Paul Hiebert (1985) argues that Christianity provides a new hermeneutic for cultural living. Every culture and every person must change in light of a new perspective—Jesus Christ, crucified, risen and exalted. Jesus came to save not cultures but people, and he came to transform them into his likeness. But whole cultures will not be transformed! The opposite is true. Church and mission history suggests that the larger culture neutralizes the church of Jesus Christ, as is often evident in the third or fourth generation of its new or renewed existence.

Transformation is neither bridging from one system to another nor transferring a Christian system to another place and people. Rather, transformation means a new hermeneutic—a redefinition, a reintegration of the lives of God's people (the church) within the system in which they find themselves living and working. Jesus said, "My kingdom is not of this world" (Jn 18:36). He thus denied the existence of a Christian sociopolitical system but called for the transformation of his disciples' thinking and social relationships with others.

The social and cultural systems of a missionary and a local, indigenous community exert powerful pressure on new believers and churches, pressure to conform to habitual standards, values and practices. Christians cannot live apart from the social games of the church or the wider society, and therefore they are subject to these unrelenting forces. Further, Christian leaders teach and practice standards and values that are inextricably intertwined with those of their social world.

Nevertheless, the gospel may become a significant powerful force in the continuous restructuring of any social environment and worldview. As believers become mature in their faith, their values and motivations reflect more and more those of the Lord Jesus Christ. Therefore Christians will experience tension and contradiction with old patterns of self-interest and greed, provoking them to contradict old social rules and judge many inadequate as they attempt to imitate the person of Christ in their lives and work. As believers increasingly obey the truth of the gospel, they will discover new ways of managing resources and relationships.

So, how can Christian workers avoid transferring their culture and nurture maturing, indigenous churches that are committed to evangelism and transformation of their local culture as disciples of the Lord Jesus Christ?

The first task is to understand our prison and the cultural prisons of others. Yet this notion of a prison of disobedience is repulsive to many.

No wonder readers resist this conceptualization of culture. A beautiful walled park in the center of Seoul contains the homes, gardens and servants' quarters of the former king and royal family of Korea, who occupied this palatial residence during the nineteenth century, the Palace of the Secret Garden. Because of his extremely high status, custom declared that the king could not leave the palace grounds; he was a prisoner in his palace. However magnificent his life was within the walls, he was a political prisoner, unable to see and experience the outside world.

Our cultural palaces are our prisons; in them we find comfort, security, meaning and relationships. Yet the wall of culture restricts our freedom and sets barriers between us and others of different ethnic origin. The splendid kingdoms of history and the nation-states of the present are many and diverse, and they have been given to Satan. Culture, economy and state are his to rule as God allows. The church is called out, the people of God, to live in a world of many cultures, as "strangers and pilgrims" (1 Pet 2:11 KJV).

The life of the pilgrim is unsettled; no single culture is adequate, settling down is temporary, and accommodation to culture is for a higher purpose. Peter tells us to "live such good lives among the pagans that, though they accuse you of doing wrong, they may see your good deeds and glorify God on the day he visits us" (1 Pet 2:12). When we enter another culture, we must examine the life and beliefs of those people; we must learn how to live good lives according to their standards; we must live in submission to their authorities; we must discover their significant questions; and we must search the Scriptures to find biblical answers to their questions and needs, recognizing their limitations of our own views.

To live as pilgrims and make pilgrim disciples, we must learn how to "live as free men . . . servants of God" and at the same time live in submission to "every authority instituted among men" (1 Pet 2:16, 13). How do we achieve both freedom and submission? We cannot get out of prison until we can see clearly the walls, the gates and the gatekeepers. We must comprehend the dimensions of our cultural prisons and discover some of the biblical keys that will allows us to unlock the chains of our cultural habits and the gates to our cultural walls. These perspectives will enable us to share our experience of freedom with others and lead them in the journey of becoming followers of Jesus Christ.

When we carefully examine ourselves, we shall be forced to admit that more often than not we conform theology to practice; we perceive the kingdom of God on earth in our own cultural terms. Only by recognizing that cultural blindness is the rule, not the exception, and that our philosophies are our windows onto the world, can we free our fellowship and our theology from the bondage of our cultural philosophies and worldview. We must look through multiple windows if we are to genuinely apprehend the transforming power of the gospel and apply kingdom principles interculturally. Each believer sees through a glass, narrow and constraining, but together as disciples with differing perspectives, we can begin to comprehend the wider impact of the Scripture in a pluralistic world.

(Abridged from "Transferring or Transforming Culture," chapter one in *Transforming Culture* [Grand Rapids: Baker, 1998], pp. 15-22.)

Sherwood Lingenfelter is an anthropologist who has served as a consultant to Wycliffe Bible Translators while teaching at SUNY Brockport and at Biola University, where he also served as provost until 1999. Since then Sherwood has served first as dean and then as provost at Fuller Theological Seminary. He and his wife, Judith, continue to lead transformative training for missionaries around the world to help them be God's agent to transform cultures.

Flying with Two Wings
The Role of Short-Term Missions

BILL TAYLOR

My evaluation of short-term missions (STM) is simple: I am in favor of them. I have led short-term trips. I am delighted to attend a growing church with a commitment to broadband short-term trips that involve youth, families and all adults. I encourage most believers to participate in at least one serious STM trip. And in 2005 1.6 million American Christians went on some kind of STM.

Some estimates say this represents about four billion dollars a year. Is this the best use of our money? I doubt today that any women or men would commit to long-term service without serious hands-on STM investment. It's the reality of our mission world today, regardless of the country or the status of missions around the world. And North Americans evidently have enough discretionary funds to travel the world on short-term service projects—and increasingly Latins, Asians and Africans are doing the same.

Many are questioning this entire venture, and perhaps with reason. Some call it mere "glorified sightseeing, funding vacationaries," and wonder whether it's worth the cost. Perhaps more seriously, are we seeing long-term change in the lives and lifestyles of the "sent ones"? If the total investment for a fifteen-person team to Peru for seven days comes to thirty thousand dollars to help build a school, what would that same investment be worth with local labor? Hmm.

So perhaps we need to borrow from theologian Lesslie Newbigin and call STM more in the category of the Christian mission of "learning," where the service opportunities include cultural exchange or solidarity learning.

Okay, let's define an STM, and clarify what makes it "short." For some, an STM means getting dirty for God in hurricane relief for three intense days; for others it's an eight-day vision trip; for others it's a three-week ministry trip (primarily in your own language), and for yet others it's a thoughtful two-year-long ministry. We are battling to keep the parameters of STM on the shorter side of things, with mid-term ministry going from three to four years. Anything more is in the category of long-term service.

Back to the flying metaphor. Short-term mission is a key wing, but only one. Both birds and planes need two to fly.

Benefits

Short-term missions have contributed strongly to God's great kingdom enterprise. Jesus had his own program of STM in the training of the twelve apostles.

I can think of ten significant benefits of short-term trips:

1. They provide hands-on, direct contact with glocal (global and local) crosscultural mission—whether close to home in your passport country or far from home. You can be very surprised at the richness of crosscultural challenges within our own borders.

2. They stimulate realistic vision for the global task and the church and have the potential of contributing substantively to the global cause of Christ. This is especially the case when they are strategic on both ends—the sending as well as the receiving. But we have to work to implement this double strategy.

3. They provide an opportunity to see God at work in one's personal life and on the "mission field."

4. They can stimulate thoughtful, significant intercession by driving home the fact that without prayer little of lasting worth is accomplished.

5. They offer reality therapy for those who see missions with fuzzy or rose-tinted glasses.

6. They can convert a person into a lifelong intercessor or missions mobilizer back home. A strategic and thoughtful STM can change a person's priorities and lifestyle, making him or her more radical in faith and future.

7. They can create within those who go a desire to serve more significantly in their home cultures and churches—using newly acquired skills and with a more global perspective. This is possible when there are substantive pre- and post-STM requirements, equipping and debriefing.

8. Short-termers can witness the impact they can make through their example, evangelism, discipleship or the use or transfer of their specific skills. Through their service they strengthen the on-site, long-term ministry.

9. They provide the foundation for their own potential long-term commitment to career missionary service. All the current servants we know (or who are in process to the field) have had a significant STM experiences that whetted their appetite for more, tested their idealism, screened their decisions and helped them discern where the Spirit would have them serve.

10. They bring glory to the living God through their demonstrated obedience to the sending Lord.

However . . .

In spite of these ten positive aspects, STM have some shortcomings. Here are seven of them:

1. *Overstated importance.* Some STM champions proclaim that they have found the decisive answer to world evangelization. This attitude can be found in some STM organizations as well as some local churches. Those who tout this view suffer from an oversimplification of the Great Commission/Great Commandment. They are looking at the world through a straw—reducing the totality to a single option—when what we need is a broader menu of perspectives.

2. *Self-aggrandizement.* Some veterans of short-term trips try to pass themselves off as missions or national culture experts.

3. *Ignored national ministries.* Short-term leaders sometimes bypass the goals and ministries of existing national churches and mission agencies. They don't understand that STM makes its greatest impact when that vision is integrated into long-range plans and programs both in the sending group and in the receiving one.

4. *Too limited, too short, too expensive.* Often long-term missions are accused of high cost and low value. But what about those nine-day, Easter-break "Win Russia for Christ" trips to sing in Moscow on Easter Sunday (especially when they miscalculate the date of the Orthodox Church's Easter)? What does it cost to send thirty high-school or college students on such a trip? Is that really the best way to use kingdom money? Instead of sending a dozen people from Boston to Indonesia for two weeks (discount four days for travel and jetlag, one for sickness, two for tourism), why not develop a really powerful trip to an inner city

in the United States, Canada or on the Mexican border—at a fraction of the cost?

5. *Exhausted long-termers.* Short-term trips can go to the other extreme by demanding too much of the field-based leaders. This saps the limited resources of national churches and expatriate missionaries. When I lived in Latin America, I finally reached the point where I was so frustrated by the demands short-term teams made on me that I said, "Don't send me one more short-termer who can't get around in Spanish!"

6. *Limited results.* We need to be wary of trips that leave little impact or require nothing after the participants return home. Generally, the shorter the trip and the younger the participants, the less that mission trip will affect their lives and those of others. But if leaders build into pre-trip training the serious home-based implications of short-term service, the investment is much wiser.

7. *False impressions.* Short-term missions may also foster an unrealistic view of the national church and existing missionaries. A short-termer can easily spend a few weeks at a location and return concluding, "Wow! These missionaries sure are lazy. We got up at dawn and slogged it out until midnight, witnessing, building the church and running Vacation Bible Schools for the kids. But those missionaries did so little!"

Sure, lazy missionaries do exist. Yet the reality is that the intensity of short-term enthusiasm simply cannot be sustained amid the daily grind of long-term ministry. When I think of most of the missionaries I know, several descriptive terms come to mind: gifted, well-equipped, dedicated, committed for the long term, quietly interceding, doing invisible acts of love, patient-

ly learning language and culture, and building trust and credibility so the gospel can penetrate with lasting power.

One of the reasons many short-term workers have such positive relationships with national believers is because they're enjoying the benefit of time-tested trust built by the on-site, long-term missionaries.

How Might We Overcome the Limitations?

I think most serious STM outreaches can address and avoid most of these problems. But too many have not; they have not built a lasting foundation and platform for STM. Perhaps they haven't developed their programs in interdependent partnership and dialogue with existing ministries on that field. Some of our older leaders struggle with the younger generations. And the fact is that too many of the younger have trouble committing to anything longer—whether a career, a job or a mission. Many of them struggle with religious pluralism and have a hard time resolving issues of ultimate authority and truth—whether Christianity as a system or Jesus Christ as Lord of the universe and hope of the world.

However, every aspect of the global mission enterprise has its challenges and problems. So let's recognize our limitations, invite and listen to outside input, and be willing to change.

Balancing Our Efforts

Should we view short terms strictly as forums for experiencing hands-on training, and focus on accomplishing the task of world evangelization through long-term ministry? My answer to that valid question is simple: an airplane needs both wings to fly. We need both—short-term and long-term missions. Shorter terms should be seen, at least in part, as hands-on training for missions. I would like to see more specific equipping for short-term missions (including what to do upon returning home) and a much larger percentage of short-termers committing to long-term missionary service.

One respected mission agency has staff missionaries dedicated full time to working with STM, and they love their assignment. Mission leaders of one agency used to question that kind of investment, but that changed to the point that now they have a higher percentage of short-termers transitioning into long-term service. That's good news. The International Mission Board of the Southern Baptist Convention recently registered 4,200 career missionaries, and over 40 percent of them served earlier on a purposeful one- to two-year venture.

The Other Wing: Long-Term Mission

Remember, most of the thousands of unreached people groups are unreached because it is tough to reach them! The reasons could be geographical or historical, ethnic or political, emotional or religious, and a combination of these factors. Yes, the Spirit of God is using the Internet, the arts and other media. Today we have a great panorama of outreach creativity (whether through sports or refugee ministries or long-term relief and development). Yet while God is the sovereign of history, I have a sense that the less-reached people groups will hear the gospel in their mother tongue, will respond in the power of God, and we will witness vital worshiping communities primarily through the work of incarnational, well-equipped, long-term servants.

This breed of crosscultural worker—I once called them an endangered species—are those who have committed for the longer haul. They are sent and supported by their churches and partners, they are well-trained servant-leaders, buttressed by faithful intercessors and shepherds who care for them on their journey. These servants learn the language and speak it profi-

ciently. They study and understand the culture, raise their families in that context and establish credibility with the people. And as they are empowered by the Spirit, they see our supernatural God at work.

Reaching the less-reached peoples of the world will take a new generation of Boomers, Xers and Millennials (and those who will follow) who decide to go for broke and serve God in longer-term ministry. They will need to intern with their local churches and get the right pre-field training for the task. They will be sent out by their churches and will work on vital teams on the field. Many of them will serve for ten, twenty, even forty years.

While a lot of these missionaries may fit our "traditional career missionary" profile, a good percentage of them will also be bivocational workers, serving as teachers, business people, engineers, entrepreneurs, consultants and healthcare providers.

Money Isn't the Answer

Would it be better stewardship just to send money instead of sending short- or long-term workers? No, that's a cop-out! It may be related to the ill-advised strategy I hear discussed in some circles—that we should stop sending "colonial missionaries" and just support "native missionaries."

I'm not the only mission leader who discerns a dangerous tendency in North America. First we cut down on screening, recruiting, training and sending long-term missionaries and then we just send short-termers. But down the road, we eliminate both short- and long-termers, and we send money instead. At the end we will send nothing!

This approach appears cost-effective and less painful at first. But it is unbiblical and perilous for the soul of the global church.

Making Changes

Since its beginning, the North American missions movement has shown vibrancy and creativity, generosity and long-term commitment, and fidelity to biblical orthodoxy and world mission. But we envision danger on the horizon. This same church in the Global North needs serious revival and transformation. Its leaders need to listen to the voice of the leaders of the global church and learn what God in his power is doing around the world. North Americans must not think that the call of God to the church on behalf of the peoples, nations and cities of the world is something that others can do alone. It's a global enterprise that invites us into all kinds of creative and strategic cooperative ventures. But it's time to develop and sustain a new heart of global interdependence, crafting mission partnerships on behalf of the church—from everywhere to everywhere. And this will affect deeply all kinds of sending, whether short term, long term or lifelong.

Global Perspectives

ROSE DOWSETT
OMF International, Scotland

Role of the Missionary

It is curious (and frankly exasperating) to have some Christian leaders from the Global South and North tell us that the days of missionaries from the Global North are over. Do they want us to be disobedient in this core part of authentic discipleship? Do they think the Lord got it all wrong? The Commission to disciple the nations is for all of us, wherever we come from. The whole church—north, south, east and west—is called to take the whole gospel to the whole world.

Attracting the Next Generations

However, those of us in the Global North do need to listen to the pain that lies behind some of the most stridently critical voices from the Majority World (Global South) church. We need to abandon power and serve in weakness, humility and crosscultural sensitivity. We need to be willing to embrace poverty and vulnerability. We need to leave behind the notion that we have the answers, and they, only the questions. We need to demonstrate willingness to serve under national leadership on multicultural teams, even when sometimes we would prefer to do things differently. We need to stop dumping made-in-the-North/West strategies for conquering the world in double-quick time and to learn instead to commit to a lifelong investment of incarnated love. We need to repent of our human (even mission) empires and to seek more profoundly only the demonstration of the kingdom of God. We need to be deeply prayerful, for truly all effective mission is the work of God.

And may I add humbly to our brethren in the rest of the world, because our failings have come more from our fallenness than from our Western-ness, all of us, everywhere, need to ask the Lord to correct our faults and lead us into lived-out truth.

Putting It All Together
Five Ways to Sort Through Your Options

STEVE HOKE

1. Find a Friend to Help You

People don't do radical things by themselves. And face it: moving into a multicultural setting in a rapidly changing and increasingly chaotic world is radical! Find a trusted friend or leader in your church who will understand your motives and mission hopes—a person who can serve as both a sounding board and a discerning listener alongside you. The kind of friend you need is not an answer giver, fixer or problem solver, but an active listener—someone who will help you hear the voice of God for your life.

2. Stretch Out Your Future on a Timeline

This is one way to identify potential roadblocks and conflicting agendas. A well-thought-through timeline will show you when you are attempting a "mission impossible" with utterly unrealistic expectations.

3. Stretch Your Faith

On the other hand, don't settle for what is merely possible. God may lead you beyond the easy or the obvious. You'll have to trust him no matter where you go, but prepare yourself for some risk-taking ventures. And be alert to this dynamic: as the Spirit stretches your faith to trust him for more, he will, at the same time, take you deeper into himself to deepen your dependence on him. As your faith ascends, you may find it founded in a deeper and deeper dependence on God himself—his attributes and character that become your rock and fortress.

4. Face Your Fears

You may have good cause to worry. Life is difficult, and you may be headed for a dangerous place. Perhaps you fear being single the rest of your life. You might fail miserably and be embarrassed before everyone who supports you. If you dredge up all the fears and look at them in the light, some will still be scary, but you may also get a laugh out of the silly scenarios the enemy conjures up in your mind. You might be needlessly afraid of being attacked by guerillas. You might have a phobia about getting shots before you go. You might not feel any more courageous after the exercise, but you won't be paralyzed by false impressions.

Psychologist and spiritual director David Benner observes,

> What we need is a knowing of love that is strong enough to cast out fear. And this is the only knowing of love that is capable of offering us the radical transformation we need. . . . What we need is a knowing that is deeper than belief. It must be based on experience. Only knowing love is strong enough to cast out fear. Only knowing love is sufficiently strong to resist doubt.[1]

5. Deal with Freedoms

To be truly free to choose the right mission opportunity, you may have to give up some of the prerogatives you think are yours. Obey God. It is not primarily a matter of finding something that "fits" you or furthers your career. The real issue is being utterly mastered by Christ. You may need to face up to a mistaken sense of entitlement. Do you somehow believe that God is rigging up the whole world to revolve around your own self-fulfillment?

Benner describes surrender this way:

> How frightening even the idea of surrender is to some people . . . only surrender to something or someone bigger than us is sufficiently strong to free us from the prison of our egocentricity. Only surrender is powerful enough to overcome our isolation and alienation. . . .
>
> Christianity puts surrender to love right at the core of the spiritual journey. Christ-following is saying yes to God's affirming *yes!* to us. If it is anything less than a response to love, Christ-following is not fully Christian.[2]

Be prepared to relinquish areas of your future or dreams that you thought were yours to pursue. If you let them go into God's hand, he has promised to give you more than you bargained for. "Whoever wants to save his life will lose it, but whoever loses his life for me and for the gospel will save it," Jesus said (Mk 8:35).

Jim Elliot put it this way: "He is no fool who gives what he cannot keep to gain what he cannot lose." We live into the legacy of freedom that Elliot left us when he chose to follow Jesus into the Ecuadorian jungles rather than remain on the safe sidelines in America.

(Adapted with the author's permission from *Stepping Out: A Guide to Short-Term Missions.* Copyright © 1987, 1992 by Short-Term Missions Advocates, Inc. All rights reserved.)

---

[1]David Benner, *Surrender to Love* (Downers Grove, Ill.: InterVarsity Press, 2003), p. 79.
[2]Ibid., pp. 10-11.

Christians from North and South pray in community

✎ Journal Worksheet Three

STEVE HOKE

Where Are You Now?

Describe any travel you have done outside your home country, including living for more than three months in another culture?

List some of the fiction and/or nonfiction books you have read that describe the differences among cultures? What stood out?

What is the extent of your exposure to attending worship services of another ethnic group? In another culture? What differences stood out?

What ethnic or culture groups do you live near that are different from your own and that you could get to know?

What country or countries do you think you'd like (or feel led) to visit?

How long could you afford to interrupt your academic program or current job to take a short-term mission trip?

What Do You Need to Do Next?

Identify a specific short-term mission trip in which you are interested.

Look at your next spring or summer vacation as a time to schedule a two- to eight-week short-term trip.

Try a weekend Urban Plunge experience to break out of your comfort zone. If you do a Google search of "urban plunge," dozens of specific weekend experiences that will submerge you in the urban environment will appear. Sort through them by location and emphasis. The following Christian organizations are only a few of the numerous church and Christian organizations that presently provide weekend "urban plunge" experiences for individuals and church groups:

Urban plunge is a weekend mission trip of Christ for the City International. You'll go to *nine* different ministries in one weekend that will thrust you into inner-city life. You'll feed the hungry, pray for the needy and talk with the homeless. You'll keep a faith journal to chronicle your thoughts and experiences of each ministry visit. www.urbanplunge.net

Urban plunge gives you and your middle-school or high-school youth, college-age or adult group the opportunity to serve agencies and organizations that are already working hard for change with Denver's homeless and working-poor populations. Through the urban plunge experience, your group can also enjoy a meal at one of Denver's ethnic restaurants, hear directly from marginalized and poor people in the community, and reflect on all you've seen and done in light of the gospel. www.servantcorps.org/urban_plunge.shtml

The urban plunge is a forty-eight hour, one-credit winter break seminar through the Center for Social Concerns, offered in most major cities in the United States. Transportation to and from the site is the responsibility of the student. Students should choose a city in close proximity to their home town. socialconcerns.nd.edu/academic/winter/urbanplunge.shtml

One or two times a year, University Presbyterian Church of Seattle, Washington, conducts a similar weekend or weeklong immersion mission experience in inner-city Seattle, called City Dive. Contact Mike McCormick Huentelmann, the director of urban ministries at <mikem@upc.org>. www.upc.org/urban.aspx?id=382

What Will the Future Look Like?

What ministry skill(s) do you need to work on the most?

What area of the world would you like most to experience? To what part of the world do you sense God's direction or urging?

Consider again the "Discovering Your Ministry Passion" reflection exercise (pp. 69-70), which helped you consider a short-term experience in light of discerning if God has given you a particular passion for a particular group of people.

FOUR

Critical Issues in Schooling and Support Raising

STEVE HOKE AND BILL TAYLOR

Having made it this far by faith is huge. The foundational issue of direction has been settled; you are committed to forging relational bridges in the body to launch you into the future, and you are considering an initial crosscultural exposure—if you haven't had a short-term trip already.

Quite naturally, a number of critical issues and questions come into focus, now that you have come this far. There are issues of the kind of educational preparation or schooling you will need and how to tackle the task of support raising. And every parent confronts questions about the options for schooling their children on the field.

So, let's walk through these issues one at a time. We will try to provide answers to questions that can be answered, but will also provide options when there are many to consider.

Educational Preparation and Basic Schooling

Basic education or required schooling? Learning or training? When we say "basic education," we are speaking of more than "reading, writing, and 'rithmetic." We mean "essential, core, foundational" as opposed to "nice to have but not essential."

But that immediately catapults us into the middle of a question that has been asked since the first century: what is needed to be used of God in crosscultural ministry? Peter was an unschooled fisherman. The apostle Paul may have had a first-century doctorate under the scholar Gamaliel. Barnabas was a Levite from Cyprus, and Luke was an M.D.. But was it their training that made them effective?

Probably not. It was their transformative encounter with the living Christ and their subsequent filling of the Holy Spirit that made them powerful. Each one ministered out of his background, training and gifting in a unique way.

We also want to avoid the cultural trap in North American society of thinking that unless you have a college degree (schooling) or have earned so many hours of Bible and missions, you are not yet qualified for service. Nothing could be more misleading. So discerning what basic education you need, really needs to be done through the Holy Spirit's voice to you in a clear and unmistakable way. Anything else will just be "going along with the crowd."

Visualizing a pyramid may help you understand the critical building blocks in your preparation for missionary service (see illustration below). Your basic education serves as the broad base. By that we refer to your experiential learning and formal schooling up to this point in your life, which for most will include primary,

Figure 2. Pyramid of educational and schooling options

secondary and some kind of college or university education. Others of you will prefer, after secondary school, some kind of vocational training that equips you for specific tasks. In this way, you are building your skill set for the future, which hopefully will dovetail into crosscultural missions.

Keeping that picture in mind, take an honest look at where you are right now. Reflect on the following questions, and dialogue with your spiritual advisers in your church or mission agencies (different organizations do have different requirements).

- What knowledge base and practical skill training do you need and want to develop for future ministry?

- What is the summary of the wise counsel you have received regarding how much formal education you need?

- Is the academic program you're pursuing or have completed adequate for what lies ahead?

- Can you supplement your basic undergraduate education with other courses?

- If not, where can you find the courses you need? Are they available in your present college or university? Can you take them as distance-learning courses, or will you have to change schools?

A new face of missions requires a diversity of skills in the crosscultural force. Here's a sampler: anything in computers, data management and website design; physiotherapy and occupational therapy certifications; electrical and mechanical maintenance abilities; teaching English as a second language. All of these the Spirit can use.

Further experience, including short-term service, your job(s), church ministry and relational experience, are the building blocks that stretch you higher and at the same time begin narrowing the structure. Practical missionary training and lifelong learning are the blocks that take you to the top of the education pyramid.

A solid general education is an invaluable foundation for long-term, crosscultural ministry for most people, and it is the educational base most mission agencies prefer. It provides a breadth of understanding and a reference point for all future training. It gives the graduate a general grasp of the liberal arts (especially social and behavioral sciences), natural science and mathematics.

When studied in the context of a Christian college with an integrating core of biblical studies and theology, the liberal arts become the "liberating arts," because they bring all of human inquiry into proper relationship with the freeing truth of Jesus Christ. Christian students in a secular college or university will have to work intentionally to make these connections. It's worth the investment. Start where you are. Ask your church or mission agency what courses they suggest or require.

If you're an undergraduate, check your experience for several major components. Most churches and agencies recommend fitting in some courses in cultural anthropology and sociology; if you haven't taken them yet, add them to your schedule in the semesters ahead. And jump at a chance for a course in linguistics. That will stretch lazy linguistic muscles in preparation for learning another language.

Also take courses about international relations or regional histories. Macroeconomics will broaden your understanding of the critical dynamics pulsing in our world today. Courses in international development will expose you to global inequities that threaten to tear our world apart along ethnic, economic and political lines. Any course that will take you out of the box of thinking that world evangelism is only about "telling others about Jesus" is a mandatory first step toward what is called "biblical holism."

Today's crosscultural servants must have a broader biblical perspective and see the gospel as ministry in word, deed (incarnational relationships) and power, as evidenced in the ministry and teaching of Jesus. The gospel of the kingdom encompasses all of these three dimensions, not one or the other. The gospel is not either evangelism *or* justice ministry, because in the heart and message of Jesus it was never either-or but both/and. Jesus looked on the poor with compassion and healed them. Jesus saw the multitudes without hope and taught them and fed them. He saw inquisitive fisherman and invited them into a life of following him. Look for opportunities, not just courses, where you can be mentored as Jesus' disciples were mentored by the Master.

Most critical to a solid basic education are some foundational courses in Bible, theology and missions. Many churches and agencies have traditionally required prospective candidates to have the equivalent of at least one full year of biblical studies and missions. However, given the changing nature of our world and the values of postmoderns, many missions are now accepting candidates with less formal biblical and mission education. It's not that less education is needed. It's just that we realize that frontloading too much formal education before a candidate has bonded with a people, ministry and country may be counterproductive.

If you have already completed your undergraduate study, find the best way to add three major components: (1) biblical training (whether acquired in a nonformal or formal setting), (2) introductions to anthropology and crosscultural communication, and (3) specialized training in a vocational skill that would give you viability in the global marketplace (see "Options for Learning," pp. 140-42).

You'll also need some understanding of the world's religions and of church history—particularly missions history. It's true: those who do not learn from history are doomed to repeat it. "World Christian Foundations," developed by the U.S. Center for World Mission in Pasadena, California, is a comprehensive attempt to meet this need through part-time distance education that you can begin right now with your pastor or qualified layperson as a mentor. You can complete a B.A. or earn an M.A. through this course, even after moving to the field.

If you can't fit in this heavy a program right away, you can get a substantial portion of it by taking the three-unit course "Foundations of the World Christian Movement." There is also the "Perspectives on the World Christian Movement" course or the *Vision for the Nations* video miniseries. For those just entering college, a freshman-level version of these programs, called INSIGHT, is also available through the U.S. Center for World Mission. (See descriptions and contact information for these in appendix 1.)

There's a rich array of educational options from which you can choose: Bible schools, Christian colleges and universities, Christian graduate schools and seminaries, local churches' credit or noncredit courses in biblical basics and an exploding array of seminars and modules on the Web. You might even consider studying in another English-speaking country or in the country where you hope to minister.

In addition, there are a growing number of summer programs, intensive courses and self-study distance-learning courses that can provide you with the basics in Bible study and missions work while you're working full time or still enrolled in college.

Some agencies and churches will take candidates with a Bible or Christian college education and send them overseas after just a few weeks of orientation. Many missionaries take additional training gradually during their furloughs and study leaves.

Other agencies are designing tracks that place university graduates overseas for two years of initial language and culture learning before bringing them back for specialized Bible and missions training that focuses on the particular people among whom the candidates have chosen to live and minister. In either case, the new pattern is evident: get your feet wet first; bond with a people; take some first steps in ministry; and then, upon your return to North America, seek further specialized training or retooling.

As you can see, churches and agencies are becoming more flexible in the design and timing of basic education programs. Whatever route you take, you will get missionary training—whether that training is formal and done in advance or through the "school of hard knocks." Regardless, the preparation that you receive will make you less vulnerable to premature and painful attrition.

A Metaphor for Ministry Learning

STEVE HOKE

There is no one right way to prepare for ministry. I got a lot of schooling. Bill [Taylor] and I both have graduate degrees. But that's not what made us competent or effective in multicultural settings.

So, it's vital at this juncture to try to pencil in the vast array of learning, schooling and training options that lie before you. Armed with solid spiritual and educational advice, you can make a wise decision.

Notice I didn't say "schooling" advice. There's a difference. We value the contribution that formal education (read "schooling") can make to missionary preparation. But both of us have also seen the negative impact of the wrong kind of schooling or too much schooling on too many well-intentioned servants who expected their formal education to make them dynamic and transformative crosscultural workers. It just didn't happen that way.

Education is about learning and broad preparation for the future, whether formal or nonformal (out-of-school education). Schooling is about taking courses that promise to prepare you for the future. Schooling is about cognitive input, degrees and accreditation. But schooling is not for everyone.

For each person, and depending on the types of content, the intentional choice of procedures and timing will result in an efficient outcome. Some people need the structure of formal education, while some learners chafe under the rules and limits of formal education.

Some of the best learners take more time, because they take initiative in seeking out the learning experience they can use the best, that will provide exactly what they need. One of my favorite mission educators, Sam, took years more time to complete his grad program than Bill or me, but no one would say those were wasted years. No, Sam knew what he wanted and took his time gathering and ordering his learning experiences. He didn't let his schooling get in the way of his education.

That should be your commitment as well. Make whatever schooling you might need fit into your overall learning pathway. Make schooling fit your needs; don't let your needs be squeezed to fit the demands of the school.

Schools are valuable for helping people learn

the underpinnings of ideas and well-connected bodies of knowledge. But unfortunately we have crammed so much knowledge and cognitive content into the curriculum of the schools, they can't even do that well.

The noted Brazilian adult educator Paulo Freire suggested that education is to liberate, not confine or enslave. This must be your perspective as you consider the almost-unlimited learning options before you.

Looking ahead to lifelong learning should not be a mind-boggling trip. Rather, it should be a thoughtful and intentional journey into a lifetime of learning and development. We cannot prescribe a lock-step curriculum for you. It has to be customized to who you are—your background, training and gifts; who God has called you to be and do; your ministry burden and passion, longing and vision; how the Spirit is leading your forward; and your mentors and individualized pathway for learning.

Let us suggest a metaphor, a mental image, that will help you visualize the various components of lifelong learning and a suggested way forward that will enable you to stay on a developmental trajectory.

The Components of Lifelong Learning

Missionary Fred Holland suggested a two-track analogy for missionary discipleship and training.[1] He identified four vital factors in a professional's lifelong learning. Two parallel railroad tracks transport a person from where he or she is at present into the distant future. The first track is that of life and *ministry experience*.

Adult learning is distinctive from childhood education in that adults bring their lifetime of relational and ministry experience with them into the educational or training encounter. They are no longer blank slates; they bring all they are and have done into that experience. The key, then, is somehow to to tap into that past experience to

"mine" what they have learned experientially, not assuming they know nothing or little about the topic under investigation. In fact, adults are best motivated to learn when they select the topic, identify the resources and go after the specific issues they want to learn more about.

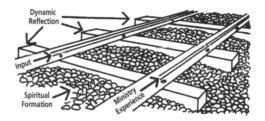

In the natural course of ministry before and on the field, there are opportunities to gain additional *knowledge* and *cognitive input* through reading, workshops, seminars and formal course work. Too often we have assumed that the heart of Christian and theological education is new knowledge. But that is too narrow an approach. Knowledge is always *instrumental*—that is, it is never a goal in itself; it is a tool that serves a higher goal: growth and development. You gain new knowledge when you become aware of an area in which you need to know more in order to grow in being and doing.

Increasingly, the Internet has made a world of knowledge available at our fingertips. But obviously our greatest need is not just knowledge, it is knowledge applied to life and to ministry situations with biblical insight. That is biblical wisdom—applied truth.

Notice that these two tracks run parallel into the distant future and never meet. So what integrates your life experience with new information and biblical insight? How do you intentionally relate what you are learning with what you are doing and how you are ministering?

Drawing from international educator Ted Ward's analogy of a split-rail fence,[2] Holland's connecting insight is that *dynamic reflection,* analogous to the railroad ties in the metaphor, links knowledge with life experience. Without conscious effort, the concepts and principles of learning are often not integrated. They float in the conceptual domain, because they have not been practically applied to a situation.

Dynamic reflection can take place in contemplative journaling and reflection. But most practicing professionals find great insight when they are able to share in integrating seminars and discussions with others. These don't have to be credit courses but nonformal learning communities designed to provide opportunities for people interested in learning about a certain topic. These could be church planters in Japan discussing what's working in gathering home groups in urban centers, or Europe missionaries gathering to learn from each other what's working in university evangelism and discipleship.

Dynamic reflection for maximum impact should be more regular than periodic, more nonformal (that is, planned and structured, but noncredit) than informal (accidental, unplanned). And integrating discussion don't need to be led by outside experts as much as they need to be facilitated by a person adept at drawing out the learnings of others.

But before we rush on, excited about learning new stuff, look back at the two-track analogy. The two-tracks are not suspended in space nor are they laid carelessly on an open field. Lasting railroad routes are carefully established on a well-formed bedrock of gravel and crushed stone. This bedrock refers to the *spiritual formation* that must underlay all lifelong learning for effective ministry. The basis of all Christian growth and ministry is the deepening character and spirituality of the disciple. Too often pastors and missionaries have tried to minister for a lifetime on the initial steps of discipleship and theological education they gained in Bible school or seminary. This is way too limited.

You cannot front-load all you need to know for the complexity and seriousness of crosscultural ministry in college or grad school before going to the field. That is an antiquated notion of professional education that has proven bankrupt across American in the last one hundred years. Current research and practice strongly suggests that the ideal way to keep learning is to look for "just in time" learning that will equip you to accomplish your next task.

Don't expect a course in church planting in seminary to complete your training for that critical task. Similarly, a college course in group dynamics will not guarantee that you'll be an effective team member. Rather, look to join a church-planting incubator or network (a network is a learning group of like-minded men and women exploring a particular subject, facilitated by an experienced church planter) engaged in cell-church planting as you are stepping into that task. Find a group of missionaries starting house groups to join for study and discussion around what you are learning. Or start a cluster group of missionaries who are grappling with reaching out to Muslim neighbors. Look for a distance-ed module or webinar on a topic of particular interest, whether that be leading multicultural teams or supervising dispersed teams.

Your learning train will stay on schedule when the two tracks of your professional learning are based on a thoughtful design that integrates all four elements. Without a firm foundation, the train will derail. The bedrock of all we do is spiritual formation, not knowledge, techniques or competency. It is the Spirit empowering what we know and who we are. Personalize your long-term growth and development plan with this learning analogy in mind.

---

[1] Fred Holland, "Theological Education in Context and Change" (unpublished D.Miss. dissertation at Fuller School of World Mission, Pasadena, Calif., 1978).

[2] Ted Ward, "The Split-Rail Fence: Analogy for Professional Education," in *Extension Seminary* 2 (1972): 5.

Options for Learning
Formal Education for Crosscultural Service
STEVE HOKE AND BILL TAYLOR

Five basic formal schooling options are described below. Match the educational mode to your needs, goals, resources, personality and learning style.

Inside the Undergraduate Classroom

1. Secular colleges and universities. Secular colleges and universities (private or state) generally offer quality facilities, diverse academic majors, large research libraries and a wide range of faculty specialization. Tuition is greatly reduced for state residents (often about half the cost of private higher education). Active campus ministry organizations can enrich classroom study with discipleship, mentoring and outreach opportunities. Many of these schools offer both undergraduate and graduate education programs.

In North America you have a menu of thousands of these tertiary schools. They range in size from very small to medium to enormous. Some are small, tucked into a rural paradise or crammed into an inner city; others are large, again either in rural or urban settings. They can be private (religious or secular in orientation) or public (supported by state funds). In contrast to many other countries, the United States does not have a "national university" funded and guided by the federal education industry. Cost factors range across the spectrum, from a relatively frugal cost at certain state universities (perhaps nine thousand U.S. dollars per year for tuition, room and board) to nearly forty thousand and more per year just for tuition and fees (2008) at high-ticket private ones.

2. Christian liberal arts colleges and universities. Christian liberal arts colleges specialize in general-education programs, seeking to give students a basic grasp of all the academic disciplines from a distinctively Christ-centered perspective. The curriculum is based on the conviction that "all truth is God's truth." It links the study of God's creation with the study of God's revelation, helping you to develop a biblical worldview. Studying at a Christian college allows you to integrate biblical training with your academic field of study. It also tends to be costly.

We live in a fragmented society that desperately needs an integrated view of life—a view that connects the pieces and offers meaning to life. Nowhere is this more important than in Christian ministry. No matter what their job description, unless believers possess an integrated, God-centered view of the world, they will have little to offer people of differing cultures. This is the special strength of the Christian liberal arts college or university.

3. Bible colleges. Bible colleges seek to develop Christian leaders who are mature in character and equipped with biblical knowledge. They have had a strong record of turning out men and women who serve as pastors, teachers, missionaries and leaders in Christian ministry. Over 60 percent of today's evangelical missionaries received some Bible college training.

At a Bible college, you'll find a large part of the curriculum devoted to biblical studies. You'll learn to study and teach the Bible, to preach and to participate in and lead Christian service. You'll be tutored in practical areas like sharing your faith, planting churches and nurturing young Christians. You will also find an emphasis on deep spiritual life and on your identity as part of a community of students and faculty committed to loving and serving God.

4. Another alternative. If you have already completed part of your bachelor's degree, you may benefit from a pattern of study that can adapt to your present responsibilities and move with you to the field if you don't finish before you go. The "World Christian Foundations" course developed by the U.S. Center for World Mission in Pasadena, California (see the contact information in appendix 1) is offered by more than one college. The material is equivalent to a traditional year of Bible with a mission perspective, but it is packaged for two years of intensive half-time study anywhere under the supervision of a local mentor. It incorporates the essentials of a three-year seminary curriculum plus a wide range of disciplines, from anthropology to hermeneutics and science to history, around the central theme of God's unfolding purpose. It is as up-to-date as you can get in terms of the overall scope of God's mission effort and is available for completing a B.A or earning an M.A. By enabling you to continue working while you study, "World Christian Foundations" can help you avoid the debt trap that ensnares many would-be missionaries.

One very important point: no missionary sending group will release you if you have a large amount of debt. At an Urbana student missions convention years ago, I (Bill) led a workshop on missionary equipping. In the question-and-answer time, a student asked me whether it mattered if he had a large loan debt after college. I said it did, and then I asked him what his debt would be. He blew us out of the room when he said, "100,000 dollars." He was a computer-science grad from MIT. I told him to get the best-paying job he could find, live like a pauper, pay his debt in as short a time as possible, save money and then go into missions. He might be able to do this in four years.

Rapidly increasing amounts of student debt for undergraduate education is a hidden time bomb. Missions strategist and mobilizer Dr. Ralph Winter, founding director of the U.S. Center for World Mission, expresses his deep concern about escalating debt in these words: "More than ten thousand dollars of student debt becomes a very serious obstacle to ever working at the modest level of missionary support."

Deciding on Your Study

How should you decide which secular school to attend if you also want to go into missions? First, seek the counsel of wise people, including your parents and your pastoral team. Listen carefully to them, then pray. Second, check out the educational track record of others you know, particularly those who have gone from the university into missions. Third, check out the liberal arts programs that will teach you how to read, think and write, or the more "marketable" ones that will give you a strong skill set in light of your academic interests. Fourth, investigate the options within your goals, desires and finances, and then try to visit the schools.

Finally, select a secular school that offers the following for you: the right academic offerings and costs according to your learning capacities and family budget; the presence of vital campus and student-led Christian ministries, coupled with a strong student-loving church with a passion for God and the world, including that campus. We cannot overemphasize the critical role of solid, campus-based Christian groups and vibrant, worshiping, intergenerational communities.

Never minimize your church experience. In both the campus ministry and church, you will find teachers of God's Word, disciplers and mentors, lifelong friends, and perhaps a husband or wife with the same passionate goals in life. Some young adults fear they will lose their faith in the secular college or university. To be honest, we have seen that happen, and it hurts;

it may have a parallel to the gradual stagnation of faith that can occur in a Christian school where the tough issues are not faced. Don't go into a secular school without the certainty that God wants you there.

On the other hand, we maintain that if the Christian faith does not work at a secular school, it surely won't work in another culture. Learn to tell the Christ's powerful story in that school and you will never forget the mistakes made, the lessons learned, the exhilaration of seeing the triune God at work in Spirit power. Make friends with seculars, New Agers, Buddhists, Hindus, Muslims, Marxists, whether they be from your own culture or not. Learn to listen to their story, and thus you gain credibility that allows you to share with them the Great Story and the way it has bisected your own life.

Moving on to Graduate Courses

5. Christian graduate schools and seminaries. Christian graduate schools are primarily concerned with biblical study and professional training for areas of Christian ministry. Graduate schools equip you with a specialty at a professional level. You can hone your professional skills in journalism, crosscultural studies, healthcare, teaching English as a second language and so on. Seminaries offer ministry preparation in areas such as missions, theology, spirituality, preaching, Christian education and church planting. Adequate professional training has become increasingly crucial for long-term missionary candidates. Some believe seminary training is mandatory for the crosscultural church planter. But the most critical issue is whether you can develop the character qualities and practical ministry skills demanded in the crosscultural setting.

Missions involve many skills in interpersonal relations, networking and resource linking, crosscultural communication and counseling, mentoring and facilitating. However, increasingly, crosscultural, longer-term servants in the less-reached world need legitimate vocations or skills for visas, as well as to "ground" ministry in a marketplace.

Each seminary has its own style and doctrinal emphasis. Some are known for training gifted preachers. Others are known for their counseling or missions programs. Still others specialize in urban ministry or international studies. If you attend seminary, the school and its faculty will have a powerful impact on you and on the shape of your theological persuasions. Select a seminary or graduate program that's compatible with your particular calling and gifting.

Yet another strong combination that is gaining traction today merges formal and nonformal training for long-term mission with key components in the home culture and strategic segments in the region or nation and culture of future ministry. More and more of these options are opening up.

A Rich Phase

Whatever avenue of training or study you choose, it can be a rich phase of your life. It's a time when lifelong friends are made and life partners are often found. Surrounded by like-minded people, you'll find freedom and support to test your calling and refine the direction of your life. But don't get comfortable in the safe environment of academia. It is designed as boot camp for what is ahead.

For colleges exclusively dedicated to thoughtful missionary training in community, check out Redcliffe College (http://www.redcliffe.org/) in North America, and All Nations Christian College (http://www.allnations.ac.uk/) in the United Kingdom.

Keys to Raising Your Personal Support

STEVE SHADRACH

I want to serve God and be obedient to his leading in my life, but I don't want to *raise support!*

If you have thought this, you're not alone. In fact, most people living a donor-supported lifestyle admit they've had feelings like this. Although this lifestyle is not a popular one in North America, where independence is highly value, it is an essential component of working with many Christian ministries.

Yes, starting from scratch and putting together your support is a huge challenge, but many come to see it as a blessing. Even though there are stresses and pressures involved in raising and maintaining a personal support team, I would not want to live any other way. The bonds I have formed over the years with our support team are priceless. The stories of God building my faith during difficult times could fill a book. And most of all, when I report to that ministry assignment, there is a sense of destiny and authority there. Why? Because I and those investing in our ministry have paid a dear price to get me to that ministry. I had better take it seriously and give it my all.

You *will* have some doubts, fears and questions. Be assured: these are normal! I still get the butterflies each time I pick up that phone to make a support appointment. If you want to be successful you'll need some guidance. Here are five simple (but challenging!) keys to raising your personal support team. Here we go!

1. Understand the Biblical Basis

Take time to study the Scriptures so you'll know exactly what God thinks about asking others to give to you and your ministry. Some choose to just pray and trust God to bring the funds in, but it is just as biblical and requires as much (or more) faith to personally invite others to invest.

Either way, we must understand that *God* is the source of our funds, not donors, our plans or hard work. In *Funding Your Ministry,* Scott Morton highlights five passages showing the validity of God's ministers being supported by others:

1. the example of the Levites (see Num 18:24); the Jews gave their tithe to the priests for support

2. the example of Jesus (see Lk 8:2-3)—many people supported Jesus and the disciples

3. the teaching of Jesus (see Mt 10:9-10)—a kingdom worker is worthy of support

4. the example of Paul (see Acts 18:4-5)—he stopped tentmaking to preach full time

5. The teaching of Paul (see 1 Cor 9:1-18)—he had the right to be supported by the churches

But first! Evaluate *your* own giving. Before you ask anyone else to give, you have to be committed to sacrificially investing in kingdom work on a regular basis too. Let's practice what we preach!

2. Kill the Giants in Your Mind

Twelve spies went into the Promised Land to take a look before the Hebrew nation was to enter and claim what God had given them. Only Joshua and Caleb came back ready to invade. The other ten spies were so terrified of the giants they saw that they confessed, "We became like grasshoppers in our own sight, and so we were in their sight" (Num 13:33 NASB). The ten had this "grasshopper perspective" and instead of trusting God and moving out with courage, they were paralyzed by fear.

It is the same way in support raising. The confidence level we have in our God, our vision and ourselves can make us . . . or break us. All of us have different "giants" in our minds that can keep us from beginning and persevering in assembling a full support team.

Some common "giants" you must conquer:

- You or your family think support raising is really just begging.

- You think you are not a worthy investment.

- You think support raising is just a "necessary evil" to be endured.

- You think people are rejecting you (or your ministry) if they say no.

Kill these giants as you fill your mind with Scripture and believe what God has said about you and your calling. Just as the Lord prepared the land for the people to simply go in and take it, we need to believe he has prepared the hearts of donors. We need to walk boldly in faith and ask them to join our vision.

3. Pray and Plan Well

Pray. S. D. Gordon said, "Prayer is the real work of the ministry. Service is just gathering in the results of prayer." Bathe yourself and donors in prayer before, during and after this support-raising journey. God will go before you. He will also build a love for your donors as you pray for them.

Create your budget. Include *everything:* your personal needs, giving, saving, debt, ministry expenses and so on. Seek to balance a lifestyle that will allow you to maximize your effectiveness, but also be above reproach in the stewardship of your finances. If you have school loans, simply include the monthly amount owed and keep going. Your donors will admire you for keeping your promise to pay it back. Commit to raising at least 100 percent of your budget *before* you even report to your assignment.

Namestorm. Now that you have turned the whole process over to God, write down *every*

person you've *ever* known. Don't play Holy Spirit by saying, "Oh, that person would never give." You'll be surprised by a few who do give—and by a few who don't! Think of people that have a heart for student work, missions or whatever group you're targeting. List churches, Sunday school classes, foundations and corporations. The bulk of your support, though, will come from individuals with whom you've been in contact over the years.

Map out a plan. Divide all the names according to cities they live in. Label each name "hot," "cold" or "medium" depending on whether they probably will give, probably won't give or might give. Next, pray over the amount you would like to ask each to give. One amount does not fit everyone; base it on what you perceive they're able and willing to give, along with the kind of relationship you have with them. You might be more comfortable suggesting a range of giving rather than a specific amount. But know that most support raisers tend to ask for too little, not too much. Remember, there is no cash-flow problem in heaven. North Americans give billions of dollars to charity each year. Give people the opportunity to invest in eternal things, and thus build up their treasure in heaven.

Plan out a map. Schedule the cities you will go to first, second, and so on, and get it on your calendar. If you want to send a letter in advance telling your potential donors what you are doing and that you'll be calling, do it. It's essential to call each person *in advance* of the trip to get an appointment. During the call, don't let them say yes or no to giving; your only objective is to get an appointment with them. Seek to line up all your "hot" prospects first, then your "medium" prospects and finally the "cold" ones.

4. Ask Them Face-to-Face

This is the key. James 4:2 says, "You do not

have, because you do not ask God." The word *ask* is used in the Gospels 113 times. God wants to teach us about asking: him and others. He wants to teach us about depending on him. Most surveys report the main reason people give is because someone asked them! It's not unspiritual or fleshly to ask. It is good, biblical and faith building to ask. Let's not hide behind our fears. Let's walk toward them and render them powerless!

If you choose to cut corners, take the quick, easy route and just send a fund request letter out or make a group presentation, you might have a 10-percent response rate. If you send a letter followed by a phone call, you might get 25 percent of people to say yes. But, if you're willing to sit down eyeball to eyeball with others and lay out the incredible ministry vision God has called you to, usually well over half will join you as ministry partners. This approach takes time and money and courage, but it communicates to the donor that they (and your vision) are so important to you that you *must* meet with them in person.

Don't be fooled. *How* you go about securing their commitment will determine the amount, consistency and longevity of their giving. My research shows that ministries that train their staff to ask for the gift (in person) raise their full budget twice as fast as groups who simply share the need, but don't ask. We have not, because we ask not.

5. Cultivate the Relationship

Youth With A Mission's Betty Barnett reminds us it's not fundraising, but "friendraising." You can have a ministry to your new ministry partner and possibly be her or his only connection to Jesus Christ or the Great Commission. Here are the ABCs (and D) of having a long and fruitful relationship with your supporters:

A. Consider tithing your ministry time to your support team: prayer, writing, calling, ministering.

B. Thank before you bank (when a new person or new gift comes in). Be prompt and professional in all your correspondence and record keeping.

C. Regularly send (or e-mail) well-written newsletters. Share how their investments are paying off, along with some specific prayer requests. Occasional postcards, phone calls and visits are great too. Beware: the main reason people drop off of support teams is that they do not hear from the recipient.

D. Win, keep, lift. When you win donors, they are now on your team. Keep them on the team by caring for and cultivating them. Periodically ask them to consider lifting (increasing) their monthly or annual gift to you.

People will stick with you for life if you appreciate them and keep them informed. View them as vital partners in your ministry, and you will gain not only lifelong supporters, but friends too. One day you'll turn around and realize how blessed you are and that you too would not want to live any other way. Trust God and begin this exciting adventure today.

Betty Barnett. *Friend Raising: Building a Missionary Support Team That Lasts.* Seattle: YWAM Publishing, 2003.

William P. Dillon. *People Raising: A Practical Guide to Raising Support.* Chicago: Moody Press, 1993.

Scott Morton. *Funding Your Ministry.* Colorado Springs: Dawson Media, 1999.

Pete Sommer, *Getting Sent.* Downers Grove, Ill.: InterVarsity Press, 1999.

If you need training, consider Boot Camp for Personal Support Raising by The BodyBuilders (www.thebodybuilders.net) or People Raising Conferences (www.peopleraising.com).

Dr. Steve Shadrach founded the ministries of Student Mobilization and The Traveling Teams. He is president of The BodyBuilders Ministry and director of mobilization for the U.S. Center for World Mission. He and his wife, Carol, and their five children have enjoyed living and ministering on support since 1986. He has taken hundreds of ministries around the world through the Boot Camp for Personal Support Raising.

 # Global Perspectives

TONICA VAN DER MEER
Principal, Center for Evangelical Missions, Brazil

Role of the Missionary

I believe missionaries from the Global North can still be useful in a number of ministries and places. The main requirement is not so much their training but their attitude. We no longer need missionaries with a "boss" or "we know better" attitude, but those willing to serve as partners or under national leadership. Global North workers can meet a need in the newer missionary sending countries for training in member care, in missionary anthropology, in how to develop and lead projects, in teaching English, business and mission, and in a number of others areas. Also, there is still a need for a unified effort to respond to the needs of children and teenagers in crisis and other social needs in big cities. Holistic mission is a key concept and a real need for those willing to serve humbly.

Recommended Prefield Training

There is a need for appropriate training for crosscultural service, for holistic mission, for understanding people from very different cultures, for servant leadership, a training that provides high academic quality, but even more, the kind of training that leads to character transformation and Christlikeness.

Character and Spiritual Qualities

These new workers need to have servant leadership qualities, a learner's attitude and a willingness to live a simpler lifestyle, to love the Lord and to love their fellow missionaries, to love national Christians and those who are lost. They must be willing to respond to unexpected needs and opportunities, be ready to persevere in difficult and painful situations and be open to receive spiritual support from local Christians.

Meeting the Educational Needs of Your Children

JANET BLOMBERG

As missionary parents move overseas, they face unique challenges educating their children. They often assume their children's education will look like what they have experienced. However, for parents of third-culture kids (TCKs), this is not necessarily the case.

To make good educational decisions, parents must understand certain foundational issues regarding education in a crosscultural context. First, they must recognize the impact of being TCKs. It shapes their children's development, impacts their worldview and affects their choices (in career, marriage and so on). For example, TCKs need rootedness in both their passport culture and the country in which they are being raised. To deprive them of rootedness in either culture deprives them of part of their TCK birthright.

Second, parents must recognize that there is no perfect option, but there are benefits and challenges to each. Unlike in previous generations, there is an ever-increasing range of choices available that includes international schools, international Christian/MK schools, boarding schools, homeschooling, national schools, online programs or a combination of these. Thus parents must carefully evaluate each option as to how it fits their goals and the values of their family, meets the educational needs of each child and works in their ministry location. They must consider whether or not an option will adequately prepare (both academically and personally) their child to reenter the passport culture. Today many parents are using multiple options at the same time in the course of educating their children.

Third, parents need a broad, long-term view of education. They must recognize that education involves not just academics but also preparing children for a fruitful life of responsible discipleship. It involves not just tests and textbooks, but skills and character. Being TCKs provides students a valuable educational experience and helps them develop highly marketable crosscultural skills. In addition, parents must evaluate their options in light of its impact on reentry to the passport culture (whether at age eighteen or earlier). It is easy for parents to focus only on the immediate goal of getting to the field and overlook the long-range implications.

Sometimes people think these decisions can be made once a family arrives overseas. However, parents need to evaluate their options and develop an educational plan for their family before they go. It is hard to make these decisions in the midst of transition, culture shock and the swirling winds of divergent opinions from family, supporters and others. Rather than extending grace, people are often quick to judge the decisions parents make, and so it can become a polarizing factor within teams and agencies. In actuality, these questions (regarding who makes educational decisions, what options or supports are funded and what policies regarding educational and family matters are in place) are things that ought to be discussed before, not after, joining a mission agency.

International Schools

Depending on the country, international schools (whether Christian or secular) may be an option. Although they wear the label "international," sometimes one culture dominates these schools in terms of the curriculum or where teachers come from. Some schools work to involve students in the local culture and teach its history and language. Others may not make this a priority. While international schools have high academic standards, excellent teachers and good programs, there are differences among them. International Christian schools are supportive of the parents' work and see themselves as partnering with them to promote the academic and spiritual growth of students. While they cost less than other international schools and offer a high-quality education, they may not offer all the specialized programs or facilities that parents want or need. Secular international schools are more expensive and thus offer more programs or have better facilities. Students attending these schools may face negative peer pressure, lifestyle issues and economic differences in comparison to other families.

Many people assume that most schools offer boarding programs, but this is not the case. In previous generations, children were routinely sent to boarding school at five or six years old. Today most students are not going until junior or senior high school, which allows them to be part of their family and bond with them. Much has also changed about boarding programs. There is now training for boarding home parents and accreditation of programs. Parents should include the children (as they become adolescents) in making this and other educational decisions. Many families working in isolated settings choose this option because of its educational, social and extracurricular opportunities. In addition, it provides a peer group for adolescents and can facilitate reentry (depending on the student's passport culture).

While separation is not desirable, parents must evaluate the long-term developmental and reentry needs of their children. They must remember they are still parents wherever their children are. Improvements in technology make it easier for parents to stay in close contact with their children.

Homeschooling

Many parents might not have chosen this option in their passport culture, but feel it is the only workable option where they are. They are attracted to homeschooling because the child remains at home and it provides educational continuity as they move in and out of cultures. Often parents welcome the opportunity it provides to involve the children in their ministry as well as to incorporate biblical and spiritual values and the local history and culture. Homeschooling gives parents flexibility, allows them to individualize instruction, and permits them to choose their children's curriculum. Some parents opt for a

packaged curriculum. Some mix and match programs. Some create their own program. Sometimes families with older students use online programs.

However, some parents are concerned about how to juggle the roles of parent and teacher or the demands of family and work. They are also concerned about the stresses or conflicts between parent and child. Some parents may feel unprepared for the task. Some parents are concerned about the lack of peer interaction for the children or of competition that may motivate their child. Depending on where the family is living, there are more day-to-day interruptions and the demands in daily living may be greater. In some cases, social interactions can be limited, especially if the national school holds classes on Saturdays or has a long daily schedule. In some countries, homeschooling may be illegal or may not be understood by those with whom the parents are working.

For parents who have homeschooled previously, it can be a very different experience overseas. Support groups or English-language libraries aren't available. Teaching and curricular resources are hard to find. There are no sports teams, musical groups or youth groups for students to join. Living in an isolated setting may intensify all of these challenges for both student and parent.

National Schools

Many missionary parents today are using national schools. It allows the child to remain with his or her parents and may be low in cost (if a public national school is used). National schools vary in quality, requirements, philosophy and methodology from country to country. Parents often choose this option because it provides friends for their child, gives exposure to the culture and helps the child learn the language. It can also be a helpful option while parents are in language school.

However, there are potential challenges. Sometimes a child is rejected by national peers or is bullied because of her or his nationality. In addition, parents must carefully evaluate the religious and political differences. Are they something a child can be exposed to or should be protected from?

Certain differences are apparent when parents visit a school: the language of instruction, class size, facilities, programs and the level of technology. However, other differences are not as apparent. Schools are not value neutral, but reflect their culture and its values. This impacts their view of the student, the teacher's approach to motivation and discipline and their definition of a successful student. For example, corporal punishment may be practiced, rote memory emphasized or subjects taught at different times or in different ways from the child's passport culture. For some students, these differences can make the transition back to their passport culture more challenging.

Above all, students who use the national school learn more than the language. They absorb the culture's values and worldview. This intensifies their identification with the culture and may create reentry challenges. Parents must understand both the benefits and challenges of using national schools and weigh carefully the impact of the child's age, linguistic background, personality, resilience, identity development and reentry needs on using this option.

Parents who use this option must carefully choose among the different types of national schools available—public, private and Christian schools. They must not assume things are going well just because the child hasn't said something, but should closely monitor the situations. Sometimes in an effort to protect their parents, children will remain silent when the situation is bad.

Variations

Often when people think of homeschooling, they think of one parent teaching his or her own children. However, parents can work together and establish a homeschooling cooperative. It enables parents to share the workload, enrich the curriculum and expand the social opportunities for their children. In establishing a co-op, parents should carefully define their goals, responsibilities and procedures.

Sometimes parents create a one-room school or a satellite school in conjunction with an existing international Christian school. Although parents still need to be involved because of the wide age span of the children or the number of grades involved, a trained teacher plans the curriculum and carries out the day-to-day school responsibilities. This option provides increased social interaction for students and may ease the transition to other options. The success of this option also depends on careful planning and clearly defined goals, responsibilities and decision making.

For parents with junior- and senior-high school students, online programs are used either to supplement their homeschooling curriculum or to provide the complete educational program. This option not only meets students' educational needs, but also creates opportunities for social interaction. Online courses can provide an alternative to boarding school or to homeschooling difficult subjects. Depending on the program chosen, it may facilitate reentry because the program is accredited.

Conclusion

Parents face repeated decisions regarding their children's education, and as their children become older they should be included in these discussions. These are complex and intensely personal decisions, but should not be allowed to become a polarizing factor. They should not be made out of fear, but by faith, depending on God's wisdom. Above all, parents must remember that being a TCK is itself an enriching, educating experience that provides a great foundation for their children to build on throughout their lives.

David C. Pollock and Ruth Van Reken, *Third Culture Kids: The Experience of Growing Up Among Worlds* (Intercultural Press, 2001). Widely acclaimed as the first and only book to fully examine the legacy of transition and change shared by those who have grown up globally, this book speaks to the challenges and rewards of a multicultural childhood. For parents, educators and adult MKs/TCKs around the world, this book brings to life the essence of the cultural, emotional, physical and geographic experiences of the nomadic life of a TCK.

Janet Blomberg and David Brooks, eds., *Fitted Pieces: A Guide to Educating Children Overseas* (SMART, 2001). Educational issues are often the greatest challenge faced by expatriate families serving overseas. This book offers hope for finding and fitting the educational pieces together. *Fitted Pieces* is designed to equip parents to make informed decisions about their children's education that are workable and appropriate for their family, whatever their situation.

"Prefield Educational Planning Seminar," cosponsored by Interaction International (www.interactionintl.org). This seminar is for parents who will be (or are considering) homeschooling or using national schools to educate their children where they will serve. Through interactive workshops, panel discussions, individual advising sessions and more, an outstanding team of MK educators and caregivers help parents develop an educational plan that fits their family and work setting.

Janet Blomberg serves as executive director for Interaction International and has worked with MKs/TCKs, parents, educators and caregivers for almost twenty years. She served as the founding director of the Asia Education Resource Consortium from 2001 to 2004, and has worked with schools and sending organizations on a variety of care, educational, program-development and policy issues as well as on the care and education needs of students and families from new sending countries. Janet speaks, provides training and has authored many articles on MK/TCK care and education. She coedited the book Fitted Pieces: A Guide to Educating Children Overseas (SHARE, 2001), and founded and edits Interact, a publication dealing with issues in MK/TCK care and education.

Survival and contrast

Top Fourteen Questions Prospective Missionaries Ask

JOHN McVAY

The following are the top fourteen questions asked on the AskAMissionary website.

Preparation and Training

1. What types of training should I consider? What major in university would be most useful in missions?

2. I have years of schooling ahead. How do I prepare and persevere? Should I skip a university degree and go into missions now?

3. How could I use my professional skills in missions?

Finances: Personal Support Raising

1. What about debt and becoming a missionary?

2. How do I raise financial support?

Raising Children and Schooling Overseas

1. How can a family with small children serve overseas? What about our children's education?

Connecting with an Agency or Church, or Going Solo

1. How do I select a mission agency? Should I join a larger missions agency or a smaller one?

2. Why do many missionaries join an agency?

Calling and Guidance

1. How can I know if God is calling me to become a missionary? Should I wait for a call to a specific country?

Practical Considerations

1. Singleness: Should I be a single missionary or should I marry?

2. Family support: Can I become a missionary if my parents object?

3. Age: Can I become a missionary if I am over age forty?

4. Facing my fears: Can I become a missionary if I have fear of living overseas?

5. Language: Can I become a missionary if I don't want to learn another language?

John McVay is a missions mobilizer who helped launch AskAMissionary.com and The Journey Deepens weekend retreats. He serves in Tulsa as chief of staff with In His Image Family Medicine Residency and Medical Missions.

⊕ Global Perspectives

HARRY HOFFMAN
Youth With A Mission, Somewhere in Asia

Role of the Missionary

Each nation has its strength and weakness. And to me the issue is now whether Western missionaries still have a role in God's global enterprise. I am a German; some of our strengths are our thinking, strategic planning and high-quality products. But we don't smile so much and often look quite serious, so we need the Brazilians to dance and laugh with. Each nation brings something unique and specific to the table, which is needed. Not always welcomed, but needed.

While each nation has a unique gifting, calling and personality, I believe the next generation in the West is even more confused about life, God, ministries and missions than my own generation. (I am forty.) Many of the younger generation are marked by divorce, abuse, addictions, sexual confusion and emotional woundedness. So young people look first for peace and healing—of self and in healing relationships. Knowing Jesus doesn't mean your life is automatically sorted out. This generation seeks good and steady relationships, people they can look up to. And you can hardly find that in missions.

I may disappoint a few people, but let me shoot straight. Many of my missionary colleagues, including myself, are strong-willed, goal-oriented, self-centered people (they call it God-centered). But we can't deal with the influx of so-called high-maintenance people with emotional wounds. Our response is, "You do pornography or have other sexual issues? Leave the field! Why are you so emotional? Then we will marginalize you!" Sometimes, when I am in a cynical mood, I call this "mission Darwinism"—only the strong survive. Ask at a field-based missions conference who has been there over ten years, and you will see what I mean.

Attracting the Next Generations

I don't know what would attract the next generation. They try the same things the former generations did. There is no fresh alternative yet. They just quit faster. Or they move quicker into a job with an international corporation and try to live Christ there, which they call "ministry" and "going into missions." I can't say this out loud though, because those terms are copyrighted for "real" missionaries. Entering business makes life more manageable for them, without newsletters and having to please their sending church with success stories and financial issues.

To ask for specific character and spiritual qualities is simply the wrong question. Unless you think mission Darwinism. Why ask? Are you strong enough to survive the battle out there? Are you too emotional? Do you have any of the five hundred personality disorders? I like Youth With A Mission. They take almost everyone, but you go through six months of community living and good teaching, and then another six months of community living and good teaching before you go into ministry full time. The issue is not competence; it is all about weakness and dependency.

People want to be taken seriously. Mission organizations can't always deal with the real person, because there is a "task" to finish. And that quickly moves them from a professed value for people to their actual priority: accomplishing the task. But people want to be known for who they really are, as nonconformist and postmodern as they might be. There is a deep longing there, in all of us, but even more in the younger generation. And that's the gospel, isn't it? God knowing you and accepting you? That's what we communicate to our target group. Maybe not so much to our colleagues though.

Health Preparations
for Crosscultural Living

BARBARA GROGG

Planning and preparing to leave for an international mission is a monumental task. Often overlooked is the need to adequately protect each mission team member against diseases that are unfamiliar to those living in developed countries. The effective missionary should be proactive, prepared and protected when it comes to personal health as well as the health of others around you. By staying healthy, you can be effective and do not become a burden to your teammates or cause a diversion from the ministry to which you were called.

Many of us fail to realize that we are placing ourselves into a category of "risky behavior." By being in close contact with the indigenous people and less-than-optimum living conditions, we may be exposing ourselves to diseases that have been eradicated in our homeland for years. To help ensure you are medically ready to embark on your mission, visit a travel medicine clinic or your healthcare provider a minimum of two months, but preferably six months, prior to your departure to allow adequate time for immunizations and ample time to budget for necessary vaccines.

Immunizations

Immunizations should form the basis for immunity to diseases that may be encountered. While costs are a consideration, the economic consequence of the disease far exceeds the initial expense of the vaccine. The following are recommended immunizations by the World Health Organization (WHO) and the national in Atlanta:

For information about specific countries, go to the Centers for Disease Control (CDC) travel website (www.cdc.gov/travel), which provides excellent, up-to-date information on a variety of topics, including current disease outbreaks by specific country. For subsets of travelers such as pregnant women, lactating mothers, those with comprised immune systems, children and infants, persons with chronic diseases or people with disabilities, the CDC website offers valuable educational materials.

Mosquitoes

Another important aspect of healthy living in many parts of the world involves encounters with mosquitoes. These pesky insects are a vector agent that carries disease-causing viruses and parasites from person to person. According to the CDC, mosquitoes are estimated to transmit disease to more than five hundred million people annually in Asia, Africa, South and Central America, and Mexico, with millions of resulting deaths.

The best approach to dealing with mosquitoes as well as other insects, thus avoiding diseases such as malaria, yellow fever, dengue fever, filariasis and Japanese encephalitis, just to name a few, is to avoid being bitten. That is easier said than done. However, with proper malaria prevention through the use of medications prescribed by your healthcare provider based on your medical history and the exact location you will be living and working, in addition to personal protective measures, that risk will be significantly minimized. Unfortunately there are many misconceptions and much misinformation about the use of antimalarial medications. Again, the CDC website has detailed information in easy-to-understand terminology about malaria as well as other mosquito-borne illnesses, prophylaxis medications and treatment of the diseases.

Information is power in travel medicine. Visit <www.mdtravelhealth.com> (complete travel health information) and <www.travmed.com> (travel healthcare supplies).

Barbara Grogg is a family nurse practitioner at Oklahoma State University in Tulsa. She is certified in Travel Health and has visited more than 125 countries, including many medical missions.

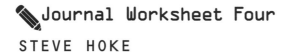# Journal Worksheet Four

STEVE HOKE

Where Are You Now?

Does your present curriculum and/or your past educational experience give you an adequate basic education, including some Bible and some social science? If it does, explain how.

If it doesn't, map out the courses or type of learning experiences that you need.

How strong is your grasp of the Bible, its structure, its message, its origins and its content?

Describe what additional preparation in Bible, theology and missions you think it would be wise to gain now.

How and when will you investigate the intensive summer courses or distance-learning options available?

What Do You Need to Do Next?

If your present education is not adequate, what steps do you need to take to supplement it or to switch to a more beneficial program?

What extension or distance-learning courses or summer intensive courses will you explore? Which schools or agencies should you contact? (See appendix 1.)

How can you arrange this new course of study? What help will you need? From whom?

What Will the Future Look Like?

If you complete the program(s) you're proposing, how will this prepare you to move ahead with advanced training at home or overseas?

How well prepared will you be to think about the world as its social and economic makeup continue to change?

World-class cities

The nobility of Africa's senior women

Phase Two

GETTING THERE

FIVE

Church and Agency
Connecting and Courting

STEVE HOKE AND BILL TAYLOR

The next critical step to consider is intensely relational. There is no formula, no preset template, no one-solution-fits-all flow chart for how to do it. And it is at this point that many prospective candidates get sidetracked or detoured. In fact, it is so personal and individualized that it is very similar to connecting with someone, liking them and starting the courting process. And it should get better and better!

The critical next question is, what is the best way to make your transition into living and ministering in another culture? Can you do it alone, or should you join up with others? Will you serve with a specific mission agency, church or denomination? The apostle Paul asked, "How can they preach unless they are sent?" (Rom 10:15). Experience shows that those who are sent within the framework of a mission agency or church denomination are most likely to be effective, long-term missionaries. The wisest sending churches are developing strategic alliances with established field-based teams or agencies.

Our strong bias is that it's best to join a team. Follow through on what you learned about body life—move out as a team, with a team, with an organization that is committed to your long-term success.

Begin with input from your home church. By now you should have a good feel for its missions heart and vision. Is its vision compatible with yours? If your church is a member of a denomination, get information about your denomination's mission first. If yours is an independent or nondenominational church, look at the mission agencies they currently support or with whom they have an existing relationship. You want to move as organically and relationally as you can. Only when there is no previous relationships will you need to start from ground zero.

Continue with the mission agency you know best. What agency or agencies do your family, missions committee and pastor recommend that you consider? Do they have a relationship with one or several agencies? What do you know about the church's missionary-sending process? Check out the organization's theology, model of ministry, vision, leadership style and ethos. Are their values a natural fit with yours?

This is so important in selecting a team. Every organization has a personality or "ethos"—an organizational culture that has grown up around how they live, work and minister together. Some are very aggressively evangelistic and replicate a particular model of ministry everywhere they go. Others move forward on relational bridges they build one at a time. Others are quite bureaucratic and have a very particular way of doing ministry. Some are conservative and cautious; others are innovative and free-flowing. Some are looking for people with particular gifts that fit their needs for church planting in Uzbekistan, for example; others empower you to do what God is calling *you* to be and do.

Like shopping for a pair of shoes or a jacket, you are looking for "fit." Is this item the right color, style and fit with your values and who you are? Does it look good and do you feel comfortable in it? Is it what you are looking for? In selecting a mission agency, you need to ask the same questions. Would you fit in their ethos—their organizational culture and style of life and ministry? If so, this is a natural place to start. If not, it's wise to continue to explore until you find at least a few other agencies with whom you find compatibility on the major issues.

Take a wider look around. There are thousands of strong churches and almost nine hundred North American agencies with a wide span of crosscultural ministry interests. They range in size from those with thousands of missionaries to those with just a handful. Some minister all over the world. Others work only in one country. Many have broad, holistic ministries—from relief and development to church planting to theological education. Others have a specific ministry, such as literature distribution, church planting, orphanages or leader development. Many are interdenominational; they have on their staff men and women from many different denominations.

Some agencies are deeply involved in church planting, while others may consider it their major role to serve the existing church. Some target specific peoples, such as Muslims or Native American peoples. Some focus on the vast "unevangelized" world or specific unreached people groups. Others have broader geographic involvement.

Check out the key source of agency information: the most recent edition of *The Mission Handbook 2007-2009: U.S. and Canadian Protestant Ministries Overseas.*[1] This triennial publication catalogs the more than eight hundred agencies in North America and describes their doctrinal emphasis, focus of ministry, size and the types of missionaries they look for. Agencies are listed by countries and type of ministry.

Call, e-mail or write to agencies. Direct your inquiries to the candidate coordinator or director of mobilization. Someone in each agency will be glad to explain its distinctive procedures, from prerequisites to application to appointment. The important thing is that you contact several agencies as soon as you have a handle on some of the questions to ask.

Local church and regional mission conferences are a fantastic opportunity to meet personally with mission agency representatives. The Urbana student missions convention sponsored by InterVarsity Christian Fellowship, in particular, is a prime opportunity to meet representatives from dozens of agencies involved in the full range of ministry, from evangelism and church planting to missions aviation, medical ministry and microenterprise development. This convention is held every three years in St. Louis. (For more information, go to <www.urbana.org>.)

The initiative lies with *you*. Remember, God wants to be in a growing relationship with you. He has a distinctive purpose for your life and a passion for you to pursue based on your unique gifting and calling. Your communion with him invites his guidance to the pathway he has prepared for you and wants you to take. That place is worth seeking in faith. Don't let anyone tell you that investigating or asking hard questions is "unspiritual." Scripture encourages the right kind of seeking, and that includes investigating ministry roles and the gifts necessary to fill them (see 1 Cor 12:31; 1 Tim 3:1).

---

[1]Evangelism and Mission Information Service, 2007; go to <www.missionhandbook.com> for more information.

How to Choose a Sending Church or Agency
A Letter to Raquel and David

BILL TAYLOR

Dear Raquel and David,

Here I am again, attempting to do a better job of answering the great question you lobbed at me during the missions conference. You are right in wanting to be careful when you consider which mission "team" you'll join. From the start, let's clarify some really crucial items.

Who sends the missionary? There's no question in my mind that ultimately you want to be sent out by your local church. Too many missionaries feel that their agency sends them out. They want their church to bless and support in prayer and finances, but not truly to send them, with all the responsibility this entails. Bad mistake! You can thank God you're in a church with a heart for its city as well as for the world and with a pastoral team that shares those powerful core values.

As we discussed the other night, there are two major ways of getting to and staying on the field long-term. One is for your church alone to send you as well as attempt to provide the critical field components: shepherding, strategizing, supervising and support system. Few churches can really do all these things well.

I'm encouraged that your church has chosen the second option: to enter into a covenant relationship with an experienced mission agency that will work with you and the church to provide these field elements. You shouldn't leave home without having that settled! Remember that joining a mission agency is similar to marriage (though it's not always for life). It's a serious, long-term, mutual commitment with heavy implications. Joining the right "ministry family" means time spent "courting," getting to know each other, evaluating the fit, knowing that God

is guiding both parties into this relationship. It's crucial that you be totally united on this. Yet remember, no perfect ministry exists.

Now, what specific items should you look for in mission agencies? Here are some guidelines to point you along the path.

What are their core spiritual commitments? Each church or agency will have a written affirmation of its beliefs. Many times this is called a doctrinal statement. Sometimes it may be less formal, as in a listing of core beliefs. Strong missiology is rooted in biblical theology. You'll want to work with a team that shares your foundational belief system, so check out their core beliefs in their doctrinal statement. Is the statement general (and probably fairly short) or detailed and specific? Some people feel comfortable in organizations that are very specific about what they believe; others prefer to work where there is broad latitude based on general evangelical orthodoxy.

Be sure you agree with your agency on some of the more challenging issues. For example, if you prefer a charismatic expression of theology, ministry and worship, but the agency you're considering doesn't endorse that option, then move on. It will be a mismatch from the start.

What's its history? How did it get started? How has it changed? How has it adapted to meet the challenges of the new millennium? Who have been its key leaders? Are any of them still around and available to talk with you? When you get a sense of team history, you can understand where the organization is and where it will probably go tomorrow. Get comfortable with this history. The group's history will reveal its flexibility and adaptability; you want to know that.

How does the church or agency articulate its purpose, goals and objectives? This information will be derived from the group's history, but you should also be able to find some clear statements that indicate where it's heading.

Consult others "in the know" to make sure these core values really work in practice. You'll want to work with a team whose goals you respect and share.

To determine whether the group works strategically, ask for its short-range and a long-range plan. How do they evaluate their progress? Learn about their decision-making process. Is it centralized, democratic, personalized, home or field-based, elected or what? What role does the national church have in evaluating the effectiveness of the mission? Does it have personnel from a diversity of cultures and nations? If not, is it moving toward becoming more multicultural? You may also want to investigate what kind of team ministry they encourage and what kind of participation they invite from its workers. How sensitive are the leaders to new ideas? How direct and open are they in resolving conflict? These few questions are critical for you to discern their ethos and style.

To what types of ministry are they particularly committed? Do they have a strong and holistic view of the Great Commission? Is their ministry based on kingdom values? Do they say they serve the church—and do they really do so? Are they exclusively "into" unreached peoples in the 10/40 Window (an area in the world that contains the largest number of non-Christians in the world, extending from ten degrees to forty degrees north of the equator—from North Africa to China), or do they have a broader perspective of global need? Will they place you in a ministry that provides a good "gift match," or do they want you to be willing to do anything? Are they ready to empower you in your calling, or do they want you to apprentice

for too long to serve their own organizational needs?

Again, the "right" answers to these questions will depend on the direction and priorities God has given you. Make sure you really can work with the ministry perspective of your potential mission agency. If you want to plant churches, but the organization you join only does evangelism and disciple-making, you will have to change.

A subset of this question deals with geography. Raquel and David, you two have expressed a desire to plant churches among less-reached peoples, so be sure the agency you choose is one that works in those contexts. Some of us seem called to a specific country or a particular ministry. We have to search for the right fit, and everything doesn't always come together. But we can try.

What kind of care do they provide, both prior to departure and on the field? Be leery of the agency that says something like, "Well, to be honest, our missionaries really don't need much pastoral care. They're all pretty strong, committed Christian leaders." You want to be sure that the organization has made a commitment to develop and nurture their people. Do they have a member care or staff development team to do this, or is that the sole responsibility of one person? Related to this is the organization's concept of the family and view of the education of children. How flexible are they in terms of gender leadership and roles for the wife? How comfortable are you with the schooling options they offer or allow for your kids?

How do they handle finances and support raising? Do they require you to raise all or part of your support? How will they help you in this? Do they have a strong training and coaching process to help you reach full funding in a reasonable amount of time? What is their administrative cost, and how is it raised? Will they allow or expect you to provide partial support for yourself on the field—through teaching or a business venture, for instance? What's their housing policy? Can you own your own home "at your own risk"? Are they a reputable organization, with open accounting and financial management? Can you respect the lifestyle of their missionaries and home staff and their leaders?

What is their relationship to your church as well as to the national church? How much are they willing to work with your church leadership as they put together the ministry package for you? Obviously, if you plant the gospel among a totally unreached people group, you hope to see the first national church. But in most countries, there already exists some gathering of national believers. How has the agency you're considering transferred responsibility and authority to the national churches in the past? Do they have an "exit plan" for how to raise up churches, turn them over and move on? What role do these churches have in the placement and supervision of expatriate missionaries?

What can you discern about the missionaries' lifestyles and unwritten rules? This is a tough one to discover, but it's really important. A friend of mind says you have to "turn on your spiritual radar system" to find this out. Ask wives and missionary children how they feel about the organization and why. Investigate the lifestyles of single missionaries. How sensitive is the agency to the issues, needs and concerns of singles, especially single women, as well as to those of married couples and families? Does your sending group have a process of discipline and restoration in the context of major personal or personnel problems?

Ask the organization's leaders what kind of expectations they have for their missionaries. Does the agency or individual offer any kind of job or role description? Who commits to fulfilling it? What types of relationships, accountability and reporting formats does the agency encourage, require or provide? What mutual commitments are made regarding furloughs? How does the agency encourage leader development and lifelong learning? How proactive are they in encouraging lifelong development through study leaves or sabbaticals?

What's their prefield orientation and language-learning policy? If they want you there only for one week of orientation, move on. One week is not enough for someone who's heading into substantive crosscultural work for a term of years. And be wary of churches or agencies that allow you to make your own decisions on language study. Basic language study of Spanish or French may take one year, but Russian, Chinese or Arabic will always take at least two. You may have to learn *two* new languages. Discern how committed they are to ongoing culture and language learning as well. You don't want your learning to stop after your first year.

Finally, remember that there are no perfect organizations. Be realistic. Beware of rapid decisions and "love affairs" with a particular team. The post-honeymoon blues can be fierce! And be sure that your church leaders participate in the final selection of your sending agency.

Take the time to get to know organizations. Find out about them and let them find out about you. It's a mutual relationship; the agencies ultimately want God's best for you.

As I reread this long letter, I hope it's not overkill. Relax, friends! Work with God in this process. And don't forget that we—your family, friends and church—are on your side.

With respect and love,
Bill

🌐 Global Perspectives

PETER MAIDEN
International Director of Operation Mobilization

Role of the Missionary

We still need missionaries from all over the world, including the Global North for pioneer, evangelistic, church-planting ministry in areas of the world where the church is not yet planted. We also need missionaries from the Global North with experience and professional qualifications to support the emerging church and emerging mission movements in the Global South. Although some of the history of church and mission in the West has been far from perfect, there is surely still a bank of history and experience that can benefit the younger church and mission movements.

Attracting the Next Generations

It's very significant that pioneer and creative church planting is still attracting the attention of the next generation, particularly in the harder places in the world. A commitment to integrated mission is also important. We also find special interest at the present time in sports ministry, arts ministry, media, Internet evangelism and so on.

Recommended Prefield Training

I believe that basic Bible and missiological instruction is still crucial. There must also be preliminary training in crosscultural understanding, interpersonal relationships and the understanding of the need for and practice of collaboration and partnership.

What the Sending Church or Agency Wants to Know About You

BILL TAYLOR

In a sense this list of key items is the flip side of my letter to Raquel and David as they consider their sending team. What does the sending team want to know about each prospective worker, as individuals and, if married, as a couple?

First, they want to hear your story. How has the triune sending God worked in your life over the years, especially in relation to your desire to engage in significant, long-term, crosscultural service. As you prepare this narrative—which you will surely give in a variety of settings—think through the components that have shaped you in life: family, personality, culture, language, nationality, studies, spiritual pilgrimage, friends, key events, marriage (if that's the case), ministry and the nudging of the Spirit toward mission.

Second, they want to discern issues related to your spiritual formation, personal maturity and overall health—physical, emotional, social, spiritual. They want to hear how the Spirit has brought about transformational discipleship in your life. Be honest with them. They may probe into some areas of your past to see if there are substantive unresolved personal, moral or family conflicts, and how you handled them. If there is serious brokenness or gender confusion or deep sin, this needs to be expressed, as well as the path to healing through which you have walked or are walking. If necessary, speak confidentially with the key leader on some of the more sensitive issues. Not everybody in leadership needs to know everything.

They also want to be assured that you have a clear sense that God is leading you into cross-cultural mission. In the case of a married couple, both have to speak to these issues. I'm a bit leery of using the language of "missionary call," but this is my personal opinion.

Third, they want to get a sense of your experience in life and ministry, what you have done, when and where. They will listen as you speak of the tough lessons you have learned and how you have persevered with your own issues, relationships, Christ and his people. They want to see how you have proven yourselves in evangelism, discipleship, leadership development and the core task you see yourself doing in the future. Here is where your experiences in short-term missions will have strengthened you. On the other side of the coin, regardless of your future assignment (whether church planting, national development, leadership training, business as mission) you need to establish that you can do your job in your mother culture first.

Fourth, they want to know about your local church relationship and involvement, knowing that it is in that primary context that your gifts and calling are discovered, affirmed and matured. Or perhaps God used a campus ministry to do the same during that special study season of life, but it's the church God will use on the lifelong journey of faith.

Fifth, they will want to know your study track record, both in formal schooling (courses, degrees, technical certifications and other key training) and nonformal equipping. I think it's right for them to seek people who have some solid biblical and missions study under their belt, so don't skimp on this one. They will want to know what you have done in the secular marketplace or prior ministry. They will want to know what kind of debts—study and other—you have that will need to be paid off. If you have heavy debts, don't be surprised if they recommend that you work like crazy to pay them off and to stay connected with them during this season. There's nothing like the freedom of living debt-free.

Sixth, they want an honest report on your personal story, your life experience, your study, your work record. This will include thoughtful references that come primarily from your spiritual leaders and work colleagues. Be dead honest with yourself in this regard. "Stuff happens," and if you leave your home, church and mother culture with deep unresolved junk, it will emerge later in life and bite you.

Finally, they may probe your understanding of working in accountable relationships and under authority. This is a delicate issue for some people, whether mission leaders or younger future missionaries. Be sure you find leaders who love and understand the qualities of the younger and older generations. But are you teachable? Do you have a sacrificial spirit? Are you willing to serve under national leaders, and if you are a man, are you willing to serve under women in leadership?

Hey, this is your story, and these church and mission leaders are friends who want to hear you out. You are part of that great epic Story of the God of mission. He ultimately is the one who invites into new life, into mission, into transformational discipleship in the vast arenas of global crosscultural ministry.

It's your journey and your pilgrimage, and our great God is with you.

Calling for the Return of the Long-Term Servant
BILL TAYLOR

It was an unforgettable experience, and I knew that my son, David, and I were witnessing a piece of history, as well as peering into the future that night in Kijabe, Kenya.

After participating in the Third International Conference on Missionary Kids (we're both MKs), we were on our way to visit the Missionary Training College, which trains Africans for crosscultural service, in Eldoret, Kenya. En route we stayed overnight with friends at Rift Valley Academy, a large mission complex in Kijabe. We providentially sat in as observers of the fellowship conference that was being held there for East Africa AIM (Africa Inland Mission) missionaries.

A Legacy of Longevity and a Glimpse into the Future?

That night AIM celebrated with gratitude the decades of service of six retiring veteran missionary couples. They shared gripping stories—of their first trek to Africa, of the 1952–1960 Mau Mau Rebellion years, of what it meant to be pioneer missionaries, of the changes experienced in their lifetimes. Now they faced the uncertainty of retirement in a far-off land, the country that had issued their passports—"home."

What astonished me was the service longevity of these men and women. It averaged forty-five years per person. Among the twelve of them, they held 540 cumulative years of service, which translates into 6,480 months, 28,080 weeks, 197,100 days. What a legacy! It was an honor for us to observe these veterans and think of that glorious day in the throne room of the Lamb when they will celebrate with African believers from different tribes, languages and political nations.

That same night the AIM multinational missionary force welcomed twenty-five single, short-term missionaries from the United Kingdom who were dedicating two years to the Bible in Kenyan schools. They were young, bright, committed, crosscultural servants, dressed in British funky styles, who would minister in English (not the mother tongue of their pupils), because their time was limited.

Were we peering into the future? Was the day of the veteran, the "lifer," the really long-term missionary over? Why have the scales tipped from the past decades, when the overwhelming number of missionaries were "career workers"? A number of reasons come to mind:

- God does different things at different times.
- Our society has changed.
- Different needs have emerged, and there are others ways of doing mission.
- The amazing Global South (Majority World)

missionary movement has exploded on the scene.

- Today's missionaries come from all over the world.

- Our culture reflects a new mentality of lower institutional commitment and higher mobility—hence a "shopping mall" mindset that wants it now but also wants the freedom to change its mind tomorrow.

A Continuing Need

So do we really need more long-term missionaries? Couldn't we send out hundreds of thousands of short-termers to complete the task of world evangelization? Wouldn't we get a better investment return on our missionary dollar if we supported fewer Western missionaries and switched our support to countless "native" missionaries? What if we invested more in media and the Internet to get the job done?

No! It would be neither biblical nor right to phase out longer-term workers, and some of my younger friends are encouraging me to reintroduce the term *career*. What's more, as Christian stewards, we reject the cost-effectiveness mentality of getting more missionary "bang for your buck." My wife and I support, personally and financially, short-term missionaries. The Holy Spirit is using them in marvelous, unique ways, particularly as they work in partnership with established churches or veteran missionaries or qualified national leaders. I respect them for their commitment, knowledge, skills and servant spirit.

But there are some things that can be done only by the long-term missionary. That's why we still need many more "lifers."

What are some distinctives of longer-term service?

- Short-termers can love the national people, but it takes the patient work of the long-term servant to learn the people's "heart language" with excellence. Speaking the

language in which the people think, dream, sing, argue and love opens the door to their hearts and souls in an irreplaceable way. The story of Jesus then flows over a bridge of integrity-built relationships.

- Short-termers can minister effectively during their limited stay, but it's the long-term servant who, over time, builds relationships of confidence with the people, understands their culture and sensitively contextualizes the gospel within that vibrant reality.

- Short-termers may make an impact, but the one who stays longer is able to invest over the years in lasting discipleship and leader development; that's a legacy. He or she will witness the rise and expansion of churches, the emergence and training of new leaders and then the transfer of responsibility and authority.

- Short-termers are missionaries also; but it is the long-term missionary who can invest in the newer generation of the Global South missionary force. The tested veterans will serve alongside and grow together with their new partners.

- Married short-termers experience brief or partial family immersion in culture and ministry. The long-term family, by contrast, experiences the joy of birthing and raising their family in another culture, with all its positives and negatives.

- Short-termers can faithfully distribute copies of the Word of God, but it takes a long-haul servant to translate the Scriptures and prepare them for publication and distribution. It often takes a lifetime to facilitate appropriate interpretation and contextualization of God's Word into the heart language.

How will these least-reached people groups hear the gospel in their own language and within the context of their own cultural reality? Through obedient servants, from cultures close and far from them.

Yes, short-termers do invest a brief segment of their lives—perhaps showing the *Jesus* film or sharing their testimonies or constructing building or doing street drama or medical care or gathering research or assisting long-term workers in scores of other creative ways. And yet others will invest short but significant segments as consultants, as investors, as encouragers. But worshiping communities of Jesus will be established among unreached peoples primarily by longer-term servants willing to invest at least ten to twenty years of their lives—perhaps even to give their lives—in order to contribute to the goal of every person hearing and understanding the gospel of Christ.

The Investment and Its Returns

When Steve and I were working on the first edition of this book (then called *Send Me!*), my friend Doug dropped by our house, and we had a rich time together. He had gone out single as a worker in Central Europe. But God had later led him to a young woman who shared the same passion and who herself had served in Romania. Married and with two children, together they have invested their lives long-term in Poland. Doug's objective was to see new churches established, to see leaders trained in the context of their ministry as well as in the emerging evangelical seminary in Poland. And he is seeing it, now playing a role as senior shepherd of shepherds, as strategist, as field leader for his agency.

Back then though, Doug jolted me with the statement "You know, Bill, I didn't go to Eastern Europe to save souls; I went to know God better. And that is what has happened to me through the long and hard work of learning the language, studying the culture and understanding the people of Poland. I know God better."

That's similar to the strong words another friend of mine says: "The purpose of missions is not to fulfill the Great Commission. Rather, it is to increase the number of people on earth who worship the one true and living God with reverence and awe, giving him the glory he deserves."

Sure, we can all say something similar. But there's really nothing like experiencing this goal and outcome over the course of years, decades, a lifetime of service.

Is there a special payoff, a compensation for longer-term missionary service? Let me answer it indirectly in the words of another colleague of mine: "We have a job that's extremely dangerous and extremely costly, with little compensation, except the satisfaction of obeying Christ among the people of the world in a distant and strange country."

As the church in a given area is born and grows and learns to reproduce itself, the long-term missionary has the satisfaction of watching the whole process, analogous to observing a baby born into your family, then witnessing the growth and development of that child into its own reproductive maturity. These, then, are some of the benefits of the longer-term missionary.

That's something Yvonne and I have discovered, even twenty-four years after we left Latin America. That investment in our earlier years of ministry continues to give long-term interest. Those lives changed so many years ago are now investing in second and third generations. And the payout just continues, to our astonishment. Recently, when Yvonne and I were back in Guatemala, some women came up and said to her, "Yvonne, it was your commitment to family that shaped us. Thank you." Some of my former students are now presidents and deans of theological schools all over Latin America. The church we helped establish is still there, struggling to renew but engaging its own future.

My mom and dad were lifers who went to Costa Rica in 1938. Well, back then there were no other viable categories. After their "retirement" from field service in Spain, they served crossculturally as Hispanic church planters back in the United States into their mid-eighties.

My wife and I served seventeen years as servants in and to Latin America. Our three children were born there, studied in a trilingual school (German, Spanish, English), and together we witnessed the book of Acts alive in the Guatemalan church. We were part of church history in Latin America. That church first met us in 1974 as North Americans, but when we left Latin America, they sent us out as part of their own missionary force, and to this day they pray for us.

Did we have tough times and wonder what was happening to us? Of course! But we hung in for a longer haul. We wouldn't trade our experience, though we might change a number of situations and relationships. But overall, the benefits of long-term missionary service were fulfilled.

Is the long-term (career) missionary a vanishing species in our North American society? Some might suggest so, but I'd cry out, "No!" I invite thousands of select short-termers to transition their rich experience into longer-term crosscultural service.

You may feel that life is just too indefinite or that global socioeconomic trends are too discouraging, and you just can't plan that far in advance. Well, you are right there; nobody knows the future. But if you can plan for short-term service in an uncertain world, that experience could equips you to aim for a long-term ministry. You might even go for forty-five years!

Commit for the long term in your own transformation discipleship to the living God. Allow him to direct you to a life of crosscultural ministry that, while deepening your reliance on him and your relationship with him, brings many more people into the diverse coalition of white-hot worshipers surrounding the Lamb on the throne.

Some Questions to Mull Over

If you want to be a longer-term missionary, what elements should you keep in mind? Here's a list:

- What are your deepest motives for desiring missionary service?

- In what ways have you already been tested spiritually in your life?

- What aspects of the global mission task seem to require longer-term missionaries?

- What does your interest and gift inventory report? What do you enjoy doing, and what are you naturally skilled at doing?

- What kinds of specific education and training do you need in order to channel your interests and sharpen your skills and gifts? How long might this take?

- What kinds of short-term ministries have you been involved in? How did they shape your life and thinking?

- In what ways is your church committed to these same passions? How can you be an integral part of the life of your church as you follow in obedience your path to the nations of the world?

 My Journey

HARRY HOFFMAN
Youth With A Mission, Somewhere in Asia

I was a German eighteen-year-old when I started searching for the sense of life, trying to fill the big hole in my heart with years of sex, drugs and rock 'n' roll. Nothing major though, but still, as a musician I was part of this culture.

My interest in other countries was awakened by a friend, so I traveled to India, Thailand and Nepal to find truth and peace there. A former girlfriend of mine became a Christian, and when I was twenty-two years old, at a very low point in my life, I gave her a call, asking for the address of a good church. When I entered the youth group during worship time, I immediately felt at home: "I've arrived! My search is over!" A very strong emotion of peace filled my heart and my body, a feeling that I has been looking for.

I had quit studying electronics at university and moved to Berlin to pursue Chinese Studies, language, country and culture, an interest that began during my India travels. At twenty-eight, I graduated with an M.A. in Chinese Studies and married my wife, whose calling for China began when she was thirteen years old. We had two children by then, and we sensed the deep longing to serve God in China through a series of events. One was a clear perception of God call-ing us to do orphanage work in China. Another one was God touching my wife's heart to actu-ally be ready to move overseas. In 1996 we left Germany and moved to China.

Now, thirteen years later, we find that life has been extremely hard. We had no clue what we had gotten ourselves into. We thought we were strong and that we had what it takes to do this. We didn't. We thought we had a God who makes us strong—but we are wounded, traumatized, disappointed, sad and now very much reality-based and down-to-earth.

These thirteen years have been costly. We are still standing though, still serving as best we can, still relating to a God who gives us peace, but whom we don't really understand. I'm still trying to make a difference for the voiceless in our society.

On the Cusp of Your Departure
A Letter to Anne and Jay
BILL TAYLOR

Dear Anne and Jay,

We are proud of you and are praying for you because we believe in you and in the global cause of Jesus Christ. We write to you on the cusp of your departure for a challenging future in a very tough region of the world, with its rich history and many cultures, and its need of ho-listic transformation—spiritual, moral, cultural and in health and education infrastructures. You have been charged with telling those sto-ries through video, and God has gifted you for these assignments. It was great having you guys here in our home, where we could talk about some of the key issues of your future. Allow us to summarize some of our conversa-tion and to extend a challenge to you before you leave.

As Yvonne and I have been mulling over who you are and where you are going, and re-flecting on our agenda items of that evening, here are some questions and recommenda-tions. We affirm your long-term commitments to Christ and mission in Africa. We want you to be "keepers," having to return home only if the circumstances and causes are totally clear. We don't want you to be painful attrition statistics.

Like we said last week, the three prime causes for attrition (early or unexpected return from field service) cluster around three sets of issues:

1. spirituality, spiritual formation, spiritual warfare; that is, weakness or inadequacy in these areas

2. relationality, working in community, on teams, with others; that is, inability to work well with or under others

3. knowledge that informs and shapes your understanding and gives you the right kind of information; that is, inadequate prefield preparation and training for the task at hand

Therefore, we encourage you to develop a core library of four to five key books in these three areas. I know you have both been reading a number of good resources, and this is encouraging. So give this some thought, talk between yourselves and some others you respect. Then send us your list of the books you want to read and want to take with you to Africa, so we can make some other recommendations.

We opened our hearts to you so that you both know that in forty-plus years of crosscultural work, we have worked hard to stay alive, grow and learn. We have been exposed to people, literature, circumstances, temptations and other testing that stretched us beyond our capacity.

A word of encouragement from another story: Michelle and Stanford have had their hearts set on mission for a long time, much longer than most. They met during a two-year stint teaching English in Hungary; they waited to get married until they were in community and under strong premarital counseling; and they were part of healthy churches; they scrimped financially during his medical studies, with Michelle working full time, even as the children started arriving.

They also had a series of well-planned short-term trips. He had been to at least three Urbana mission conventions and she perhaps two. As you guys did, they profited greatly from the Perspectives course; they read like crazy; they put themselves under the mentorship of two wise mission veterans; they grappled with the strongholds of both family lines; they got vitally involved in a strong, mission-minded church; they investigated places where Stanford's medical training would fit. They applied to a small but growing mission agency and have gone through their own pre-field training.

Michelle and Stanford will go to Africa on a two-family team, and their colleagues are equally prepared for ministry. Between them they have seven children! They are on the cusp of their departure to another challenging place in Africa to do missionary medicine. And we are proud of them, grateful to God for the privilege of having walked with them for almost twelve years. They, and you guys, are the future of global mission from the Global North.

Finally, when is your last Sunday at your sending church? I would love to drive up and just be present. Also, is there any chance you can come down for a last day to be with us before you leave? We can talk, pray, laugh, weep and enjoy each other's presence, even as we release you to the sending God.

Jay and Anne, our dear younger friends and fellow servants, the blessing of the High Three be upon you.

Yvonne and Bill

Raising the Standard for Missionary Care

NEAL PIROLO

The days of the missionary as a lone ranger or superstar are over. They never should have been. Mission agencies, churches and even missionaries now agree that the mission process requires a well-trained and coordinated team of diverse skills. Mission is a team effort.

William Taylor's book *Too Valuable to Lose* (William Carey Library, 1997) emphasizes this point. In trying to identify the cause(s) of missionary attrition, 453 mission agencies from 14 sending countries were asked why their missionaries were leaving the field. The research found that 29 percent quit for "reasonable" reasons: a spouse died on the field, a child became chronically ill and so on. But this left a shocking 71 percent who left for what they called "preventable" reasons.

Those reasons were grouped in three very major categories:

1. Many lacked clear direction from God to go. In other words, they had gone to the field when missionary work was clearly not for them.

2. Many lacked sufficient or proper prefield training.

3. Many lacked sufficient ongoing care and nurture. It is to this third pressing issue that these very practical suggestions are directed—to raise the standard for missionary care.

Confirming the Call Before They Go

Last Sunday I listened to a twelve-year-old-girl read a Scripture—actually she started to read it, but stumbled over the words. And never finished it. It was her "confirmation" that she was supposed to go to an African nation to participate in an evangelistic crusade.

"It will cost three thousand dollars. Can you help me?" she asked the congregation. Until this moment, no one except her parents had heard of her knowledge of "God's will" for her. I am not saying it is not his will, but I do ask, "Where was her support team that spent time in fasting and prayer to hear from the Holy Spirit and discern the will of God for her young life?"

The pattern for Barnabas and Paul is clear in Acts 13. The Holy Spirit directed, "Set apart for me . . . " (Acts 13:2). If Barnabas and Saul, leaders in the Antioch church, returned from Jerusalem filled with excitement about the regions beyond and submitted themselves to the church leaders for the confirmation of their call, why do some believe that is not necessary today? And yet, the countries of the world are strewn with people (I dare not call them missionaries; the very word means "sent ones") whose call was never confirmed, but claimed. Again, I cannot say that they did not hear from God. But it is a valuable safety net to have a team of people who have committed themselves to the task of discerning and confirming the call along with the one sensing the call.

It was this confirmation that served as an encouragement to a missionary who was concerned with his youthfulness once he got out there. Timothy received two letters of encouragement from his supporting mentor, Paul. "Don't let any one look down on you because you are young," wrote Paul to his mentee, timid Timothy (1 Tim 4:12). "Fan into flame the gift of God, which is in you through the laying on of my hands [that is, when we commissioned you]," Paul later coached (2 Tim 1:6). There it is! A group of committed and mature people—a team—had been involved in sending young Timothy to the region of Ephesus.

Prefield Training

"Oh, God called me. I don't need any training. He will just tell me what to do." I cannot count how many times I have heard those words spoken to me by zealous young (and not so young) missionary hopefuls. A seasoned missionary heard that a young, attractive lady from his church was planning to go to West Africa. Her youth pastor had said, "God called you? Then go! He will lead you." Frank, the missionary, let me know that he had encouraged her on a number of occasions to call me about training.

Time went by. Finally she called. I thought, "Great! She can attend our next ACTS 29 Training Course in Tijuana." My thoughts were interrupted by her reason for calling. "Yes, Frank encouraged me to call you. I leave tomorrow. But I do have one question: 'When I get there, do I call the American embassy to pick me up at the airport?'"

A bit extreme? Yes, but the fields of the world are strewn with people who lack the skills of living and ministering in a second culture. Where was her team, beginning with a knowledgeable youth pastor, guiding her through the mine fields of preparation? For it is spiritual warfare in the most intense battle of all time in which new missionaries are preparing to engage.

The Rest of the Team

In delineating the mission process, Paul spoke of the need for missionaries with the question "How can they hear without someone preaching to them?" (Rom 10:14). Clear. Simple. Easy to understand.

And how we yearn for more to respond to his call to go. However, Paul did not stop with that question. He asked one more: "And how shall he preach unless he is sent?" Why has this question been ignored for so long? In the gapless logic of Paul, by putting this question last he was giving it the greatest emphasis. Yet, today, the "rest of the team"—those who serve as senders—are, at best, given only an afterthought. It is vital that we raise the standard of missionary care. Missionaries are too valuable to lose.

By the time a missionary's call has been confirmed, all six areas of care that Paul, the apostle, said he needed should be in place and "up and running." Experience has shown that each element is as vital for missionaries today as it was for Paul two thousand years ago. Those who have taken the time and energy to build a strong personal support team will echo the truth of Scripture: "And how can we preach [how can we be effective] unless we are sent?"

Moral Support

Moral support comes easily from those with the gift of encouragement. Solomon said, "A word spoken at an appropriate time is like golden apples in a silver bowl" (Prov 25:11). There are some people who can see and help others to see the silver lining through the blackest of clouds. They are the ones who see the glass half full instead of half empty. The ones who see things more and more from God's perspective and are willing to voice their encouragement for the risky exploits of those ministering in a second culture. The ones who recognize their role is to speak courage and holy boldness into the lives of crosscultural workers who often minister far from their support team.

Logistics Support

Practical logistics support is needed. By this time, the missionary should be working toward being unencumbered of all the details of daily living, that he or she may "please [the] commanding officer" (2 Tim 2:4). What to sell? What to give away? What to store? Where to store it? Who will check in on Grandma? Who will be responsible for . . . everything?

These are the details for a group of people with organizational skills who will become a part of the missionary's team. Promptness of action, concern for details and sound business practices are just three of the characteristics needed for these support team members.

Prayer Support

Prayer support is of first importance. In fact, it stands alone and above all other considerations in the care of missionaries. It is not the "God bless all the missionaries" generic prayer. Rather, it is the effectual, fervent intercessory prayer of righteous people (see Jas 5:16). A powerful intercession team requires people who make the commitment: "Ever since I first heard about you, I have not ceased to pray for you" (Col 1:3-4); people who know how to "tell God the details of their [missionary's] needs in earnest and thankful prayer" (Phil 4:6); people who know how to "stand in the gap, and fill in the hedge" (Ezek 22:30). Prayer is not asking God to do something he is loathe to do; it is integrating and interposing in today's world God's plan of the timeless ages through conversation with and listening to Abba.

Communication Support

Those responsible for communication support should develop a network for the various types of communication media and who will send and receive which: praise and prayer notes, general newsletters, emergency issues, care package and so on. Are there restrictions on what may be sent? Postage requirements? Insurance? Customs? Confidential terminology for restricted countries? The intercession team, of course, will have the priority in this network. We want their prayers to be offered with understanding based on up-to-the-moment information.

Financial Support

Oh, yes, lest we forget, it will take a team of people looking to increase their heavenly portfolio of investments. Wow! Doesn't that sound a lot better than "I hate the thought of raising support"? That process—raising support—is almost as difficult as raising the dead. But, a focus on investments brings life.

Certainly, those with the gift of giving will find it easier to manage this portfolio. However, everyone who really believes the Word—"Store up for yourselves treasures in heaven, where moth and rust do not destroy" (Mt 6:20)—should be anxious to consider if this is where God wants their investment to go. It is the missionary's privilege to invite others into a wider and deeper biblical understanding of stewardship and investment in an eternal portfolio—the kingdom of God.

Reentry Support

"What's the big deal? He's just coming home!" Research from the past fifty years reveals that reentry is usually the most difficult time in the life of a missionary. Expecting their return home to be natural and effortless, missionaries confront "reverse culture shock"; they now are unsettled by the values they see in their own nation. Reentry care needs to be in place even before the missionary leaves.

It is those emergency trips home that can be the most difficult. Further, a missionary may do well on one reentry, but that does not guarantee that the next one will be so easy. In addition, each family member, as an individual, has specific needs at reentry. (The severity of the need for personal care at this juncture in the life of a missionary prompted me to write *The Reentry Team: Caring for Your Returning Missionary* [see www.eri.org].)

From the time when God begins stirring a heart to go to the harvest fields of the world, through the person's time of confirmation, training and preparation, through time on the field, and until she or he is fully integrated into the home culture at the end of the missions career, a missionary desperately needs care.

It Takes a Team

This total care unit needs training not only in the skills required, but also in being a team. Part of the dilemma facing the sports world right now is that so many are trying to be superstars and not giving consideration to the team. Yet the impact of the global missionary movement is of far greater consequence than any World Cup; we are handling the eternal destiny of souls. Each team member needs to know how his or her part fits into the whole, how to relate with the other members, how vital his or her role is and how individual lack of effectiveness may detract from the goal.

And, finally, we all must regard our investment of time, money, prayer—whatever it is—as a privilege. God is sovereign. He will be "exalted in [all] the earth" (Ps 46:10). As Mordecai prophesied to his niece Esther, "Salvation will come. God will save His people. But who knows but that such an hour as this, you have been called to the kingdom?" (Esther 4:14).

If you listen carefully, you will hear these words of encouragement echoing down through the corridors of time. For, I believe with all of my heart, that each of us has been called to the kingdom of God for an hour such as this. What a privilege to be about our Father's business!

Neal Pirolo is the founding director of Emmaus Road International (www.eri.org), an organization that sponsors seminars and publications to mobilize churches, train crosscultural teams and network fellowships with national ministries around the world.

Challenges of Single Women
Results of a Field Survey
PETER'S WIFE

It is a little known fact that close to 60 percent of the Western missionaries in the last two hundred-plus years of the modern missionary movement have been single women. They are in many ways the hidden treasure of this movement, but they have not always been treated as such.

A recent survey of single women conducted by Allyson (a pseudonym to protect her status in a limited-access country) sought to identify some of the unique issues and problems that single women face.

Many of the problems they mentioned are common to anyone serving outside their culture. The lack of communication with people at home, the glazed-over looks when they share their stories, the expectation that those serving overseas need much less money to live on and really should live on a lower standard than others, and the fear of loss of support when they are "out of sight."

But single women have some additional stresses because they are serving outside their culture "alone." They may be part of a team, but without the committed relationship that marriage affords, they have some special needs. Even before going overseas, while raising support, they already feel the stress of their "aloneness." They feel that they always have to be "on" without a break, because they can't share the responsibility for raising support. Often single women are asked to speak in women's and children's meetings, but have difficulty meeting the person who can make financial support decisions. They also sometimes have to deal with combative people who don't think single women should serve overseas.

We want to do what's loving for these women, so we want to know what will help.

These women would like their sending organization to help them in ways that would benefit anyone else they are sending out. Some organizations place a lot of emphasis on knowing where their people feel called to serve. Perhaps it would be better to consider the team they should serve with first. This may reduce the attrition rate caused by conflicts with other workers on the field.

Providing a mentor was a common request among those surveyed—someone to walk them through the process of support raising and practical needs, such as how to get visas and what to take or leave behind. They wanted help planning a timeline, so everything wouldn't come down to the last month. They thought they'd also benefit from regular meetings with a mentor with overseas experience to help them become aware of what they would be facing, so they could adjust their expectations and deal with the heart issues of leaving.

Once on the field, single women face some stresses uniquely theirs. One woman said the hardest part was being forgotten by families going to lunch after church on Sundays. Several mentioned the lack of a man to champion their ideas to the team; they felt the married women's ideas had a fair hearing in the team planning. Another felt the couples took advantage of her by expecting her to baby-sit. One said that the community of single women is generally young, and they do not want an older single woman tagging along with them. How sad!

Some concerns were the same whether they served on a team or not: wondering if they would ever marry, loneliness, not having a sounding board, concerns about how to develop close relationships with other women and meeting social needs. In addition they feared for their safety. They didn't feel they had the same protection and covering as married women. Another common concern was dealing with what their singleness meant in their host culture. In the United States, singleness is often celebrated as independence, but overseas it is often seen as a curse.

Depending on the nature of their calling, some always had to do their work on their own. For these women, loneliness and making decisions alone were additional stresses.

There is much that can be done to help single women. The number-one thing churches and sending organizations could do to help is in communication. A point person or team would keep close contact, yet understand that it is not always possible, when overseas, to keep in touch. Others should know enough about the worker's situation to be able to ask appropriate questions and show concern. They should share the woman's needs with the church and share news from home with her. Phone calls and e-mails would also help single women feel less isolated. Mostly they don't want to be a name and picture on the wall, but a friend and sister remembered often.

Receiving occasional "care packages" and being pampered a little and made to feel special would go a long way toward relieve their special stresses.

A visit from someone from home would help too. Experiencing is the key to understanding, and understanding is the key to caring. Single women want to be able to share their home, their work and their burden with someone from home. A pastoral visit or one from the overseas director or another woman who could share her concerns would be most appreciated.

Finally, the home church should be the single woman's primary prayer support. They should know enough about the field that they can pray specifically and diligently. Recognizing that many of the battles single women face are spiritual in nature can help them persevere in prayer, even when they don't know specific details.

When single women contact their home office, they want their communications to be taken seriously. Like anyone serving overseas, they would like their sending organizations to provide training materials and worship CDs. They would like conferences and seminars so they can grow and stay connected with others doing similar work in their part of the world. They want encouragement, coaching and someone with whom to be accountable.

The most helpful field visits would be those with someone who will take time to talk and get down to deeper issues, such as with more experienced or retired workers, particularly women who can share what they went through and how they resolved their struggles.

Finally, single women face many challenges on home leave. A couple of months before they are due to be home, they would like someone to tell them the current styles and cultural trivia so they don't feel so "foreign" when they start meeting people at home. It would be helpful if they could be provided with a car, a place to stay and help getting things done. Many need additional financial support to be able to pay for rent, for traveling to see family and supporters, and merely for living in their home country.

To have others host an open house in their honor so they can make contact with lots of people quickly would conserve their time and strength when they first return home. To have someone help organize speaking engagements and support-raising events would be invaluable. They want to be able to tell their story and have times of prayer for them and their work.

Many mentioned that they didn't want to be put on a pedestal. They wanted people to be real with them, to talk to them about what is going on in their lives, to seek them out while they're home, to act interested in what they have been doing. They wanted to be encouraged and loved. They also wanted people to understand that they need rest when they feel overwhelmed and time to adjust to being home.

Perhaps with better understanding of what single women serving outside their home culture need, we all can do our part to support and encourage them.

Peter's Wife (www.peterswife.org) is a resource website for women living crossculturally.

My Journey

PETER TARANTAL
Operation Mobilization, South Africa

I grew up in Cape Town, South Africa, during a time that Charles Dickens would describe as "the worst of times," the difficult days of the apartheid regime. Our primary concern was to survive and to dream of a day of liberation.

When I was twenty, God powerfully intervened in my life when I became a follower of Jesus Christ. Within two weeks, I had embarked on a four-year, part-time discipleship program. I got involved with the youth and did some itinerant preaching. I felt I was doing my bit for God. Besides, I was living in one of the most beautiful places on the planet!

Occasionally, Caucasian missionaries came to speak at our church, bringing slides of their work and speaking too long on each slide. Conclusion: missionaries are boring people—Caucasian, older and you had to be close to a hall of famer to be one. Another significant myth I believed was that black people were the objects of missions; therefore, the thought never entered my mind that I could be a missionary.

In 1986, I attended a myth-buster event that would change the course of my life. The Doulos, an Operation Mobilization (OM) ship, docked in Cape Town. I attended a youth leaders' conference onboard and met vibrant young people with a zeal and passion for God. All my negative beliefs about missions were demolished. I purchased an *Operation World* book, which en-

couraged me to pray for the nations of the world. While praying for laborers, I sensed that the Lord wanted me to be the answer to my own prayer.

I joined OM the next year on their two-year program, hoping to go on the other ship, the Logos, in Latin America at that time. I was challenged however to stay on in South Africa to help mobilize the South African church for missions. (Because of the nation's isolation from the rest of the world, few South Africans were involved in missions at the time.)

This was not something I wanted to do. I agreed to pray about it, however, and that became a dangerous prayer. I stayed in South Africa—for twenty-one years now! I have worked in Eastern Europe for short stints as well as on the OM ships, but I have served mainly in Africa.

My life has been influenced by OM's founder, George Verwer. He models to me big-heartedness and generosity, the value of being willing to take risks, and transparency and willingness to change. This is reflected in the organization.

As one who is now a bit more senior in years, I am convinced that we need to see a new generation of leaders raised up who will carry the baton of missions. It will be people "from everywhere to everywhere."

Good News and Bad News in the North American Missions Movement

MICHAEL JAFFARIAN

Good news: Much is being done. Christians in North America are giving about six billion dollars per year to overseas missions. They send and support about forty-three thousand long-term missionaries. As a result, people around the world are coming to Christ. Though other national missions movements are growing strongly, the United States sends almost four times as many missionaries as number two (South Korea).

Bad news: Much more could be done. Maybe six billion dollars sounds like a lot of money, but then, Americans spend fifteen billion per year on pet food and fifty billion on toiletries and cosmetics. I used to serve in Singapore, a nation much smaller than the United States, less wealthy and relatively new to the cause of world missions. In the early 1990s Singapore was sending missionaries at twice the rate of the churches of North America—when you compare the number of missionaries sent with the number of Christians back home.

Good news: Our missionary force is growing. Right now the number of long-term missionaries sent and supported from North America is growing, year by year. We have been in a growth trend since the late 1990s.

Bad news: Our missionary force is smaller than it was. The high point was around 1988, when the number of long-term missionaries from North America was about 44,600. There was a decline for several years until the trend bottomed out and growth came again in the late 1990s. The main reason for the decline was the retirement of many in the post-World War II generation. Immediately after World War II, many new missionaries went out from North America, in a movement fueled by evangelical revival and a mobilization rhetoric that said, "We've won the war and saved the nations from tyranny; now let's go preach Christ and save them from hell!"

Good news: **Some *newer, innovative churches* are strong in world missions.** I use the term "innovative churches" as a catchall to describe churches with praise bands, seeker-friendly churches, purpose-driven churches, emergent churches and the like—the fastest-growing churches today. Almost all new churches planted today are innovative churches. Some of these are giving sacrificially to send missionaries and to help the poor and oppressed. Some are developing short-term mission trip programs that feed effectively into long-term service. Some are instilling a missional vision in every member, to make an impact for the kingdom of God at home and to the ends of the earth.

Bad news: **Most *newer, innovative churches* are weak in world missions.** Innovative churches tend to be most burdened about the people who are lost and needy in their own cities and communities. They give serious effort to developing new ways to evangelize and minister that are attractive, persuasive and effective among emerging generations. That's a good thing. There are more than two hundred million people in the United States and Canada who are not evangelical Christians.

But outside these two countries, there are well more than five *billion* people who are not evangelical Christians. Those statistics do not tell us who is saved and who is lost, but they give some idea of the global imbalance. Traditional churches tend to be much stronger in world missions than the innovative churches—giving more, supporting more and sending more. As traditional churches continue to decline and innovative churches continue to grow, what will it mean for the future of missions from North America?

Good news: The churches of North America are sending a lot of people on short-term mission trips. The best estimate is that about 1.5 million Americans go overseas each year on these mission experiences, usually for one to two weeks. This is now the single most prominent feature in the missions programs of North American churches. Many of these programs are good: participants get missions education, they provide real help to overseas ministries, and they experience Majority World poverty face-to-face.

Bad news: The churches of North America are sending a lot of people on short-term mission trips. The North American missions movement is now sending more than sixty times as many short-term mission participants as long-term missionaries. In other words, for every long-term missionary overseas there are more than sixty mission-trip participants. Let's be honest. Though many mission trips are good, many others are a waste of time and money, and some even do more harm than good. The best research now shows that most people who go on mission trips get excited about world missions, they pray more, they give more . . . but then that vision fades, and their involvement drops back to where it was before. The number going on mission trips has exploded; the number going long-term has not. Most of what we hope to see happen in the world for Christ requires long-term commitment, long-term language and culture learning, long-term relationships and long-term sacrifice. I am praying that churches will retool their short-term trip programs to produce more long-term missionaries.

The ultimate good news is, well, the good news. God loves us, God sent his Son to die for us, Jesus rose from the dead, he will forgive us if we believe, and we can live as God's children in this life and forever. We rejoice in the good things happening in and through the North American missions movement; we pray and weep over the bad things.

One last statistic: 1.9 billion. That's the number of people in the world who have yet to hear the gospel for the first time. They have not heard it through literature, through radio, through a church, through a missionary, through a national believer or through any other means. Tragic! Almost none of the 1.9 billion live in North America. Pray over what the churches of North America should be doing for the 1.9 billion. Then pray over God's calling on your own life.

Michael Jaffarian is a missionary researcher with WorldVenture (formerly the Conservative Baptist Foreign Mission Society) and senior research associate with Operation World. He served for six years as executive director of the Singapore Centre for Evangelism and Missions and for seven years as a research associate for the second edition of the World Christian Encyclopedia.

✎ Journal Worksheet Five

STEVE HOKE

Where Are You Now?

Obviously the organization you connect with is organically linked with your ministry burden or passion. It is based on a laser-sharp sense of God's call on your life that you are now ready to take this next step—to make initial connections with agencies that are working in areas that fit with your passion.

What missionaries have you met from whom you'd like to learn more? How can you contact them?

Does your church have an active missions program? *If so,* who are the key people who could tell you more about the agency or agencies your church is related to? Schedule a meeting with them. *If not,* what steps do you need to initiate to make initial connection with several mission agencies that you want to learn more about?

If you're a member of a denomination that has a sending agency, how can you and/or your church leaders contact them?

What city, nation and unreached people group(s) is your church targeting?

In what country would you like to serve, or what unreached people(s) would you like to play a part in reaching?

Do you have friends who are also looking to make contact with an agency? What are they discovering?

What Do You Need to Do Next?

Spend some time reflecting on your life and ministry values. It is vital that you are clear on what you value before you begin selecting a church or agency with whom to affiliate. It is like joining a family. List below five to eight core values that are important to you (for example, teamwork, leader development, committed to incarnational ministry, holistic scope of ministry).

What ethos would you like to find in your ideal mission agency? List several elements of that ethos below (for example, an empowering environment, supportive leaders, focus on the poor, focus on church planting, supportive of women in ministry and leadership, a safe environment).

When will you check out your church's mission program? Set a date or deadline and write it here.

If you're a member of a denomination, set a date for contacting the candidate secretary or writing for information. When will you look at other agencies beyond your church or denomination, if necessary?

What Will the Future Look Like?

What criteria will you and your church use to determine which mission agency is the best fit for you? List below the value-based criteria that you think are most important for you to find.

What limitations on debt, family size, theology and so on do you need to be aware of in relating to an agency?

What do you need to hear from the Lord during this time of exploration? Be attentive to what the Spirit is saying to you on daily basis.

Latin servants on assignment in Delhi, India

SIX

Ministry Role and Assignment Search

STEVE HOKE AND BILL TAYLOR

The next two steps—seeking out the place where God wants you to serve and getting hands-on training—overlap with discovering the right agency. Each one influences the others. So steps five, six and seven should all be tackled simultaneously, as a single unit.

It's necessary to ask God specifically about the role you are to play in seeing him plant a strong, vibrant church in a part of the world where Jesus is not known. You are not a pawn for some Christian agency to move around as it desires, irrespective of your gifting and calling. Rather, you are a crosscultural servant who brings a sense of passion and calling to serve God's purposes in a specific way. You seek to find the team with which you can best fulfill that calling. You want to join a team that will steward your life with great care.

The core profile of the crosscultural servant is just one of the roles essential to the decade ahead. Church planting remains a critical role. There are nearly two billion people in some 6,500 people groups who live with little or no culturally relevant Christian witness. Unless many Christians, from many places, go specifically to these unreached peoples with an understanding of their language, their culture and their needs, no new church can be established among them.

But other roles are needed, too. We have listed a range of missionary roles that focus on and supplement church planting. We've also listed the types of preparation required for them. Maybe there's a certain role that fits you, your training, your experience and your gifts. If God has specifically equipped you to serve as a teacher to MKs, for example, then go ahead.

There's no need to feel guilty about filling a much-needed support role. Similarly, if God has shaped you to be a nurse or to serve in a helping profession, that is no less significant than being an evangelist.

I spent my first thirty years obediently seeking God's role for my life, but wrongly assuming that if church planting among unreached peoples was the greatest need, I should sign up to fill that need. Only after completing graduate work, knocking on multiple doors and gaining initial field experience, did I discover that God had neither gifted nor called me to be a church-planting Paul in Southeast Asia. I was a come-alongside encourager-teacher, like Barnabas. For the past thirty years I have pursued my passion in over forty nations—to equip and encourage frontline crosscultural workers. That's a rather specialized role, and it took some time to find it, prepare for it and then fit into it.

Regardless of what you now see as the role to which God is calling you, you'll find it extremely helpful to think about and focus on a particular people group. Ask your church or agency to help you study a people group or perhaps several people groups that occupy the same region or the vast unreached cities of our globe.

Look for evidence of God's leading: a match between your natural abilities, learned skills and spiritual gifts and the characteristics and situation of the people. Avoid making quick judgments or being too easily attracted to (and distracted by) certain jobs or the prospect of an exotic adventure. Hawaii is no longer unreached. Neither is San Diego, Cancun or Monte Carlo.

Patiently wait for God's leading to be reinforced by other indicators or "wisdom signs." Prayer, "divine appointments" (those uncanny times when God providentially leads across your path just the person you need to talk to), confirming spiritual counsel, an overriding sense of his peace and even circumstances, to some extent, can serve as wisdom signs.

The apostle Paul was "called" into full-time ministry at his conversion on the Damascus road (see Acts 9), but he wasn't "sent" until he was released by the first church in Antioch a number of years later (see Acts 13). If Paul could wait for confirmation and specific direction, so can you. "Calling" and "timing" are two crucial but very different issues to keep balanced.

Let's clarify a possible misperception. Though there is a sense of prophetic urgency in the New Testament to reach the unreached, the weight of Scriptures makes clear that God is not in a hurry. God grows things over time. In the very passage in which Peter urges his readers in Asia Minor to hasten the Lord's return ("speed its coming," 2 Pet 3:12), he reminds them that God "is patient with you, not wishing for any to perish but for all to come to repentance" (3:9). So which is it? Is he patient, or is he in a hurry?

God's heart weeps for every person who dies outside a redemptive relationship with him. Yet he is not rushing around the earth, accelerating the flow of redemptive history in ways that our Western approaches to "managerial missions" try so hard to do. There is a divine tension between God's compassionate heart for all peoples and a divine patience that is also shaping the lives of his servants around the world to be the godly disciples he intended.

What if you don't know where you're supposed to go or have no geographic preference? What if you don't know of any unreached people groups? The suggestions listed below were gathered from others who have faced the same predicament.

- Tune into the clues around you. Learn about the particular people group or geographical focus your home church emphasizes. Pray regularly for specific unreached people(s), nations and cities listed and described in *Operation World,* the best geographical prayer digest. Be aware of the people God brings into your life (divine encounters), friends who have a similar burden, international students you encounter who are all from a certain part of the world or a growing concern about a special people to whom God clearly indicates he wants to lead you. As you tune in to the clues around you, tune in to the voice within you that will help you see the patterns and connect the dots.

- In a journal, keep track of insights or strong interests as they develop. Each week, review what you've written, reflect on it and see if any patterns, divine encounters or contacts with a particular people in a particular part of the world have emerged. Be attentive, as well, to what God may be teaching your church about their missions focus. Like Habakkuk of old, find a quiet place to meet Abba regularly; keep watch to see what God is saying; discern the voice of God as he speaks; and "record the vision"—write out or journal your dialogue with God (see Hab 2:1-3). The essence of biblical journaling is writing down your prayer and God's answer.

- Be open to visiting regions within the vast unreached world. For many, short-term mission trips become an eye-opening exposure to particular peoples, needs and projects. They do not gain that vision and passion until they get out of their comfort zone and into the war zone. That's just the way it works for many.

- Interview missionaries and international students who have come from similar regions or who are from a particular people group. Learn all you can. Keep track of your insights. The website AskAMissionary.com has collated the answers from such interviews into hundreds of FAQs.

- Be up-front about a call that conflicts. If you sense a growing call to a people group other than those emphasized by your home church, it's time for intensive prayer, deeper discernment and sensitive communication. Take the initiative to share clearly and honestly with your leaders how, where and why you think the Lord is leading you. Ask them to pray with you about your direction. Seek their participation in your decision so they can have a shared sense of ownership in your plans as you move forward. Ultimately we would affirm that God's Spirit will speak directly to you—and then you'll have to step out in holy boldness.

- Be encouraged, and also be faithful. God wants to reveal himself and his heart to you in a very personal way. As you seek to draw closer to him through intentional study, prayer and listening, you will probably find yourself drawn to a particular people group. This listening-to-God process is much more organic and relational than you may have been led to believe. God really wants you to be clear about his purposes and his calling. That's why the psalmist continually visualizes God's Word, direction and words as illuminating light, light that eliminates darkness, shadows and doubt. Once illuminated, however, you need to take the next step.

- Step out in faith. If after extended prayer you still believe God is directing you to missions, but you have no sense of leading to a particular people, the Lord may want you to step out in faith. He may be asking you to move in obedience like Abraham— not certain where you're headed, but knowing that he will point the way.

Most sending agencies and sending churches are happy to walk with you during your process of searching for a role and an assignment. They're interested in matching your gifts with the task to be done. They want to see you placed on a team where your abilities and gifts will complement the mix of the rest of the group.

You will probably be asked to take personality inventories and tests on things like vocational and role preferences, psychological background, conflict-resolution style and linguistic ability. While these exercises may seem like a lot of paperwork, they're not busywork. All the information you gather will help you, your church and the agency determine what you're well suited for. Research and experience have shown that for success in language learning, for example, motivation is as important as natural aptitude. Keep in mind, too, that these are tools for self-understanding and assessment, not final answers.

Remember in all of this that the sovereign Spirit of God is at work around the world completing his purposes. Within that macrosphere, the same Spirit also speaks in a still, small voice to you and me, providing the courage and the direction we need to keep in step with him. The enemy often intervenes with subtle but distracting voices that raise doubts, questions God's direction and seeks to block any momentum and excitement the Spirit has created in you. Can you see now the Spirit's purpose in teaching you to discern his voice in this initial decision-making process that will equip you to discern his will and make wise decisions for a lifetime of ministry?

There is no need to be in a hurry. God may be shaping your character in ways that are prerequisite to you serving effectively overseas. The issue is not geography, but spirituality; not timing, but teachability.

Tuning in to the Spirit for this role and assignment search will place you in a posture of learning and listening that will last your lifetime.

The Missionary Preparation Matrix

STEVE HOKE

There are thousands of unreached people groups with no Christian witness. Each requires a well-trained team of church-planting missionaries. But other roles are needed too. In table 3 we have tried to show the different kinds of training needed for different tasks.

Step	1	2	3	4	5	6	7	8	9	10
Types of Mission Roles/ Careers	Spiritual Formation	Body Life	Exposure	Basic Education	Agency Connection	Role and Assignment Search	Hands-On Training	Apprenticeships	Lifelong Learning	Finishing Strong
Agriculturist	X	X	X	X	X	*	▵	?	X	X
Church Developer/ Church Renewal Specialist	X	X	X	X	X	X	X	X	X	X
Church Planter	X	X	X	X	X	X	X	X	X	X
Community Development Worker	X	X	X	X	X	X	X	X	X	X
Evangelist/Discipler	X	X	X	X	X	X	X	X	X	X
Field Researcher	X	X	X	X	X	X	X	X	X	
Health Specialist	X	X	X	X	X	X	X	*	X	X
Journalist	X	X	X	X	X	X	*	—	X	X
Medical Doctor	X	X	X	X	X	X	*	Y	Y	X
Member Care Counselor/Specialist	X	X	X	X	*	X	*	*	X	X
MK School Teacher/ Administrator	X	X	X	X	*	X	X	—	X	X
Nurse/Pharmacist/ Lab Technician	X	X	X	X	X	*	X	—	X	X
Pastoral Mentor/Coach	X	X	X	X	X	X	X	X	X	X
Pilot/Technician	X	X	X	X	X	*	*	X	X	X
Secretary/Admin. Asst.	X	X	—	X	X	X	*	—	X	X
Tentmaker	X	X	X	X	*	X	*	—	X	X
Theological Educator	X	X	X	X	X	X	X	—	X	X

* Specific to technical skill

? Requirements are variable, not specific

— Not needed

A Prophetic Call to "Sub-merge"

JOHN B. HAYES

Sub-merge: Living Deep in a Shallow World (Regal, 2006) is a manifesto, a prophetic call to join what God is doing among poor and marginalized communities, those who are shut out from or cannot find footing in the market-driven economies of the world. Our planet is spiritually, socially and environmentally at risk, and the vulnerable poor are the first to pay the price. How we respond to this situation, individually and collectively, matters deeply.

Sub-merge is also a message of hope to Christians around the world, especially First World Christians who yearn to respond to the poor personally but don't know how or are fearful they will be burned out in the process.

In InnerCHANGE, we believe that one response needed today is to create unique orders: mission communities that are part team, part tribe, part family. We have journeyed to a place beneath the consumer mirage of status, style, spending and speed. We have experienced change from *sub-merging,* what we call going beneath the surface of a consumer society's demands and aspirations and finding life with Christ among the poor. On this journey, we have learned ways to live deep in this shallow world. *Sub-merge* is written to share some of our insights in this adventure and to outline what we believe are imperatives for other emerging orders in this new world.

Living deep is something that only God can lead us to; it is a direction, not an accomplishment. Living deep concentrates on the welfare of God's people and the pursuit of his Word. By "shallow world" I refer to the "world, the flesh and the devil," to quote Martin Luther's summary of the forces that assail us and take us in a direction counter to the kingdom (see 1 Jn 2:16). I believe the anesthesia of First World affluence enhances the shallow world's pull and makes living deep that much more challenging.

Society and culture are changing so rapidly that many of the church's traditional responses are being called into question—in particular among the poor. Lessons from forgotten Christian history need to be unearthed. The ground has moved beneath the church's feet, and for the most part, our attention has been elsewhere while it happened. *Sub-merge* is an effort to see that the terrain we stand on is new ground, new opportunity. This new ground requires deeper spirituality and a deeper sense of community.

Deeper Spirituality

As I spend time with young people in the United States and other parts of the West, I find a generation of Christian disciples with an increasingly postmodern outlook and set of expectations. This younger generation seems disenchanted with a faith life that peaks on Sundays and wrestles the remainder of the week in a spiritual crawl space. As I have listened to young disciples, I sense that they do not want to attend church services that confuse worship and entertainment, joy and *en*joy.

As we have "sub-merged" among the poor, we have embraced a spirituality centering on an upside-down-kingdom Jesus. Christ reminds us that the last are truly first, the leader is servant, the poor are blessed, and the rich go away empty-handed. Through the years, I have observed that Christian missionaries who have emerged from the mainstream church have often inadvertently communicated that Christianity is a middle-class, Western phenomenon. Consequently, conversion in the field sometimes appears more cultural than spiritual. In Jesus, however, God stands with the poor and the outcast as he promised to do in Matthew 25, and he is available to be met among them in a vital and personal way. We have only just begun to glimpse a spirituality we do not deserve and cannot earn but desperately want more of. This meeting with God's Son among the poor is personal without being exclusive, freeing without being individualistic and full of a grace that allows us to celebrate who we truly are, not just who we hope to be.

I believe that God is calling for a new kind of missionary with a more holistic understanding of mission and self. Too often, sending entities communicate that mission is primarily a profession. On the other hand, too often churches give the impression that mission is a short-term adventure or rite of passage for the young. As I have heard Fuller Theological Seminary professor Dr. J. Robert Clinton state, "Effective ministry flows out of our being, not just our doing." We must equip our young Christian workers with the conviction that mission is both a vocation and a way of living that is redemptive in our fullest selves.

Deeper Sense of Community

"New wine," Jesus said, "must be poured into fresh wineskins" (Lk 5:38). Old wineskins, stiff with use, burst when new wine is poured into them. The loss is double, as Jesus pointed out, because the wine is spilled and the skins are ruined. New wineskins, new mission vehicles, are necessary to mature and preserve the fresh expressions required to help the maturation process of emerging communities and the gifts God has given them.

Although two-thirds of the world's human beings live in poverty or hover close to it, only a small fraction of Christian workers actually go to live and work among them. According to statistics pieced together, only about 6 percent of mission workers actually minister as poor to the poor, and that figure may be generous. We have a math problem. Either God is not calling many to do this, or we are not hearing him. If the good news were a marketable product like Coca-Cola or Pepsi, a 6-percent reach to two-thirds of the world would mean that someone in marketing would be fired. Not so in Christendom. Nevertheless, God is well able to work with the many or the few.

Still, as I encounter mission workers among the poor worldwide, the quality of people and their level of commitment excite me. Likewise, I am encouraged by the emergence of new incarnational mission entities targeting the poor and marginalized. Servants to Asia's Poor, a pioneer among Protestant agencies among the poor in the 1970s, has been followed by Urban Neighbors of Hope, Word Made Flesh, Servant Partners, Emmaus and others. In the United Kingdom, there is a host of new creative entities, Urban Expression being the one I know best. In the developing world, too, are fresh expressions of church planting and mission among the poor, some entirely comprised of nationals, such as Life Way, based in Nairobi.

Mission man-hours are declining ever more rapidly. Some of this has to do with money. Despite strong, sustained economic growth worldwide during the 1990s, missions giving declined. Nowhere is this disparity more apparent than in the United States. In a land of plenty, missions are on a starvation diet. However, the fall-off in missions is about more than changes in giving patterns; it is also about changing attitudes.

Identifying and helping current and future apostolic communities mature and develop is crucial. To sustain workers in challenging ministry among the poor long-term, we must move from training to developing, or forming, individuals. To form individuals and help them gain a sense of their unique destinies, we must first *see* them. At InnerCHANGE, we have discovered that communities, with their effort toward transparent relationships, "see" more accurately than organizational hierarchies do. Orders, which have their emphasis on collective life, can be ideal places to both sharpen and sustain individuals.

At InnerCHANGE, we are aware of how young we all are in the journey among the poor as communities of mission workers. Although God has done much in and through us that is dear to us, we are painfully aware that our work will appear small in the world's eyes. In "sub-merging" among the poor, we have found that the world looks different from the way it does on the surface. We have seen God in a different way. We have seen him redefine success and adjust the way we see beauty. Sub-merge joins with and stands on the shoulders of many vital prophets and missionaries whom God has raised for work among the poor.

My prayer as you begin your journey with Jesus is that you capture something of what it means to live deep in a world of tragic and overwhelming human need, while being simultaneously pressed by culture to lead shallow lives. Speaking for all of us who work among the poor, we hope that this book contributes to your journey of faith with Christ, who "sub-merged" for us and expresses himself so vividly below the surface of a shallow world.

(Abridged with permission of the coauthor from John B. Hayes, *Sub-Merge: Living Deep in a Shallow World* [Ventura, Calif.: Regal, 2006].)

John B. Hayes has had a lifelong interest in the needs of the poor. He and his wife, Deanna, are general directors of InnerCHANGE, a mission order than works among the poor in five countries, sharing the good news in words and works through personal relationships. John has lived among the poor on the most overcrowded street in Southern California, the inner city of San Francisco and now lives in one of the poorest neighborhoods in London. John graduated from Princeton and received his master's in International Relations from Yale.

# Global Perspectives

BOB CRESON
President/CEO of Wycliffe USA

Role of the Missionary

Jesus' global call to "go" and make disciples as we are going extends from the heart of a God, a passion he has for pursing men, women and children right into eternity that will continue until Christ returns. While this global call has not changed, the diversity of people God is calling has changed. Where we get confused in the Global North is when we forget that we are working alongside mature believers from the Global South who are fully capable of leading, planning and strategizing. Our unique opportunities right now are to see God working through this diversity and not try to control it.

Attracting the Next Generations

Some things never change. As they have in the past, recruits for Wycliffe USA want to make a difference in the lives of people and have an impact for the kingdom—whatever their length of service. What's changed is the urgency they feel (impatience for results) and their broader interest in things like human rights, justice and meeting physical needs. It is not always a foregone conclusion that there is a connection between Bible translation and these issues, but there is. Our recruitment has been increasing (up 10 percent over each of the previous two years), so there is still broad interest in Bible translation. We are finding that *commitment* is being redefined by recruits into shorter terms of service; it is not necessarily for a long-term "career" as it has been in the past.

Character and Spirituality Qualities

Demanding Christian spiritual maturity that we in the Global North see as "heartiness" and a no-sin mentality is not helpful either, and even counterproductive (often seen as hypocritical). We're on this journey together, imperfect people living and working in community. Recruits need to demonstrate maturity in terms of a love for God, love for others, an ability to live and work successfully in community and an ability to deal successfully with life issues based on biblical values.

What About the Poor?

PAUL BORTHWICK

Certain verses in the Bible exist to rattle our cages. They explode off the page to wake us up and cause us to reevaluate. Jesus' words about the separation of the sheep and the goats certainly qualify (see Mt 25:31-46). The Lord awakens his followers to the real definition of the gospel by explaining that God's judgment will be based on how we cared for people in need.

He reminds us that a visit to a prisoner, compassion to the impoverished (the giving of food to the hungry, drink to the thirsty and clothes to the naked) and a visit to the lonely reflect our true love for him. If we are the people of Christ, we're supposed to be characterized by hospitality to the outcast and outreach to the poor. Omitting these practices results in eternal judgment. Sounds harsh, but it accurately portrays Jesus' concern that our faith touch the disadvantaged.

James put it more bluntly in his letter designed to remind us that "faith without deeds is dead" (Jas 2:26). "Faultless" religion, he writes, is "to look after orphans and widows in their distress and to keep oneself from being polluted by the world" (1:27).

James wrote to people preoccupied with status, especially in 2:1-13, on the issue of showing partiality to the rich. In contrast to their natural inclinations, he exhorted them to demonstrate their faith by reaching out to the statusless—namely widows and orphans. Giving to those who cannot give back marks our religion as "pure and faultless."

Jesus and James both endorse the same truth. They tell us that the genuineness of our faith, our outreach and our Christlike love can be evaluated with one question: how does our faith take expression in caring for the poor?

The question stirs our guilt and causes us to wrestle with responses like, "But Jesus, what about all these other good things I'm into?" But we're still left with the provoking question,

"How does our Christianity demonstrate itself in our outreach to the poor?"

Dr. Ron Sider rocked the Western Christian world almost thirty years ago with his book *Rich Christians in an Age of Hunger.* He recently began challenging Christians to pragmatic ministry to the poor by joining in a covenant he calls "The Generous Christian Pledge."[1] He encourages every Christian to undertake a lifestyle mission for the poor. The pledge reads:

> *I pledge to open my heart to God's call to care as much about the poor as the Bible does.*
>
> *Daily, to pray for the poor, beginning with the Generous Christians Prayer:*
>
>> *Lord Jesus, teach my heart to share your love with the poor.*
>
> *Weekly, to minister, at least one hour, to a poor person: helping, serving, sharing with, and mostly, getting to know someone in need.*
>
> *Monthly, to study, at least one book, article, or film about the plight of the poor and hungry and discuss it with others.*
>
> *Yearly, to retreat, for a few hours before the Scriptures, to meditate on this one question: Is caring for the poor as important in my life as it is in the Bible?—and to examine my budget and priorities in light of it, asking God what changes He would like me to make in the use of my time, money, and influence.*

The cage-rattling statements of Jesus and James demand a response. The Generous Christian Pledge is a great place to start.

Paul Borthwick, D.Min., along with his wife, Christie, serves on the staff of Development Associates International (www.daintl.org) focusing on leadership development in the Majority World. In addition, Paul teaches missions at Gordon College in Wenham, Massachusetts, serves as an Urbana/ Missions Associate with InterVarsity Christian Fellowship and mobilizes others for crosscultural missions. Rick Warren, author of Purpose Driven Life *cites Paul's books* A Mind for Missions *and* How to Be a World-Class Christian *as "books that should be read by every Christian."*

---

[1]For more information, write to Evangelicals for Social Action, 6 East Lancaster Avenue, Wynnewood, PA 19096.

Wall poster of AIDS and Malaria control

Serving the Poor
Steps to Relief and Development Ministries

SAMUEL J. VOORHIES

The Dilemma

They won't hire you unless you have experience. You can't gain experience unless you get hired. What do you do?

Development agencies generally do not consider anyone for an international assignment unless she or he has had overseas experience. Most young people don't have that experience.

After being asked about this numerous times by young people seeking to become involved in missions through a relief or development ministry, I began to reflect on my own experience and that of others with whom I have worked in recent years.

It Was Only a Dream

Thirty years ago, like many young people today, I had a dream about serving God overseas. A dream about sharing the gospel with those who had not heard and giving practical assistance to those suffering from abject poverty and injustice. That's really all it was, a dream, not something I thought could really happen. Growing up in the swamps and bayous of Louisiana, where my family made a living hunting and trapping fur-bearing animals, I knew little about overseas missions. But I did have a burning desire to live for the Lord and to serve him in whatever way he wanted me to. I was exposed to international missions only after going to Wheaton to complete a master's degree in Christian Ministries.

At Wheaton, I met professors and students from Asia, Latin America and Africa. My roommate was a missionary kid from Zaire. We used to lie out on the soccer field at night and dream about being in Africa together one day. He planned to complete his degree and return to

Africa with the same mission agency as his parents. But I didn't even have a home church and knew nothing about mission organizations.

My future wife, Emily, had completed her master's at Wheaton and was working with Living Bibles International (LBI). After we married, Emily was asked to take a position in LBI's Africa office, based in Nairobi. After prayer, supplication and six months of marriage, we began our "faith adventure" in Kenya. Through a series of contacts and relationships, I was invited to work with the Evangelical Fellowship of Kenya, assisting in training pastors and church leaders across the country.

So our African adventure began. We had the most privileged experience one can imagine, working with African national leaders who had vision for their continent. We thought we would be there a year and then carry on with our careers. The Lord had other plans. After our first year, the Lord gave us great affirmation from our African colleagues that he was calling us to this ministry for a long-term commitment. We did. Now, twenty-five years later, we are still participating in ministry in Africa.

Six Ideas for Getting Started

How do you get started? What is the key to getting your foot in the door of international aid agencies carrying out Christian relief and development activities?

1. Have faith and take risk. The key ingredients are faith (being willing to dream) and a willingness to step out in faith. This has to be a call, not just a professional career path. You must be willing to take some risks. There is no clear-cut path or formula. Most of the people I know have a similar story to mine. They did not prepare for and then get started on a career path of Christian development work (though this may be changing as we now see graduate programs of study in the area of international and community development).

2. Have a technical skill. Finish your degree and have a technical skill to offer. The work of Christian relief and development involves very practical skills. A few areas that are always in need include public health, agriculture (especially extension), finance, logistics, adult education and training, and communication (video, photo journalism and computer skills).

A young man from California was between his college degree and graduate school and wanted an "overseas experience." Through a contact with Opportunity International, he went to Zimbabwe for a year to work with the local agency. He was able to help them set up computer programs for processing loan applications and to do some basic computer training. It was a good experience for him, and he made a useful contribution. Where it will lead, only the Lord knows; but he has gotten started.

3. Study a second language. Having a second language and an appropriate technical skill can sometimes be as helpful as having experience. This is particularly true for short-term, well-defined roles that are often needed in emergency situations.

4. Look for short-term opportunities. Look for short-term missions or study opportunities. Often you can do a semester or year overseas as a part of your program. Do a semester at an African university, school of agriculture or department of sociology. I recently met a young man in northeast Zimbabwe wearing a T-shirt that claimed North Carolina as home. A committed Christian, he had been in Zimbabwe for the year on a Rotary scholarship, doing part of his master's degree in conjunction with the University of Zimbabwe. As part of his community service (a requirement of the Rotary program), he was teaching English as a second language to Mozambique refugees. From Zimbabwe, he went to Geneva to volunteer at the United Nations refugee headquarters.

5. Be prepared to volunteer. Even after graduation, look for short-term and volunteer opportunities. A nonpaying role without any guarantee of a paying job or future opportunity may not be what you had in mind after graduating. But it may be what it takes to get started. That's what happened to Cheryl and Randy Lovejoy. After graduating from college, they participated in a short-term (six months or longer) mission in Mexico. It gave them a language and a grass-roots crosscultural experience. Because of this initial short-term experience, their technical skills and their language capacity, they were offered a contract position with World Vision in Mozambique.

You may need to start in an area that is not aligned to your long-term career, but just gets you on the field. Once you are there, you are getting experience and will make key contacts for the future. The job the Lovejoys were offered was not something that either wanted to make a career, but being on the field enabled them to make contacts that led to other opportunities.

6. Not just through Christian organizations. Overseas missions opportunities do not come just through Christian mission organizations. Many folks have gotten their start as Peace Corp volunteers—not a high-paying job but an opportunity that provides language and crosscultural training and grass-roots community development experience.

International aid agencies include not only Christian organizations but government and private as well. These organizations will continue to respond to the ongoing disasters of famine and war. Such organizations include the United Nations aid agencies, United States Aid for International Development (USAID) and a host of private (nongovernmental) agencies dealing with health (International Medical Corps), agriculture (Heifer International) and housing (Habitat for Humanity), to name only a few. These provide opportunities for professional work and get you to the places where the poorest and most unreached peoples are located.

What Is Your Dream?

While living in Nairobi that first year, I became acquainted with World Vision through friends in a home Bible study. As a result of those relationships, they later offered me a job. Since then I have traveled across thousands of miles of bumpy roads, slept in numerous villages and had the privilege of working with and learning from nationals seeking God's help to overcome seemingly impossible odds of poverty in some seventy countries—all since that first dream out on the soccer field of Wheaton College just twenty-nine years ago.

What is your dream? How will God be using you a few years from now? Get started now. It will come sooner than you think.

Samuel J. Voorhies, Ph.D., has almost thirty years of crosscultural international leadership and management experience in nongovernmental relief and development and has traveled and worked in some seventy countries. Having lived in Africa for twelve years, Sam has worked in twenty-five African countries, as well as another forty in Europe, Asia and Latin America. His vision and passion have focused on building national leadership to lead sustainable programs.

Your Professional Skills Can Have Kingdom Impact

LANDA COPE

The God of Scripture is Lord over all of life, not just the spiritual and not just our worship. Once we erase the lines between the secular and the sacred parts of our life, we are free to explore a more connected plan.

Your professional background or "domain" is one of the arenas God wants to use to restore a broken world. While business is one of the major domains, it isn't the only area. Consider the following six critical domains: economics/business, science/healthcare/technology, arts/communication, education, law/government and social work.

God is inviting us into difference-making on such a grand scale that it's not part time with what's left over. It's discovering how your profession becomes the means to kingdom impact, for it's not just *what* you do, but *why* you do it, *how* you do it and *where* you do it that can begin to make the difference.

Understanding these domains can help you intentionally turn professional capacity into kingdom resources. Your professional expertise, training, experience, influence, connections and opportunities are about more than a paycheck. Your work is a distinctive and holy calling, part of God's greater purpose for your life and his world. Consider the suggested biblical themes for each domain as a means to deepen and broaden your scriptural base.

Economics/Business

Themes to discover when studying economics in the Bible are ethics and principles of finance, loans, agriculture, the worker, labor, the manager, inheritance and wages. God's promises to Israel as they left slavery in Egypt were not isolated to blessings of an unseen nature. He promised he would bless them in every area of life, including their crops, livestock and business; if they would obey him, they would not have poverty in their land.

The Hebrew mind could not grasp a concept of blessing without it being manifest in tangible as well as intangible ways. The goodness of God was tied in part to having enough food, clothing and shelter. Blessing was practical and material. God's financial instructions led to economic development, the elimination of poverty and blessing others. The domain of economics reveals Jehovah Jireh, God our Provider.

The primary attribute of God that economics is responsible for is goodness.

Science/Healthcare/Technology

Themes to consider when studying science in Scripture are health, nature, hygiene, medicine, engineering, technology and ecology. Its purpose is to discover and steward God's material creation, leading us to awe, wonder and solutions. Today many Christians believe, or at least behave as if they believe, that by virtue of our faith, we are alienated from science, that it is a battleground where some are trying to disprove the existence of God. Others feel it is the lesser plane of the "material" and not as important as the "spiritual" realm.

This can be a grave danger in a world where some of the most important moral issues are being asked in the realm of science. Science is, of all the domains, the most limited, because the scientist cannot discover anything

that God has not created. God uses his natural laws to humble us and reveal his awesome power and wisdom. This domain reveals the Creator.

The primary attribute of God that science reveals is order and power.

Arts/Communication

Themes to consider when studying the arts in Scripture are music, design, sport, dance, culture, dress, poetry, literature and crafts. Everything God made is beautiful. Nothing in the universe is without color, form and design. He turns ashes into beauty. He is our song, the Potter, the Lord of beauty. The arts reveal the Creator through music, words, color, design, balance, movement, harmony and rhythm. The psalmist charges the sun, moon and stars to praise him, and there are physicists today who think it is completely possible that the heavens do vibrate in perfect harmonic chords.

God renews and restores us through beauty. He created us to need and to celebrate beauty and joy. Christian artists are part of God's answer to that world of need. The domain reveals God as the Song of Songs and the Potter.

The primary attribute of God revealed is beauty.

Education

God originates and encourages wisdom, knowledge and education. Everything in Scripture is about learning. The Bible is a book inspired by God for our education and understanding of his ways. For the Hebrew mind discipled by the teaching of Moses, the concept of "knowing" included "application" or "action." Most educational systems are based on the concept that you can "know" by retaining information *about* a subject without being able or needing to apply any of it. This is not a biblical assumption. God gave the responsibility for the education of children to the family, not the government or the church. Parents can delegate their authority, but if they abdicate their support or if their role is ignored or even denied by the institution, then those schools have very little legitimate authority over the children.

The domain of education reveals God as the great Teacher, Rabbi. The primary attribute of God that education reveals is wisdom.

Law/Government

When we study the domain of government in the Bible, we are looking at areas like legislative, executive, judicial and military functions of government. We are looking at law, national and local authority, relationships between nations, rules of war and areas of community development related to government. We are looking at the roles and actions of judges and kings and those who worked for them in official capacities.

The primary purpose of government is to serve the population of a nation by providing an objective, trustworthy source of justice. In Deuteronomy we find that government is ordained by God and gets its authority from the people. The character of political leaders is important; it is to be representative of all the people and is to provide a source of just resolution of conflicts.

The domain of government reveals God as the King of kings. The primary attribute of God that the domain of government is responsible for is justice.

Social Work

Social work is hard to study as a separate category in the Scriptures. As it is practiced today, we find that it seems to combine the elements of most other domains and is focused for the good of the family and community. The study of other domains gives insight into the purposes of God for social work in the twenty-first century.

The attributes of God most clearly demonstrated in this domain are his compassion and restoration.

Landa Cope is the founding international dean of the College of Communication for Youth With A Mission's University of the Nations. Since joining YWAM in 1971, her work in missions has taken her to more than 110 nations. She is the author of Clearly Communicating Christ, a book about Jesus-style communication, and The Old Testament Template. In 2005 Landa founded the Template Institute (www.templateinstitute.com), which is committed to providing seminars and materials for the development of biblical thinking in the professions as well as a comprehensive biblical approach to issues in the public forum. For additional articles from Landa, visit <www.templateinstitute.com>. (Although this article is the product of a talk given by Landa, it has never appeared before on any of her websites.) Landa currently lives in South Africa.

Al fresco school in Africa

Healthcare and Missions

JOHN McVAY

Many countries and cultures do not accept "traditional" missionaries. But in many of those same places, professionals from overseas are welcomed and respected. Healthcare professions that open doors include physicians, nurses, nurse practitioners, pharmacists, physical and occupational therapists, public health consultants, healthcare educators, community development and more.

Visit AskAMissionary.com for answers to questions such as

- I'm just beginning university and I have a heart for both healthcare and church planting. How do I choose between these—or can I do both?

- I'm just beginning university and I'm interested in healthcare. What major do you recommend?

- I'm in nursing. Should I get further training in community health, home health, pediatrics or obstetrics, etc.? Should I get a master's degree?

- I'm a medical student. What specialty do you recommend for healthcare missions?

- I've graduated as a healthcare professional. How much theological training should I get?

Even better, meet medical missionaries and connect with dozens of agencies.

Learn from workshops on healthcare missions at conferences such as these:

Global Missions Health Conference
Louisville, Kentucky
www.medicalmissions.com

Healthcare Ministry and Missions Conference
Pasadena, California
www.healthcaremissions.org

World Medical Mission Conference
Ashville, North Carolina
www.samaritanspurse.org

Since information changes from time to time, we suggest as an online companion resource to *Global Mission Handbook* that you bookmark The Journey Deepens (www.thejourneydeepens.com). Under healthcare missions are lists of current conferences and medical missions networks.

John McVay is a missions mobilizer who helped launch AskAMissionary.com and The Journey Deepens weekend retreats. He serves in Tulsa as chief of staff with In His Image Family Medicine Residency and Medical Missions.

🌐 Global Perspectives

DAVID TAI-WOONG LEE
Director of Global Leadership Focus; Founder and Director
of Global Missionary Training Center, Seoul, Korea

The Role of the Missionary

Let's take a close look at the New Testament as we address this issue from two sides. First, the entire church, whether North or South, should engage in missions according to the pattern that is given in the New Testament in all stages of her life cycle, even in today's globalized world. The Western church, therefore, should not dismiss evangelism, church planting and holistic ministry from their missions agenda.

Recommended Prefield Training

Second, each church has liberty to construct it own strategy. There are a number of areas where the Western church has advantages over the non-Western one. It is in these areas that the West can truly partner with the non-Western church. For example: offering expertise in missionary training by sharing resources and personnel; creating a friendly atmosphere for the non-Western missionaries to minister alongside Western missionaries in international mission organizations; forming authentic partnership infrastructures in the fields so that non-Western organizations can benefit without being engulfed in the formation of unnecessary duplicative international organization that lack identity in the sending bases; and providing aid in crisis situations.

One thing that the Western church should not do is to retreat into her own hemisphere and focus on only her own back yard. It will take no less than a global missionary force to evangelize the whole globe. Until then, churches on mission in both North and the South must engage in missions globally with full speed and full force, following these New Testament patterns.

Removing the Fear Factor

STEVE HOKE

Making major decisions absolutely petrifies many Christians. In fact, the more riding on the decision, the greater their fear factor. But that was never what Abba intended.

Decision making is a very natural part of following Jesus and is meant to be a spiritual practice that becomes more and more organic and relational the longer we journey with Jesus. The further along we walk and the greater the intimacy, decision making becomes less of a harried search for a hidden treasure as it does hearing and discerning the voice of the Spirit within us. The Spirit, as the divine encourager and wise counselor, is obviously concerned with clear communication and unity of heart. Elisabeth Elliot calls seeking guidance "affirming the will of God." It's not so much about discovering the mysterious as it is affirming the obvious.

I grew up in a Christian environment that held to a particular approach to decision making—the divine blueprint approach. We were told to look for the one perfect plan for our lives—or the perfect spouse. We were encouraged to search Scriptures and hunt for signs, trying to uncover the map of our lives that God has drawn.

In 1980 I found an excellent book by a Bible professor that expanded my understanding of Christian decision making. Garry Friesen's *Decision Making and the Will of God* (Multnomah Press, 1980) includes a forceful critique of the blueprint school and presents an alternative— the wisdom school. Friesen argues that God gives us moral will and grants us principles (wisdom) by which we are to live, acting in accordance to these principles. We make our choices based on these principles, and as we grow in wisdom, we apply this godly sense to our daily circumstances. Friesen rejects any implication that we are like pawns on a chessboard that God merely moves around at his will. We are told not to expect that there is just one answer to God's will for every decision we face. Several may be possible.

I initially designed the "Decision Making Worksheet" after reading Garry's book in 1980 and finding his summary of the "wisdom signs" extremely practical in making major decisions.

A more recent author, Gordon T. Smith, in *Listening to God in Times of Choice* (InterVarsity Press, 1997), argues for a third way, and this is the basic approach we encourage here. Gordon suggests that we develop discernment as a spiritual discipline. By stressing the personal aspects of growing in our relationship with Abba, we come to understand the personal and relational nature of his will, not just in times of crisis but throughout our daily lives. We grow into an interactive relationship with God's Spirit, who longs to speak into our lives on a daily basis. You can see that this kind of Spirit-guided conversation is neither a written "blueprint" nor a fixed "wisdom sign" or printed road map.

Smith writes,

Another concern I have is that the wisdom model takes little if any account of our emotions, which have a powerful effect on how we think and can easily shape and potentially distort the decision-making process. Further, the wisdom model fails to deal adequately with the reality of mixed motives that inevitably shape the process of making a choice.

He rightfully suggests that we need a model for both small and major decisions and discernment "that enables us to come to terms with our emotional makeup as well as the motives, confused or otherwise, that influence our thoughts."[1]

Consider the following very practical approach to sorting through all that Scripture says about wisdom, listening and guidance as it relates to some of the major decisions you will be making about moving into crosscultural ministry. It is meant as an essential approach to discerning God's voice, not turning the spiritual into a mechanical formula.

Christian decision making involves freedom and risk. Scripture teaches us to confirm God's moral will (as revealed in the Bible) by following certain indicators—"wisdom signs." These signs are specific biblical ways the Holy Spirit guides us in our decision making.

Types of Decisions

Christian decision making can be divided into two categories. The first involves *areas that are specifically addressed in the Bible*. These are the revealed principles and commands of God, which must be obeyed. Those scriptural guidelines—both exhortations and prohibitions— shape our lifestyles as believers.

The second category involves *areas where the Bible gives no command or principle to fol-*

low. In these situations, it's the believer's responsibility to freely choose his or her own course of action within the boundaries of biblical guidelines.

Now, how do these apply to the specific decisions we face on the journey—what is our ministry burden and passion, for example, or which church to attend or which mission agency to contact or whether we're to marry and have children? Does God provide help for these life decisions beyond the general guidelines set forth in his Word?

We believe that the triune God is a personal and loving God—not a detached, aloof being. Abba invites us to know him and tells us that he has counted the very hairs of our heads. The Spirit is given to guide, encourage and empower us. Jesus lives within us. Since he's so personally involved in every aspect of our lives, how, then, do we understand his mind for us when we face a specific decision?

Seven Wisdom Signs

Scripture describes the following seven wisdom signs. These indicators can help you discover and affirm the Lord's will for your life.

1. Common sense. God created people with a natural ability to make sound judgments based on facts. It's a form of wisdom that's part of God's grace to humans everywhere (see Prov 1:1-3; 3:5-6; 4:11).

When it comes to selecting a mission experience, common sense tells you to compare things like the mission organization's purpose, values, vision, ministry, leaders, supervision, fields and costs. It causes you to look at your own abilities, experiences and spiritual gifts.

Common sense works as a wisdom sign because it affirms or denies our basic intuitive response to an idea, person or option—as long as it harmonizes with the moral will of God and does not contradict what he has already revealed in Scripture.

2. Spiritual counsel. The book of Proverbs teaches that there is balance and wisdom in seeking the wise counsel of mature believers (see Prov 10:23; 15:22; 19:20; also Heb 13:7-8). These may include parents, close friends, teachers, pastors or others in spiritual leadership. They are not so much "subject-matter experts" as they are additional discerning ears in the process. The Christian corrective to the extremes of individualism is the wisdom and support of the Christian community of faith of which you are a member.

When you're in the presence of wise Christians, ask questions. Lay out your concerns and invite their perspective. Listen to how they navigate solving a problem or sorting through multiple options. Distill their years of insight into principles that you can apply to your situation.

If the advice of certain counselors conflicts at points, evaluate the reasons behind their differing viewpoints. Keep in mind the strong points of each type of counselor: your parents probably know you best; teachers and professional counselors can help you uncover conceptual blind spots you've overlooked; pastors and other spiritual counselors can help frame facts and situations into proper spiritual perspective.

3. Personal desires. Spiritual growth makes a significant impact on your personal desires. The psalmist wrote that when you delight in the Lord, he gives you the desires of your heart (see Ps 37:4; Prov 21:21). What is your heart's desire as it relates to stepping into your part in God's foreign policy? Is your heart to work among migrant gang members or to reach homeless people in Amsterdam? Does your heart beat as you establish house churches in Russia or as you teach and equip emerging leaders in Central

Asia? As you mature, your motives and desires often reflect God's desires. But your personal desires are never authoritative and must always be judged against God's Word.

When two options you are considering seem truly equal, this wisdom sign tells you to choose the one you would enjoy most. Follow your heart! That is the incredible freedom of the exchanged life.

4. Circumstances. The situation and context in which you will find yourself become vital ingredients in decision making. You are not a disembodied saint floating eerily through chaotic times. You are a particular person with very unique wiring and calling, whom the Spirit has placed in a specific set of circumstances "for such a time as this" (Esther 4:14). Context is vital to understand and is the setting into which God speaks.

Carefully analyze your situation (see Prov 16:9, 33; 20:24). As you contemplate missions involvement, your situation will include factors like timing, people, events, circumstances, cost, travel and so on. Every option has its advantages and disadvantages. Try to discern the more subtle meaning and consequences of your decisions. For example, what is God saying to you through your recent encounter with a leader from a particular ministry? What interruptions and circumstances have suddenly presented you with fresh options? What is God saying through your recent impromptu ministry to those in need around you?

Writing down an insight or idea is a simple antidote to emotionalizing your decision or becoming a victim of your own impulsiveness. We are not suggesting that you spiritualize every event or seek spiritual truth hidden under rocks. Rather, become aware that God does use circumstances to shape our character and to provide guidance toward or away from his purposes. Become more attentive of how the Spirit uses the elements and dynamics of your daily reality to help you make decisions.

5. Scripture. God's moral will is objective, complete and adequate as revealed in his Word. Yet the Bible does not tell us the precise answer to every situation. What it *does* teach us is to acquire wisdom and to apply it to our decisions (see Prov 6:20-23; 8:10-11, 32-33; 9:10).

We've all heard the jokes about people opening their Bibles and trusting the "fickle finger of fate" to point them to the exact verse to inform their decision. Once a close friend of mine, trying to select a seminary, opened and pointed to a verse. When he read, "Grace be unto you," he immediately applied to Grace Seminary. That's a stretch, and a misuse of how the Spirit intends to speak to us through the written Word.

We've all had spontaneous ideas pop into our heads. Those inner impressions can come from a variety of sources—God, Satan, past experience, habituated behavior, stress, the flesh, immaturity, indigestion or insomnia. Each must be judged by God's Word. After thoughtful reflection, you may conclude that an impression or feeling is actually a good plan—a wise way to serve God. Or you may decide it's foolish and ought to be ignored.

6. Prayer. Prayer is simply conversation with God—your means of communicating with God to understand his mind and his guidance. It's a two-way conversation: you share your heart and needs and requests; God, in turn, shares his heart of love, insights and words of direction. In most decisions, this is where the battle is fought (see Eph 6:18). The time you spend thinking and gathering information about a decision should be matched with daily conversations in prayer. At times it helps to focus these prayers by writing them down. I have known people who agonize over major decisions, but spend less than five minutes a day praying about them. If you are trusting God as your loving Father, doesn't it make sense that he is eager to answer your requests for wisdom through the intimate channel of prayer?

The "Decision-Making Worksheet" on page 203 is meant to be used as your prayer journal—listing what you've thought, heard and discovered, and then dialoguing with the Spirit to get his input. I have found the worksheet helps me keep track of the incredibly specific insights and words the Spirit speaks back to me. It doesn't de-spiritualize the process at all. It keeps me much more dependent and responsive to all that the Spirit does want to communicate with me.

7. Previous experience. Life is a classroom, and you don't want to return to elementary school if you can help it! Be smart. Reflect on your past decisions—and those of others—to learn how they were good and how they were bad (see Prov 10:24; 21:1). Write down any critical decisions that influence where you now are and what options you have before you. The "Symbol Timeline Exercise" (pp. 249-51) is just one very helpful way to answer the question "How has God been working in my past, and what has he been saying to me?" The final step in completing your timeline is in distilling the spiritual insights and leadership lessons the Spirit has been teaching you over the years. The timeline is merely a way to capture years of spiritual insights.

In reflecting on your past experience, for example, you may detect a pattern of pain and difficulty when you move into isolation and greater growth and blessing when you are in authentic relationships and closer accountability. Or you may discern a pattern of rapid growth when you have an intentional mentor and see periods of malaise and wandering when you get too detached from wise counselors.

Romans 8:28 says that God is at work in every decision you make as a Christian committed to his will. This means that when you make the best decision possible, you can trust him to work out the results for good.

Decision-Making Worksheet

The following Decision-Making Worksheet can serve as a model of a "balance sheet" of the pros and cons for each specific decision you're facing. It's a simple, logical tool to help guide your thinking and reflection. It is not meant to take the mystery out of the process but to remove the mystical. By referring to the seven wisdom signs listed in the left column of the worksheet, you are seeking to listen to each of the major areas of guidance mentioned in Scripture in your decision-making process. Meanwhile, don't forget that God has committed himself to be at work in your deliberations for the ultimate purpose of his greater glory.

Personal Experience

When facing a major decision, I start a separate worksheet for each option I'm considering. So, if I were evaluating schools, I might have one worksheet for each of the three schools I was considering. Or, for a move I was praying through, I might create a worksheet for each option. I record the pros and cons as I carefully work through each wisdom sign. This may take days or sometimes weeks. Some may see this as too mechanized or lacking spontaneity, yet that same person will take weeks with a pro-and-con list to evaluate what car or computer to purchase. So if the decision facing you is an important one, I think it's worth the effort.

I find the process is a discipline that helps

me be more prayerful and careful. It doesn't make it easier; it just makes the issues clearer. In every decision I've made since high school, it has clarified my need to wait on God. It doesn't replace dependence; rather, it makes painfully obvious the areas in which I really am totally dependent on the Lord.

Use the worksheet as a spiritual decision-making aid; it's not a gimmick or a Ouija board. But if you've been confused by the number of options you face, and the details and issues seem to multiply, this tool is guaranteed to spotlight the wisdom factors you should consider.

Process

As you take time to think and pray through what insight and wisdom you've gained from each wisdom sign, write down those insights in the appropriate column. When you've completed your spiritual "homework" prayerfully, you may find that one option very clearly outweighs the pros or cons of another option. And that's the purpose of the tool—to help you determine which option would be the wisest decision to make.

Peace

When the wisdom signs seem to point toward a particular choice, bathe your final decision in prayer. When you sense God's *peace* about that option, you can be pretty sure it's a wise decision. That is the practical pattern Paul suggested to the Colossian Christians (see Col 3:15). Let God's peace be the final confirmation ("umpire") that you have made a wise decision, and move out confidently in obedience.

We recommend Gordon Smith's *Listening to God in Times of Choice* (InterVarsity Press, 1997) as a helpful primer to take you deeper into the art of discerning God's will.

Note: You may want to make copies of the worksheet to write on so you can evaluate more than one option.

David G. Benner. *Desiring God's Will.* Downers Grove, Ill.: InterVarsity Press, 2005.

Dallas Willard. *Hearing God: Developing a Conversational Relationship with God.* Downers Grove, Ill.: InterVarsity Press, 1984, 1993, 1994.

[1]Gordon T. Smith, *Listening to God in Times of Choice* (Downers Grove, Ill.: InterVarsity Press, 1997), p. 102.

Decision-Making Worksheet

STEVE HOKE

Description of decision to be made:		
Date:		Deadline:
WISDOM SIGNS	PROS	CONS
Common Sense		
Spiritual Counselors		
Personal Desires		
Circumstances		
Scripture		
Prayer		
Previous Decisions		
Peace		
Conclusion		

🧳 My Journey

ROSE DOWSETT
OMF International, Asia, Scotland

I tumbled precipitately into Christian faith as an unhappy, philosophically Marxist teenager. Challenged by a school friend, I read the New Testament on a dare, confident I could disprove the resurrection. I read it right through, three times in three weeks, and discovered that I was wrong and Jesus is most gloriously alive. My previous allegiance to Marxism had given me global eyes, and while reading the New Testament I immediately spotted the inescapable missionary dimension of authentic Christian discipleship. I couldn't see why the church didn't seem to notice.

A praying peer group at university (most of us went on to serve in Asia), encounters with lively and joyful missionary speakers, friendships with Asian students, a supply of riveting missionary books, three years of staff work with Inter-Varsity U.K., a week caring for shivering leaders of Asian IVCF movements at an exceedingly cold and wet Keswick Convention student camp, unexpected engagement to a colleague diverted to the Philippines—all these and more conspired, in the goodness of God, to take me, by now a member of OMF International, to be seconded to IVCF Philippines. Eight years of walking with God through wonderful friendships, political upheaval, violence, life-threatening illness, satisfying ministry, seeing God doing beautiful things—these stretched my faith and changed my life.

Reassigned in 1978 to Scotland—another foreign country for us—I had trouble making sense of it all. But the Lord tenderly opened up new areas of ministry, which I gradually came to see could not have happened without all that had gone before. We are still passionate about world mission, still reaching across cultures, still learning more about trusting God and about worship through life as well as lip.

"Get Smart" About Missions

JANET COCKRUM

Most people say, "I'm willing to go, but planning to stay." You need to reverse this and say, "I'm planning to go, but willing to stay."

That simple statement by my pastor, Dr. Don Hoke, changed the way we approached missions. If you aren't planning to go, you never get off the dock, step in the boat and leave land. If my husband and I hadn't been intentional about moving forward with the education, applications, integration and mentoring required by our agency and home church, we would have never gotten beyond the "willing to go" mindset.

I always think of the old *Get Smart* TV show when I reflect on this challenge. Every show started with Agent Smart having to move through a series of security doors to get down to the home office. Every door was closed, but Smart kept moving forward. A door wouldn't open until Smart was right in front of it (sounds like today's motion-activated doors). At any stage along the way, one of those doors could have remained closed, and he would have been shut out from the home office and his next assignment.

I approached getting to the field with this visual picture. God could open or shut any door as we moved down the path to Spain. It was actually liberating to keep moving forward, focused on being obedient to the calling and listening to God's voice on the journey.

What are some of the doors that must open as one moves toward missions? There are the obvious ones of training, education, legal requirements, agency requirements, concerns of aging parents, educational needs and interests of children, and of course the big double garage door of fundraising. But there are also doors that you don't expect to see and suddenly you are on an unplanned detour.

My husband and I were three weeks from completing our mission training. We were moving forward in our support raising. We had rented our house, found a new home for our beloved dog, dropped the kids off at college, quit our jobs and were looking at departure dates. We had been hit with many little surprises in recent months. Two car wrecks, infections, allergic reactions to medications, major dental issues and financial concerns. Every week the "attacks" seemed to accelerate. We recognized them as attempts by the enemy to discourage and distract us. We drew strength from a team of friends who prayed with us. We saw God bring healing, bring hope and keep the joy in our lives.

We were three weeks from completing our prefield training when we found out our son had some serious problems with his knee. As we were driving up to Washington, D.C., to apply for our visas, we got the call from the orthopedic surgeon that our son didn't need surgery on his knee, but he needed to see a blood-cancer specialist to be analyzed regarding a serious problem with his blood platelets. We were stunned, overwhelmed, devastated and blinded with pain. We didn't think we should continue the visas process, because who knew if we would even be considering missions now. We

cried and prayed, and then we determined that we needed to at least apply for the visas, because one thing was certain: we couldn't go to Spain without them. So this was one more door that we were letting God open or close.

Our prayer warriors labored with us over this burden. The amazing news from the doctor was that Chad was completely healed and that his blood was normal. How we celebrated answered prayer!

We continued to bask in this news for the next three days until the most stunning unexpected unbelievable and unplanned event happened. My athletic, disciplined husband dropped dead in minute twenty-eight of thirty on the treadmill. He had full cardiac arrest and was dead for five minutes. God had a cardiac doctor thirty seconds away from him at the gym. There was a fireman working out, who called for the defibrillator. There was a sixteen-year-old young man who had been trained one week before how to use it. This was critical because certain brain damage starts at eight minutes. There was an emergency nurse there who joined this team to help save Mark's life. One week later he had quadruple bypass surgery. This was a giant door and one that was really heavy, but God opened it. Mark made a complete recovery, and the doctors gave him the okay to go.

Four months later, our tickets were bought, and we were busy saying our goodbyes. With five days left to departure, I had a full seizure. It was so powerful that it broke the right side of my back. I had never had a seizure, and there was no history of seizures in my family. We cancelled our tickets, and I was sent to bed for a month to heal. Once again we saw in big letters "detour." We were delayed, but kept moving forward and were amazed as God threw open the door that had "health concerns" written on it.

Two months later, we finished saying our goodbyes, and I flew off to Spain in a back brace and with the overwhelming commitment of our family and friends to be praying for us. The enemy wanted to distract, discourage and destroy our plans to bring the gospel to Spain. His scheme failed miserably, because it resulted in a deepening interest and eagerness of our supporters to pray for us. It grounded us in the assurance of God's love and watch care as evidenced in his provision during our personal health crises.

How many times we have reflected on the challenge that helped us get on the field. We weren't just committed to think about missions or "willing to go." We intentionally planned to go

and kept going forward. There is a home office and an assignment waiting for you at the other end of those doors. Get smart about missions and let God be the one who directs your steps.

Dr. Janet Cockrum has the heart of a teacher and mentor. Her passion is praying for young people to know the transforming power of the gospel, to experience intimacy with God and to hear his call. Her years as a teacher, athletic director, and adjunct professor of marriage and family laid the foundation for her new role as the director for interns and recruitment for World Team Spain.

Journal Worksheet Six

STEVE HOKE

Where Are You Now?

Do you know some missionaries who are attempting to reach an unreached people? Where are they now or are they intending to serve? If you don't know any missionaries personally, this becomes a very practical discovery task to find and dialogue with at least two.

Is your church supporting missionaries or national workers who are reaching unreached peoples? If not, find some nearby churches that have an intentional focus on launching into new, unreached territories. Make an appointment to dialogue with them about how they came to this strategic focus.

How familiar are you with different cultures and people groups from around the world?

List the top three people groups that currently interest you.
1.
2.
3.

What Do You Need to Do Next?

When will you discuss the needs of the world with your church or a mission agency? Which one(s)?

When and how will you do your own investigating on unreached people groups or other major unevangelized parts of the world with whom you might become involved?

What continent?

What region or nation(s)?

Which people group(s)?

List at least three specific learning objectives you will set for yourself as you research unreached people(s):

1.
2.
3.

What Will the Future Look Like?

What *kind* of missionary do you believe God is leading you to become? (In other words, what will be your special niche within a church-planting assignment or on an outreach team?)

What insight has focusing your ministry burden and passion brought to your decision-making process?

Where do you believe God will have you serve?

With what church or agency might you serve?

With what people group or geographic location will you be involved?

List the questions and concerns you still have and that you are praying through.

Keep track of the insights and answers that the Holy Spirit brings into your heart and mind.

What additional insight is the Spirit giving you as you wait on him for your future? (Use whatever additional paper or means your prefer to record these answers to prayer.)

SEVEN

Hands-On Missionary Training

STEVE HOKE AND BILL TAYLOR

Let's assume you've completed your basic academic training. Let's also assume you've had serious on-the-job ministry training within a local church or community—and (hopefully) have been gainfully employed in the meantime.

Assuming all these things means that by now you have probably spent at least one brief period in another culture and perhaps as long as two years in a ministry-focused local or international short-term or crosscultural experience. You've been stretched. You've been shaken. And you've grown stronger as a result.

Now it's time to figure out what kind of training you're going to need. Our focus here is to highlight practical equipping for the particular kind of ministry work you will do on the field. We know of some church planters whose only stateside ministry experience was discipling high-school students and teaching an adult Sunday school class. This is neither adequate nor realistic practical training for persons who will be ministering in multilevel, multicultural contexts. We've heard of others who arrive to serve on a team who have never, ever lived in community or worked closely alongside others in a working team.

By now you may have determined the kind of missionary role you want to fill. This workbook uses church planting as a sample role for you to consider. But bivocational (tentmaking) ministry and training other missionaries are examples of other vital roles toward which God may be directing you. As you know by now, we're assuming that all these roles contribute to the ultimate goal of taking the gospel to a group of people who have never heard it before and being used by the Holy Spirit to plant a community of Jesus-worshipers.

Perhaps God has shown you a particular continent, country or people group among whom he wants you to minister. Maybe you've had the opportunity to study the many needs for a holistic ministry that have been identified there. You may feel led by the Spirit to attempt to reach a particular one. Or you may be part of a church with a particular missions focus, such as sending church-based teams to plant churches among an "adopted" unreached people group or nation. Or you may be from a church that is committed to translating the language of an unreached people group.

All these factors will affect the extent and type of practical missionary training you will need. It will require time and actual ministry experience to develop competencies in all three of the dimensions described in the profiles: character and spirituality qualities, ministry skills and knowledge. You'll need to drive your foundations deep into the substrata of God himself.

Master the Fundamentals

First, you must build a solid God and Word foundation—a strong working knowledge of Scripture that establishes your faith, undergirds your values and guides your behavior. Second, you must have a good grasp of the cultures within which the Scriptures were written. That involves knowledge of the biblical history and culture, as well as a growing sensitivity to the cultural issues in introducing Jesus into another culture. Without this, you will be unable to communicate God's Word effectively to another culture. Third, you will dream of the day when this living Word comes supernaturally alive in a new culture.

Your biblical knowledge is to be valued, not because it affords prestige or power, but because it is useful for guiding your ministry. It enables you to be and do what would otherwise be impossible. That's why we've focused first on character qualities ("being" goals) and ministry skills ("doing" goals). Those first two qualifications help you determine what knowledge you need to acquire for effective missionary service.

Build a Solid Set of Ministry Skills

If your work on the field is to be effective, your missionary training should be intentional and purposeful. Your early on-the-job training in a church was meant to expose you to the range of ministries needed in a church and to stretch your ministry "muscles" while letting you try your hand at teaching, witnessing, discipling, equipping and releasing others, and so on. This practical training phase of your preparation is a time in which you need to sharpen the specific ministry skills you will most likely use overseas. Hopefully you were part of a church-based cell group that witnessed growth and even multiplied itself.

Know Your Role as You Focus Your Training

The most relevant preparation for church planting overseas is participation in and significant responsibility on a church-planting or community-building team *at home*. Similarly, the most relevant preparation for teamwork overseas is active engagement in a ministry team stateside. Witnessing in your neighborhood, relating to the needs of your neighbors, initiating relationships in your apartment complex, starting evangelistic Bible studies, creating cell groups, raising up leaders from the harvest and discipling new believers to the second and third generation are critical church-planting skills. These are practical traits you can acquire, develop and refine in your own community and congregation.

Have an Adequate Missiological and Theological Preparation

This includes an understanding of God's purposes in history, how his Spirit has worked in the history of the church, how theology has developed and the way men and women through the ages have worked out their understanding of what God has been saying to us. But keep it practical. The purpose of this study is to help you be more effective in living and equipping others to live meaningful, Christ-centered lives. Your knowledge is never an end in itself.

Avoid simplistic mission slogans and sloppy reductionism of the Great Commission. Develop a strong theology of creation and of kingdom values. Many missionaries have greatly benefited from one to three years of formal studies, but it doesn't work that way for others. The "Perspectives on the World Christian Movement" course is the single best introduction to a theology of international missions. If you haven't yet taken the course, now is the time to do so. (See appendix 1 for details.)

Get Broad Training in the Social Sciences

The social sciences, especially anthropology, sociology and political science, go hand in hand with the history and present effectiveness of missionary work around the world. Anthropology enables you to consider the origin and nature of cultures—your own and that of the people you will be serving. Sociology provides a vocabulary and mental models for understanding how people establish rules for living together. Political science gives you tools for understanding the dynamic tensions that flow (or rip) through societies and how societies organize themselves politically. As missionaries learn about the beliefs and customs of a people, they discover effective bridges for the communication of biblical truth.

Focus on Language and Culture Learning

No effort should be spared here. Wise churches and most sending agencies have a clear policy that lays out the orientation, cultural study and language proficiency expected of all missionaries. However, because this can be one of the most difficult parts of practical missionary training, some churches and agencies ease off requirements in this area.

Actually, churches and mission agencies should encourage missionaries to do *more* than the required minimum. There are hundreds of missionaries who would say with regret, "How I wish that years ago we had spent the time and the effort to become fluent in the language. The demands of family, the needs of the field and the 'tyranny of the urgent' drew us into ministry with less-than-adequate language literacy. Our ministry could have had much more impact."

Language acquisition and culture learning go hand in hand. It's difficult to really understand a culture until you can *think* in its terms— until you can use its idioms, laugh at its jokes, weep at its pain. Thinking culturally requires fluency in the language, and not just the trade language used in the cities, either.

As a friend of ours says, "You want to communicate fluently in the language that people think in, dream in and make love in." Some of the best training in language acquisition is given in combination with stateside prefield orientation workshops. A number of agencies have moved all their cultural orientation training to the field, so it is given "in context"—on the ground and in the country in which actual ministry will occur.

Most North Americans have little training in language learning and language theory. The majority of us are monolingual. The rest of the world is not. That puts us at a distinct disadvantage when it comes to learning a language. Therefore, a basic understanding of language theory or linguistics may prove useful before you plunge into learning a new language. In addition, it's even more useful to study some of the new language-acquisition techniques that have recently been developed.

One of the most effective language-acquisition methods is to learn among people who speak the language. Tom and Betty Sue Brewster pioneered the LAMP (Language Acquisition Made Practical) method in the 1970s. It emphasizes learning simple phrases and repeatedly using them while living with a host family or conversing regularly with a local "language helper" from your target culture. "Learn a little and use it a lot," is their motto. This total-immersion approach to learning language and culture is the most natural way of "bonding" with your new culture. Today it is widely practiced by many mission agencies as a primary language-acquisition technique.

As the world becomes more urban, there's a growing emphasis on preparing missionaries to live and minister in cities. Missions internships in urban centers throughout North America provide ideal preparation for incarnational living among city dwellers, especially the urban poor. For instance, each summer several mission agencies and local churches jointly sponsor an eight- to ten-week urban internship in Los Angeles. Missionary appointees learn while ministering in a context similar to that of the "target people" to whom they'll eventually go. Each participant lives with a family from the ethnic group with whom he or she plans to minister.

Faculty come from participating churches, mission agencies and nearby seminaries. The participants' training includes highly interactive, on-site cultural exposure and investigation, language acquisition, spiritual formation (including biblical study and reflection), team building and leadership development. Similar training programs are conducted by other agencies and churches in other major cities such as New York and Chicago.

Several other innovative language study programs, like that of the Russian Language Ministry at Columbia International University in Columbia, South Carolina, have arisen in response to the growing demand of North Americans who are moving to Eastern Europe and regions of unreached peoples. Based on recent developments in linguistics and language learning, these U.S.-based programs provide a solid foundation in language basics within a stable, familiar environment before you move overseas and encounter cultural and language stress. Thankfully, there are two-week intensive courses that provide language learning skills for you. Check out these two missionary training organizations that offer intensive, short-term workshops in language acquisition:

Don't fall into the trap of thinking you will have to learn only one language in your lifetime. God may move you to another field. The future of missions will see an increasing redeployment of missionaries from one country to another, often in mid-career.

Having an ability to learn other languages increases your flexibility, making you ready to take new assignments elsewhere in the kingdom. And don't let a negative experience of trying to learn a language in high-school prejudice you. Your classroom attempts may not have been a true test of your abilities at all.

Despite the diversity that has enriched North American culture, we have tended to see it as a rather bland "melting pot" of many cultures rather than as a "stew pot" or "tossed salad" of coexisting, rather distinct cultures and peoples. Certainly the new century has ushered in an emphasis on diversity and inclusiveness, and the postmodern generation has a broader perspective on culture and the world than did most of our ancestors. Yet the headlines frequently testify to the fact that North Americans still tend to *react* to differences, rather than accept and celebrate them. Thankfully, this situation is radically changing as the "nations" pour into North America.

The history of missions includes countless examples of sincere but sad attempts to reach a people—attempts made by missionaries who understood neither their own culture nor the culture of the people they were trying to reach. Learning about the culture right next door to you will start you on the path toward learning to be a "cultural detective"—naturally inquisitive and genuinely interested in learning about other people and comprehending their ways of life. The first step is to understand yourself and your own cultural background and biases.

For resources on schools and other sources of practical missionary training, including language and culture learning, check out appendix 1.

Missionary Training International
www.mti.org (see Program in Language Acquisition Training [PILAT])

Center for Intercultural Training
www.cit-online.org (see Programs, then Core Five, then Cultural/Language Reasons)

Why Overseas Missionary Training Works

ROGER CHARLES

Rice paddies surrounded the seminary where Dirk studied church planting. Friends debated the theory and practice of Muslim evangelism over heaping bowls of rice and chili peppers. The competing melodies of Indonesian church music and the call to prayer at a dozen nearby mosques set the mood for his theological studies. Crowded dorms and buses and the lack of clocks and electricity taught Dirk volumes about the values and realities of ministry in another culture. The farmers in his village church grew to respect the foreigner who was first a learner, then a teacher.

After graduating from the Indonesian seminary, Dirk wrote, "I have found that my impact on Asians is largely measured by Asia's impact on me. Overseas training has brought me thousands of miles closer to the hearts of those I want to serve. I believe this extra cultural learning has added an incarnational freshness to my ministry that rings true with the lifestyle of Jesus and the apostles."

Taking the Plunge

Dirk and many other aspiring missionaries have experienced the strengths and weaknesses of overseas training. Many came from strong churches and top Bible schools, yet they recognized gaps in their crosscultural preparation. Overseas training provided the right tools for their job and exposed them to real crosscultural living. Though they went about it in different ways, cultural immersion was their common goal.

Missionaries often mistake plunging into ministry for plunging into culture. They pay for a fast trip through language school by enduring years of slow and pain-filled ministry. Some are disillusioned and discouraged when what were great ministry skills and experience in the United States are not immediately useful overseas.

Swimming is best learned wet. Before missionaries face the pounding surf of full-time ministry, they need a chance to paddle around, flounder and right themselves in shallower waters. The mistakes that knock them down need time to be transformed from failure to insight.

Slowing down at the beginning for a mixture of formal and nonformal on-site training can immensely accelerate their ensuing climb up the learning curve to high-quality ministry.

Seminary Overseas

Dirk's seminary classes were all taught in the Indonesian language. He planted and pastored a church on weekends. He interned on a local missionary team. Academically, he could have done better in America. But his experience has made him a cultural insider with a large network of Indonesian pastors and leaders. He's now teaching and writing training materials with a distinctly Asian focus and flavor.

Of course, full-time theological training is not for everyone, even when linked with plenty of hands-on ministry. Australians Barry and Mary entered the same seminary program as Dirk, but unlike him they did not have a mission board to shepherd them. The Indonesian school's demands were overwhelming and not geared for a foreign family. Barry and Mary decided to slow down and study part time. That helped.

After a year of language and a year of part-time studies, Barry and Mary found their ministry niche on a team targeting a large unreached people group. Now they can start this focused ministry, having already overcome many family and cultural problems.

Seminary anywhere is difficult. In another language it is often incomprehensible. For those interested in a year or two of study near—but not immersed in—a foreign culture, seminary programs in English are available in the Philippines, Singapore, India and several African and Latin American countries.

Wading in Gradually

Sharon was headed for Thailand. She received one month of candidate orientation in the United States, then three months of training in Singapore. There she was directly exposed to Asian cultural issues. She studied culture and missions with full-time missionaries. She learned to eat hot sauce on rice by adding one drop each day. Her entry into the culture and language of Thailand, which is so radically different from that of the United States, was moderated by a general introduction and immersion into Asia.

Sharon's cultural training was just beginning when she went from Singapore to Thailand for twelve months of language school. Then, for her first term, her mission gave her a culturally intense assignment and evaluated her language progress quarterly.

Sharon spent that first two-year term living in a Christian girls' hostel, surrounded by Thai friends, Thai food and the Thai language. After leading Bible studies and worship for hundreds of evenings over those two years, Sharon's degree of language fluency and cultural adaptation astonished her family, friends and even other missionaries.

Building on Short Terms

Overseas training is the logical extension of "see it first" ministry visits. Cultural immersion provides purposeful mastery of the cultural adaptation skills necessary for an interested visitor to become an effective resident. Amy took this route. She had gone on several short-term trips to the Philippines. Those experiences whetted her appetite for missions and gave her a desire to return as a long-term missionary.

She enrolled in the Asian studies program at the University of the Philippines. For two years she studied in the city and ministered in a church in the countryside. Amy wrote a thesis on traditional Filipino healing and spiritism, gaining a much deeper understanding of these crucial spiritual issues than do most of the busy long-term missionaries.

At her graduation awards banquet, following several dull speeches in English by Filipinos, Amy gave a glowing speech with a Christian message in clear, formal Tagalog. She received thundering applause. Cultural immersion had turned a bold short-term visitor into a powerful crosscultural communicator.

Cultural Apprenticeship

Dave and Eve had been on short-term mission trips before their local church sent them to Hong Kong as full-time missionaries. Their assignment was to assist a Chinese friend who was researching the church in mainland China.

While studying Mandarin, Dave began writing a prayer guide on the Chinese church. His cultural and political understanding grew rapidly. Without shepherding and supervision, however, his family was nearing burnout. Dave linked up with an effective field team and found the right balance of cultural apprenticeship with Chinese friends and ministry apprenticeships with American missionaries. Thereafter his ministry to China and his web of relationships grew rapidly. Their "let's be learners first" attitude propelled Dave and Eve into a strategic program, which trains overseas Chinese to minister in mainland China.

Jack, on the other hand, leaped right into an intense international apprenticeship. He was a former Marine, but boot camp never prepared him for the challenges of ministry in inner-city Manila. After a few months in a language immersion program, Jack joined an inner-city ministry to the poorest of Manila's street people. He lived with a band of Filipino street evangelists. The twenty of them slept in a room with narrow bunk beds crammed only eighteen inches apart.

Jack ate, bathed and slept "ghetto Christianity." He followed a Filipino leader everywhere for the first months, then was increasingly sent out to minister on his own. This was cultural boot camp in its most intense form. But in his two years on the streets, Jack won more souls than many lifelong missionaries in Manila and was frequently told by Filipinos, "You speak Tagalog better than we do!"

Seasoned Missionaries Too

Veteran missionaries can also benefit from overseas training opportunities. After losing his visa as a religious worker in a Muslim country, Rory fulfilled a long-time dream by reentering the same country as a student. He learned a new regional language and had a chance to study the culture more deeply than when he'd been a busy church-planting missionary. Also, he was able to maintain old relationships with his disciples and to mentor informally new missionaries who came to "his" country as tentmakers.

Ray, a senior mission agency administrator, decided to complete a doctorate in management in the Philippines rather than in the United States because the school there had a program in English and the location would enable him to spend time with his children, who were in an academy in Manila.

Ray spent one school quarter each year in the Philippines and maintained his ministry and administrative roles in another country the rest of the year. One product of his studies was the creation of an on-the-job training program for new field leadership within his agency. The agency had run similar programs in the United States, but they were much more expensive to maintain. Ray's experience gave his agency the expertise needed to plan a new, less costly approach, while providing him with a valuable advanced degree.

Finding Overseas Programs

The cost of overseas missionary training is often quite low—especially compared to the high cost of seminary and the higher cost of first-term burnout. However, finding a well-rounded program that will stretch you without breaking you may take time.

Christian international students and missionaries from your country of interest can provide insight into the missions training options available in their homeland. Missions professors and missions agency leaders are often also aware of good programs and the costs involved.

Variety is essential to missionary life and training. The best training experiences include most of the following personal spiritual preparation: language learning from people, not books; living with nationals; some structured goals and activities; a national and a foreign mentor; occasional fellowship and spiritual support with missionaries; adequate rest and recreation; a supportive home church and mission committee.

Just as some people can handle spicier food than others, some potential missionaries are able to handle more aggressive training programs. But don't overestimate your capabilities. Generally, you should settle for a balanced diet of training with a distinctly foreign flavor. The spiritual food served up by missionaries who train overseas will taste a lot more like home cooking to the people they serve.

(Adapted from *Missions Today '96* with permission of the publisher. Evanston, Ill.: Berry Publishing, 1996.)

Roger Charles (a pseudonym) has participated in cultural immersion programs in several countries. He currently trains Asians in crosscultural communications, comparative religions and New Testament theology.

Customize Your Prefield Training

STEVE HOKE

There's a world of learning beyond the classroom. It's practical. It's guided. It's culturally specific. And it's offered by some of the finest agencies in the world. More and more, mission agencies are designing their training for the specific fields and people groups they serve. These in-house programs will teach you principles and skills that are best learned on the job. The instruction begins at home, intensifies on the mission field and covers the following ten critical dimensions.

1. Ministry Philosophy

The core values and beliefs that guide every missionary effort are better caught than taught—best learned by rubbing shoulders with missionaries and national coworkers. The conceptual foundation for a missions philosophy is presented in a prefield orientation or candidate school that lasts from one week to three months. You'll see it at work when you get to the field. Principles from Scripture, research and field experience are shared to help you develop spiritual, crosscultural and relational skills.

One mission executive says, "Our four-month prefield training program is the single most important factor in preventing field casualties." Yet hearing about an agency's philosophy while sitting in Denver is one thing; learning it in incarnational ministry in Calcutta is the real thing. No matter what the ministry, new missionaries develop their own personalized philosophy of ministry best in the crosscultural crucible. Another exec explains: "We are looking for team players, but we fully expect to help new staff learn how we disciple, build and plant new churches. Once we find strong players, we're committed to making them even more effective through teamwork."

2. Message

Each mission crafts and channels the gospel message in creative ways that reflect its style of ministry. Campus Crusade, the Navigators and InterVarsity are just three groups that have helped successive generations of young people share their faith through distinctively clear and concise presentations. Initial workshops familiarize you with the basic presentation style of an agency, while on-the-job training and practice in the "seminary of the streets" expand your understanding and hone your skills.

There are also rich messages in a mission's "hidden curriculum," which comprises the values, beliefs, lifestyle, language and culture it has developed over the years. Spontaneous expression of an ongoing gratitude to God for his grace and his goodness is the "life message" characteristic of one particular mission. A mission's "message" will rub off on you as you work alongside them.

3. Money

Some of the finest coaching input you can receive on stewardship of time, talent and treasure comes from prefield training programs. The essentials of trusting God for every detail of life—living by faith—form the bedrock of missionary support raising and are taught by veterans who empathize with you in this faith-building process. Skills in budgeting and handling money are developed under experienced tutors. The basics of both "friend raising" and fundraising are mastered under caring mentors who walk with you through the process. Over the years, field missionaries have learned that support raising is the single greatest impetus for ongoing spiritual formation. (See 4.5, which lists resources for personal support raising, pp. 143-46.)

4. Meaning

The shape, color and flavor of a message influence the meaning it conveys. Mission agencies help you comprehend the implications of Jesus' message both for your own life and for the lives of new disciples. Inservice training can foster greater spiritual effectiveness and power in your own life. This, in turn, invests your communication with renewed vigor and meaning for others. Each mission's distinctive programs add layers of meaning to Christian ministry that are unique to their approach. What were formerly only clichés or concepts soon become life-changing truths. You're introduced to new ideas before you go, but you'll find nourishment in these truths when you digest them for yourself in the heat of battle.

5. Methods

Mission agencies teach fresh and different ways to communicate the good news across language and cultural barriers. Ministry methods vary from personal evangelism and discipleship programs to specialized linguistic and anthropological training. Missions typically teach the use of ministry skills and specialized materials during on-field internships that last from one month to two years.

They involve informal meetings and interviews, formal classes and scheduled practicums in areas such as lifestyle evangelism, discipling others, urban church planting, street preaching or leader training.

Increasingly, missions have target peoples, which demands customized strategies. Focused outreach to Muslims, Chinese, migrant workers, Hindus, Buddhists or animists requires intensive, specialized, on-field training by skilled national and missionary practitioners. Language learning is best done on-site as well and can last from two months to two years before fluency is developed.

6. Models of Ministry

Each mission has developed a design or pattern for the way it does ministry, whether evangelism, discipleship or church planting. This becomes a framework within which ministry is planned. Many missions intentionally teach the principles that undergird their approach to ministry. Approaches vary from street theater and preaching to cell-group evangelism in high-rise communities, from research-based church planting to holistic engagement in hunger relief or community development, or university evangelism. An agency's model of ministry can enhance your own emerging view of crosscultural mission and stretch you into more creative means of reaching people for Christ. You should observe critically and listen carefully—trying to detect the pattern of coworkers, willing to adapt your own ideas of how missions should be conducted.

7. Models and Mentors

Every mission has its share of gentle giants. They may be the formal leaders or the informal, unobtrusive leaders who influence an entire movement. Time alone with them is a powerful training experience—life-on-life exposure to God's "Hall of Famers." They aren't flawless, but they know how to play the game. Two key character qualities to look for are faith and dependence.

If you really want to distill the experience that people like this carry, you may need to seek them out and ask for time alone with them. If you can, design an internship or apprenticeship under the guidance and mentoring of a veteran missionary or national pastor whose character and life you respect and whose ministry you want to emulate. Don't be afraid to ask, "Will you mentor me?"

8. Management Style

Within days of joining a mission agency, you'll begin to pick up pointers and principles of managing ministry, leading or stewarding others, and working with people. Take advantage of opportunities to learn lessons from godly men and women on faith, courage, planning, organizing, leading, imparting vision, facilitating, coaching and evaluating ministry.

Every mission agency has a distinctive style of management or leadership. Some are very Western in their approach, setting measurable objectives and evaluating progress. Others are much more relaxed in how they recruit, train and guide the flow of ministry. Some exert considerable control over lifestyle and ministry. Others allow more freedom and empower greater personal responsibility. Some are rigid, others flexible. Try to discern which leadership style fits you best. Learn all you can ahead of time about the dynamics and "chemistry" that make these teams work.

9. Member Health

More and more mission agencies are realizing the importance of providing balanced TLC for their missionaries. This includes proactive training and lifelong opportunities for learning, as well as appropriate reactive care of missionaries and their families. A brief prefield orientation is helpful, but it is inadequate for lifelong effectiveness. The initial training must be followed by specialized equipping on the field and supplemented with study breaks and ongoing educational opportunities on furloughs.

Some missions have significant infrastructure and staff to serve missionary needs; others are quite lean and can offer little care. Some offer mid-career assessment and career counseling; others can only listen, encourage and refer you to skilled professionals. Some agencies are developing reentry workshops to help returning missionaries decompress from the pressures of crosscultural living. These workshops involve reflecting on their experience in groups with other missionaries and talking about their expectations of what lies ahead. The key to healthy reentry is knowing how to maintain your spiritual, relational and physical strength despite a radically different schedule and setting.

Churches and agencies are also increasingly concerned with missionary care and nurture, with helping their missionaries develop personal programs that keep them plugged in and turned on. Caring for the education, transitions and well-being of missionary kids is another significant ministry of larger organizations. Counseling services, career assessments and retirement planning are areas that round out a mission's care program.

10. Mobilization

Mission agencies can also teach you to be more effective in mobilizing others for missions. Your experience can be a great magnet for others, convincing them of the need to become world Christians. You can allow your own experience of crosscultural ministry to serve as a powerful model. A mission agency can help you be on the lookout for those who will respond to the burden of your heart for missions and who will share in the challenge to pray, give and serve.

After your formal training, you can look forward to discovering a unique world of learning. It's personal. It's powerful. It's life changing. Be prepared to meet some of the finest teachers and godly mentors in God's academy. Unlike formal programs burdened with requirements and financial costs, mission agencies provide personalized training—custom fit to your gifts and background. These nonformal programs will give you hands-on expertise in face-to-face ministry that has direct impact on peoples' lives, teaching you skills that are best learned on the job. The instruction you've already received has only just begun. It keeps getting better. And so will you.

(Adapted from *Missions Today '96* with permission of the publisher. Evanston, Ill.: Berry Publishing, 1996.)

There are numerous other prefield orientation programs that have distinguished themselves over the years as being at the top of the list. Many agencies do their own in-house prefield training.

Missionary Training International (ww.mti.org) provides a range of language acquisition, prefield and reentry training workshops in a highly interactive format (mostly two- and three-week modules).

Center for Intercultural Training (www.cit-online .org) provides an even wider range (up to eleven weeks) of language acquisition, prefield and reentry training workshops in a highly interactive format.

Gateway Training for Cross-Cultural Service specializes in missionary preparedness (www .gatewaytraining.org).

Africa Inland Mission sponsors Training In Ministry Outreach (TIMO; www.timo-aim.com), an innovative on-field training for all arriving members of their multicultural church-planting teams in Africa.

Institute of Strategic Languages and Cultures (www.strategiclanguages.org) is an interdenominational organization committed to providing essential crosscultural and linguistic training for missionaries who are preparing to serve Christ among Arabic, Chinese and Russian-speaking peoples.

Tom and Betty Sue Brewster. *Language Acquisition Made Practical*. Pasadena: William Carey Library, 1976.

My Journey

DAVE LIVERMORE
Cornerstone University, Michigan

As far back as grade school, I was convinced I was going to be a missionary. By eleven, I had the next twenty years of my life mapped out. My parents, while affirming my desire to pursue a life serving in global mission, cautioned me against too dogmatically scripting what it would look like. I was convinced they were crazy. I had heard from God! Or so I thought.

Nearly thirty years later, my life looks very different from what I had scripted. I couldn't have possibly imagined the realities of the twenty-first-century world and church. I never guessed there would be more missionaries coming from the Global South than the North. I never conceived of the global connectivity existing as a result of technology and travel. But the recur-

ring thread in my life has been a continual longing to join God in revealing his glory wherever I am and discovering my role in his work through the community entrusted to me.

I regret spending way too many hours obsessing over my plans and not enough time praying and processing my dreams in community. I celebrate family members, mentors and friends who encouraged my calling and tempered my overzealous ambition.

I regret too often comparing my missional significance and impact with whoever impressed me last. I celebrate having a community who helps me find my own voice, calling and place in Christ's worldwide revolution.

God has consistently helped me discern my

role in mission through community. From my parents and the midsize Baptist church I grew up in, to my best friend and wife, mentors, peers and, increasingly, through dear friends in and from dozens of countries around the world, I find safety, accountability and clarity about my role in global mission through community.

On-the-Ground Training
The TIMO Case Study

DAVID HENNIGH

"In the context of relationships, TIMO [Training In Ministry Outreach] exists to effectively train long-term missionaries in team settings, in order to make disciples of the lost."

Background

In a meeting with Dr. Ralph Winters in the early 1980s, the director of Africa Inland Mission, Dr. Dick Anderson, questioned the most strategic means for reaching the unreached. Out of that conversation, an AIM committee drafted a rough strategy, which was the beginning of TIMO. This evolved into what today has becomes one of AIM's premier training and outreach programs.

Training In Ministry Outreach is a two-year program[1] with two goals. The primary purpose is the training of new missionaries in the basics of evangelism and church planting in the local context. The second goal is the establishment of a church among an unreached or under-reached people group.

The primary goal is accomplished through the recruitment and preparation of an experienced missionary to implement and facilitate the two-year program. The choice of team leader is crucial to the success of a team. The team leader, using the TIMO "Team Leaders Manual" and "Curriculum Guide" provided, leads the team through the two years, through both example and teaching. Obviously, the team leader carries the greatest responsibility in making the program work to its potential.

The secondary goal is accomplished through the team living out their two-year experience among the host people group. They learn language and culture, build relationships and through those relationships share Christ naturally. The curriculum and training help them to do that, hopefully, more effectively.

The two years are laid out chronologically as follows:

All team members are required to arrive on-site at the same time, to allow everyone to process the same information together. The first two weeks are spent in an orientation to TIMO and going through a modified version of LAMP (Language Acquisition Made Practical), produced by veteran linguists Tom and Betty Sue Brewster. Often (but not always) these two weeks of sessions are held off-site but preferably in the same language group. There are practical things dealt with during this time as well.

Following orientation and LAMP, the team moves to the site, where they are given a few days to settle into their new homes. They then spend a week living with a host-culture family chosen by the team leader. The purpose of this week is to begin observing the lifestyle, language and culture of the host people group by total immersion in it. Often, lasting relationships come from this "Home Stay." Following that, team members are given a short time to adjust and settle, then their TIMO experience continues.

The team leader often finds language helpers to assist each team member with daily language sessions. During this time, the tools gained from the LAMP course are put to work. Much of a team member's day is then spent practicing their new language in the community among the people. Weekly team meetings begin, with the team spending the day in prayer, Bible study, worship, curriculum study and a business meeting.

The remainder of the first three months, called Orientation Unit, has the team grappling with what it means to live crossculturally, understanding culture stress, learning how to resolve interpersonal issues and concentrating strongly on language. The second unit is a study in prayer and spiritual warfare and various views regarding the topic. The third is a study on crosscultural communication, including an ethnograph. The fourth is a study on evangelism and church planting in a crosscultural context. The fifth unit has to do with discipleship, and the final (sixth) unit is the closure unit, where issues of transition and handing over ministries are discussed.

Though it varies for every location, never do TIMO teams start formal ministry before six months (and it is usually much later), because the desire is to have them learn first, understand and then for the type and method of their ministry to emerge naturally and organically when they are ready. What that particular ministry looks like can vary widely from team to team, and it should. For many teams, for example, "storying" or "narrations" have become an important element of ministry for communicating the gospel effectively.

Ministering in various African countries and contexts, TIMO embodies the missionary spirit

of flexibility, which adapts to meet the needs of a given situation. As a result of this flexibility and adaptation, TIMO teams can look very different from each other, causing some to wonder, "What is it that makes TIMO, TIMO?" Many are not used to being a member of a values-driven ministry, but a program-driven ministry.

The twelve values listed below are the non-negotiables found among any TIMO team. They encapsulate our philosophy and desires for our team members through their TIMO experience. These are TIMO's core values, which we hope by the end of two years participants will have adopted as their own.

- *Reaching the lost with the saving news of Jesus Christ.* The lost can be the classic "unreached," who have yet to be exposed to the gospel, but also those who have yet to respond positively to the claims of the gospel. This is the central value of TIMO. In general, TIMO will not work where the gospel is already being effectively proclaimed by another group, but will instead seek out groups of people who are most needy from an evangelistic viewpoint. Our motivation is to see the kingdom of God increase through people beginning a relationship with the triune God.

- *Commitment to the local language and culture.* Critical to effective proclamation is articulating the gospel in the context and mother tongue of the hearer whenever possible.

- *Relationships, relationships, relationships.* All mission work involves relating: with our Lord, our teammates and fellow missionaries, our national church partners and those to whom we minister. TIMO encourages its members not only to offer their skills and giftedness but their entire selves to the ministry. This is costly and painful but also brings its own rewards and glorifies God. Our goal is to be able to say along with the apostle Paul, "We loved you so much that we were delighted to share with you not only the gospel of God but our lives as well" (1 Thess 2:8).

- *Lifestyle and proclamation evangelism.* Incarnating the truth of the gospel message in our lives and verbally proclaiming that same message should be two sides of the same coin. One without the other creates imbalance.

- *Living among those to whom we seek to minister.* A logical outgrowth of commitment to local language, to learning culture and to lifestyle evangelism is living among those to whom we minister.

- *Entering with a learner's attitude and posture.* Though we come with knowledge of a relationship of which many are ignorant, we enter in the posture of a learner and sharer, trusting the Lord to provide opportunities to share our knowledge of the gospel. But if we are serious about learning language and culture, and earning the right to be heard, we must come as learners and servants rather than as experts.

- *Simpler lifestyle.* Seeking to have a minimal amount of possessions frees us from the bondage of material things. A simpler lifestyle also removes some of the barriers between nationals and us. Cost effectiveness is a third reason why TIMO embraces simpler living.

- *Teamship*—they will know we are Christians by our love. As Jesus told his disciples, functioning as a loving, committed team is eloquent testimony of who we are following. Teamship is critical. TIMO trains its members in becoming a smooth, fully functioning team, but it expects that love and commitment for each other will be the undergirding strength of the team—not technique.

- *Prayer is ministry.* Prayer is not just what we do before we go and minister; prayer is kingdom work, the battle itself and not just preparation for the battle. TIMO emphasizes the range of biblical prayer as ministry throughout the two-year program.

- *Training is for a lifetime.* TIMO does not aim to complete a missionary's training, but rather attempts to model patterns of learning for a lifetime. A continual upward spiral of spiritual, emotional and mental growth is the goal for every TIMO alumnus.

- *Ministry flows out of being.* Who we are impinges directly on what we do. We can offer only what we have. We are often the first and only message they see and hear. Mature ministry results from a mature relationship with our Lord, so as vital as ministry is, TIMO stresses that one's personal relationship with Jesus will always be the most essential aspect of our lives.

- *High view of the local church.* The local church is God's primary model for evangelism and discipleship. There are other valid, biblical forms for increasing and maturing the universal church, but we believe the local church, with its support, accountability and variously gifted members working as the body of Christ, is the most powerful and effective means for sustained numerical and spiritual multiplication. Therefore, TIMO is committed to planting local churches and working alongside the local church to see the spontaneous expansion of the kingdom.

Today TIMO participants are spread through-out all of AIM, with a significant percentage in top leadership. After twenty-three years, around 60 percent of TIMO participants are still with AIM with a further 15 to 20 percent with other ministry organizations. A significant percentage of those remaining are in full-time ministry within their home context. TIMO alumni are highly sought after within AIM for strategic outreach because of the preparation they have been given.

David Hennigh was born to missionary parents serving in Tanzania with AIM. He and his wife, Julia, arrived in East Africa in 1990 and led the fourth TIMO team. Since then, they have led two more teams and were in their fourth team when David became the director of TIMO in 2002. For more information on TIMO, go to <www.timo-aim.com>.

---

[1]TIMO teams normally last two years, but some go a bit longer. The curriculum is based on a two-year schedule, regardless of the actual length. Three years is the longest team to date. When you read "two years" in this document, remember that it can be longer.

Teamwork at the Jesus Restaurant

SCOTT OLSON, RICK KNOX AND SUSAN PEARSON

Great teams have four strengths: *Vision* lets them create the future together. *Trust* leads them to practice vulnerability. *Diversity* helps them value each other's uniqueness. *Longevity* ensures that their contribution will last. Let me show you what that looks like in our refugee ministry team in Athens.

At the Athens Refugee Center (ARC), we minister to some of the world's most brutalized families and individuals. We feed the hungry. Provide clothing to those with none. Hear endless stories of betrayal and abuse. Care for widows and orphans in their distress. And tell them the story of Jesus.

Why? We share a vision of men and women from many nations who become transformed by the power of God into potent witnesses to their own people. Together with them we are creating a future where God's kingdom figures prominently.

This team of men and women from Australia, England, Canada and the United States serves hand in hand with colleagues from Albania, Greece, Iran, Kurdistan, Russia and the Philippines. Some are volunteers; others, full-time missionaries. We serve soup in Jesus' name to more than 1,400 people a week. Over countless cups of tea, we build friendships and listen to their life experiences. We (and our indispensable short-term volunteers) do all the cooking, cleaning, dish washing and serving. We have to work through frequent misconceptions, miscommunication and frustration. Being honest and open with each other is hard work! But doing the truth in love is worth all the effort.

Most of our clients come from a Muslim background, and God uses our multilingual team powerfully among them. Consequently, many have put their faith in Christ. Susan Pearson tells about "Ernie" and his family:

When the Iranian government rid the country of thousands of Afghani immigrants in late 2007, "Ernie," ten, and his family traveled to Turkey, then to Greece. His mother, "Fatima," had been a teacher in Iran and spoke English well.

Shortly before Christmas, when she came to the ARC to get food for their family, Fatima brought her two boys.

I met Ernie and his younger brother in the Kids' Room, where I helped my Canadian teammate, Carolyn, with the childcare. Ernie really wanted to learn English. So one of our short-term helpers photocopied a workbook for him, and I spent over an hour going through it with Ernie. He soaked it up like a sponge. I suggested that he work on it at home with his mother. Soon Fatima asked Carolyn and me to tutor both Ernie and his younger brother; before long, both of us were meeting with the boys at their home.

Through Christmas outreaches, our team fed and gave gifts to nearly 1,200 people. We know of twenty-three who put their faith in Christ. Afterward, Fatima and ten to fifteen other women began attending the Bible class taught by Kallie, my Greek colleague, at the Persian Christian Fellowship.

Fatima gladly received a Farsi Bible and soon was deluging us all with questions about faith and comments about Islam. She and her husband, "Achmed," clearly wanted their kids to be free to choose their own faith. But Fatima was sure that if *she* were to convert to Christ, it would destroy her mother.

As Easter approached, Fatima and her family began planning to move to Germany, where her mother already lived. Kallie prayed that Fatima's mother would release her from Islam's grip. The next day, during a phone call, Fatima's mother told her, "You're an adult. You must choose for yourself."

During a macaroni dinner at the Persian Christian Fellowship, Fatima excitedly related her mother's decision to Kallie. She pleaded, "Can I pray right now? Let's do it." And so they did.

Three days later, she came to Carolyn and me, worried about a habit Ernie had developed. "He won't stop reading the Farsi Bible," she said. "He knows more than I do. But how will he learn English?" We assured her that this was a great problem to have, and that Ernie would do fine with English. "Why not read it *with* him, and discuss it," we suggested.

Two days later, they left for Germany. A month later, Fatima called Kallie. "Please get a Farsi Bible for my husband," she begged. Now, that is the kind of request we love to grant!

These two long-term missionaries, a Canadian and American, were happy to help children while their parents were being cared for by Greek, Kurdish, Persian and other team members. While they served tea and built friendships, God was drawing another family out of darkness into the Light.

We'd be lying if we said we always got it right. But when our team members in Athens are driven by a common vision, will trust one another enough to be vulnerable, delight in their differences and are determined to stay with it over the long haul. They are a *great* team. They make disciples who infect our world with the glory of God.

Scott Olson is the president and CEO of International Teams (USA). Rick Knox and Susan Pearson have both served in key leadership positions with International Teams for a number of years.

Development Roles for the Viable Missionary

BRENT LINDQUIST

This sidebar gives my perspective on a seminal article: "The Viable Missionary: Learner, Trader, Story Teller" by Donald N. Larson.[1] Don was a mentor for me from 1975 to 2000, and I am honored to share this review with the emerging generation of missionaries.

Don always made a big deal about how missionary development begins at home, but even more importantly, missionary development continued and is enhanced through involvement with the local people as resources and surrogate family members. All too often, the new missionary has some blind spots about what he or she needs to know and understand and learn in order to move toward effectiveness in living, witnessing and working.

Don's article illustrates the developmental process new missionaries needs to go through to become effective persons of influence, ensuring they develop an understanding of the experience, background and worldview of their host community. The three roles are learner, trader and story teller:

1. The **learner** role emphasizes language learning as the primary symbol of identification with the host community. Through full-time work with language helpers and coaches, and lots of time spent in the community practicing, by three months the learner has established numerous relationships which have helped her or him to initiate conversations, make statements and ask and answer simple questions.

2. At the fourth month, the **trader** role is added, where insight and experience is "traded" with the hosts. This includes sharing of cultural experiences through pictures and other means so both the learner and host learn about worldview and relationships. At the end of this period, the new missionary is well on the way to being established as a learner and as one who is interested in other people.

3. In the seventh month, the role of **story teller** is added to the others. Stories about Bible times as well as personal encounters and faith in Christ are learned in the host language to be retold. These are incorporated into the daily cycles of events and situations. At the end of this cycle, the new missionary has made acquaintances and friends, and hopefully has left countless positive impressions as a learner, trader and story teller, and is ready to add new roles, really throughout the rest of her or his career and life.

Space is unavailable here to discuss this in more detail. As a member-care resource person, I marvel at this approach. Though it is simple, it makes room for many perspectives. It drives the new missionary to the hosts, facilitating interaction with a built-in tendency toward closeness, if not intimacy. It avoids a tendency toward separation and autonomy, with the concomitant problems of loneliness and depressed reactions. And it moves the new missionary into an active-learning, relationship-building, incarnational emphasis replicating the original incarnational Life we strive to emulate.

While many situations have changed in the thirty years since this article was originally published, there remain many key concepts to be refined and developed for the effective use of these developmental roles.

---

[1]First appeared in *Missiology: An Annual Review* 6, no. 2 (April 1978).

Brent Lindquist, Ph.D., is the president of Link Care Center and consults with mission organizations on member-health issues.

Global Perspectives

DOUG MITTS
Europe, Greater Europe Mission

Europe needs the well-trained missionary. Europeans live in an educated, largely secular and refined culture and welcome help from those who seem qualified to give it. Europe has tremendous spiritual needs and therefore has use for a wide variety of ministries missionaries can provide.

The missionaries who come for the long term will be better utilized if they assume the role of a facilitator, encourager and coach. They must be able to come alongside national leaders to develop in them the courage, character and skills necessary for this tough ministry. From the start, they need to ensure that resulting ministries reside in the hands of Europeans.

It's strategically important that long-term missionaries be trained in language acquisition, cultural adaptation and crosscultural communi-

cation. They must also have relational skills (for both the sending and the receiving culture). They must be able to handle their missionary dreams being radically reworked upon meeting the reality of the host culture.

These new workers must come already with a deep spiritual life steeped in the habits of Scripture and prayer that results in an application of truth. Only this allows them to become better lovers of God and others. Their life must manifest evidence of the Spirit's leadership. Lastly, they must be growing in self-awareness, humble, owning responsibility for their actions, gracious toward others who hurt them, living responsively to Christ in a fallen world and authentically before others, with a deep desire for harmony in the body of Christ.

Missionaries Know How to Read Romans 13

CHRIS HOKE

Jesus and his apostles got arrested. A lot.

They didn't see it as a tragic lapse into sin, nor fear that they were dishonoring God. "Most of the brothers," Paul wrote to his satellite communities from a jail cell, "have been encouraged [and given confidence by his imprisonment] to speak the word of God more courageously and fearlessly" (Phil 1:14).

They knew their entire calling, mission and message of the kingdom of God on earth would clash on the deepest levels with all human kingdoms.

From the Christmas story (Jesus' birth) to the Easter story (Jesus' death), our Lord was at odds with both his own culture's governance (temple authorities) and the foreign rulers (Herod, Caesar and other Roman powers). This is our story. The kingdom, the government of heaven is at hand. At the gates. Invading. We're the heralds, the frontlines of heaven's invasion on earth. To call Jesus Lord, to say Christ is King, was—and still is—to say this: Caesar is *not* the king. Nor is any president—of any nation.

This is where international missionaries learn the secret of God's politics. Having left the land of their upbringing, their hearts and minds are free from the idolatry of patriotism and nationalism. They can see governments for what they are, not intoxicated by the ancient drug of pride, propaganda and religious rhetoric. Missionaries enter a nation with an entirely *other* (read "holy") mission. (Try reading Jesus' Sermon on the Mount alongside any political, economic or law enforcement model or foreign policy.)

Sadly, most American Christians grow up doing something no missionary child would do: pledge their allegiance, with hand over heart, ritually, to a national government and its icon. I believe this prevents American patriots from reading and understanding clearly Paul's famous comments in Romans 13 on submitting to governing authorities. While the domesticated church in America has used these verses to justify a naive faith in the nation's character and rule of law, missionaries in China, Iraq, Rwanda and North Korea, as well as in Hitler's Germany and Pinochet's Chile in years past, know that these verses must be read in the fuller context of the apostolic mission.

That is, the thrust of Paul's whole argument leading up to it in Romans 12 is how to respond to human evil, corruption and persecution in their context: "Do not be conformed to this world, but be transformed by the renewing of your mind" (v. 2 NASB). "Give preference to one another in [showing] honor" (v. 10 NASB). "Bless those who persecute you; bless and do not curse" (v. 14 NASB). "If your enemy is hungry, feed him . . . for in so doing you will heap burning coals on his head. Do not be overcome by evil, but overcome evil with good" (vv. 20-21 NASB).

In the same way, honor and submit to such governing authorities: don't conform to their unjust laws and authority, but submit to their unjust (and inevitable) punishment as Christ modeled on the cross—to subvert the world's system. To overcome evil with good. To be a witness (Greek, *martyr*) for God, converting the nation to heaven's ways and governance.

Chris Hoke ministers among migrant workers and gang members in Burlington, Washington, and commutes between Central American jails and the Skagit County Jail to forge bridges for youth on the margins. He recites a different pledge of allegiance now than he once did in school.

The future of India's mission leaders

📋 My Journey

GIO[1]
from Guatemala to North India

I came to know Jesus in 1982 at age fourteen, and our first evangelical church experience in Guatemala impacted all of us—my mom and us four kids. Two years later, during the church's first missions conference, Obed, one of the youth leaders, asked me to meet him for breakfast with a missionary on a short home leave.

It was intriguing to me how a man from El Salvador could be a missionary in North Africa among Muslims. I didn't know that a Latin could be a missionary! As he shared with us, he told us how he was a hydrological engineer and used that as a needed and legitimate platform to work long-term in the country where he was serving. That year I committed my life to missions, and I decided to study engineering in order to serve in a closed country.

My options after graduation were going to seminary, serving with Operation Mobilization or studying abroad. Thanks to a generous scholarship, I was able to study in an excellent Christian university in the United States, and was sent as a "missionary" by my church elders to study engineering. In that university I served as leader of the Students Missions Fellowship and led two summer missions projects. I met my wife in college, an MK from Africa. The children started coming soon after, and now we have four, ages four, six, ten and fourteen.

I returned to Guatemala and worked for a few years as an engineer, thus fulfilling the scholarship requirements. My wife and I helped established a new church in the city and were involved in the first missions committee of the church. After seven years, my wife asked me when we would go to the mission field. I told her, "The day God sends us a specific invitation, where I can use my skills, then I will quit my job." A good managerial answer, I thought. I believed it, but I was buying time.

The next morning, a fax came into my office from SIM (Serving in Mission). A computer expert was needed in Ethiopia as soon as possible. Were we available? I knew God was calling us. I decided I was not going to rationalize this one, so I quit my job.

It took eleven months for our visas to come through. We spent a two-year term in Ethiopia, where we saw many come to Christ. I was also able to help in computers and other technical things, as well as youth ministry. When time came to leave Ethiopia, we committed to long-term service in missions and returned to Guatemala for a season to be with family and our sending church. The personnel directors challenged us to open our eyes to Asia, living among and serving a large Muslim population. We have been here, with our four children, for almost eight years.

It is tough here, and we sometimes wonder what will happen. But we have seen the hand of God in powerful ways in our lives and in bringing Muslims to himself. I want to be a channel of God's love to the nations.

---

[1] The author's name has been changed to protect identity.

✎Journal Worksheet Seven

STEVE HOKE

Where Are You Now?

How would you rate the amount and quality of data you now have about churches, schools and other sources of practical missionary training?

What information do you have about graduate schools or advanced training in culture and language?

What other languages can you read or speak? Have you ever studied another language? How did it go?

What situations have you been in that required you to understand a culture quite different from your own? How did you learn about the culture? How well did you adapt to it?

Whom do you know that may be able to counsel you on practical training or schools?

Pastors:

Missionaries or mission leaders:
Christian staff on campus:

Friends at church:

Teachers:

What Do You Need to Do Next?

Talk with your church leaders or mission organization about practical training programs and look through the resources in the appendices. Then, list three training programs or schools you're interested in exploring further:

1.

2.

3.

When will you discuss ways and means of learning language with your church, school counselors and mission agency?

When and how will you work out an integrated program of language and culture learning?

Which school(s) will you visit, call, e-mail or write? When?

What Will the Future Look Like?

With some understanding of your financial situation, how much time should you plan to set aside for further training or education, if any, at this time?

What specific languages will you need to know to reach the people to whom you feel God is leading you?

What language school or program might you attend for language acquisition in this country? List your top options. Then rank them by considering quality, location, scheduling and tuition.

1.
2.
3.

How would gaining some actual on-the-job field experience reshape your training plans?

Would it be best for you to "sandwich" your schooling within a meaty layer of field experience?

How does all this relate to your marriage or family plans?

Phase Three

GETTING ESTABLISHED

EIGHT

Apprenticeships and Internships
STEVE HOKE AND BILL TAYLOR

Experts agree that the ideal place for practical, hands-on missionary training is as close to the target location as possible. Neither suburban Wheaton nor Colorado Springs are ideal training sites to help candidates gain firsthand experience in multicultural, urban living. For that reason, more agencies are carefully designing very practical, field-based orientation programs for newly arriving missionaries in each region in which they minister.

Historically, an *apprenticeship* is a system of training a new generation of skilled crafts practitioners. Apprentices build their careers from apprenticeships in a particular craft they have selected for a profession, whether blacksmithing or glass blowing. Most of their training is done on the job while working for an employer who helps the apprentices learn their trade, in exchange for their continuing labor for an agreed period after they become skilled.

A field apprenticeship is a way of training a new generation of missionaries to be effective in the craft of crosscultural ministry.

An *internship* is a temporary position with an emphasis on on-the-job training rather than merely employment, making it similar to an apprenticeship. Interns are usually college or university students, but they can also be high-school students or post-graduate adults seeking skills for a new career. Student internships provide opportunities for students to gain experience in their field, determine if they have an interest in a particular career, create a network of contacts or gain school credit.

A *field internship* (sometimes called a "new staff" position) is an opportunity to develop basic skills in crosscultural communication and understanding in your hosts' language and culture upon arriving in your host culture. It generally entails no other ministry responsibilities; your only job is to become proficient in the language and culture. Hopefully, a qualified and experienced missionary or national leader will then work with you to build your ministry on what his or her experience can teach.

We will use the two terms—*apprenticeship* and *internship*—interchangeably.

If you're still in college, being an intern in crosscultural service may seem years away. It probably is. But one way to prepare for the future is to understand it better. While we can't forecast exactly what the future holds, we *can* make plans and decisions that affect it.

Your expectations will significantly shape the nature of your experience. When you take a new job, it seldom turns out to be all you expected it would be. New experiences are like that. The same will be true of your first crosscultural assignment. That doesn't mean you should expect to be "bummed out." But you should, by faith, hold your initial expectations loosely. Bring them before the Lord with open hands, willing to let him shape or replace them. Mission is going to be tougher than you imagine, but hang in there. It's worth it!

Your crosscultural experience will stretch you and deepen you. Be ready for the most intense period of personal, family and ministry growth in your life. The spiritual battle will stretch you and build your spiritual muscles. Living in community with a multicultural team of Christians will feel like a crucible experience—being crushed under pressure and remolded amid heat. Anticipating that experience with realistic faith will increase your dependence on the Lord and your commitment to being a vital member of your ministry community. And if you are married (with or without children), prepare for added stresses and challenges.

There is much you can do to understand what it will be like. Ask your church and mission agency questions that will help you prepare. A template for a first-year internship experience is described below. Also pay especially close attention to "Barefooting," a description of one couple's actual internship in Caracas, Venezuela. As you read these, seriously consider how you can adapt the model to your own situation to maximize your first year on the field.

Model for a First-Year, On-Field Internship

STEVE HOKE

The following outline of an actual training model describes the procedure, assumptions and activities that could guide your first year on the field. It is meant to give you a clear idea of the expectations, opportunities and resources available. This model may be adapted by your church or agency.

Assumptions

You have completed both a pre-field orientation workshop and language acquisition workshop before going overseas. This training has given you an overview of the requisite attitudes, sensitivities and skills for culture learning. You have gained some advance exposure to your new language through Berlitz, LAMP or an equivalent intensive language-learning program.

Beyond the general prefield orientation to crosscultural living and communicating, the best place to learn culture-specific information and language is in the host culture. "Bonding" with the local people and their culture is critical to your long-term success in feeling at home in your new culture. (See Tom and Betty Sue Brewster's book *Language Acquisition Made Practical* [Lingua House, 1976] for practical steps toward bonding with your host culture.)

Language learning *is* ministry; hence, a deep commitment to gaining language proficiency as soon as possible (up to two years of full-time study), while continuing to bond and build relationships with host nationals, is necessary.

New missionaries should be exposed to as little nonpreparatory ministry experience as is reasonable (that is, without taking time away from the priority of language study). A *guided internship* during your first year of language and culture learning is more effective and desirable than a completely spontaneous and unguided experience. You should have a mentor or coach to facilitate your entry, language learning and general acculturation.

Learning Objectives

Upon completion of your first (or second, depending on the language) year in your expected location, you should be able to

- carry on a simple conversation about spiritual matters (at an entry level) with a national, with 80-percent accuracy and comprehension

- explain the history of the city and culture in which you live, highlighting key persons and events that have significantly influenced them, as well as describe several possible entry points for effective relational ministry

- evidence a respect, sensitivity and appreciation for the local culture, including its history, cultural values, food and lifestyle

Procedure

The following activities describe the type of learning activities that can be customized into a one-year internship experience:

- "Bond" by living with a host family for three weeks during your first six months on the field.

- Find and develop a relationship with a reliable cultural "informant" and model (if different from your tutor or host family).

- Consistently attend language classes and/ or meet regularly with your language tutor.

- Develop a close relationship with a national family or couple, and vacation with them.

- Experiment in hospitality with your neighbors and new friends in your neighborhood. Learn how the locals do meals together. Become as creative as you can to adapt to their style of eating and hospitality.

- Participate in a national-led small group or cell group.

- Attend a national church with services in the national language.

- Attend a church camp or retreat.

- Attend the national church's version of leadership training.

- Attend and observe at least three national cultural or religious festivals and celebrations.

- Visit three to six other national churches,

across denominational lines.

- Conduct a personal prayerwalk in your host city, and join others in other cities if possible.

- Be praying that the Holy Spirit will identify the "worthy person" (Mt 10:11) that he has prepared ahead of time, a bridge person for you into a neighborhood or avenue of ministry. Just as Jesus instructed the first disciples to "search" or "inquire" as to who that person might be, be attentive to the people God has prepared ahead of time to assist you in the new culture.

- Read and study the briefing information prepared by your agency for "your" country (a compilation of key background articles, book chapters and other written resources that your organization may have created for new missionaries).

- Visit at least two other cities and areas of interest in the country, with an eye toward observing regional distinctives, differences and similarities, and toward learning about national history and culture.

- Keep a personal journal for the first twelve months, making entries at least weekly. Use your journal to guide intentional, critical reflection on your spiritual formation and culture learning.

- Compare this general model with "Barefooting" below, a first-year itinerary of a real-life missionary couple in Caracas, Venezuela.

- Spend consistent time with your missionary mentor *and* a national cultural informant. Let the local people be your experts on the ground.

🌐 Global Perspectives

BRENT NEELY
Middle East

Role of the Missionary

The world scene is inextricably intertwined and globalized. Yet it is surely debatable as to

whether we are embarking on an era of global, pluralist community or moving into intensified clashes between civilizations and economic strata. This is an era of transnational corporations, transnational terror and, at the very same time increasing tribalism, nationalism and strengthening of traditional identities.

On a practical level, everything from the development of indigenous churches and sending bodies to anti-Western perceptions to tightening visa regulations and access restrictions to the decline of the U.S. dollar—all combine to call for a reassessment of the role of the Western missionary.

- A role for the Western missionary must remain, theologically, as long as there is a viable Western church. The nonmissional church is an unhealthy church.

- It must also remain because the current world reality is a global reality. Beyond that, there is plenty of biblical warrant for a tangible expression of the intercultural, globalized body of the Messiah.

- Perhaps the best way to characterize the ideal role of the Western worker is "partnership." However, defining a balanced theory of partnership is hard enough, let alone seeing it work in health.

I would argue that "true engagement" implies people-sending and not simply "funding international ministries." A finances-only basis for mission and ministry is, I think, ultimately a weaker and inadequate model. It is sometimes assumed that because a worker from the Global South does not bear the baggage of the Western colonial and imperial legacy, their entrance to a given culture will be much easier. At times this is the case, but at times this overlooks other prejudices, hurdles or crosscultural adjustments they will indeed be forced to grapple with.

Attracting the Next Generations

I sense there is a yearning for adventure and the attraction to the "other," the exotic, the difficult or the unconventional among many younger workers. They seem to want to be less tied down, less restricted by convention or mission bureaucracy, and so on. I think variety and travel (not just "to" the field, but as a ministry style "on" the field) is important to many. I suspect that as visa regulations become increasingly tighter (rising nationalism, terrorism and economic migration issues all driving this trend), specialized skills will become more important and will attract the appropriate personnel.

Recommended Prefield Training

I suppose the old cliché still holds: the prime directive for mission work is "flexibility, flexibility, flexibility." But we can approach the issue at an even more fundamental level. As in most things in life, deep character precedes skill and gifting in the divine hierarchy of values. This certainly continues to hold true for crosscultural endeavors.

Among other things, I would characterize our current Western culture as individualistic, creative, youth-oriented, pluralist and directed toward personal fulfillment. However, against this backdrop I do feel a need for a healthy, renewed emphasis within the community of faith and mission on certain values that might ring slightly "old school," but which, nonetheless, I think are actually biblical, life-giving and productive. I am thinking specifically of the qualities of submission (and the various ways and arenas within which that can be teased out) and perseverance (that is, a long obedience with a lessened emphasis on personal attainment or fulfillment).

Barefooting

Your First Year in the Field

STEVE HOKE

First Six Months

Your first three months in Caracas are to be spent doing nothing but getting settled into a national home or your own place and adjusting to your new culture.

During this time you will

- find housing and furnishings
- meet your neighbors
- immerse yourself in Spanish study (classroom, tutor, relationships)
- learn where to change money
- learn how to get around using buses, taxis and the subway
- learn where the post office and stores are located
- visit several different churches and ministries
- learn how to use the phone, pay bills, pay rent and so on
- find a Venezuelan mentor or helper (or "adopt" a family)
- obtain your *cedula* (official ID document), health certificates and driver's licenses

During your second three months, you will add to your adaptation skills by doing things like these:

- opening a bank account
- purchasing a car (note: some may want to wait longer on this)
- finding a church home

Second Six Months

During your second six months, you will expand your knowledge and relational base by doing things like these:

explore ministry possibilities

visit and become acquainted with various re-

sources and ministries in the city, including Christian bookstores, the Caracas Ministerial (local pastors ministerial association), the Evangelical Alliance and theological education centers

- continue relationship building in your new church home
- read the following: daily newspaper, weekly magazine, a recent book that evaluates Venezuelan culture

Third Six Months

Begin structured ministry.

Expand your cultural understanding by attending or visiting the following:

- a wedding
- a horse race
- the theater
- a funeral
- a soccer match and a baseball game
- a *barrio* (only after checking with your director regarding safety precautions)
- the beach

Your ministry should gradually become more clearly defined. You will have a clearer picture of what you will do, where, with whom and what skills you will need to do it.

Fourth Six Months

Focus on ministry development. Some cautions:

- Watch the time you spend exclusively with people of your own nationality or ethnicity.
- Limit your time on e-mail. Already we see new missionaries misuse their time this way.
- Give your cyberspace correspondent (even family) time to ponder the differences in time zones and currency exchange.

- Don't let other technology neutralize personal relationships.

- Do not use DVDs from home as an escape or unhealthy crutch.

Adapt this template to your setting, to your needs and to your family. Notice that the emphasis is on practical, hands-on learning interactions, not reading books on the topic. The more time you spend on the streets with local people, the greater will be your pace and depth of culture learning

▣ My Journey

REUBEN EZEMADU
Christian Missionary Foundation, MANI (Movement for African National Initiatives), Nigeria

It was in 1971 that I first heard from the Lord that he had called me to serve him "after the order of Paul." Being just one year old in the Lord then and in my fourth year in high school, I did not have a proper understanding of what this meant until much later. The striking confirmation came by word of prophecy. All I could do then was to continue to share my faith with fellow students at school.

After graduating from high school, I spent two years in a section of Igboland (Ohaozara in the present Ebonyi State, Nigeria) where the dialect and culture are different from my own, even though I am an Igbo. I taught at a primary school there and was involved in church-planting activities under the Assemblies of God Church. I led outreach programs with our youth into the interior places of that region, often engaging in spiritual warfare with the priests and practitioners of tradition religion.

In 1974, I began study at Jos Campus of the University of Ibadan. This was my first major exposure to people of other tribes than mine, providing me a great opportunity to learn more about people other than my tribesmen, to relate to and fellowship with believers of different tribes and churches. Evangelism within and outside the multicultural university community offered me more opportunities to widen my worldview and appreciate some of the richness of other cultures. I later transferred to the Ibadan main campus, and we continued in weekend rural outreaches as students from the Christian union in a dominantly Yoruba culture.

During the one-year, compulsory, post-graduation National Youth Service program, I was posted to serve in Borno State, a strong Kanuri Muslim enclave, yet another different people group, socially and religiously proud and self-effacing. This year afforded me and my Christian colleagues the privilege of penetrating the strongholds of Islam with the gospel, with limited but abiding results of four people we reached, discipled and envisioned. All of them eventually became Christ's servants among their people. One leads the Kanuri Project, a Bible translation program under the Churches of Christ in Nigeria to spearhead the translation of the Bible into the Kanuri language and the promotion of reading and using the translated Bible among the Kanuris.

To crown it all, the Lord gave me a crosscultural marriage to a lovely Yoruba lady, Bosede. She has been a partner, supporter and encourager in the Christian Missionary Foundation, a crosscultural ministry both of us pioneered and have led for the past twenty-seven years.

Baggage Claim Exercise

TED WARD

Expatriates and missionaries sending baggage to other countries were required to fill out detailed Baggage Declaration forms, listing the contents of their suitcases, crates or shipping barrels. In the same way, this exercise provides an opportunity for people to look at their "cultural baggage." In this context, cultural baggage refers to the values, habits, lifestyle and expectations the sojourner takes along into the overseas assignment. The exercise can be done alone, but best results come when shared as a small-group exercise with peers experiencing entry into a new culture.

Individuals will prepare their own responses to a list of self-perception and self-assessment questions. Then groups of two to four people each will be formed to discuss the items.

Individuals should write their responses to the items on the Baggage Declaration. (The two forms, Baggage Declaration and Baggage Checklist, should be reproduced for each participant.)

Baggage Declaration
Personal characteristics.

In your own country, what do people notice when they see you coming?

In the country where you are planning to go, what will people notice when they see you coming?

What do you try to avoid?

What do you most enjoy?

Relational style.

What sort of people do you prefer to work with? Indicate major characteristics, traits or qualities.

What sort of people do you prefer to be with for social and recreational activities? Indicate major characteristics, traits or qualities.

How do you feel about *authority?*

How do you feel about *equality?*

How do you relate to beggars and panhandlers when they confront you on the street?

How do you react when invited to a formal or prestigious event?

As each individual completes the Baggage Declaration, ask him or her to pair with another person who is done to compare and discuss their Baggage Declarations while waiting for the others to finish. When everyone has finished writing, go to the next step, Baggage Checklist.

Explain or read aloud the following to everyone:

As we all know, when you enter any country, there are some items you are not allowed to bring in. At the level of personal judgment, there are things you know that you should leave home. The next part of this exercise asks for some careful judgments about what you carry into the country and what you leave home.

Baggage Checklist

Make a list of your cultural baggage and indicate items that fall into each of these three categories:

1. Must carry. My professional or career (ministry) role absolutely requires that I not leave these items behind—whether or not I might want to.

Give one example here:

2. Would like to leave behind but probably can't. My judgment is probably better than my capability of following through. I will try not to take these things, but they may show up as embarrassing "stowaways."

Give one example here:

3. Must be left behind. My overseas assignment will be a new page in my life as long as these items are concerned. I will not take them along.

Give one example here:

Debriefing

Discuss the meanings and share a few examples of each of these items as individuals suggest them.

Next, each individual should fill out the Baggage Check form.

Share by grouping people in sets of two or four when they complete the writing. Put the following questions on a whiteboard or flipchart to guide the discussion:

- What "baggage" might embarrass you if you take it overseas? Why?

- What can you do about things you should leave at home? (Be specific—discuss particular items.)

- What sort of help will you need to follow through on your good intentions? (Again, be specific—talk about particular items.)

Find examples of each of the following (if they are on your lists) and discuss what can be done:

- matters that might give offense

- sources of "personality clash"

- matters that will interfere with one's major purpose in being overseas

(Adapted from *Living Overseas: A Book of Preparations* [New York: Free Press/Macmillan, 1984], pp. 302-5, with permission of the author.)

Ted Ward taught at Michigan State University for thirty years and then at Trinity Evangelical Divinity for fifteen. Ted's influence on the development of educators spans the university, the seminary and the Christian college. There is hardly an evangelical theological institution in North America, not to mention in many countries of the world, that doesn't have at least one faculty member who has been directly touched in some way by his passion for the educator as facilitator of the learning community.

BAGGAGE CLAIM FORM

CATEGORIES OF CULTURAL BAGGAGE	MUST CARRY	WOULD LIKE TO LEAVE BEHIND	MUST BE LEFT BEHIND
Appetites (for foods and other things)			
Attitudes toward other people			
Feelings about my country and other countries			
Habits (especially things I do without thinking)			
Things (yes, things— for example, your microwave oven)			

Why I Love Failing Spanish 1

JANET COCKRUM

I grew up in California and studied French for two years. I can't tell you how many times I have regretted that decision now that I live in Madrid. My one and only Spanish phrase was "Yo quiero Taco Bell." I'm fifty-one years old and fighting for last place in my Spanish class with a few Asians who can't roll their Rs and a few other internationals who drop the last syllable of every word and are completely impossible to understand.

I go to school five days a week for two hours each day. I will be repeating Spanish 1 for my third semester in the fall. I have a Ph.D., and I thought that moving into the role of student after twenty years as a professional teacher would be a difficult role to fill. I thought I would hate language school, and I thought it would be nothing but hard work and a place of discouragement for me.

Then my husband (three years of high school and two years of college Spanish) was placed in my class. Great. I would be living full time with my tutor and the teacher's pet.

All I can say is that everything I thought about language school was wrong. I love it! I am having the best time going to school, and I have friends from over fifteen countries around the world. We are a little community. We are a family struggling through cultural and language acquisition together.

Half of the students in our classes are young girls living as nannies in Spanish homes. They are verbally abused at times, they are overworked, they are unappreciated, and they are lonely. Other students have left their family, their friends, their culture and are sharing rooms in apartments with strangers. They have little money, they have no friends, and they are looking to build a better life for themselves. There is

little joy in their lives. There are others in the class whose husbands have high-paying jobs, and they are learning Spanish so they can shop and function in the country. It's more of a hobby for them, not a skill that they need to get a job.

We are a mixture of cultures, ages, genders and language skills. We are united by our common goal to learn Spanish. A room full of strangers needs someone to reach out to initiate interaction and start the process of becoming friends. The dynamic of a mature, fun couple was a magnet to the lonely, needy, friendless youth in our class.

My husband and I choose to sit apart from each other in class. We partnered with different students in class for activities. We invited the students for coffee after class and would practice our Spanish and then quickly move to some form of broken English/Spanish interaction that just involved friends finding ways to talk. We had the students over for meals, went shopping, gave the students rides to government offices to get their papers processed, offered advice about marriage, being a nanny and even dealing with a bad employer. We were their friends.

God put me in language school where there was fertile ground waiting for me to plant the seeds of the gospel. I got to lovingly water and care for this lovely place five days a week. I am continuing to be surprised by the life sprouting in the garden, and I am anxiously waiting to see the harvest God will yield.

God used language school as the place that I fell in love with the people in Spain. He opened the doors for ministry in an area and in a way I never imagined. It was as easy as being a friend.

At the end of our first semester of class we had an international party. I showed my newly created slideshow with music and pictures that captured the faces and places we had been during our fall class. As the images crossed the screen, the words sung by Alison Krauss expressed our experience beautifully, that things are said best "When You Say Nothing at All."

I couldn't say or understand much Spanish that first semester, but I didn't need words to speak God's love. His love said it all in my smile, the touch of my hands and the truth in my eyes—that God was going to lovingly catch them wherever they would fall. Let me tell you some ways we said it best.

Sarah was a very outgoing twenty-year-old from the Czech Republic. She became a regular in our after-class coffee gatherings and other activities. As the semester was ending, we planned a small birthday lunch for her, and I told her to invite whoever she wanted. As I prepared for the gathering, I had an overwhelming conviction that God wanted me to read a passage of Scripture to Sarah at the party. I wasn't sure if this was a good idea, but I had a strong impression from the Holy Spirit that I should do this.

As our celebration was winding down, I told Sarah I had a special present for her. It was something I wanted for my own children, and it was a gift I wanted to share with her. While I read from the Bible, the tears flowed from her face. She cried for almost ten minutes, and the other students listened as she thanked me for this gift, saying, "I always knew there were people like you out there, but I had never met anyone." The next day she e-mailed me this note:

> Thank you very much for your very special present. . . . It really touched my heart! I had no words yesterday, I really wasn't able to describe my feelings. . . . I wanted to ask you if it is possible to copy me the page of Bible you read yesterday. . . . I'd love to have these words always with me.

Two days later Sarah was in our house to spend the night, and we had our last meal together before taking her to the airport and her departure from Spain. We gave her a Spanish/English Bible because we didn't have any other translation we could give her. She cried with joy as she opened her present, and she wrote me this note the next day:

> Just arrived home. . . . I've already told my family about some our experiences and the beautiful friendship between us . . . and as well I've read them the part of the Bible which you read me on Monday. And thank you very much for the really special present from yesterday (I've read approx. 20 pages) and I have to say that it's really the greatest present I could ever get! My favorite sentence is this one (and during it I'd like to say you good-bye for today): 'I ask God from the wealth of his glory to give you power through his Spirit to be strong in your inner selves, and I pray that Christ will make his home in your hearts through faith." . . . Thank you, God bless you.

In the first month of my second semester of Spanish 1, Zuzca came to class weeping and distressed. She was a nanny for a family involved in the occult, who treated her badly. She didn't have any money, but she was looking for someplace else to live and for a new job.

When Zuzca shared her plans to move on in a few weeks, the mother in the house exploded and in anger and manipulation tried to break Zuzca's will and to force her to stay. She began to "prophesy" evil things that would happen to Zuzca if she left their home. When this failed, she kicked Zuzca out and told her to get her stuff after school and leave for good. As Zuzca entered class an hour late, we stopped our instruction, and she tearfully shared this story with us.

The stunned class sat there and tried to find

words of comfort. I whispered to my husband and then told Zuzca that we wanted her to come home and stay with us. The swearing, brassy girl from Slovakia was now a broken child who needed love. We went and got all her things and brought her home to our apartment. We shared God's love with her by meeting her needs for food and shelter and a safe place to stay.

The woman had prophesied that Zuzca would never have any friends and wouldn't find a job or a place to live. I hugged Zuzca and said, "Look, we are your friends, and you can stay with us. This lady was wrong. God says in the Bible that he loves you and how precious you are to him. You are welcome to stay in our home, and we will help you."

"You are my Spanish family," a tearful Zuzca replied. Later that night I asked her if I could pray for her to find a job, a place to live, to have peace and to know how much God loves her. She let me pray for her.

In a very short time God has done all this and much more. Our friendship with Zuzca has deepened, and even though she never returned to our class, we have been able to stay in touch and share God's love in word and deed with her. Throughout the semester, other classmates would ask us about Zuzca, and we were able to give updates and greetings from her to the teacher and other students.

Our kindness to Zuzca led to new relationships with other young folks who were a bit edgy and who hadn't expressed an interest in getting to know the older, not-so-hip couple from America.

It even touched the heart of our teacher, impacting her in a way I didn't know until my last day of class. I had to miss the last few weeks of language classes because I was going to the States for my son's graduation from college. I said a simple goodbye to the class, and as I left, I gave my teacher a big hug and Spanish goodbye. She looked at me and said, "I love the way you love."

I replied, "Marta, it's God love in me that you see, and it's his love that is flowing from me to you. He loves you too." She nodded her head. The gospel was planted, and I am anxiously waiting on the harvest.

In the fall I will be the only student repeating Spanish 1. Everyone else passed the exams and has moved on to more-advanced levels, even my husband. I don't mind being left behind. The friendships with my classmates will continue to grow as we greet and meet over coffee or plan nights on the town or dinners in our house.

There's a whole new batch of immigrants who will be joining me in Spanish 1. I know a lot more Spanish now, but I won't forget that the smile on my face, the touch of my hands and the truth in my eyes will say it all. God's love can speak even if I say nothing at all.

Dr. Janet Cockrum has the heart of a teacher and mentor. Her passion is praying for young people to know the transforming power of the gospel, to experience intimacy with God and to hear his call on their lives. Her years as a teacher, athletic director and adjunct professor of marriage and family laid the foundation for her new role as the director for interns and recruitment for World Team Spain.

✏️Journal Worksheet Eight

STEVE HOKE

Where Are You Now?

How does your church or mission agency prepare new missionaries for field service?

Describe your picture of a good internship or apprenticeship so you can compare it with what churches and agencies are actually doing.

So, how does all this sound to you? Journal your emotions, fears, thoughts, questions, ideas . . .

What are your initial responses to hearing about the importance of practical, in-field language learning?

What are the first things you'd like to learn upon arriving in another culture?

What Do You Need to Do Next?

Here are some questions to ask a church or mission agency about its first-year training program:

- By the time I arrive on the field, how much orientation will I have received?

- Where and when will my language learning take place?

- What responsibilities will I have while I'm studying the language?

- How long will all this take?

- Where will I be assigned after language learning?

- Will a missionary mentor or coach work with me? How? If not, how can I find one to assist my initial on-field learning and acculturation?

- How can I participate in the life of the national church *and* mission agency while on the field?

- What first-term traps or barriers should I seek to avoid?

- What competencies should I be building right now?

Whom do you know that has recently arrived overseas and seems to be adjusting well? E-mail or call them and ask them about their first impressions and reactions.

What Will the Future Look Like?

What apprenticeship or internship programs exist related to the ministry location you're seeking?

What professional or missions associations should you relate to or join? What missions magazines or journals should you receive and read? Other intercultural journals or books?

What are several ways you could keep abreast of developments and changes in missions as well as related to the country where you may live?

Take time now to journal about the kind of communicator and servant you would like to be upon arriving on the field. Try to capture, at this early point in your journey, the passion God has given you to be an incarnational witness who ministers out of an intimacy with Abba and lives out the fragrance of Christ living in you.

NINE

Lifelong Learning

STEVE HOKE AND BILL TAYLOR

Caution: For those of you who are young adults, some of the following material may not appear to be highly relevant to you right now. Those of you who are older can rapidly discern the relevance of the following reflection exercise. Regardless of your age and experience, spend some time here. If you are younger, ask a mentor to work with you through the reflection. Another thing to keep in mind is that these exercises might best be done in small groups.

- A missionary of twenty years finds herself asking, "Which way next?"
- A mission leader realizes he is merely reacting to the demands of ministry. He has no focus and has lost sight of his unique giftedness and calling.
- The wife of a missionary has always sat in the shadows. She has significant capacity to minister, but no one has helped her clarify her ministry. Yet she has consistently devoted her efforts to helping and caring for others.

These are all-too-familiar scenarios of missionaries who lack a perspective on their past and a focus on their future. Probably it's not their fault. We need to revise our concept of what a "term of service" means. The future of missions will bring much more mobility to our missionaries. Job contexts will change or tasks will be completed or more visas will be denied or children will need special secondary education opportunities. Your crosscultural skills may be used in different countries or regions of the world. And as your gifts and skills mature, God will open up new and creative areas for you to grow as a person as well as in ministry.

The task of learning never ends. One challenging aspect of missionary life is that situations will always be new. There will always be fresh opportunities to learn and do new things. Your perspective on ongoing personal and professional development will be critical to your

long-term effectiveness. Continuing to learn and grow as you minister will keep you fresh and on the cutting edge.

Dr. J. Robert Clinton, professor of leadership at Fuller School of Intercultural Studies, writes, "The single most important antidote to plateauing is a well-developed learning posture. Such a posture is also one of the major ways through which the Spirit gives vision."[1]

Getting sidetracked by the "tyranny of the urgent" and getting stressed out over trying to do too many tasks in too little time are just two of the typical traps encountered by the busy missionary who neglects his or her personal development. All too often, what's missing is a broader, long-range perspective on what is important.

Clinton has correctly observed, "The difference between leaders and followers is perspective. The difference between leaders and effectiveness is better perspective." More than ever before, missionaries recognize that leadership is demanding and difficult. If missionaries are to finish well in life and ministry, they need all the perspective they can get.

So, how do you continue to develop a broader perspective? How can you keep learning and growing?

- *Read consistently.* A distinguishing mark of effective leaders is that they are readers. Create your own annual reading list by gleaning the key books you need to read from the annual *Christianity Today* list of the year's best books, as well as from listening to what your leaders and colleagues are reading.

- *Read widely.* Include in your reading selections from daily newspapers, weekly news magazines, Christian and missions journals, and current writings on theology, missiology and ministry. Feed your heart by reading from both historical and contemporary books in spirituality and spiritual formation.

- *Pursue ongoing education.* Use home assignment (furlough) for specific courses or degree programs. The wisest investment is to map out a long-term learning plan that includes further graduate work, or at least periodic attendance in workshops, courses and seminars at a level that will enable you to stay on the cutting edge of ministry.

- *Plan a study leave.* Take a study leave, take advantage of distance learning or enroll in webinars, modules or courses on the Internet. Many mission agencies have provisions that allow veteran staff to take a year or more to complete graduate programs that will enhance their ministry effectiveness.

- *Take a sabbatical.* Mission agencies are increasingly seeing the "return on investment" in creating a program that allows their missionaries to take sabbaticals of three to nine months every seven years. Given the rigors of crosscultural ministry in the difficult places of the world, sabbaticals no longer appear to be an option; they are mandatory. Sabbaticals are structured to focus on personal development and spiritual formation away from the demands of daily ministry for an extended time. Several model programs are listed below for you to consider.

The development of a mature Christian leader takes a lifetime. God refines our character, values and leadership skills throughout our life. Your development as a leader is the function of many events, people and circumstances—process items—that leave an imprint on your

life and priorities. These milestones teach us significant life and ministry lessons. Reflecting on God's ongoing work in our life teaches us to recognize his activity. All leaders can point to critical incidents in which God taught them important insights that shaped their development.

Personal Timeline

Your responses to God's shaping can be tracked on a timeline that helps evaluate your development, reveals your unique processing patterns and provides a lifetime perspective. The Symbol Timeline exercise on page 250 will help you chronicle how God has directed your life and shaped your identity. You can gain insight for future ministry direction and decisions by comparing your development with the generalized development patterns of other Christian leaders or missionaries. This insight contributes to gaining a godly perspective.

Ministry ultimately flows out of being. Take time to create your personal timeline, and you'll accomplish an invaluable step toward gaining perspective and direction for the rest of your life.

Because God changes us through our life experience along the journey of faith, setting aside intentional time for personal growth and development should be a vital component of every missionary's ministry plan. We have tried to make it clear that we don't assume that all the preparation and training you need will be academic. Much of it will depend on the personal and professional growth goals you set for yourself. With this in mind, a second way to be intentional in your lifelong development is to set goals for personal growth.

The Personal Development Plan introduced on page 260 is a reflective, goal-setting worksheet and action plan. It is designed to map out specific growth and learning objectives in the three profile categories: character, skills and knowledge. This exercise may help you piece the tasks and growth areas you've noted on previous pages into a coherent whole.

The Personal Development Plan can be used once to help you establish new direction for your learning, or it can be adapted and used annually as a self-study guide to assist you as you analyze and shape your lifelong learning process.

Coming up are two short, practical exercises (in place of the journal worksheet in this section), the "Symbol Timeline Exercise," below, and the "Personal Development Plan Worksheet," on pages 260-61. You will want to work through these exercises to gain a clearer perspective on your past and to develop a personal growth plan for the future.

Bob Buford. *Half-Time: Changing Your Game Plan from Success to Significance.* Grand Rapids: Zondervan/HarperCollins, 1994.

J. Robert Clinton. *The Making of a Leader.* Colorado Springs: NavPress, 1988. <www.navpress.com>

———. *Focused Lives.* Altadena, Calif.: Barnabas Publishers, 1995. <www.barnabaspublishers.com>

———. *Reading on the Run: A Continuum Approach to Reading.* Altadena, Calif.: Barnabas Publishers, 1995. Clinton has designed a reading continuum that identifies different techniques for approaching the reading of a book for information, moving from less intense and less in-depth to highly intense and in-depth reading. Each type of reading has different goals and employs different techniques for getting the information desired. Methodologies along the continuum include scan, ransack, browse, pre-read, read and study levels.

Bill Hybels. *Making Life Work: Putting God's Wisdom into Action.* Downers Grove, Ill.: InterVarsity Press, 1998.

Richard A. Swenson. *Margin: Restoring Emotional, Physical, Financial and Time Reserves to Overloaded Lives.* Colorado Springs: NavPress, 1992.

Christianity Today publishes an annual listing of its books awards in categories ranging from fiction to missions. Go to <www.christianitytoday.com> and do a site search for "book awards."

---

[1]J. Robert Clinton, *Focused Lives* (Altadena, Calif.: Barnabas Publishers, 1995), p.503.

Gaining Perspective
The Symbol Timeline Exercise
STEVE HOKE AND TERRY WALLING

You may want to do this alone or in a small group of fellow pilgrims. Take a few minutes to graphically capture your life pictorially, from birth to present, on a timeline. Use any symbols (figures, buildings, people, key words and so on) that you find helpful to illustrate the progression of your personal journey. Include key people, circumstances and events that have affected your development. Note significant dates and places, transitions and changes.

PERSONAL TIMELINE

BIRTH

PRESENT

Upon completing your first draft, look back over your timeline to glean insights and convictions that can guide your development. What patterns do you see in your responsiveness to God? What major lessons has he taught you? In what situations have you learned the most about yourself? About God? About ministry?

Notice how . . .

- God has used key people, circumstances and events (process items) to influence your development.

- Your life has gone through various phases or seasons of growth (development phases).

- Your life experiences, both positive and negative, have launched you to a greater level of growth and ministry. Many of these experiences serve to develop your life and ministry values.

This simple timeline should provide you with a big-picture view of your life and Christian growth. This perspective can give you new insights and encouragement about God's ongoing faithfulness and work in your life. It may also help you articulate to others how he has shaped your walk with him thus far.[1]

After you complete your timeline, go to page 00 and complete the Personal Development Plan Worksheet.

---

[1]You can find this at <www.churchsmart.com>. Go to Products, then Product Categories, then Leadership Development. Go to page two of four, "Focused Living Resource Kit: Perspective Workbook." If you want to do an expanded personal timeline with more complete directions, coaching helps and interpretive principles, refer to Terry Walling excellent workbook *Perspective: Personal Mission (Calling) Statement* (St. Charles, Ill.: ChurchSmart Publishers, 1998).

Living with the Darkness in Our Past
BRENT LINDQUIST

Unfortunately, this side of heaven most of us will continue to carry the burden of our "dysfunctionalities." Whatever the health of our family, we bring to our mission life a number of issues that simply do not go away. Some of these are actually intensified in the crucible of crosscultural living.

Just what is this "baggage"? It can be a large number of things, but it is usually clustered around dependencies, addictions and dysfunction. Dependencies are our weakness or proclivity for going back to or repeating behaviors that are not enhancing our interpersonal, emotional or spiritual development. Addictions refer to the fact that these behaviors can become situationally uncontrollable, or worse. Dysfunction refers to our general adjustment or stance toward life when we, in effect, normalize the brokenness in maladaptive ways.

We get to this place by experiencing life and then not effectively experiencing healing. For some reason, the trauma from before becomes stuck, and we are unable to work our way out. Or the work that we do consists of repeating the destructive behaviors in an effort to "medicate" our symptoms. Pornography, Internet overuse, drugs and alcohol are all readily available for us to become dependent on, or addicted to. These issues can become viral, infecting every aspect of our life: interpersonal, emotional and spiritual.

While there are issues and treatment designs that go far beyond the scope of this sidebar, there is one ultimate principle that knits most together: in our weakness, God is strong. For me, this stance grounds me in the perspective that I really have no power over how things have become. Healing begins, and more importantly continues, when I give up. I turn to my community for help. This includes my heavenly Father, friends, family, coworkers, specialists—anyone who can help me make the choice to change and build with me a new community of change.

If you are a potential missionary, now is the time to face your past. Accept it, and then gather the resources to change. Keeping it hidden will only make it stronger. If you are a leader responsible for the next generation, model your own woundedness and healing journey. Build into your corporate structure a place for accountability, follow-through and follow-up. And in our weakness, he will be stronger.

My colleague Paul Mavrogeorge, M.A., L.M.F.T., has written an incredible workbook, *Breaking the Cycle,* which allows the reader to work on any number of dependent or addictive processes, including Internet pornography. It is available from the author at <mavrogeorgeconsulting@gmail.com>.

A helpful book on understanding change in community is Alan Deutschman, *Change or Die* (Los Angeles: Regan Books, 2007).

Brent Lindquist, Ph.D., is the president of Link Care Center and consults with mission organzations on member-care issues.

🌐 Global Perspectives

PETER TARANTAL
Operation Mobilization, South Africa

To Whom Does the Task Belong?

"Africa's hour has come!" These were the opening words that rang out at the welcome of 520 leaders to the Movement for African National Initiatives (MANI) Consultation in Nairobi during February 2006. The atmosphere was electric, with many participants ululating at the prospect of Africa becoming a meaningful player in world evangelization. There was an understanding and powerful commitment that we need to move from being a recipient of missions to becoming a contributor. This crystallized for me the optimism currently felt in the Global South, where the church is growing at a phenomenal rate.

With the new sense of ownership for missions currently experienced in the Global South (GS), what is the future role of missionaries from the Global North (GN)? We are deeply grateful for the contribution of the church in the GN, often at great sacrifice. The GN church has so much experience in missions. We would simply reproduce more mistakes if we did not capitalize on that experience and encourage new forms of serving crossculturally.

I also propose that leaders from the GS and the GN co-mentor one another, though not all people have the appropriate giftings to mentor. But they can all reproduce themselves in valuable ways, pouring their life, spirituality and giftings into younger leaders, peers and colleagues.

A model of missions we encourage the church in the GS to embrace is that of proximate missions, reaching out to people of a similar ethnolinguistic group in close proximity and who are more or less in a similar economic bracket.

When we meet in global forums, we must come as equals. There is a temptation for those who have financial and power resources to want to dominate the agenda. The temptation for those from the GS could be one of triumphalism because of our numbers and what God is doing in the Global South. Both attitudes are wrong.

Attracting the Next Generations

From where I sit, the global ministries that will attract the next generation of missionaries will offer cutting-edge experiences and take them out of their comfort zone. I sense anew in many young people the radical desire to lay down their lives for the cause of Jesus Christ. With attrition discussed in missions these days, ministries with an appropriate infrastructure to care for their people will be successful both to attract and to keep this next generation.

Recommended Prefield Training

To minister effectively in these clusters of global villages with their constantly shifting geopolitical scene, all of us must be equipped both to live and to minister crossculturally. The two are not necessarily the same. I have noticed a lack of solid Bible teaching in many who have joined our training program in South Africa. Training with an emphasis on the Word will be most helpful. We also need to be willing to be exposed to new models of mission. We need to marry theory and praxis. As my good friend Bill Taylor would say, we need to be "reflective practitioners."

Character and Spiritual Qualities

I appreciate stickability in leaders who work with me. In Operation Mobilization, we say that our OMers need to be *FAT* people: flexible, adaptable and teachable. I also enjoy working with those who have an appreciation for diversity and can embrace a variety of people. We need to be lifelong learners. When I was twenty, I knew everything, but the older I get, the more I realize how little I know. I appreciate and need more creative people.

On the Bench
God's Shaping in Isolation
SHELLEY TREBESCH

"Will I ever effectively minister again? In my home context, I led Bible studies and shared about my life following Jesus. Now I do nothing. I just sit and study all day. When I try to speak, people make funny faces or laugh at me. I feel useless."

This young crosscultural worker is experiencing (and being transformed by) the pain of isolation. Isolation is the setting aside of vocational ministry or work for a period of time. This "setting aside" happens either voluntarily due to factors such as entering crosscultural service (during language learning), study leaves and sabbaticals, or involuntarily due to sickness, injury, prison, organizational discipline and so on.

Whether voluntarily or involuntarily, you can expect significant periods of isolation throughout your lifetime, especially in crosscultural ministry. In each of these, God works to bring transformation resulting in deepened spirituality, changed character traits and behavior, creativity and breakthroughs in ministry.

Normally, isolation involves four stages:

1. stripping—removing our external identity; eliminating the "doing" identity

2. wrestling—struggling to understand who we are without "doing." One may experience intense feelings of insecurity or inferiority during this stage.

3. transformation—God bringing changes and good things he intends through isolation

4. expansion—transformation leading to increased ministry responsibility, spiritual authority and breakthroughs that strongly impact ministry

Decide now to embrace isolation when it occurs. Here are a few ways to use the time:

- Deepen your relationship with God. Practice the spiritual disciplines, study the Word (even prepare materials for the latter) and try different practices of prayer (for example, contemplative, listening, journaling).

- Be open to healing, character formation and personality transformation. It may be helpful to explore your life story and take personality inventories.

- Find a supportive community—on-site and via e-mail or Skype.

A final word: stay in isolation as long as required. Often it's painful, so we do whatever's necessary to leave, to fill our lives with ministry activity once again. Resist this temptation! The Lord has precious treasures awaiting you in isolation.

Shelley Trebesch serves as director for member development for OMF International and is assistant professor of leadership at Fuller School of Intercultural Studies. In this role, she seeks to enhance the effectiveness and potential of 1,400 OMF workers all over Asia who serve in a variety of ministries, including church planting, relief, development and medical services. Shelley also teaches, leads and consults in other organizational contexts internationally.

Living Under an Open Heaven
Reflections on Genesis 28 and 35

BOB EKBLAD

Departure from family, homeland, traditions and the land of slavery are everywhere in Scripture as precursors to revelation, fruitfulness and every kind of blessing. Whether you leave in response to God's call or are driven out by forces that oppress (consider Hagar and the children of Israel), an exodus is key to faith. Have you considered all that God wants to do as you anticipate leaving your land of comfort and identity?

Jacob leaves Beersheba ("well of the vows," a place of accommodation?) in Genesis 28:10, on his way to Haran ("cross-roads, paths," the place of Abram's original call and departure). Jacob flees the righteous wrath of his older brother, Esau, whom he has just robbed of his father's blessing through premeditated fraud, lies and trickery. Far from every security, with a rock under his head as a pillow, fugitive deceiver Jacob dreams of a ladder ascending to heaven. Angels are ascending and descending. God appears beside him and says,

> The land on which you lie I will give to you and to your offspring; and your offspring shall be like the dust of the earth, and you shall spread abroad to the west and to the east and to the north and to the south; and all the families of the earth shall be blessed in you and in your offspring. Know that I am with you and will keep you wherever you go, and will bring you back to this land; for I will not leave you until I have done what I have promised you. (Gen 28:13-15 NRSV)

Jacob names the place Bethel—God's House.

The men I minister among in jail are always surprised that God doesn't arrest Jacob and take him back to face justice. People expecting compliance with laws or other prerequisites in exchange for divine favor are intrigued that Jacob is running away and then just sleeping when God gives blessings and promises. Such grace and extreme promises of blessing to the bad guy are unheard of, especially among criminals.

I have felt compelled to share these reflections in France, Korea and here at home over the past few months. Is this good news too good to be true? How can we stay in this place of grace, where help comes under an open heaven and God promises permanent presence and fruitfulness in every direction?

Jacob isn't won over immediately. Right after waking up he even says, "If God will be with me, and will keep me in this way that I go, and will give me bread to eat and clothing to wear, so that I come again to my father's house in peace, then the Lord shall be my God" (Gen 28:20-21 NRSV).

It takes Jacob twenty-one years of working, an "infinite" amount of time (seven is symbolic of a totality of years for each of his two wives and herds) to make him finally flee Laban's oppression. A wrestling match with God, who blesses him yet again, and his enemy brother's surprising forgiveness finally win him over. Now he is ready for God's call to live in a place of perpetual grace (see Gen 35:1).

Limping, Jacob's hardships and experience of divine grace have made him truly understand what is required. He tells his family to put away their foreign gods, purify themselves and change their clothes—and they do it. Jacob and his people strip themselves of every competing security as they head toward Bethel (the House of God).

What would this look like for us today? What are the gods we lean on that need to be put away so we can live under an open heaven? In a church I visited in France, culture and the generous social system stood out as potential idols. In Korea they were parental approval, upward mobility and honor. In our Burlington church it is money, materialism, sports, self and nation.

I find myself continuing to ask the Spirit to show me what I am leaning on that is keeping me from Jesus' life of freedom and fruitfulness. I want to see God's love and grace poured out through me and others in every direction—north, south, east and west. I long to live in God's house 24/7—here and now, before and after I die.

Let's head toward Bethel now, laying aside every weight and the sin that clings so closely, fixing our eyes on Jesus—our only security.

Dr. Bob Ekblad is executive director of Tierra Nueva, an ecumenical ministry among migrant workers, inmates and the marginalized in the Skagit Valley of Washington. Bob and his wife, Gracie, were missionaries to Honduras in the eighties and now travel around the world sharing with ministries in Europe, Africa, Korea and Latin America the mix of social justice, charismatic and Word-centered traditions that are blending in the jail ministry in Washington.

Practical Ways to Give Roots to Missionary Kids

RUTH VAN REKEN

So how do you help missionary kids (MKs) send down deep roots wherever they are living? Here are some practical gardening tips.

Build Strong Ties with Your Nuclear Family

This is the group that will stick together, no matter how many times friends change. Some ways to do this include the following:

- Set aside at least one time each week when you close out the rest of the world and do something as your own particular family. Get away from your station, or work, if there will be too many interruptions. Make it a regular part of your schedule.

- Travel to the key spots in your host country that you all want to visit. Whether it's climbing

Mount Fuji in Japan or Mount Kenya in Kenya, seeing Victoria Falls in Zimbabwe or Iguassu Falls in Brazil, memories built in the garden spots will last a lifetime.

- When you travel back and forth to your host and home countries, get off the plane in Europe, or wherever, and find a place to stay and tour together as a family. This builds family memories and history uniquely yours.

- Make family traditions that can be replicated no matter which country you are in. For us, it was something as simple as a particular assortment of breads and sweet rolls made for Christmas breakfast each year.

Build Strong Ties with Your "Extended Family"

Your kids may grow up far from blood relatives, but God will send you aunts, uncles and grandparents where you are. There are always some around that particularly fit in with your family somehow. Foster these relationships so your children have the experience of growing up in a close community, even if you're far from relatives. This is also an important way for singles to be incorporated into the family structures of the mission and also to have their great gifts benefit your children enormously.

Give Gifts That Reflect the Country You Are in or Places You Have Traveled

These "sacred objects" eventually become the MK's walking history that she or he can cart around the world in all future years. It helps to connect all the places and experiences of life. Creative adaptation will free you from the guilt of not buying your kids the latest toy-of-the-week in States. They'll thank you for it.

Stay in the Same Area, Even House, Each Furlough

It is important for children to have a sense that there is at least one physical place that is home, even if they travel a lot. Maybe it is Grandma's house or a house you buy and keep for furloughs. Hopefully you'll go to the same church each furlough, too. (One hint: As your kids get older, don't necessarily drag them with you to visit every church. At some point the churches have to understand, and your child may be much happier staying with Grandma and going to his or her own Sunday school class while you go off and do your thing.)

Basically, Have Fun

Expect God to be faithful to you and your family. Enjoy the kids he's given and the huge world to explore together. Don't ever let the pressure of busyness and the short-sightedness of stick-in-the-mud families steal the exuberant joy of your family.

(Adapted by Ruth E. Van Reken from the workshop handout "Principles for Missions," prepared for Mercy Ships seminars, March, 1999, Lindale, Texas.)

Ruth E. Van Reken is a second-generation MK who grew up in Nigeria and raised her own three MKs in Liberia. She is cofounder of the annual conference "Families in Global Transition," coauthor of Third Culture Kids: The Experience of Growing Up Among Worlds *and a speaker to many communities around the world on issues relating to internationally mobile families. For more information, go to <www.crossculturalkid.org>.*

Schooling Resources for Missionary Kids

RUTH VAN REKEN

Numerous individuals and several Christian organizations provide a range of training to help missionary parents to understand their options for schooling in another culture. The organizations listed below are those providing the widest range of training and consulting to parents and MK schools:

Dr. Janet Blomberg leads Interaction International (www.interactionintl.org), an organization committed to addressing missionary parents' educational concerns, including briefings, reentry workshops for MKs, materials and homeschooling consulting and training.

SIETAR (www.youngsietar.org) is an international training organization with a long-term interest in third-culture-kids issues.

Ruth Van Reken (www.crossculturalkid.org) offers articles, workshops and a range of other training resources.

Find information about the "Families in Global Transition" international conference at <www.figt.org>.

David Pollock and Ruth Van Eken. *Third Culture Kids: The Experience of Growing Up Among Worlds.* Yarmouth, Maine: Intercultural Press, 2001.

Mission to the World (www.mtw.org) offers some workshops and resource to their parents on the field.

Taking Sabbaticals Seriously

STEVE HOKE

Sabbaticals in missions are a recent innovation with a long history. The biblical principles and precedent for sabbatical are found in the Old Testament. Just as the seventh day was set aside as the Sabbath day of rest (see Ex 20:8; Deut 5:12), so the seventh year was set aside as the Sabbath year (see Lev 25:1-7). The people and the land were to have a year of rest to allow time for physical and spiritual replenishment (see vv. 4-5).

The idea of setting every seventh year aside in the academic environment became an assumed benefit for tenured faculty as far back as the Middle Ages. Only recently have churches (Protestant and Catholic) and Christian organizations permitted a form of sabbatical for personal and/or professional development.

The following proposal is drawn from the practice of several mission organizations that have found their sabbatical program to be the single most effective means of holding on to their top leaders and building deeply into their souls.

Purpose of a Sabbatical Leave

A sabbatical is established for the development

of church and mission agency staff members to facilitate their maximum personal and professional growth. The simple purpose is to encourage staff to focus periodic and extended time for renewal and growth. The objectives are

- to provide three months to a year away from full-time ministry responsibilities every seventh year for intentional reflection on ministry; and
- to provide an intensive time for physical refreshment, spiritual enrichment and ministry development.

Rationale for Extended Time Away

Since people are the church's and missions' primary resource for kingdom ministry, these organizations share the accompanying stewardship responsibility to shepherd and develop their staff. Lifelong training and continual growth toward spiritual maturity is vital for the continued development and effectiveness of cross-cultural missionaries. Rather than merely providing reactive crisis intervention, agencies and churches need to create systems of preventive care and nurture. The developmental sabbatical is one pivotal step to better care for our most important resource—the field missionary.

J. Robert Clinton's research indicates that 90 percent of leaders face isolation. (The principle is, when God wants to use a person greatly, he will hurt them deeply; see 2 Cor 1:3-4.) Therefore, all Christian ministry staff will benefit greatly from this process at some time in their life.

More missionaries may be in isolation or boundary phases than is known. The sabb. process will help surface this reality and en. preventive and developmental assistance rath than crisis intervention. Positively, patterned a. ter the Scripture rhythm of one year off every seven, organizations are finding that leaders fly higher and further when renewed with such an extended time away on a consistent basis.

Length of Time

The typical sabbatical may last three to twelve months, depending on the goals and circumstances of the proposal. Staff on a sabbatical program should be eligible to receive a normal salary and benefits during the entire period.

Types of Activities

The following is a list of typical activities undertaken during a sabbatical, but is not to be taken as exhaustive:

- spiritual retreat for reflection and personal growth under a spiritual director
- pursuit of spiritual growth in a particular area of concern or in a capacity to be tapped in the next phase of ministry
- time to reflect, recharge and refocus before assuming a significantly new or wider responsibility in leadership
- research and study on a specified project related to ministry assignment (but sabbaticals are *not* primarily study leaves to finish academic work)
- research and writing projects
- enrollment in a course of study, exchange teaching or ministry designed to upgrade professional qualifications or to prepare for a new assignment within the organization
- professional internships
- creative projects in the arts related to one's ministry assignment

Reporting and A-

Providin-

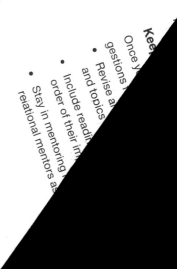

Christianity Today has an archive of articles on sabbath practice and how to plan and take sabbaticals. Go to <www.ctlibrary.com>, search for "sabbaticals," and go from there.

The Navigators hosts a three-and-a-half-day Sabbatical Orientation Workshop every March and October at the Navigators headquarters in Colorado Springs. This workshop will equip you with a few foundational sabbatical skills, assist you in drafting a sabbatical plan and set a tone for your sabbatical. For more information, e-mail their People Resource Team at peopleresources@navigators.org or call (719) 594-2555.

Personal Development Plan Worksheet

STEVE HOKE

Instructions

Work across each row of the chart on page 261 from left to right. Don't just write down things that would be nice to know or that you want to learn. Focus on the specific training areas that relate to that dimension of formation (character-spiritual formation, ministry formation or knowledge goals).

Start by identifying your *developmental needs.* This will keep you focused on your "felt needs," which is vital, because you probably won't work at these skills unless you really feel they're an area of need.

Recording measurable *learning objectives* will help you identify specific bytes of growth that you can achieve. Describe them in a way that helps you think of ways to measure whether and how well you have accomplished them.

Jot down *learning resources* that come to mind. If you're lacking information here, ask your pastor, friends or mentor for additional ideas. Visiting a Christian bookstore should be enough to help you to identify a dozen books on just about any ministry topic. If you're on the field, talk with coworkers and network by e-mail with friends who may be knowledgeable about resources you could use. Look over the resource books listed at the ends of chapters in this book and in appendix 2. Ask your leaders for books they recommend.

Set realistic *dates for completion* in the timetable column. For example, don't try to complete all objectives by December 31; rather, spread them out over the course of the year so you'll always be working on something and won't be overwhelmed by everything at once.

To increase *accountability,* ask your pastor, field leader, mentor or coach to review and sign your plan. At a specified date, get back together and update her or him to find out how well you did.

ping It Current

ou've written a Personal Development Plan Worksheet (PDP) action plan, here are some sug-
or keeping it current:

d update your PDP annually, including specifics, such as emphases for your quiet time
to study.

g goals. List the top ten to fifteen books you want to read each year. Read them in
portance to you.

elationships for growth and accountability. Write in the names of your peer or
well as selected "upward mentors."

Table 9.10

PERSONAL DEVELOPMENT ACTION PLAN for _____ TEAM ROLE: _____

DEVELOPMENTAL NEED What specific knowledge, attitude, skill or character trait is needed? What results will be achieved by filling this need?	OBJECTIVES/METHOD What measurable learning objectives (specific action steps) do you want to set for yourself to meet the development needs? What types of learning experiences will be most helpful? What needs to be designed?	RESOURCES Which coaches or mentors, books or materials, training courses or experiences will be needed?	QUESTIONS Questions to ask your mentor or supervisor	TIMETABLE When will action steps be taken?
Spiritual/Character Formation:				
Ministry Formation:				
Strategy Formation:				
Other:				

Supervisor's/mentor's signature _____ Date _____ Your signature _____ Date _____

TEN

Finishing Strong and Well
BILL TAYLOR AND STEVE HOKE

It's those old shoes that sit to the left of my desk. I turn my head and gaze at them. They seem to stare back at me, now dusty, at times dusted, now silent, then talking. They belong to an old marathoner friend of mine who has finished the last race in a life fully lived.

Back in the early nineties I had called him on the spur of the moment and asked him to send me a pair of his really old shoes. He laughed, asking why in the world I would request that. I said, "I want tangible, shoe-leather evidence of how to finish well after years of life, marriage, parenting, crosscultural ministry, leadership, laughing, loving and serving."

A few days later they arrived by snail mail, in a cardboard box. I sat and gazed at those cracked, worn shoes, thanking God for what they represented. This veteran had begun his marathon with Christ as a teen. He was the promise of his uncle's business in Atlanta until he informed his uncle that business was not his passion; Jesus was. The reprisal came rapidly; the angry uncle disinherited his nephew.

Yet this set the runner free for a God-driven future. He married a life partner in the race, and together they began the marathon of life and ministry: studies at Moody Bible Institute were balanced with pastoral ministry in a Swedish Covenant Church in East Chicago, Indiana. A daughter came into their world. They were turned down by two mission agencies for "health reasons." But they persevered, and another sending body took them on in 1938. Following linguistic studies in the then-young Wycliffe Bible Translators program, they sailed on a banana boat for Latin America. A son was born soon after.

The race continued. After a decade of service they returned for further studies at Wheaton College, sensing the need to upgrade their skills. Over the next decades their race took them to three Latin American countries for ministry. Then for twelve years the runner was CEO of a mission agency in the United States.

As this creative man approached his sixtieth birthday, he and his wife informed the mission leadership of their desire to return to field-based ministry in Spain. They would serve under a much younger man, whom the runner had recruited for Spain years ago. The board was stunned, and the chairman admonished him, "Sir, no president of a bank ever returns to become a teller." To which the runner quietly replied, "I do not work in a bank."

They served in Spain for five years, developed a vibrant camp and conference center west of Madrid, turned it over to Spanish leaders and then returned to the States. What now? These battle-worn veterans could have opted for retirement, but their spirits were strong, and the body still had more laps to go. Back in their geographic roots, they planted Hispanic churches. Today eleven Spanish-speaking churches in the metropolitan Atlanta area owe their existence to this vision.

But I'm most impressed with the deep character of this runner. He had a unique combination of natural and spiritual abilities: visionary leadership and administrative gifts, coupled with spiritual insight and sensitive pastoral care, and a robust sense of humor. He could really laugh. The runner was not threatened by younger or more brilliant leaders, and he opened space for them to emerge into leadership. He mentored an unusual number of young Latin leaders during his career. He recognized his wife's gift blend and released her for complete parallel fulfillment. He was a strong leader, and servanthood marked his style.

Those old shoes. I cannot get away from them. The runner's pace slowed down, Alzheimer's took his mind. His life partner was taken by dementia. They were deeply in love with each other, read actively and into their mid-eighties taught weekly Bible classes. He once told me that the two of them laughed a lot—at things, at each other, at other people. I have sweet memories of the last conversations with him until That Disease robbed his keen intellect.

Two lasting memories stay with me. He was seated on his bed in the assisted-care home, slowly looked me in the eye and said in that shaking voice, "Bill, do you see that lovely lady over there? She's my wife and the most beautiful creature in the world."

Toward the end, I visited them, and his eyes caught me coming across the room. He took my hand, looked straight into my eyes and barely got out the stammering words, "Bill . . . you . . . taught . . . me how to . . . finish . . . well. And I'm . . . trying . . . to do . . . that . . . right now." I wept. He died at age eighty-eight, weighing sixty-five pounds.

Why this story of the old shoes?

I tell it because I, at the tender age of sixty-eight, personally need ongoing encouragement to keep my eyes on the ultimate goal, not the management goals of an organization or ministry; not the false, self-imposed goals of a society that values high productivity; not those measurable and tangible outcomes, an ever-increasing profile of apparent success (whether you get there by the humble route or not).

All of us, women and men, younger and older, need to be wary of the traps set out for us.

Some of them will simply trip us up for a while; we will recover, possibly through confession of sin and restoration or simply through the natural path of maturation. But other traps are deadly and can destroy our lives and ministries, our integrity and our families.

So let's take a careful look at something that may be distant theory for many of you, namely, finishing well. The least you can do right now is know yourself and anticipate the potential minefields out there, discerning some of the dangers and learning from those who have battled to finish well.

Two Case Studies from Scripture

Check out Daniel, that great public servant, one of God's bivocational workers, professionally agile enough to serve through at least five different despotic regimes. Perhaps he sets our standard. Early in his forced international study program, living in exile, this brilliant youth made some radical choices. He purposed in his heart that he would not cave in to the cultural, religious and power pressures of his world. It was a scary option, but when he made that radical decision, God empowered him to keep his commitments. Even in his fading years, he remained faithful to those personal vows, and when he might legitimately have shaved his standards to avoid hungry lions, he stayed firm. And for that reason the High God calls him one "greatly loved of God." Why? Because he finished well.

Study the life of Paul the apostle, another example. He writes from prison: "I have fought a good fight, I have finished the race, I have kept the faith" (2 Tim 4:17). Paul had lived long enough to see some of his friends and ministry colleagues withdraw from the race or capitulate to the cultural and religious pluralism of his day. But Paul wanted to finish well, and he did—executed by the Roman Empire as a threat to the imperial system.

What Does Finishing Well Mean—
and Not Mean?

Finishing well does not mean someone who completes her or his personal career, regardless of the vocation, on top of the pile, lauded as a great example of modern ministry productivity. Finishing well does not mean banquets celebrating retirement or biographies or sharing your secrets to success or having your own video ten-step program. It does not mean prizes given to the spell-binding speakers, the writers of self-help books, the powerful motivational speakers, the evangelical celebrities, the prophetically gifted ones, the great public intercessors, the international missions mobilizers or legendary missionaries. Nor is it the high prize given to parents who claim, "I praise God that all my children are on fire for God and serving him."

So, what does finishing well really mean? It means coming to the end of the life race with authentic faith and personal integrity. I have two passions in life related to finishing well, and I measure them simply. First, I want to come to the end of my life still holding to a working conviction of the truth of Christianity, as well as integrity in life and toward my wife and my children. At my funeral I want my kids to say, "Dad loved Mom to the end, was totally faithful to her and did not sacrifice us on the altar of his traveling ministry." That's my bottom line. The second passion is to do all I can to contribute toward the goal that every person in every generation in every culture has a legitimate opportunity to hear and understand the gospel of Jesus the Christ in order to make a legitimate decision for or against. It's only fair.

Finishing well in crosscultural ministry does not mean you have to stay a missionary or stay in the same geography or culture all your life. The future crosscultural servants will serve with greater mobility, according to global and local needs, based on context and opportunity, skills and gifts. He or she will seek to expand the kingdom into the tough unreached areas, committed to building up the church of Christ everywhere in the world. The fuller meaning of the Great Commission equally balance the Great Commandment with the proclamation of the gospel and the edification of the church. Ultimately the key is not vocation or geography or role in society, but rather integrity, passion for the living God in Christ, service to the community of faith and commitment to make Jesus known.

Finishing well is done in community: your extended family, your spiritual family and your church family, your colleagues in ministry and your intercessors, your mentors and your fellow believers from different nations and cultures. Finishing well also means completing in the right manner the different stages of your ministry and assignments, not just the final one.

Too many of us have suffered from the image of the Christian life as the Summer Olympics, and I write these words in the middle of the 2008 Games. We honor and exult in those who jump the highest, run or swim the fastest, endure the most and, above all, those who get the gold medal—or eight or more of them. Who remembers any bronze medalists of any Olympics, much less those who finished last in any event? (Actually, I do know the story of some of the last-place finishers, and their stories are much more moving.)

But it helps me to think of the Christian life rather as a lifelong pilgrimage more akin to the small-town Special Olympics. These latter games are significant because it does not really matter who wins. As those runners and swimmers come close to the finish, they cross to the cheer of the coach and crowd. That's a better analogy for us. The Christian life is Special Olympics, and the key is for each of us, regardless of age, gender and vocation, to cross that final line, flailing. We finish. And our Coach welcomes us.

Finishing well may mean completing life with broken dreams, unanswered prayers and unfulfilled desires, with children who may or may not be walking with Christ. It may mean that there are few publicly recognized evidences of high productivity or tangible value. This is particularly a problem for those of us who live in cultures that reward efficiency, effectiveness and measurable, busy productivity.

Why Do So Many Not Finish Well?

Over the years, I have gathered observations on some of the major traps we encounter along the journey. Some have called these development stoppers. Others, like J. Robert Clinton, have written insightfully on these themes.

All of us have a weak side, and the sooner we recognize it and shore it up, the better off we are. You may say, "I'm too young for all of this to make sense, and it sounds negative, so why waste my time here?" Well, let me assure you, this is no waste of time; but you may have to take that on faith from someone who has traveled further along the path and has seen a lot along the way.

Here are some of the major traps the can ensnare us in crosscultural mission.

Financial mismanagement. Watch out for money problems, particularly if you come from a background of poverty or if you come from privilege and wealth. In ministry you are closer to poverty and may have to deal with those realities.

Sexual sin, whether as a single or a married person. This is a danger for both women and men today as never before. Many of our younger missionaries come from broken families and have been sexually active prior to encountering Christ. Others struggle with gender confusion until being set free by the Spirit of God.

Temptation patterns can reemerge later in life and cause a fall. Married men tend to succumb to infidelity more than married women, and the reasons are diverse. Not all marital infidelity leads to a broken family, but broken trust is very difficult to recover. We also know now that Internet porn is destroying too many male missionaries, even in remote areas of the world.

Serious family problems. These are often due to the lack of authentic and loving parenting, creating psychological and interpersonal problems in our marriages and families. They must be addressed with wisdom and courage. Remember that no perfect families exist. Nevertheless, contend for healing and restoration and for establishing new patterns.

Power abuse. Most missionaries will not make much money, but some substitute for that loss. They struggle to submit to authority but then when they get it, they misuse it in a destructive way. Over time, some of you will emerge into leadership. Recent studies in global, crosscultural mission document the destructive power of toxic leadership, which causes premature and painful attrition.

Pride and ambition to "get to the top" of the ministry ladder. It's surprising to observe the machinations—many times couched in humility—that people use to work their way into the high echelons of leadership and influence. Remember Peter: "Humble yourselves before the Lord, and he will lift you up" (Jas 4:10).

The inability to turn over leadership and authority at the appropriate time. There are simply too many examples of men and women who won't let go at the conclusion of their term of leadership or when facing retirement. The results are evident, damaging many individuals and organizations. Some call this "founder's syndrome."

Testing in the middle years of ministry. At certain points in life, the living God invites his servants into deeper levels of brokenness and suffering. This may come as a result of our own sin, and we will reap the consequences, or it may come at the hand of others. Yet brokenness may be a sovereign and complex invitation to follow the path of the suffering servant Messiah.

Why does God do this to us? Perhaps he's in the process of deconstructing us, of purifying us or of preparing us for the next stage of ministry. Ironically this next stage might mean ministry from the sidelines, away from the dangers of the spotlight. It might mean we will end up walking with a "life limp," as Jacob did after the battle with the angel. I am moved by Isaiah's record, "Yet it was the LORD's will to crush him and cause him to suffer" (Isaiah 53:10). In all cases it means the downward path of mobility—to the cross.

This kind of testing brings out the best or the worst in us. When God invites us into the pathway of brokenness, he does not force it on us, but rather gives us a choice. If we say no, his blessing may not be removed, but we will not be what we could have been in his original purpose of growth through suffering. Only when we submit in humility to the deconstruction and reconstruction will we be the person God wants us to be.

Coasting to the end. This is a peculiar pitfall, fallen into by those who have simply run out of vital energy for the task or perhaps who struggle with dry rot of the soul. So they maintain the system, play the game, go through the routines of ministry and external religious behavior. But their heart is not in it. And neither is the power of the Spirit.

Spiritual warfare. We must be able to discern the personal, unique weak spots where our arch-enemy attacks us. They may have deep roots in our background, in biological factors, in personality weaknesses. But one thing you can be sure of: the enemy will throw all he can at you to take you out, and he often attacks the most vulnerable in a family.

What Are the Antidotes?

There is good news. First of all, the triune God is on our side: his Spirit lives in us, and his Son advocates for us before the Father. Let me suggest some brief things to keep in mind, forged in the context of decades of crosscultural ministry in Latin America as well global ministry with the World Evangelical Alliance.

Deal with your weaknesses. Identify your personal weaknesses of character and spirituality, and then shore them up. Some of these are "hidden addictions" of mind, will, emotions and behavior, to which we must be sensitive. God will use different means to reveal them to us.

Develop a sensitive heart to the panoply of sin and the ways in which you are vulnerable. Maintain a tender heart to the loving and sovereign Father, Son and Spirit, and practice a daily lifestyle of confession and repentance.

If you marry, never forget your vows. I made some mistakes as a husband in my early years of ministry in Latin America. Fortunately they were not "big sin" issues, but simply a notable lack of sensitivity to my young bride struggling to learn a foreign language, living in a crosscultural setting, growing her own identity as a woman and as a woman in ministry, and balancing the demands of small children with the expectations of "being a missionary." I was a missionary kid who had returned "home," thus unable to identify with her battles. God used Yvonne to show me where I needed to change and grow.

Be wary of the seduction of travel invitations. This is especially true when you have children at home. I am thankful for the guidelines Yvonne and I developed early on to control these glorious invitations to save the world. We also saw too many colleagues who were out there doing their thing but losing their children or their marriage, or both.

Grow an accountability community. Find one key person or a small group. You cannot be truly accountable to or fully open and honest to many people. Choose carefully with whom you will share your deepest struggles, as not all people can handle such knowledge.

Be wary of the attacks of the enemy. Be especially wary when you are alone, such as when you travel in ministry. I prefer to have a colleague stay with me in a hotel room so we can help strengthen one another's resolve to avoid toxic TV programs and movies or Internet temptations.

Have people praying for you. Ask God to help you develop a prayer shield of deep friends who will become serious intercessors for you. Some of these will stay with you all your life, while others will be with you for a season.

Keep growing spiritually. Commit to building your inner landscape of transformational spirituality. Select key writers who touch you deeply. Return to the classics of Christian spirituality, and drink deeply from them. A few contemporary writers also have much to say to us, among them Henri Nouwen, Dallas Willard and Eugene Peterson.

Never stop learning, reading, studying, expanding your horizons. If married, encourage each other to grow as you read and study. Develop a lifetime perspective on ministry and personal growth in Christ.

Be a mentor and find a mentor. Commit to being mentored and to mentoring others. This is something we will develop in the last chapter.

One Key to Avoiding Becoming a Statistic

I've reviewed everything that Steve and I have written so far. To a degree we write to avoid preventable, painful attrition. One of the most important things is to begin grappling with many of these themes within the aid of your church community prior to field departure:

character and spirituality issues, emotional maturity, the ability to serve creatively under authority, life in community, gifts that emerge and are tested and evaluated in the context of the local church, completion of basic education, spiritual warfare.

We cannot underscore enough the importance of a strong church community for future missionaries. The church is the missionary seedbed, the principal selector and screener, the fundamental equipper, the prime sender and intercessor base. The wise church will partner in prefield training with specialized schools and should engage in a strategic partnership with a field-based agency for proper supervision and shepherding of their workers.

Final Thoughts on Finishing Well

I primarily want to encourage you. I suspect that most of you (congratulations for having gotten this far with us!) are younger disciples of Christ, and you are thoughtfully and deeply committed to the crosscultural telling of the Great Story. Jesus is unique, period. I hope this chapter on finishing strong and well is not theoretical for you. We yearn to see you, and your inner you, on God's pathway to the world, on your own long-distance pilgrimage, surviving and thriving with integrity until the end.

So be strong hearted, be of good cheer. We and a host of witnesses are with you and for you.

Oh, by the way, that veteran runner and his shoes? I well remember one of my last telephone conversations with him. We concluded the conversation with my words to him: "Dad, I really love you and Mom."

And so, the old shoes still rest on the bookshelf next to my computer desk. My folks have gone Home now, but the shoes keep talking.

A Personal Checklist

What people do you know who have finished well or are finishing well.

What lessons can you learn from their story? Jot down several of the principles that stand out from their life.

How about some you know who have not finished well in their Christian life? If it's helpful, write down some of the names that come to mind.

What were the primary causes that hindered them? What were the traps they fell into?

What can you apply from their stories for your own life?

What are some of your own weaknesses that need to be shored up?

What might cause you to struggle with finishing well? Identify any personal, family, financial or situational issues that might take you out.

In what ways does the story of the veteran runner and his shoes encourage you?

What About Missionary Attrition?

BILL TAYLOR

I was involved in coordinating a 1994–1996, fourteen-nation study of the attrition of long-term missionaries. By *attrition* we mean departure from crosscultural ministry, for any reason. We discovered that approximately 5.1 percent of the long-term mission force left the field each year, and 71 percent of that figure left for "preventable" reasons.

What does that mean? Let's estimate the current long-term, international, crosscultural missions force at 150,000 strong. An annual loss of 5.1 percent means 7,650 missionaries leaving the field each year. Over a four-year term, this figure jumps to 30,600. This is the total loss for all reasons.

The "preventable" percentage of 71 percent of that 30,600 gives us an attrition of 21,726 long-term missionaries over a four-year term. The financial implications are striking and calculable, but the human implications are staggering. We want to reduce this preventable attrition in all ways that we can.

As we have stated elsewhere, the prime causes of premature or preventable attrition were clustered around these issue:

- inadequacies related to spiritual formation and character, or a misunderstanding of the cost of service

- problems related to interpersonal conflict—within the family, with fellow missionaries or with national workers

- the absence of the right kind of study and purposeful knowledge that would have prepared them for their particular ministry

In our research, we also discovered a number of attrition categories, with some overlap in the groups:

- normal attrition, unavoidable or expected, such as death, retirement, conclusion of the work contract or development project, political unrest

- unpreventable attrition, such as issues related to the education of children, health reasons or a change of job with transfer to another ministry, conflicts within the family or team members, or diminished financial support

- preventable attrition for painful reasons, such as emotional or moral issues, lack of prayer or funding, miscommunications of job description and expectations, disagreement with the sending agency, conflicts with peers, lack of call, inadequate pre-field training

Significantly, the top reasons for field departure were markedly different from the older sending countries (United States, Canada, Germany, England, Australia, Denmark) and the newer sending countries (Brazil, Costa Rica, Nigeria, Ghana, Philippines, Singapore, India, Korea).[1]

Some ten years later, a research team followed up this attrition research with a study that focused more on missionary retention issues. It also clearly indicated the best practices of sending churches and mission agencies regarding retention.[2]

[1]For more on this, read William D. Taylor, ed., *Too Valuable to Lose: Exploring the Causes and Cures of Missionary Attrition* (Pasadena, Calif.: William Carey Library, 1997).
[2]Peruse the outcomes of the twenty-nation survey on missionary retention by Rob Hay and team, *Worth Keeping: Global Perspectives on Best Practice in Missionary Retention* (Pasadena, Calif.: William Carey Library, 2007).

Six Characteristics of Leaders Who Finish Well

E. DAVID DOUGHERTY

Reflecting on a lifetime of biblical leadership research, Dr. J. Robert Clinton's comparative study of biblical and recent historical leaders reveals that few finish well and those who do display six factors in their life and leadership.[1] This provides a growth template for contemporary leaders who desire to make their leadership count with eternal results.

Introduction

A repeated reading of the Bible with a focus on leadership reveals four crucial observations fraught with implications:

1. Few leaders finish well.
2. Leadership is difficult.
3. God's enabling presence is the essential ingredient of successful leadership.
4. Spiritual leadership can make a difference.

And what is true of biblical leaders is equally true of historical and contemporary Christian leaders. It is the first observation to which I speak here. Identifying the fact that few leaders finish well was a breakthrough warning for me, which has led to a lifetime of further study.

The Six Characteristics

While there may be other characteristics of ef-

fective leaders, certainly these are extremely important ones. Not all six always appear in a leader who finishes well but at least several of them do. Frequently, effective leaders who finish well will have four or five of them in their lives. And some, like Daniel in the Old Testament and Paul in the New, demonstrate all of them. What are these six characteristics?

1. The leader maintains a personal, vibrant relationship with God to the end. Daniel is the classic Old Testament leader who exemplifies this. In the New Testament, Peter, Paul and John all demonstrate this. See their last writings—the tone, the touch with God, the revelation from God, their trust in enabling grace for their lives.

2. They maintain a learning posture and learn from various sources. Enduring leaders continue to seek truth and greater understanding, and they exhibit an insatiable thirst for God's Word. They live in a posture of humility, eager and willing to learn from anyone they can. Daniel is again the classic Old Testament leader who exemplifies this. See chapter 9 of the book of Daniel for a late-in-life illustration of one who continues to study and learn from the Scriptures. Paul and Peter are the classic New Testament leaders with a learning posture (see 2 Pet 3:18; 1 Tim 4:13).

3. They manifest Christlikeness in charac-ter. This is evidenced by the fruit of the Spirit in their lives. Once again we can turn to Daniel, who exemplifies godliness (see the summary references to him in Ezek 14:14, 20). In the New Testament, note the evidence of character trans-formation in Paul's life (see 2 Tim 2:24 and an il-lustration of it—the book of Philemon). These were men who over a lifetime moved from strong personalities with roughness in their leadership styles to strong personalities with gentleness.

4. Truth is lived out in their lives so that convictions and promises of God are seen to be real. Joshua's statement in his closing speech, about God's promises never failing him, demonstrates this characteristic of some-one believing God and staking his life on God's truth (see Josh 23:14). See the many truth state-ments Paul weaves into his two letters to Timo-thy. See, for example, his famous, stirring con-victions echoed in Acts 27:22-25.

5. They leave behind one or more ultimate contributions. In a study on legacies left be-hind by effective leaders who finished well, I have identified the following categories: a mod-el life, a ministry model that others emulate, an extensive and effective public-speaking minis-try, righting wrongs, founding new organiza-tions and ministries, launching movements, re-searching what has happened and why, abilities in writing or music, and mobilizing and equip-ping others. Of course, in addition to these standard categories are also unique legacies that leaders leave behind.

6. They walk with a growing awareness of a sense of destiny and see some or all of it fulfilled. A sense of destiny is a leader's inner conviction, arising from an experience or a se-ries of experiences in which there is a growing awareness that God has his hand on the leader in a special way for special purposes. Over a lifetime, a leader is prepared by God for a des-tiny, receives guidance toward that destiny and increasingly completes that destiny. No biblical leader who accomplished much for God failed to have a sense of destiny, one that usually grew over his or her lifetime.

Conclusion

Will you be in the list of those missionaries and mission leaders who finished well and left be-hind a legacy—an ultimate contribution for Christ and his kingdom.

A leader ought to want to finish well. Dr. Clin-ton says, "I never give this warning, 'Few lead-ers finish well'; and this challenge; 'Do you want to finish well?' without an overwhelming re-sponse. Yes, I do. Then heed these six factors. Take proactive steps to develop these charac-teristics in your life. Finish well!!!"

E. David Dougherty has been a leader development specialist with OMF International since 1995. He was also the coordinator for the LeaderLink pro-gram sponsored by Mission Exchange/CrossGlobal Link. He is currently a leadership coach serving a number of evangelical mission organizations. Con-tact him at edaviddoug@gmail.com.

[1]Drawn from the research and writing of Dr. J. Robert (Bobby) Clinton.

The Old Runner's shoes

A Personal Effectiveness Checklist

STEVE HOKE

The following checklist will help you evaluate your development in light of the six characteristics of effectiveness described by J. Robert Clinton. After each statement, circle the number on the continuum that most accurately describes your current practice of that habit. Circle 0 if that habit is not present at all; circle 5 if you feel you are practicing that habit consistently with effectiveness.

	Very poor					Excellent
1. I maintain a personal, vibrant relationship with God.	0	1	2	3	4	5
2. I maintain a learning posture and can learn from various sources.	0	1	2	3	4	5
3. I manifest Christlikeness in character as evidenced by the fruit of the Spirit.	0	1	2	3	4	5
4. Truth is lived out in my life so that convictions and promises of God are seen to be real.	0	1	2	3	4	5
5. I am leaving behind one or more ultimate contributions.	0	1	2	3	4	5
6. I walk with a growing awareness of a sense of destiny and am seeing some of it fulfilled.	0	1	2	3	4	5

Total your score for the six habits.   **Total:** _____

Your score profiles your relative strengths and weaknesses in each of the habits. You should base your interpretation not on the total score, but on how your scores on each habit compare with the others. This can help you determine where you need to focus your efforts.

My Journey

JIM TEBBE
Interserve in Pakistan, Bangladesh, Jordan, Cyprus;
Urbana in the United States

My first crosscultural ministry experience was to my "passport country." I grew up in Pakistan, the son of a Presbyterian missionary educator. Like most missionary children, I returned to my home country for college education. At Indiana University, InterVarsity Christian Fellowship was used by God to form me in my spiritual life. InterVarsity taught me how to study the Bible, share my faith and lead and disciple others while I myself was being discipled.

It was at InterVarsity's Urbana student missions convention that I stood in response to an invitation to commit to crosscultural mission service to the Muslim world. The person who was to become my wife stood with me. I never lost sight of that call, although it took several more years and seminary studies at Gordon-Conwell before we were released to go.

My second crosscultural ministry was in the Muslim world. We were partners with the agen-cy Interserve for twenty-five years, working in the Pakistan, Bangladesh and Jordan, ending up in mission leadership in Cyprus. We raised our four children overseas, and the richness of fellowship, ministry and life is more than I ever thought I would know.

Our third and perhaps most challenging crosscultural ministry experience was our return to the United States to direct the Urbana Student Mission Convention with InterVarsity. North American student culture had changed enormously since I was a student. And while God's call to his mission remains unchanged, issues in missions have changed dramatically. But the organizational, cultural and missiological challenges of Urbana, while difficult, have also been fulfilling. My experience in crosscultural ministry has truly been one where "the blessing of the LORD brings wealth, and he adds no trouble to it" (Prov 10:22).

The Power of Mentoring

STEVE MOORE

Leaders naturally take initiative. Perhaps that is why it is so frustrating to stand on the outside looking in. But almost every young leader can relate to the feeling of having something important to contribute, but not having a window of opportunity or a platform for influence. One of the most powerful bridges for young leaders facing a challenge of this nature is the right kind of mentor. No biblical character understood this better than the apostle Paul.

The relationship between Paul and Timothy has been referred to so often by church leaders that their names have been co-opted to represent the interaction between a mentor and a mentee. When speaking to a Christian leader, you would not be misunderstood if you asked, "Who is your Timothy?" In his final epistle, Paul reaffirmed his value for developing others in an exhortation to Timothy: "And the things you have heard me say in the presence of many witnesses entrust to reliable men who will be qualified to teach others" (2 Tim 2:2). We are accustomed to thinking of Paul the mentor, but rarely has he been viewed as the one benefiting from a mentoring relationship.

Early in his ministry Paul found himself run out of Damascus by Jews who had conspired to kill him. He went to Jerusalem hoping to connect with the disciples. Paul was filled with a sense of destiny flowing from the message given to him by Ananias (see Acts 9:15-19). He had become "more and more powerful and baffled the Jews . . . by proving that Jesus is the Christ (v. 22). But in spite of his radical about-face, zealous ministry and personal giftedness, upon arriving in Jerusalem, Paul was on the outside looking in. He "tried to join the disciples, but they were all afraid of him, not believing he really was a disciple" (v. 26).

Almost every young leader can relate to this stage of the apostle Paul's journey. Overflowing with zeal, passion and a growing sense of confidence in terms of leadership skills, he found no one who was willing to give him a chance to make his mark. He sensed God's call and wanted very much to make a difference. He probably asked himself, "Why can't other leaders see what I have to offer?" Sound familiar?

Thankfully for Paul and the early church, Barnabas was willing to listen to this leader-on-the-fringe, believe in him and take a personal risk to connect him with the apostles (see Acts 9:27). Do you understand how God wants you to respond to this kind of challenge? Are you proactively seeking a Barnabas-like mentoring relationship that can shape your heart and help bridge this important leadership gap?

Mentoring: A Definition

The simplest definition of mentoring is relational empowerment. In sentence form, mentoring has been defined as a relational experience where one person is empowered by another through the sharing of God-given resources.[1] The inter-

dependence between the two key words in this definition, *relational* and *empowerment,* can be described this way: the level of empowerment that results from mentoring is directly proportional to the depth of the relationship.

A deep relationship between mentor and mentee opens the door for greater levels of empowerment. Yet it is important to clarify the relational component of mentoring as something that should not be confused with disproportionate amounts of time or social contact. Your mentor does not have to be your best friend in order to empower at deep levels. But he or she does need to be someone you trust, can be vulnerable with and respect. This line of mutual trust is critical if the relationship is to generate more than superficial results. One of the often-misunderstood and unintended consequences of mentoring is the limit placed on empowerment based on a superficial (in terms of trust and honesty) relationship.

Mentor Functions and Network

One of the common myths of mentoring is that of the "ideal" mentor. The fact is, there is no one person who will be able to provide all the input you need. It is much more practical to think about mentoring in terms of the functions mentors perform.[2] Table 4 outlines one view of the different ways mentors interact with mentees.

When seeking a mentor, it is important to consider the specific mentoring functions you need most and to enlist a mentor who can serve in that role. Pursuing a focused mentoring relationship that springs off a particular mentoring function will help your mentor cut through the fog and confusion associated with a more general approach.

Over a lifetime, a balanced network or constellation of mentoring relationships would include upward mentors, who speak into your life; downward mentees, who are receiving assis-

Table 4.

	Mentoring Functions	**Central Thrust of Empowerment**
Intensive	Discipler	Instruction in the basics of following Christ
	Spiritual Guide	Accountability, direction and insight for questions, commitments and decisions affecting spirituality and maturity
	Coach	Motivation, skills and application needed to meet a task or challenge
Occasional	Counselor	Timely advice and correct perspectives on viewing self, others, circumstances and ministry
	Teacher	Knowledge and understanding of a particular subject
	Sponsor	Connects mentee with people, resources and opportunities
	Contemporary Model	A living, personal model for life or ministry, who is not only an example but also inspires emulation
	Historical Model	A model character from history, either biblical or historical, who has positively impacted your life

(Source: Clinton and Stanley, *Connecting* [Colorado Springs: NavPress, 1992], p.42. Used with permission.)

tance and input from you; and peer mentoring relationships, in which there is a mutual, give-and-take sharing from people inside your church or organization (and from outside as well).

Back to Barnabas

Consider the example of this kind of mentoring network[3] as seen in the life of the apostle Paul in the book of Acts.[4]

Paul's journey into the inner circle of early church leadership clearly hinged on his relationship with Barnabas. But after putting his personal credibility on the line to introduce Paul to the apostles and sponsoring him into the leadership team, Barnabas was most likely among the "brothers" who felt it was better for Paul to leave Jerusalem and "sent him off to Tarsus" (Acts 9:30).

This is an important point we dare not miss. It's obvious that Barnabas was both accepting and trusting of Paul. But the fact that Barnabas listened to Paul, believed in him and took a personal risk on his behalf did not immediately transfer into a formal ministry role for Paul. In fact, it culminated in Paul being sent to Tarsus, where he would move out of the biblical narra-

tive and into anonymity for at least a decade.

Too often young leaders want a mentor as long as she or he will say what the young leader wants to hear or will provide an immediate connection with a more highly visible leadership role. While it is clear Paul was seeking a place where he could use his gifts and live out his calling, he did not rebel against the advice he was given or interpret it to be a desire to hold him back. We see the beginnings of becoming a good follower.[5]

Perhaps the manner in which Paul responded in this crucible moment was what brought him to Barnabas's mind while serving as the leader of the primarily Gentile (multicultural) church in Antioch (see Acts 11:25-30). Clearly Barnabas would have remembered what Paul shared with him in Jerusalem about Ananias's explanation that Paul was to be God's chosen instrument for the Gentiles. What better training ground could Paul have to prepare for this life purpose than in Antioch? It was in Antioch alongside Barnabas that Paul refined his understanding of Gentile evangelism and gained valuable experience in the methods he would use for making disciples outside a Jewish context.

What Paul Might Have Learned from Barnabas

The value of people development. Barnabas was intentional about engaging Paul, in drawing him into a place of service that matched his destiny and in creating a role aligned with his gifting and calling. The time they spent together in Antioch was marked by a teaching and equipping/releasing ministry. This value shaped Paul's leadership style.

The importance of generosity. Barnabas entered the New Testament narrative when he sold his island real estate on Cyprus and laid the money at the apostles' feet (see Acts 4:36-37). It was a natural extension of Barnabas's leadership to respond to Agabus's prophecy about a famine by collecting funds and bringing the offering to Jerusalem (see 11:28-29). Paul's values concerning the use of money and his generosity were shaped by his mentor, Barnabas.

Integrity with finances. Barnabas influenced Paul not only with regard to giving money, but also to handling it with integrity. Paul's desire to be careful with funds was, I believe, an outgrowth of his time with Barnabas. Paul enlisted Titus's help with future collections, perhaps in part because Titus had been converted in Antioch and would have been familiar with how Barnabas handled things.

The ministry of encouragement. Barnabas was nicknamed the "Son of Encouragement" (Acts 4:36) for his contagious spirit and willingness to pour courage into others through verbal affirmation and appropriate words of praise. Paul's appreciation of encouraging others was no doubt influenced by Barnabas, who had encouraged him at a time when no one else would listen to him. When the Jerusalem church leaders needed to send an overseer and interim pastor to Antioch, notice that they selected bicultural Barnabas, the natural spiritual cheerleader. He was just what the exploding church needed (see Acts 11:22-26).

Making the Most of a Mentoring Relationship

It is clear from Paul's journey that the mentoring relationship with Barnabas played a critical role in preparing him for all that God had intended. There is no evidence Paul took the initiative with regard to his connection with Barnabas. But that should not stop young leaders from actively seeking out wise and experienced mentors to help them along in the journey. Here are a few practical pointers to consider as you seek to make the most of a mentoring relationships:

- Be specific in outlining what mentoring function you need and are asking your mentor to provide, and what specific goals you have in mind. A vague and general request for a mentor will rarely produce the same kind of response as a specific and well-thought-out proposal.

- Emphasize your respect for your mentor's time and define your expectations for the relationship. Your mentor may misunderstand your request as a desire for a time-intensive, socially driven relationship. Don't allow that to create a barrier from the start. Acknowledge your awareness of your prospective mentor's busy schedule and explain that you are asking only for a limited amount of time focused specifically on the goals you have articulated.

- Affirm your commitment to follow through on any projects or assignments your mentor may give you, to the best of your ability. Some mentors are understandably skeptical because they have tried to help people before, only to discover the commitment level was not sufficient to bring about the desired growth. Going public with your intention to apply yourself to this learning relationship will both encourage your mentor and deepen the resolve in your own heart.

- Offer to compensate your mentor in some

way, as appropriate. If you are approaching a high-level leader who is routinely asked to mentor others, it may be necessary to demonstrate how serious you are by offering to pay for his or her input, even if it is by doing volunteer work to help compensate for the time you are taking.

Ideas for Application and Reflection

- Make a list of the most important areas in which you desire to grow right now. Then review the chart of mentor functions and try to determine which kind of mentor would best fit each item on your growth list. Who do you know that may be able to mentor you in your most important growth goals?

- Think about a past mentoring relationship you have had. Now review the tips in this article for making the most of a mentoring relationship. How could following these have enabled you to get even more out of that relationship?

- Review the mentoring network diagram and write down the names of key people who fit in each quadrant for your life. On which quadrants should you be focusing now? Are there noticeable holes in your network?

- Which mentoring functions do you do best? What should you do now to help prepare yourself to be an effective mentor?

Steve Moore is president and CEO of The Mission Exchange.

[1]This definition is taken from the NavPress book *Connecting: The Mentoring Relationships You Need to Succeed in Life* by Paul Stanley and J. Robert Clinton (1992).

[2]This idea of mentor functions is also outlined in *Connecting.*

[3]Clinton and Stanley refer to this as a mentoring constellation. When using Paul's life as an example, it is worth noting that Paul had scores of lesser-known mentees beyond Timothy and Titus. Acts 20:4 lists six, in addition to Timothy. It is also worth pointing out that Barnabas functioned both as an upward mentor and later as a peer. Luke was in the inner circle of Paul's relationships, but as a Gentile physician was able to speak into Paul's life from a non-Jewish perspective as an external peer mentor.

[4]Paul testified to being "thoroughly trained in the law of our fathers" by Gamaliel (Acts 22:3). Luke was a close companion of Paul, but as a Gentile physician, he brought an "outsiders" perspective that is associated with external peer mentoring. Peter visited the church in Antioch, where Paul served with Barnabas and referred to Paul as a "dear brother." He read Paul's epistles, acknowledging their inspiration as well as the profound truths they contained (see 2 Peter 3:15-16).

[5]Paul later testified to the fact that Jesus himself confirmed that he should leave Jerusalem and reaffirmed his call to the Gentiles (see Acts 22:17-21).

Mentoring That Makes a Difference

SHELLEY TREBESCH

@%$#, %!, $%#&!

Loud expletives, seemingly never-ending. The team members and I looked at each other, shrugged and wondered what had happened to Jason. Normally a quiet, steady, dependable, young Chinese American man, Jason had come out of the shower and announced he was leaving Mumbai and going home.

I had noticed a change in Jason over the weeks since our arrival in Mumbai. In the begin-

ning, he couldn't wait to get out into the streets and train stations where we made contact with street children and endeavored to build relationships of trust. Jason dived in, even initiating ideas and working longer hours. Eventually, however, I noticed him withdrawing his hands from the child beggars and standing aloof from the crowds. Jason's teammates pursued him, but he rejected their gestures of support and care. He hardened his face and gritted is teeth each day on the crowded buses and trains of Mumbai. He cringed as he was touched and jostled by the people.

I asked Jason what happened in the shower. He said a huge cockroach ran across his foot, and so he beat it to death (while shouting the expletives). And now Jason wanted to return to the States, several months into his two-year commitment to live among the urban poor.

Eventually Jason shared more of his story. It was easy to see why he unraveled. The firstborn son of immigrant parents, Jason worked hard and excelled in academics and leadership. He became a Christian in his first year of university. Following Jesus meant being open to a life of service, which eventually led him to choose India and the urban poor. His parents, not Christians, were disappointed Jason did not pursue a "normal" career, but thought he would eventually "grow out of it." Now, facing the first major failure of his life, Jason prepared to return home to his parents in shame.

Jason's story is similar to most stories of those transitioning into full-time vocational ministry, especially those who serve in a crosscultural context. It's likely he would leave ministry without a mentor or coach to offer perspective and to journey with him through this important transition. For new ministers and their mentors, here are the key touch points to remember.

A Safe Environment of Trust

Jason and others in the first stages of ministry often face situations where they come to the end of themselves, where they lose control, perhaps for the first time. Often just creating a safe, loving environment accelerates the process. Losing control, especially for highly competent, success-oriented achievers, is earth shattering. For these young adults, pursuit of success and the appearance of "having it altogether" have been primary motivators. However, Jesus invites them to dependence on him and others. That's very difficult if you're used to doing it on you own.

The mentor creates the safe context, asks the deep questions (about the pursuit of achievements, for example) and provides connection for sojourners like Jason moving from reliance on self to interdependence.

Transformation

Transformation, in and through the early stages of ministry, focuses on character, particularly as it relates to trust and obedience. God continues the process of moving us from reliance on self to dependence on him and others. For independent "control freaks" like Jason, losing control feels like a free fall. Nothing is the same. Old coping mechanisms do not work. Everything unravels.

The coping mechanisms, such as performing for love or refusing to trust, often form in our early years because of pain and dysfunction. These habits empower survival for a time, but ultimately they block goodness and love coming from God and others. In the early years of service, God provides many opportunities for healing and change.

Transformation comes when one dares to embrace the freedom of dependence: asking for help, receiving help; admitting weakness, receiving grace.

Mentors journeying with new workers in these early years must reassure and offer support. They can absorb some of the anxiety of being out of control, but ultimately this road must be chosen by the mentees. They must risk to let go and trust.

Ministry Skills

Early vocational ministry provides ample opportunities for developing ministry skills. In fact, the most important word a new worker like Jason must say is *yes*. Say yes to writing and leading a drama; say yes to leading Bible studies; say yes to practical projects like feeding the hungry or building a home; say yes to crosscultural experiences. Over time, saying yes to a wide variety of activities enables gifts to emerge and develop. Over time, we have increased understanding of our gifts and, therefore, can later say no.

Mentors provide help in this time by coaching toward skills through demonstrating, practicing with mentees and giving feedback.

Habits for the Long Haul

Twentysomethings often live to the fullest, ignoring reflection, sleep, proper nutrition, stable finances and so on. This was certainly true of Jason; he felt invincible. While this is okay for a time, new ministers must eventually establish life-giving habits in order to serve—without burnout—for the long term.

Mentors can encourage essential spiritual practices (prayer, devotion to the Word, community, service) and healthy life practices (eating right, getting enough sleep, generously and wisely managing finances). These habits help the new worker be in ministry for the long haul.

Wrestling with Call

Three to five years after beginning vocational ministry, the new worker often loses the passion she or he first had for serving. The practice of doing ministry no longer provides motivation or energy. Hitting this wall often signals a call to move from "doing" to "being" and a recommitment to service. Because this period feels insecure and unfulfilling, young ministers may leave their work during this time. Mentors bring needed perspective and help new workers to understand who God has created them to be and to negotiate their deepening commitment.

Numerous mentors are needed for this key stage in the early years of ministry. Churches and mission agencies must prepare for this critical juncture.

Shelley Trebesch is assistant professor of leadership at Fuller Theological Seminary. She also serves as director for member development for OMF International. In this role, she seeks to enhance the effectiveness and potential of 1,400 OMF workers all over Asia, who serve in a variety of ministries, including church planting, relief, development and medical services.

 # Global Perspectives

JAMIE WOOD
National Director, Pioneers New Zealand

Role of the Missionary

In today's globalized missions context, the role of a missionary from the Global North must include a strong emphasis on servanthood. For teachers, evangelists, church planters, financiers, business people, medical or development workers, the attitude of Christ is more important than any other trait, skill or resource. True humility recognizes what one has and makes it available for kingdom purposes, with the realization that the offering has no more nor less worth than the different offering of others within the global church.

Attracting the Next Generations

I would like to use the term "holistic mission," but I fear it is swinging wildly toward an altruistic "good-works" bent. Gen Y (the Millennials) tend to be more cause-oriented than Gen X. Despite being technophiles and heavy consumers, they are easily engaged in justice-oriented causes, fair trade and debt/poverty relief. But there is a danger that the Lord who came to set the captives free may be sadly missing from the activism.

One could easily blame this shift on postmodernism and its demand for tolerance as a top-level value. This purist view of postmodernism would argue that there is no place for a global Christian story or its exclusivism (that is, that Jesus is the only way to be restored to a right relationship with God, our fellow humans and creation). However, we must also blame churches that teach an insipid and escapist Christianity of personal prosperity and fail to wrestle with our world's pain.

Global ministries that will attract the next generation are activist (in a truly holistic sense), small-team oriented, strongly egalitarian, highly flexible (within the parameters of the organizational raison d'être), preferring relationships over regulations, open to free debate and critique, and willing to live in the tension between helping to facilitate a personal vision and advancing the wider vision of the team and organization.

Recommended Prefield Training

I dream of an apprenticeship model of on-field training and experience backed by assigned academic reflection and closely monitored by one-on-one mission mentors and coaches. Where are the mentors willing to engage in such a discipleship model? The teachers aren't on the field and the field workers haven't got energy (or perhaps the gifts) to teach this way. Information technology can help bridge the gap, but no effective model is yet apparent.

Character and Spiritual Qualities

Those from Gen Y willing to engage in mission need to first and foremost be worshipers, people absolutely committed to Christ, willing to lay down their lives for him. The sense of allegiance must be strong enough to carry them through the pain that is par for the course in crosscultural ministry.

They must understand what faithfulness is and remain faithful to what he calls them to be and do, no matter what the cost. They need to be absolutely convinced that this life is merely a training ground for something to come that will far exceed their every hope and fulfill their deepest desires, that the trials they will experience will be light and momentary in comparison to the reward they will receive.

They will want to work alongside people with backgrounds different from their own, but they'll need to appreciate others in a deep way, willing to understand and willing to be misunderstood. They must be prepared to work through conflict and seek to maintain strong relationships through the misunderstandings—willing to lay down their own rights at times.

While they will likely have a short-term focus, they'll need to maintain a long-term purpose: that people from all nations will be blessed through them, the spiritual offspring of Abraham. Now, that would be a global force to be reckoned with!

✎ Exercise
Finding Personal Mentors
STEVE HOKE AND TERRY WALLING

By this point you have clarified your past shaping and processing by drawing your personal timeline. You have sharpened your future direction with the development of your personal calling statement. The final question is, who will help you accomplish your mission?

Are you looking for a person who can give you perspective and provide wisdom, support, resources and guidance as you seek to grow and develop into the person and leader that God intends? Do you desire to help others grow and achieve a level of effectiveness that they have yet to experience? Do you desire to influence the next generation of Christian leaders?

This exercise is meant to be completed in tandem with Steve Moore's earlier explanation of mentoring, with its inspiration and insight drawn from the foundational work on the topic by Paul Stanley and J. Robert Clinton, *Connecting* (NavPress, 1992).

What Is Mentoring?

Mentoring links leaders to the resources of others, empowering them for greater personal growth and ministry effectiveness. Mentoring is "a relational experience in which one person empowers another by sharing God-given resources."[1] Mentoring is making the mentor's personal strengths, resources and networks (friendships and contacts) available to help a protégé (mentee) reach his or her goals.

The mentor is the person who shares the God-given resources. The mentee is the person being empowered. The interactional transfer between the mentor and mentee is called empowerment.

- Mentors offer empowerment resources. The relationship between mentor and mentee may be formal or informal, scheduled or sporadic. The exchange of resources may take place over a long time or just once. Such empowerment usually occurs face-to-face, but it may happen over a great distance (especially today, using telephone, fax and e-mail).

- Mentors empower mentees with encouragement and timely advice gained through life and ministry experience.

- Mentors model habits of leadership and ministry, and challenge mentees to gain broader perspectives and new maturity. These lessons build confidence and credibility in mentees.

- Mentors link mentees with important resources, such as books, articles, people, workshops, financial resources and opportunities to minister with the mentor.

Three Kinds of Mentoring

"Christian workers need relationships that will mentor us, peers who will co-mentor us, and people that we are mentoring. This will help ensure a balanced and healthy perspective on life and ministry," says J. Robert Clinton in *Please Mentor Me*. Lifelong leadership development is greatly enhanced by a balance of three kinds of mentoring relationships: upward mentoring, co-mentoring (internal and external) and disciple mentoring (see the sample mentoring constellation below).

1. Upward mentoring pushes leaders forward to expand their potential. Upward mentors are typically older, more mature Christian leaders who see the bigger picture and how a leader's current situation fits into that picture. Their experience and knowledge base is more advanced than that of the mentee. They give valuable advice and challenge the mentee to persevere and grow.

2. Co-mentoring is alongside mentoring that comes from peers who are either inside or outside a leader's daily frame of reference. *Internal comentors* are peers in your ministry environment who are at approximately the same level of spiritual maturity. They provide mutual growth and accountability, contextual insights within the organization and friendship during difficulty. *External comentors,* because they are outside your ministry situation, can provide an objective perspective and can challenge your thinking and acting.

3. Disciple-mentoring means empowering younger or less experienced leaders. It engages you organically in the lives of emerging leaders whom you need to identify, select and help develop. In these relationships you provide acceptance, perspective, a listening ear, safety, accountability, challenge, insight and critical skills for new leaders.

Building a Mentoring Constellation

Initiating the mentor relationship is most often up to you, the mentee. Reflect on the following questions as you begin looking for the right mentors in your life:

What type of help do you feel you need most?

What are your mentoring issues (needs)?

In the space below, list at least three prioritized goals for your life and ministry for the next year. Next to each goal, list the name of a potential mentor. Who are the people you would like to approach to mentor you?

Life Development Goals   **Potential Mentors**

1. _____   _____

2. _____   _____

3. _____   _____

Ministry Development Goals   **Potential Mentors**

1. _____   _____

2. _____   _____

3. _____   _____

Now plot your potential candidates on the mentoring constellation below, keeping these tips in mind:

- Think outside the lines—geographical, departmental and organizational.

- Where would they fit in your constellation?

Sample Mentoring Constellation

The following example shows the three kinds of mentoring and the types of mentors that can guide your development.[2]

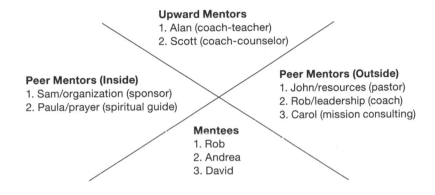

Upward Mentors
1. Alan (coach-teacher)
2. Scott (coach-counselor)

Peer Mentors (Inside)
1. Sam/organization (sponsor)
2. Paula/prayer (spiritual guide)

Peer Mentors (Outside)
1. John/resources (pastor)
2. Rob/leadership (coach)
3. Carol (mission consulting)

Mentees
1. Rob
2. Andrea
3. David

Figure 10.8. A mentoring paradigm

Leaders don't always have mentors for all the quadrants. That is normal. But long-term lack of one type of mentoring is dangerous. Begin praying for balance in the mentors God will give you.

Guidelines for Mentoring Relationships

The "Ten Commandments of Mentoring" below, developed by Stanley and Clinton, will help guide your mentoring relationships to greater effectiveness.[3] Use the first five as a general guide; don't hamper the relational aspects with too much formality.

1. *Establish the relationship.* Sometimes mentoring relationships just happen. Sometimes they are developed intentionally and cultivated. Mentoring has a better chance for empowerment when a relationship is clearly established. The stronger the relationship, the greater the empowerment.

2. *Purpose.* Jointly agree on the purpose of the mentoring relationship. By spelling out the expectations, you can avoid unfulfilled expectations and disappointments.

3. *Regularity.* Determine how often you will meet.

4. *Accountability.* Determine the nature of accountability. Agree together on how the accountability will be set up and monitored. You can use written reports, phone calls or general verbal feedback.

5. *Communications means.* Set up clear lines of communication. Discuss when, how often and by what means you will interact.

6. *Confidentiality.* A mentoring relationship must honor the participants' personalities and feelings about confidentiality. Clarify that personal issues will be treated as confidential unless you agree otherwise. This is an essential step for establishing a "safe-place" environment where transparency can flourish.

7. *Life cycles of mentoring.* Periods of mentoring vary in length of time for empowering to happen. Don't expect a mentoring relationship to last forever. Set realistic time limits for the type of mentoring you choose. Have periodic check points and exit points when both parties can leave without endangering the relationship.

8. *Evaluation.* Effective mentoring relationships need to be evaluated periodically to prevent stagnation. Wise mentors use the three dynamics of attraction, responsiveness and accountability to evaluate the ongoing state of the mentoring venture and make midcourse corrections. A joint evaluation is best.

9. *Expectations.* Unmet expectations are the root of most disappointing mentoring experiences. Use evaluation and feedback to modify your expectations so they fit your real-life mentoring relationship. While you will seldom reach ideal expectations, you can reach realistic ones.

10. *Coming to closure.* Begin with the end in mind. A positive ending for a mentoring experience involves closure, in which both parties evaluate, recognize how and where empowerment has occurred, and mutually end the mentoring relationship. Whether you are the mentor or mentee, bring closure to the mentoring relationship when you feel there has been sufficient growth, you move overseas or you both sense the time is right come to closure.

Keith R. Anderson and Randy D. Reese. *Spiritual Mentoring: A Guide for Seeking and Giving Direction.* Downers Grove, Ill.: InterVarsity Press, 1999.

Mindy Caliguire. *Discovering Soul Care.* Downers Grove, Ill.: InterVarsity Press, 2007.

———. *Spiritual Friendship.* Downers Grove, Ill.: InterVarsity Press, 2007.

Gordon MacDonald. *Mid-Course Correction: Re-Ordering Your Private World for the Next Part of Your Journey.* Nashville: Thomas Nelson, 2000.

Paul D. Stanley and J. Robert Clinton. *Connecting*: Colorado Springs: NavPress, 1992.

Terry Walling. *Finding Personal Mentors Workbook.* St. Charles, Ill.: ChurchSmart, 1998. (Check out this book for a fuller discussion of the terms and types of mentors.)

---

[1] Paul Stanley and J. Robert Clinton, *Connecting* (Colorado Springs: NavPress, 1992), p. 33.

[2] *Check out* Terry Wailing's *Finding Personal Mentors Workbook* (St. Charles, Ill.: ChurchSmart Resources, 1996) for a fuller discussion of terms and types of mentors.

[3] Paul D. Stanley and J. Robert Clinton, *Connecting* (Colorado Springs: NavPress, 1992), pp. 197-208.

Helping TCKs Finish Well

RUTH VAN REKEN

One of the greatest aspects of a TCK or MK (third-culture kid or missionary kid) lifestyle is the fun it can be. In his book *Living Overseas,* Ted Ward emphasizes the importance of enjoying the adventure "of living."[1] Parents of TCKs don't need to wake up at 3:30 a.m. feeling terribly guilty because they've imposed a horrible experience on their children.

Ironically, the richness of their lives can become so routine that TCKs and their families forget to notice it. People who live in the foothills of the Alps soon take them for granted. Those living in tropical climates beside an ocean beach become so accustomed to waving palms and the roar of the sea, they rarely pause to wonder at the beauty. What's exotic and exciting to others has become ordinary for them.

How *do* third-culture families make the most of their experiences in other cultures and places? Here are some practical tips.

Set Aside Special Times and Make Family Traditions

Close out the rest of the world and plan some family time at least once a week. This might be a weekly outing, table games together one evening a week or some other activity the family enjoys. In cultures where visitors chronically stop by with no warning, families often have to leave home and find a park, beach or restaurant to have this kind of uninterrupted time together.

Traditions bind people and groups together because they are visible markers affirming a shared history and celebrating a current unity of thought, purpose or relationship. Every nation and ethnic group has them, and hopefully every family has them. Traditions help families everywhere build their unique sense of identity and give each family member a sense of belonging as well.

Third-culture families have at least as much need for traditions as other families do—maybe more. But because they won't always be around to go to the family reunions stateside, they may have to do a little more conscious planning to develop traditions that are transportable and can be replicated in different places. Be creative with how you celebrate the "big four" holidays: Thanksgiving, Christmas, Easter and birthdays. These traditions can be as simple as giving each family member the chance to pick the menu for his or her birthday supper every year or as complicated as making a piñata stuffed with candy for a particular holiday once a year.

Ideas from different places can be incorporated to help each tradition become a marker of family history. In Liberia, a hot-dog roast on the beach defined Christmas Eve for some expatriates—not a traditional custom in most snow-covered lands, but a nice one to carry back home as a distinctive reminder of that family's history.

Build Strong Ties with Community

TCKs usually grow up far from blood relatives, but there can be substitute aunts, uncles and grandparents wherever TCKs live. Sometimes these people will be host-country citizens; sometimes they will be from the third-culture community itself. Parents can foster such relationships by inviting these special people to join in celebrating the child's birthday, allowing the child to go shopping with them or taking trips with them—whatever is appropriate for the situation. This "created" extended family gives TCKs the experience of growing up in a close community, even though they are not blood relatives. As TCKs remember their childhood, some of these relationships rank among their fondest memories.

Build Strong Ties with Extended Family

Relatives back home are another important part of a TCKs life. Relationships with them need to be fostered also. A great way to do this is by bringing a grandma, grandpa, aunt, uncle or cousin out to visit. This not only helps TCKs get to know their relatives better, it also lets relatives see TCKs in their own environment—the place where these TCKs do, in fact, shine. On top of that, TCKs love to return "home" and to be able to talk to family members who know what they're talking about. But even if relatives cannot make such a trip, it's important for TCKs to maintain contact with them as much as possible through letters, e-mail, faxes, phone calls and pictures. Facebook, MySpace and Twitter are just three of the recent online social networking forums, which greatly facilitate these international conversations.

Developing closeness with relatives at home is especially important if and when the time comes for TCKs to repatriate while parents continue living overseas.

> During the four years that Lois attended university in the States, she never once received a care package or an invitation to visit during the holidays from any of her numerous aunts and uncles. Lois was a good kid, and her relatives were warm, caring people, but it apparently never crossed their minds that she might need them. Lois was too shy to ask, and her parents never thought to alert their brothers and sisters that Lois would need care from the extended family.
>
> Fortunately Lois knew one family's friends from her early childhood, who opened their hearts to her. Now, many

years later, Lois's own home is continually open to other TCKs whose parents are overseas.

Build Strong Ties with Friends

To begin with, TCKs should work at making new friends everywhere they go, so that they won't try to escape the challenges of entering a new culture or dealing with reentry into their home culture by isolating themselves. Friends from the past are also important because they validate the TCK experience and prove that the third-culture world and experience aren't a dream. It's also important, when possible, for TCKs to attend school reunions and to visit the home or homes of their childhood.

Return to the Same "Home" During Each Leave

Whenever practical, third-culture families should return to the same place (at least for a short time) each time they go on home leave (furlough or "home assignment"). Children who change worlds every two or three years, as well as those who stay in one host country their whole lives, all need the sense there is at least one physical place to identify as home in their passport country. When staying in the same physical house isn't possible, families should try to locate nearby so TCKs can have the same school, church and friends. It's also helpful when taking trips to visit friends or relatives in other places to stay long enough to establish at least some basis for a relationship that can be built on during the next leave.

While it's good to foster all these relationships in the home country, families shouldn't spend the entire leave visiting people. When every evening is spent with the adults chatting happily in one room and the TCKs and children from the host family eyeing each other warily in another, and every night is spent in a different bed, the overload can be stressful. Third-culture families should also plan trips to amusement parks and regional scenic attraction, nights in motels, camping trips or other private times during their travel stateside to reinforce their sense of being a family and having an identity in this land as well as in the host country.

When Traveling Between Countries

As families go back and forth between host and home countries, they need to get off the plane, find a place to stay and tour the countries in-between. Making stops along the way not only expands the TCKs world but also creates memories that last a lifetime. Courtney had this to say about her experiences of travel:

> My memory is much bigger than most of my friends', because of all the exciting places my parents took me on our trips between Saudi and America. When we went to England or Germany, for example, knowing I loved art, my mom would take me to the museums while my sister and dad went off on other excursions. I learned so much by absorbing the cultures we encountered.
>
> My parents may not realize that the most profound thing they did for me was take me to Dachau. I must have been about eleven or twelve. We walked the grounds; I cried; we looked at everything. My parents did not protect me; they exposed me to everything, including the crematoriums, gas chambers and the photos. When you read about World War II and the concentration camps, I can't imagine how you can truly understand it without seeing it. I just stood there, overwhelmed, and thought, "I am filled up when I think of all that I've seen and touched, and how much I want to return and touch them all again."

Explore and Become Involved in the Surroundings

Don't neglect actively learning about the history, geography and culture of the host country. Make it a family goal to travel throughout the entire country and come to know it as your own. Families should pretend they're tourists once or twice a year and plan trips just to see the sights. Courtney's parents also helped her to explore their host country, Saudi Arabia. My parents often took us out into the desert to look at various natural treasures such as sharks' teeth, sand roses and arrowheads. It was exciting to imagine this place under water millions of years ago. These may seem like simple memories, but they've left Courtney and me with a deep sense of connection to our past.

As a corollary, a common regret we hear from TCKs is that they never really got involved with the surrounding culture when they were children. Whether it happened because they went off to boarding school or played only with expatriate friends, many consider this a loss. As adults they realize they could have learned so much more and wish they had studied and even mastered the language or taken time to learn how to cook the wonderful local dishes they enjoyed when they went out.

Acquire "Sacred Objects"

As already mentioned, artifacts from countries where they have lived or visited eventually become the TCKs walking history to cart around the world in future years. It helps connect all the places and experiences of their lives. During her childhood, TCK Sandra acquired a set of carved ebony elephant bookends, a lamp (with a base including more elephants), feather paintings and other ebony carvings to hang on the wall. At university and in the sixteen locations where she has lived since her wedding, when the bookends are in place, the paintings and carvings hung on the wall and the lamp turned on, she's home.

In the end, a German TCK, Dirk, summed up best what we are trying to say. When we asked him what he thought of his experience as a TCK, he said, "The thing I like best about my life is living it!"

That's what it's all about: living and enjoying the world of TCKs.

(Adapted from chapter 15 of Van Reken's *Third Culture Kids: The Experience of Growing Up Among Worlds* [Yarmouth: Maine: Intercultural Press, 2001].)

Ruth E. Van Reken is a second generation TCK (or MK) who grew up in Nigeria and raised her own three TCKs in Liberia. She is cofounder of the annual conference "Families in Global Transition," coauthor of Third Culture Kids: The Experience of Growing Up Among Worlds *and speaks to many communities around the world on issues relating to internationally mobile families.*

---

[1]Ted Ward. *Living Overseas: A Book of Preparations* (New York: Free Press, 1984).

Our Last Words and Your Journey
Looking Back and Moving Ahead

STEVE HOKE AND BILL TAYLOR

Well, that's just about it. You have seriously embarked on the process of charting your own journey to the peoples of the world. If you've made it this far, it's been by faith, hard work and endurance. Congratulations! You are to be commended.

We trust that as you've worked through the counsel in this book and taken the first steps on this pilgrimage that you have grown in substantial ways—in your character, in your church base, in your ministry effectiveness and in your overall knowledge. We hope that you've seen more clearly as you look to the future and as you feel God's empowering presence as you step out in obedient faith. You certainly have enough contact addresses, web pages and further resources to keep you going for a while.

Maybe you haven't always known exactly where you were going, but you've been aware of God's guiding presence with you. You've sensed God's touch in your life, either lightly or strongly. You've seen tangible answers to prayer—and perhaps some prayers that were not answered.

You're able to deal with a bit more ambiguity in life. You've possibly already experienced some painful failures in your personal life as well as in relationships, or the brokenness that comes from your family system and in ministry. That's all part of the package of transformational discipleship. You've experienced some divine encounters with God and perhaps with other people. You've entered into a relationship with a mentor who is giving you input and counsel.

Overall, we trust that you have made definite progress in your journey toward active long-term service to Christ in the vast least-evangelized parts of the world. Or perhaps the Lord has confirmed your role in another region of the huge world of human and spiritual needs where your unique gift mix and skill set will be used best. But wherever you are at this point, our prayer is that you will stay focused first of all on knowing God and second on building his cross-cultural kingdom by showing his love in practical ways, by making disciples and by planting churches. As you go on in life, we hope you will grow stronger with that high goal of finishing well—whether in your home country or in an adopted one.

The journey of faith is a lifelong process. God's pattern for working with his people is to develop them over a lifetime. That's why the Christian life is best described as a lifelong pilgrimage. You will be tempted to get discouraged; you will be tempted to sin, to quit, to throw in the towel. You will meet lovely and apparently peaceful Hindus, Buddhists, Muslims or seculars, and these relationships may trigger an internal warfare as you battle with profound spiritual doubt, even wondering whether it's necessary to claim that Christianity is unique among the other faith systems. You will have to grow in your understanding of how to narrate the saving story of God and to discern the thresholds that people must cross before they entrust their lives to our Lord.

You will be heartbroken when your friends and apparent believers slip away from Jesus. You may get physically sick, worse than you ever imagined you could, even wanting to die and get it over with. Hey, that's part of the deal. Remember Jesus. But when the temptations come to chuck it in, remember also that your ultimate desire is to love and honor the triune God.

Most of you will start your global race strong, and the majority of you are young (at least younger than the two of us—but then, it's pretty easy to be younger than we are). Begin your race with commitment and determination, and continue with patient endurance (see Rev 14:12) as the decades roll by. You may serve for five years or more—or less—in crosscultural ministry, then return "home" radically changed and forever internationalized. Or you will sign up for longer terms of service, extending your crosscultural ministry segment by segment.

The most important thing is not where you geographically work out your discipleship to Jesus, but the reality that you pursue him passionately, wherever. So stay focused for the distance, and get ready to be changed by the living God who brings glory to his name, and rejoice when it happens that he invites you to be a part of it. Enjoy your seasons among the people of every nation, tribe and language who will one day worship together with you around the great throne of heaven.

That's a vision worth living and dying for!

Appendix 1

RESOURCES

With appreciation to Dave Imboden (GoConnect.org) and John McVay (AskAMissionary.com) the key compilers of this section.

Since resources change from time to time, visit the above websites for updates and live links. Also browse TheJourneyDeepens.com, the online companion to this edition of *Global Mission Handbook*.

Next Steps in Your Global Mission Journey

<www.goconnect.org/nextsteps> (for everyone)

<www.perspectives.org> Next Steps (especially for alumni of the Perspectives course)

<www.urbana.org> Next Steps (especially for alumni of the Urbana student missions conference)

<www.PreparingToGo.com> (resource center for aspiring missionaries)

<www.thejourneydeepens.com> (weekend retreats and monthly fellowships for prospective missionaries)

<www.finishers.org> (especially for adults in their forties and fifties)

Missions Opportunities

The Journey Deepens <www.thejourneydeepens.com/opportunities.asp>

<www.ShortTermMissions.com> (comprehensive, all ages; one-week to three-year opportunities)

<www.MNNonline.org> Mission Trips (comprehensive, all ages)

<www.MissionFinder.org> (comprehensive, all age; short-term and career opportunities)

<www.urbana.org> MSearch (opportunity database for students)

<www.RightNow.org> ServeNow (opportunities and counsel for those in their twenties and thirties)

<www.MissionNext.com> (opportunities and counsel for ages twenty-four to forty)

<www.Finishers.org> (information, coaching and pathways for mid-lifers)

<www.ServantOpportunities.net> (information and opportunities for mid-lifers and older)

<www.goconnect.org/opportunities> and <www.goconnect.org/strategies>

Events

<www.takeitglobal.org> News (calendar of North America missions events)

<www.lausanneworldpulse.com> (calendar of both North America and internationally)

<www.goconnect.org/conferences> (categorized for students, churches, citywide/ entire church and finishers)

<www.brigada.org> (weekly e-newsletter that includes upcoming events as they are announced)

Answers

<www.AskAMissionary.com> (over four hundred answers to questions pertaining to becoming a missionary plus blogs, podcasts and videos)

<www.urbana.org> Next Steps > Ask Jack (hundreds of answers questions about missions, God's will and many other key issues)

Prayer and Country Resources

The book *Operation World* by Patrick Johnstone and Jason Mandryk contains vital information and prayer points on every country in the world (www.operationworld.org)

Global Prayer Digest (www.global-prayer-digest.org), available in a monthly booklet or daily e-mails, includes condensed missionary stories, biblical challenges, urgent reports and accurate descriptions of unreached peoples

<www.goconnect.org/content/view/1145/183/> (global prayer campaigns, training, books, magazine, articles, websites, quotes, videos, MP3s and children's prayer resources)

The book *Prayerwalking: Praying On-site with Insight* by Steven C. Hawthorne (Creation House, 1993) provides practical insights for a prayerwalk in your community or on a mission trip

Courses

"Perspectives on the World Christian Movement" <www.perspectives.org>—a fifteen-week course (typically one evening per week) that unfolds God's plan for the world and different roles for individuals and churches. Every prospective missionary should take this course.

INSIGHT (INtensive Study of Integrated Global History and Theology) is a one-year, college-level training program of the U.S. Center for World Mission that prepares future world Christian leaders through the intensive study of God's purposes throughout history. College-age students study the span of history chronologically throughout the year with other subjects, such as anthropology, philosophy, literature, Bible and missions. Classes are discussion-based with a focus on independent and investigative learning. Students can earn up to thirty-six college credits or gain a certificate in Bible and mission, offered at several locations around the country. Visit the website to learn more: <http://www.uscwm .org/insight>.

The **World Christian Foundations** study program invades the mainstream curriculum, the legendary "liberal arts" curriculum, and it invests it at every point with missions-oriented content and perspective. This teaches people everything they would normally learn in college and seminary (aside from vocational specialties) and does so with a broad four-thousand-year, global-mission perspective.

This unique curriculum can be studied anywhere in the world with a qualified face-to-face mentor. Northwestern College offers the course at the undergraduate level as a degree completion through their Alternative Education department. William Carey International University offers the curriculum in a graduate education program. For more information, contact:

USCWM Mission Training Division
World Christian Foundations
1539 E. Howard Street
Pasadena, CA 91104
Email: wfc@uscwm.org
Website: www.worldchristianfoundations.org
Phone: 626-398-2106

Vision for the Nations is a thirteen-week, video-based, Sunday school/Bible study curriculum, which introduces missions to your church from four perspectives: biblical, historical, cultural and strategic. This set includes: thirteen lessons featuring some of America's foremost mission educators; a leader's guide with reproducible handouts; a participant's reader, with reading, study assignments, a synopsis of each video lesson, and overviews of key mobilization resources, ministries, networks and seminars. View more information here: <www.uscwm.org/ mobilization_division/resources/resources. html>. You can order it from the William Carey Library, <http://missionbooks.org/>.

Foundations of the World Christian Movement course. This course provides a chronological overview of the historical and cultural aspects of the global development of the biblical faith and the Christian movement, with special attention to the biblical foundations for addressing the roots of human problems around the world. Foundations is being offered throughout the year in the form of an online educational experience where students from around the world take the course with one another via the Internet. <http://stores.lulu.com/foundations>

The workbook and course *Experiencing God: Knowing and Doing His Will* by Henry Blackaby (rev. ed., B&H Books, 2008) is designed to be studied daily for three months. Knowing God does not come through a program, a study or a method. Knowing God comes through relationship as God reveals himself, his mission, his ways and he invites you to join him where he is already at work.

"Encountering the World of Islam" (www.encounteringislam.org)—a semester-long course on Islam that gives a working knowledge of the Islamic faith and an understanding of how to share with Muslims the life of Christ

Boot Camp for Personal Support Raising (www.thebodybuilders.net)—a two-day seminar that trains Christian workers how to get to their ministry assignment quickly and fully funded

Tentmaking and business in missions seminars, conferences and courses

Global Opportunities, <www.globalopps.org>

Business as Mission Network, <www .businessasmissionnetwork.com>

A comprehensive directory of missions courses

<www.goconnect.org/introtomissions>

<www.AskAMissionary.com> Courses

Missions Resources

<www.goconnect.org/resources> (annotated

links to about anything you could need regarding missions)

<www.missionaryresources.org> (an assortment of articles, links, books, videos and discussion forums)

<www.missionresources.com> (resources from A to Z for missionaries and Christians worldwide)

<www.mislinks.org> (directory on practical missions, regions of the world and so on)

<www.oscar.org.uk> (UK information service for world missions)

<www.worldevangelicals.org/commissions/ mc/> (the website of the Mission Commission of the World Evangelical Alliance, linked to 128 national alliances and 50 missions movements around the world)

Unreached and Least-Reached Peoples

<www.ethne.net> is perhaps the most up-to-date global network focused on the least-reached peoples of the world, with key voices from both the Global South and the Global North.

<www.adopt-a-people.org>—Adopt-A-People Campaign, facilitated by the U.S. Center for World Mission, provides a thorough e-manual on how to adopt an unreached people group, case studies, a list of sending and service agencies participating and an introductory video.

<www.adoptapeople.org>—Adopt-A-People Clearing House, facilitated by GAAPnet, is for those who want to report their involvement in and adoption of a people group, or to find others who have adopted the same group so they can begin networking and possibly partnering with them. Also provides services for churches looking for guidance and assistance in adopting a people group.

<www.joshuaproject.net>—Joshua Project provides a regularly updated listing of the least-reached people groups of the world and their current status of engagement. Additional

web pages for churches and individuals provide guidance and help with missions involvement.

Help for Your Church

<www.goconnect.org/goteam> is a directory of mobilization ministries, resources, conferences, seminars, consulting and coaching to help missions take deep root in the life of your church.

<www.goconnect.org/networking> provides links to local and regional mission training opportunities and services for many United States metro areas as well as a growing number of citywide mission activist networks.

<www.acmc.org>—Advancing Churches in Missions Commitment (ACMC) is a ministry network of missions-active churches and organizations through which your church can get specific, practical assistance tailored to your church's global outreach needs. ACMC will help you mobilize your congregation, build vision and become strategically involved in world evangelization

Periodicals

Ask A Missionary quarterly e-mail newsletter on becoming a missionary, with answers, missions magazines, books, conferences and Internet sites. Go to <www.AskAMissionary.com> Newsletters.

Daily Connections daily e-mail or RSS feed (www.goconnect.org/daily) you in touch with trends affecting missions in the North American Church, upcoming conferences, events, articles, strategies and resources.

Lausanne World Pulse monthly e-magazine (www.lausanneworldpulse.com) provides missions and evangelism news, information and analysis.

Mission Frontiers (www.missionfrontiers.org) hard-copy magazine published bimonthly by the U.S. Center for World Mission and dedicated to fostering a global movement to establish an indigenous and self-reproducing church-planting movement among all unreached peoples as soon as possible.

Connections: The Journal of the WEA Mission Commission (www.weaconnections.com) is published three times a year, providing a global roundtable for mission leaders and writers from all around the world. Go online for full access to current and past issues.

Mission Maker Magazine (missionmakermagazine.org) is an annual, hard-copy magazine with articles, resource catalog, mission opportunity listings and missions directory indexes.

Momentum (www.momentum-mag.org) is a monthly e-zine that provides information and inspiration to help believers passionately, quickly and effectively obey the Great Commission and reach the unreached peoples.

Perspectives in Practice is a monthly e-zine that inspires Perspectives alumni and others with testimonies, practical tips and ideas to get involved in going, sending, praying, welcoming, mobilizing and business as mission. Go to <www.perspectives.org/pip>.

Peter's Wife (www.peterswife.org) is a monthly e-mail newsletter with help and encouragement for missionary wives and moms.

Women of the Harvest (www.womenofthe harvest.com) is a bimonthly e-mail newsletter with articles by women who know the difficulties of adjusting to a new culture, stumbling over a new language, finding a place in ministry.

Appendix 2

BIBLIOGRAPHY

This annotated bibliography tracks the themes developed here in the *Global Mission Handbook*. In preparation of this list, I (Bill) asked about twenty of my colleagues around the world for their recommendation.

Should you read all of these? That's up to you. Should you acquire them? Perhaps that's a good place to start, and then set yourself on a robust long-term reading journey that will stretch your heart and mind, and better prepare you for the critical tasks ahead in world mission.

For more, visit these websites of mission publications: <www.missionbooks.org> and <www.worldchristian.com>

The Challenging World We Live In

Miriam Adeney. *Kingdom Without Borders: The Untold Story of Global Christianity.* Downers Grove, Ill.: InterVarsity Press, 2009.

Adeney will always stretch your heart and mind for world mission. This is her latest, written for Urbana 09, where she surveys Christians on a global canvas. Adeney, with her broad crosscultural experience, narrates stories from Latin America, Africa, Asia and the Muslim world—places inhabited by real Christians with real challenges and joys. Her topics include local theologies, indigenous leadership training, sustainable development, church growth, persecution, trauma counseling, ecology, world religions and teaching media from songs to the Internet. This is a superb primer.

Thomas Friedman. *The Lexus and the Olive Tree.* New York: Farrar, Straus and Giroux, 1999.

———. *The World Is Flat.* New York: Farrar, Straus and Giroux, 2005.

———. *Hot, Flat and Crowded.* New York: Farrar, Straus and Giroux, 2008.

Friedman is a *New York Times* political columnist with superb global and cultural insights. I especially like Friedman's first book, his introduction to globalization, full of stories and statistics. The others follow similar themes, though I doubt that the world really is as flat as he thinks it is.

Jonathan Hill. *What Has Christianity Ever Done for Us?* Downers Grove, Ill.: InterVarsity Press, 2007.

Hill's cultural survey is packed with events and people, and creatively illustrated. He establishes the powerful impact that Christianity has had on the Western world—culture, thinking, the arts, the landscape, education, society, spirituality, ethics and social justice.

Philip Jenkins. *The Next Christendom: The Coming of Global Christianity.* Oxford: Oxford University Press, 2002.

One of the best-researched overviews of the spread of Christianity. The triune God has moved South, yet without abandoning the North. The book challenged both the media and the academic world's bias against the Christian faith. However, most of us in the global mission community already knew what he researched and wrote on. Some of our Global South colleagues are not as enthusiastic about the book.

———. *The New Faces of Christianity: Believing the Bible in the Global South.* Oxford: Oxford University Press, 2006.

Jenkins follows up his earlier book with a very helpful look at how Christians in the Global South approach Scripture differently from those of us in the post-Enlightenment North.

David Lundy. *Borderless Church: Shaping the Church for the 21st Century.* Waynesboro, Ga.: Authentic Media, 2005.

Lundy, international director of Arab World Ministries, writes from long experience. I like his take on global realities and ministry today. He engages issues of postmodernity and globalization, with helpful local-church case studies.

Jason Mandryk, ed. *Operation World.* Authentic Publishing, 2010.

This will be the latest update of the missions classic that combines more information and more spot-on prayer requests than you can imagine. Few mission leaders have been without the earlier editions. For decades it was edited by Patrick Johnstone, who has passed this torch to his younger Canadian colleague, Mandryk. The most recent edition came out in 2001, and the world has changed radically since.

Stan Nussbaum. *A Reader's Guide to Transforming Mission.* Maryknoll, N.Y.: Orbis, 2005.

Nussbaum helps tie together the major themes from Bosch's 1991 masterpiece, *Transforming Mission: Paradigm Shifts in Theology of Mission.* Nussbaum has crafted a readable and relevant, but challenging, book.

Bob Roberts Jr. *Glocalization: How Followers of Jesus Engage a Flat World.* Grand Rapids: Zondervan, 2007.

A Christian counterperspective to Friedman. Robertson is a pastor with a solid biblical grasp of how to keep a local church locked into God's global agenda.

Richard Tiplady, ed. *One World or Many? The Impact of Globalisation on World Mission.* Pasadena, Calif.: William Carey Library, 2003.

Tiplady, a younger British mission leader, edits the only book on globalization with evangelical writers from Asia, Latin America, Africa, North America and Europe. Prepare to be stretched.

Gene Wood. *Going Glocal: Networking Local Churches for Worldwide Impact.* St. Charles, Ill.: ChurchSmart, 2006.

A pastor takes a fresh look at how local churches of any size can engage in global ministry, regardless of their location and resources. His goal is to link one hundred thousand local churches in going glocal (being rooted and engaged locally as well as globally).

Evangelism; Religious Pluralism

James Choung. *True Story: A Christianity Worth Believing In.* Downers Grove, Ill.: InterVarsity Press, 2008.

Choung creatively weaves the story of the epic narrative of God, presenting the gospel in a, fresh, engaging and relevant fashion.

Don Everts and Doug Schaupp. *I Once Was Lost: What Postmodern Skeptics Taught Us About Their Path to Jesus.* Downers Grove, Ill.: InterVarsity Press, 2008.

Stories of postmoderns who have followed Jesus and the particular "thresholds" that they cross in coming to faith.

Ajith Fernando. *Sharing the Truth in Love: How to Relate to People of Other Faiths.* Grand Rapids: Discovery House, 2001.

Ajith is a gifted evangelist and apologist who speaks out of his lifetime of experience in Southeast Asia as director of Youth for Christ in Buddhist Sri Lanka.

————. *The Christian's Attitude Toward World Religions.* Wheaton: Tyndale House, 1987.

This wise and gracious Sri Lankan writes from his own context—Christian minority faith in a Buddhist society. Few have his authority in speaking on this theme.

Terry Muck and Frances S. Adeney. *Christianity Encountering World Religions: The Practice of Mission in the Twenty-First Century.* Grand Rapids: Baker, 2009.

A recent contribution about engaging with people of other faiths, focusing on "giftive mission," rooted in the picture of a free gift—the gospel message—with historical examples.

Lamin Sanneh. *Whose Religion Is Christianity? The Gospel Beyond the West.* Grand Rapids: Eerdmans, 2003.

Born in Gambia and a Christian convert from Islam, Sanneh is a professor at Yale Divinity School. His is a remarkable example of worldview transformation by Christ, and he is a world-class apologist for the Christian faith. This work helps us respond to the challenge that Christianity is a Western faith.

John G. Stackhouse Jr., ed. *No Other Gods Before Me: Evangelicals and the Challenge of World Religions.* Grand Rapids: Baker, 2001. And Timothy C. Tennent. *Christianity at the Religious Roundtable: Evangelicalism in Conversation with Hinduism, Buddhism, and Islam.* Grand Rapids: Baker, 2002.

These two are just samplers of many solid books that help us understand the uniqueness of trinitarian Christianity in a world of radical pluralism—religious, cultural, moral and personal.

Mission and the Bible; Contextualization

Richard Bauckham. *Bible and Mission: Christian Witness in a Postmodern World.* Grand Rapids: Baker, 2003.

This pithy, four-chapter book by a professor of New Testament at St. Andrews University, Scotland, is excellent. Initially given as lectures in the United Kingdom and then in Ethiopia, this book bears the mark of authentic Christian thinking on missions.

Paul Borthwick. *A Mind for Missions: 10 Ways to Build Your World Vision.* Colorado Springs: NavPress, 1987.

While a bit dated, this thoughtful, short book is still on target and offers exactly what the title says.

Rose Dowsett. *The Great Commission.* London: Monarch Books, 2001.

In my estimation Dowsett has done the best job in helping us rethink the robustness of the Great Commission of our Lord. Avoiding simplifications (reductionism), she weaves Scripture, history and personal experience to help us think clearly about the Great Commission. What more could you want?

James F. Engel and William A. Dyrness. *Changing the Mind of Missions: Where Have We Gone Wrong?* Downers Grove, Ill.: InterVarsity Press, 2000.

Writing on the cusp of the new millennium, Engel and Dyrness have engaged churches and sending agency in a dialogue that causes both to grapple with radical, global mission changes. The book provoked a healthy controversy and discussion. While even some good friends disagree with them, it's still worth reading.

Samuel Escobar. *The New Global Mission: The Gospel from Everywhere to Everywhere.* Downers Grove, Ill.: InterVarsity Press, 2003.

Veteran Peruvian missiologist, longtime International Fellowship of Evangelical Students worker and now resident of Spain, Escobar has done an excellent job in this short book. Few people write with such gracious eloquence and substance, presenting the newer face of world mission, whether from the margins of the immigrant (legal and otherwise) or mission to a post-Christian and postmodern world.

A. Scott Moreau, Gary R. Corwin and Gary B. McGee. *Introducing World Missions: A Biblical, Historical, and Practical Survey.* Grand Rapids: Baker, 2004.

A companion to Mike Pocock, Gailyn Van Rheenen and Doug McConnell, *The Changing Face of World Missions: Engaging Contemporary Issues and Trends,* (Grand Rapids: Baker

2005). This book develops the concept of mission as found in Old and New Testaments and in history, and explores candidates, sent ones and senders in those contexts. It concludes with a strong section on the contemporary world.

John Piper. *Let the Nations Be Glad! The Supremacy of God in Missions*. Grand Rapids: Baker, 2003.

Piper's bestselling book remains a seminal one on the theology of mission—what he calls "doxological mission"—for this generation. He establishes more clearly than any other author the indisputable integration of worship as the ultimate goal of the church and the purpose of mission: "Missions exists because worship doesn't."

Mike Pocock, Gailyn Van Rheenen and Doug McConnell. *The Changing Face of World Missions: Engaging Contemporary Issues and Trends*. Grand Rapids: Baker 2005.

This superb reader has a chapter on most of the topics in the article "The Global Canvas," plus many others. The title says it all.

David Sills. *The Missionary Call: Find Your Place in God's Plan for the World*. Chicago: Moody Press, 2008.

Probably the most complete, practical and biblical discussion of the topic you will ever find. You may have to wade through some of the material, but you won't regret reading it. Bob Creson, president of Wycliffe Bible Translators USA, recommends it to all their candidates.

Missionary Life and Work; Crosscultural Communication

Janet and Geoff Benge. *Christian Heroes: Then and Now*. Seattle: YWAM Publishing, 2006.

This easy-to-read series of thirty missionary biographies (about two hundred pages each) will keep you on the edge of your seat. These realistic, newly written biographies are designed for older children, but are rich for all ages.

Thomas Hale. *On Being a Missionary*. Pasadena, Calif.: William Carey Library, 2003.

Written by a veteran medical missionary to Nepal, this is a highly readable, practical compilation of the ideas, experiences and insights of more than one hundred missionaries. It's my top read for this category.

Paul Hiebert. *Transforming Worldviews: An Anthropological Understanding of How People Change*. Grand Rapids: Baker, 2008.

This is one of Hiebert's last books, published just a year after his death. He gives us essential Christian and anthropological reflections for anyone trying to understand differing worldviews—from rural oral societies through modernity, postmodernity and even post-postmodernity. It is a vital and challenging read. (Read anything by Hiebert, and you will be a better crosscultural servant.)

Glenn M. Penner. *In the Shadow of the Cross: A Biblical Theology of Persecution and Discipleship*. Bartlesville, Okla.: Living Sacrifice Books, 2004.

Why have we waited so long to have something of this quality and depth? Rooted in serious biblical study through all of Scripture, it helps you build a personal, working theology of suffering, persecution and martyrdom. Not for the faint-hearted!

Tom Steffen and Lois McKinney Douglas. *Encountering Missionary Life and Word: Preparing for Intercultural Ministry*. Grand Rapids: Baker, 2009.

Out of decades of experience, you have here, perhaps, the most comprehensive discussion of just what the title says. it's a great companion to Hale's book.

Richard Tiplady, ed. *Postmission: Mission by a Postmodern Generation*. Carlisle, U.K.: Paternoster, 2002.

Pithy and spicy, this jewel emerges from the "Holy Island Gathering" in 2001, at which a small group of Gen-Xers thoughtfully reflected on mission for and by their generation. This book irritates a few older mission leaders but gives hope to many others.

Holistic Mission

Tim Chester. *Good News to the Poor: Sharing the Gospel Through Social Involvement.* Leicester, U.K.: Inter-Varsity Press, 2004.

Formerly an international researcher for Tearfund UK, Chester now leads a group of church mission initiatives into an unchurched British community. He speaks with familiarity of poverty in many different countries and contexts, and does an excellent job of showing the biblical imperative for holistic mission.

Jayakumar Christian. *God of the Empty-Handed: Poverty, Power and the Kingdom of God.* Monrovia, Calif.: MARC, 1999.

Christian, who has worked with the poor in India and elsewhere for more than thirty years, explores the relationship of poverty to powerlessness, masterfully integrating anthropology, sociology, politics and a biblical theology. He includes seven pragmatic responses to the poor and identifies key guidelines for re-equipping grass-roots practitioners and missionaries who work with them.

Tim Dearborn. *Beyond Duty: A Passion for Christ a Heart for Mission.* Monrovia, Calif.: MARC, 1997.

Dearborn was a Presbyterian missions pastor before directing World Vision's Institute for Global Engagement. This is a superb six-part study of the role of God's people throughout the world, designed for small groups and classes.

Gary A. Haugen. *Just Courage: God's Great Expedition for the Restless Christian.* Downers Grove, Ill.: InterVarsity Press, 2008.

Haugen, author of *Good News About Injustice: A Witness of Courage in a Hurting World* (InterVarsity Press, 1999), is president of International Justice Mission, a ministry of radical hope that rescues victims of violence, sexual exploitation, slavery and oppression around the globe.

John B. Hayes. *Sub-merge: Living Deep in a Shallow World.* Ventura, Calif.: Regal, 2006.

The founder of a Christian order among the poor, Hayes invites today's Christian radicals to "plunge in, go deeper, and sub-merge yourself!" Learn what it means to do more than give a handout, and discover how to build authentic, faith-based relationships among the poorest of the poor.

Dewi Hughes. *God of the Poor: A Biblical Vision of God's Present Rule.* Carlisle, U.K.: Authentic Media, 1998.

Dewi is the theological adviser to Tearfund UK. The book comes in two sections: biblical foundations and practical applications. It contains illustrations from around the world.

Bryant L. Myers. *Walking with the Poor: Principles and Practices of Transformational Development.* Maryknoll, N.Y.: Orbis, 1999.

As a veteran international development specialist, Myers provides a masterpiece of biblical integration and application that draws widely on the best Christian and scientific sources of holistic development. Myers challenges us to follow Jesus by respectfully embracing the poor. This is a needed corrective to a very Word-oriented evangelical missions enterprise.

Spiritual Formation; Spiritual Warfare

Clinton Arnold. *Three Crucial Questions About Spiritual Warfare.* Grand Rapids: Baker, 1997.

Perhaps the most balanced and helpful work on the topic, rooted in Scripture and reality, avoiding the extremes.

David G. Benner. *Surrender to Love: Discovering the Heart of Christian Spirituality.* Downers Grove, Ill.: InterVarsity Press, 2003.

A compelling reminder that it is our surrender to love that allows us to offer it to others in power.

———. *Sacred Companions: The Gift of Spiritual Friendship and Direction.* Downers Grove, Ill.: InterVarsity Press, 2002.

An inviting, encouraging and direct introduction to the ancient practice of the church of being in accountable spiritual relationships.

Bruce A. Demarest. *Satisfy Your Soul: Restoring the Heart of Christian Spirituality.* Colorado Springs: NavPress, 1999.

The most helpful overview of the disciplines and spiritual formation and direction I've found (Steve).

Richard Foster. *Celebration of Discipline.* San Francisco: Harper and Row, 1980.

This classic by Quaker spiritual director Foster outlines ten classic spiritual disciplines for personal and community growth into Christlikeness.

A. Scott Moreau. *Spiritual Warfare: Disarming the Enemy Through the Power of God.* Colorado Springs: Shaw Books, 2004.

A valuable series of study guides on twelve topics based on inductive Bible study. This is a gem for anyone in missions.

———. *Essentials of Spiritual Warfare: Equipped to Win the Battle.* Wheaton: Harold Shaw, 1997.

Other missiologists have cited this short book as the best introduction to spiritual warfare on the market. It is a balanced understanding that is biblically based, personally relevant and culturally sensitive.

M. Robert Mulholland Jr. *Invitation to a Journey: A Road Map for Spiritual Formation.* Downers Grove, Ill.: InterVarsity Press, 1993.

A clearly written introduction to the transformative nature of intentionally choosing to start the journey of spiritual growth and formation.

Henri Nouwen. *In the Name of Jesus: Reflections on Christian Leadership.* New York: Crossroad, 2002.

One of the most powerful books on true spirituality, especially relevant for all who are Christian leaders or aspire to be. I have given away more copies of this book than any other in my life. It is deceptively brief.

———. *The Way of the Heart.* San Francisco: HarperSanFrancisco, 1991.

This beloved devotional author and spiritual director suggests solitude, silence and prayer as the core dynamics of a deeper walk with Jesus.

Eugene Peterson. *A Long Obedience in the Same Direction: Discipleship in an Instant Society.* Downers Grove, Ill.: InterVarsity Press, 2000.

This spiritual counsel by one of the wisest and tested shepherds of the Global North, rightly dissects our penchant for instant spirituality and leadership, and calls us to perseverance and endurance in the lifelong journey of faithful discipleship. (Anything by Peterson will be healthy for you.)

Dallas Willard. *Renovation of the Heart.* San Francisco. Harper, 2002.

This is arguably the most accessible writing of Willard, who dissects the Christian life into its component parts and then puts them all back together into a riveting guide to personal transformation.

Finally, here are two key resources on spirituality you must acquire.

Adele Ahlberg Calhoun. *Spiritual Disciples Handbook: Practices That Transform Us.* Downers Grove, Ill.: IVP Books, 2005.

This project is best done in small groups. It introduces you to the classic spiritual disciplines that have shaped God's people throughout history. Don't go anywhere in the world without these two!

Gerald L. Sittser. *Water from a Deep Well: Christian Spirituality from the Early Martyrs to Modern Missionaries.* Downers Grove, Ill.: IVP Books, 2007.

I have found this to be one of the richest and most inviting sources with which to deepen and grow my own spiritual life. Just the stories of the early church are worth the book, but it takes you into today's world as well.

Appendix 3

THREE SMALL-GROUP LEADERS GUIDES

1. GLOBAL MISSION: A Practical Workshop to Explore Next Step Realities
Scott White, Lake Avenue Church, Pasadena, California

Goal: Provide a small group (twelve-person maximum) where individuals can seriously investigate whether God might be moving them toward crosscultural ministry.

Method: The Global Mission Workshop is rooted in the InterVarsity Press *Global Mission Handbook,* which walks the reader through issues of personal, spiritual, educational and vocational evaluations, while exploring potential ministry opportunities for the future.

Each week, the workshop reviews one chapter, which covers approximately thirty pages of reading and worksheets. A number of issues from the reading are discussed, but the focus throughout remains personal, as group members wrestle interactively to better face the realities of their personal next steps of obedience in missions.

Participants each week have the opportunity to interact with a different, experienced missions specialist, who serves as a resource as they discuss and consider the realities of missionary service. These specialists include a veteran missionary worker, a missionary-care specialist and a personal discipleship or development leader.

Through these various elements, the workshop provides a space to learn, ask the "scary" questions and explore the future with others on a similar pilgrimage of discovery. The result is not to turn out "missionaries," but to assist participants as they consider their personal and individual potential next steps in mission.

The Global Mission Workshop is by invitation or application only. Classes are on five consec-

utive Tuesday nights a few weeks after the conclusion of the spring Perspectives course.

The weekly format is as follows:

First Half

Interactive discussion based on handbook:

- Identify key issue or questions for small-group and large-group reflection.
- Participants do homework on their own ahead of meeting to be prepared for conversations and topics.

Second Half

Interaction with mission professionals: There are missionaries on home assignment and locally based crosscultural workers. In both cases these are practitioners who believe that spiritual formation is critical for success, not merely technical expertise in their area of focus.

Specific Weekly Focus

- Church planters—personal and professional issues and "calling"
- Missionary-care issues—personal and emotional realities and challenges for crosscultural workers
- Personal development—spiritual disciplines, mentors and life decisions
- Personal mission statements with reflections and responses from the workshop coaches to each participant

Other key element: each person is paired with two partners for prayer and discussion for the duration of workshop.

2. THE JOURNEY DEEPENS MONTHLY FELLOWSHIPS

John McVay, TheJourneyDeepens.com

The purpose of these monthly fellowships is to provide a vehicle for future missionaries that can carry them all the way to the mission field. These groups rest on two core beliefs:

1. The most encouraging person for me to regularly meet with while on my journey to the nations is another person on the journey. We share the same commitment. We face the same difficulties.

2. Currently no vehicle exists that can *continuously* help prospective missionaries all the way to the field. Regular participation in such a group can provide that continuity.

Membership. Open to anyone seriously considering becoming a missionary. New members join at any time. Current members leave the group for the mission field, but continue relating with the group. New groups form when membership grows beyond eight people.

Facilitation. Group members with leadership gifts start, coordinate and facilitate the monthly meetings. A coleader is recommended so that the group continues when the leader leaves for the field.

Coaching. A variety of missions professionals (missionaries, trainers, recruiters, mobilizers and so on) can be invited to help coach the members of the fellowship. Together, the members and the missions professionals design content for the monthly meetings based on the needs of the members.

Content. The *Global Mission Handbook* may be used in a variety of ways as a primary reference tool for these groups. Some examples include (but are not limited to)

- *Launching a new group.* With an opening orientation during the first month, work through the chapters of the *Global Mission Handbook* in each subsequent monthly meeting. Have a small-group discussion of journal and worksheet entries completed by the group members each month.

- *Needs-based application.* Select sections of the *Handbook* that each member needs based on where they are on their journey. This may be done with guidance from an outside mentor. If enough group members are on the "same page," that chapter can become the content for the monthly meeting.

- *As a reference guide.* Coaches and the group leader personally assign homework and suggest application ideas and steps based on various chapters of the *Handbook.* This method works well when new members join after most of the group has already worked through the entire book.

Editors' note: The Journey Deepens Monthly Fellowships are one adaptation of the ministry category called Fellowships of Future Missionaries. This approach has various names and formats as it is adapted by different local churches, citywide mission networks, existing mobilization ministries, mission agencies and campus ministries.

3. THE JOURNEY DEEPENS WEEKEND RETREATS

Don Parrott, The Finisher's Project, and John McVay, TheJourneyDeepens.com

The Journey Deepens weekend retreats for prospective missionaries are based on three principles:

- *Retreat.* Participants retreat from their

normal environment, with all of its distractions and materialistic messages, and enter into an environment that encourages quiet time, prayer, reflection and listening to others who also are looking for something new.

- **Relationships.** The Bible teaches that God desires relationship with his people and that he works through his people to accomplish gis plans. The Journey Deepens seeks to help people establish a closer relationship with God through corporate worship and prayer. This environment allows plenty of time for interaction in small groups and in one-on-one discussions with each other and with missionaries. These interactions provide opportunities for participants to process what they are hearing and what is in their hearts, and to receive validation of their callings to missionary careers.

- **Reinforcement.** Challenging talks, small-group discussions, conversations with missionaries, book and video resources, and follow-up communication help participants maintain their commitment to the path God has called them to take. The biggest challenge for most participants in any training is to apply what they have learned. The Perspectives national director wrote of the retreat, "[It] has what future missionaries need: support, encouragement and accountability. We don't need more options; we need to sit down and plan our next steps."

The core of the retreat and the key distinctive is the discussion groups comprised of six prospects and two mentors who meet four times throughout the weekend. The discussion questions for these four sessions are selected from different chapters of the *Global Mission Handbook.*

The retreat has separate groups for college students and high-school seniors, young professionals in their twenties and thirties, adults of any age, singles and married couples. These connect with others like themselves, compare maps of their journeys and discussing their compass with coaches who have journeyed into missions already.

Attendance is fifty to one hundred people. People are not overwhelmed with too many choices. Subjects covered in the general sessions, small groups and one-on-one time with the missionary mentors include these:

- I feel a pull from God to the nations. What should I do next?

- Which of my gifts and interests could I use in another culture?

- How can I deal with school loans?

- What's involved in raising prayer and financial support?

- How do I discuss missions with my family and my church?

- If God leads me to stay and send others what would that involve?

As additional study guides to *Global Mission Handbook* are developed, these will also be posted on TheJourneyDeepens.com, the online companion resource to this edition of the workbook.

Along with being the curriculum for these small-group study options, *Global Mission Handbook* is a member of the Perspectives Family of resources, along with a workbook and live interaction that advance the global purposes of Perspectives.